Supervision of Instruction
A Developmental Approach

CARL D. GLICKMAN
University of Georgia

Allyn and Bacon, Inc.
Boston   London   Sydney   Toronto

1985

Dedicated to the cathedral builders

Library of Congress Cataloging in Publication Data

Glickman, Carl D.
    Supervision of instruction.

    Bibliography: p.
    Includes index.
    1. School supervision.   I. Title.
LB2822.G57   1985   371.2   84-29986
ISBN 0-205-08468-0

Series Editor: Susanne F. Canavan
Designer: Jane Schulman
Production Coordinator: Helyn Pultz
Production Services: Total Concept Associates
Cover Coordinator: Christy Rosso
Cover Designer: Robert Northrup

Printed in the United States of America

10 9 8 7 6   89 88

Contents

CONTENTS

Contents

CONTENTS

Contents

Contents

   and Without   379
The Door Is Open   380
The Role of Supervision and
   Supervisor   381
What Is School Success?   382
A Final Note   382

Appendix A   What Is Your Educational
                  Philosophy?   387

Appendix B   Skill Practice in Nondirective
                  Behaviors   393

Appendix C   Skill Practice in Collaborative
                  Behaviors   397

Appendix D   Skill Practice in Directive
                  Behaviors   401

Appendix E   Example of Letter Initiating Peer
                  Supervision   405

Appendix F   Example of Behavioral-Objective
                  Curriculum   409

Appendix G   Webbing Curriculum   412

                  Indexes   415

                  Author Index   415

                  Subject Index   418

Foreword

I went to Indianapolis recently to look for an apartment. After almost thirty years of teaching and research at the university level, I had decided to go back and work in the public schools. My new position had a fancy title, but, simply stated, it was supervision. I wanted to try to practice what I had been professing.

During the course of searching for the apartment, I had a revealing experience. In retrospect, it probably should not have been such a sharp, dramatic insight, but at the time I stopped dead in my tracks and made an exclamation. This is what happened.

My daughter, who lives in Indianapolis, had taken me on a tour of the city to point out various apartment possibilities, and eventually we started to visit one apartment complex after another. My wife was not with us, so my daughter and I had decided simply to scout around and get some idea of what was available. I would come back at some later time with my wife, and then the two of us would decide where to live.

Late in the afternoon we drove into the parking lot of what appeared to be a very exclusive, elegant place. The parking lot was secure. There was a doorman. The floors inside were polished marble, and deep mahogany and shiny brass were everywhere. Crystal chandeliers hung in the outer office, and a quiet air of charm and class permeated the atmosphere.

When we finally got to the model apartment, plush carpets, expensive furniture, and unique art objects gave the apartment an especially impressive appearance. Our perceptions were confirmed when the manager mentioned (what seemed to me) an exorbitant monthly rental, "plus utilities." I was ready to get back in the car and continue our search

Then my daughter said, "But Dad, this seems so small. I don't think you and Mom would be comfortable in this place, even if it was less money. It seems so crowded, plush furniture and all."

"How many square feet are there here?" I asked the manager.

"Nine hundred and five square feet," he replied.

And then it hit me. "Nine hundred and five square feet." That is precisely the number of square feet in a typical classroom, where a teacher plus twenty-five or thirty students live and work and try to learn, day after day, week after week, month after month, year after year. What seemed too small for my wife and me was exactly what teachers and students have as a work space every school day.

Most families of four usually feel they need fifteen hundred to two thousand square feet of living space, if they can manage it; but teachers and their students are jammed together, hour after hour, every day, trying to create experiences for themselves that will be helpful and positive. Nobody said that teaching would be easy— that much is sure; but the complexities of teaching and learning are both exacerbated and obscured in the pressure of the confined space that we call classrooms. Years ago, Jackson wrote about this in *Life in Classrooms,* but on that day in Indianapolis it seemed real to me.

Nine hundred square feet, one teacher, and thirty students— that is the reality Carl Glickman deals with in this book. The confinement, the pressures, the conflicts, the purposes, the materials, the relationships, the opportunities—this is what teaching and learning are all about. What can any person who functions in a supervisory role do to help teachers in their demanding and sometimes demeaning job? How can supervision enable teachers to do better what they are already trying very hard to do—help students learn? These are the kinds of questions Carl Glickman addresses, and answers, in this book.

I first met Carl Glickman several years ago when we were both on the faculty at the Ohio State University. Although our interests were similar in many ways, we were members of different departments and never had an opportunity to work together closely. Eventually he moved to the University of Georgia, but we stayed in touch through professional organizations and incidental meetings. When he asked me if I would be willing to read his manuscript and perhaps write a foreword, I jumped at the chance. I like the way Carl Glickman deals with the reality of schools and schooling. I like the way he applies research from various disciplines to the problems and possibilities of education. I like the way he invents new and better theory by mixing what he knows from research and practice and conceptualizing supervision in unique, creative ways.

Some writers conceptualize a textbook in such a way that they actually reconceptualize the field. I think Carl Glickman has begun to do that with this book. Compared to other areas in education—instruction, curriculum, administration, guidance—supervision has been an underdeveloped field. With few exceptions, textbooks filled with anecdotes and how-to-do-it illustrations have been the norm in supervision. This book is clearly different.

Glickman begins by building a solid base of knowledge from which supervision can proceed: what schools are like; what they can become; the forces that affect teachers' development as people and professionals over time; and what supervision is and what it might become. Drawing on research from many fields, he describes the theoretical underpinnings of supervision and offers a series of specific propositions.

Following the development of the knowledge base, Professor Glickman describes the interpersonal skills, technical skills, and tasks of supervision in ways that are not also theoretically defensible but practical as well. It is the unique blend of theory and research with practice and application that makes this book substantially different and qualitatively more provocative and exciting than many other books about supervision available today. The discussion is always in depth. Studies are not merely cited but analyzed in detail. Practical suggestions are not just hinted at but are spelled out at an operational level, sometimes with several variations.

The thrust of Professor Glickman's thesis is that teachers are different; that teachers can learn; and that schools can become different, better places if those who work with teachers day in and day out accept the reality of teacher differences and the reality of teachers' learning. Furthermore, there is no one best way to supervise. Glickman spells out a rationale for adapting supervision— creating different ways of working—to make the supervisory effort meet the needs of different teachers and the needs of the supervisor in a goal-oriented process that will help students learn. The development of this learning-oriented rationale is one of the important contributions of this book.

Student learning is what schooling is all about. Schools exist to help young people learn. The way to do that, Glickman believes, is to help those who work with students become different, better people—more knowledgeable, more sensitive, more thoughtful, more resourceful, more flexible, more creative, more intelligent human beings.

Carl Glickman has laid out a plan of action for supervision that is rational, empirically based (experimental and experiential), comprehensive, and practical. He urges educators to become cathedral builders (rather than bricklayers) and to serve "a cause beyond oneself." *Supervision of Instruction: A Developmental Approach* is an in-depth description of why such goals are achievable and how they can be achieved.

FOREWORD

Classrooms are only as big as a small apartment. Most teachers need all the help they can get in their efforts to help young people learn. This book goes a long way toward helping those who function in supervisory roles rethink their basic purposes and reexamine their traditional ways of working.

Jack Frymier
Indianapolis Public Schools

Preface

In writing this book, I was guided by one central question: What do we know about schools, teachers, human development, and supervision that supervisors can use to help their schools become more successful? Drawing applications to supervision from three areas of study—effective schools, teacher and adult development, and supervisory practice—will help school faculties become more reflective, collective, and productive. As educators move into higher stages of abstract thinking, creativity, and commitment, the prevailing stagnation in our schools will dissipate.

It is time to move beyond the national and state commission reports about what is wrong with our schools ("An Open Letter to the American People," 1983; Tanner 1984). As local school boards and state legislatures take actions to remedy the external factors related to school improvement (teaching scholarships, career ladders, increased salaries), those who work within schools must alter the work environment to make our schools truly professional places for teachers. Until we recognize the need to provide school environments of stimulation, challenge, and encouragement for all educators, the educational environments for our students will remain the same—or, as John Goodlad (1983, p. 19) wrote, possibly "... worse; more boring, less fun, more repetitious, still fewer encounters with significant educational problems."

Schools have indeed been in peril, but we also have cause for rejoicing: Some schools are succeeding, and in a smashing way. This book is written for those people in instructional supervisory roles who will lead a rejuvenation of their local schools.

Supervision refers to the school function that improves instruction through direct assistance to teachers, curriculum development, in-service training, group development, and action research. The audience for this book includes those involved in school supervision from preschool through twelfth grade. Examples and research are drawn mainly from a substantial body of research on effective schools, teacher and adult development, and supervisory practice, as well as my own experiences as a public school teacher, supervisory principal, government education analyst, and professor of supervision. A significant influence on this book has been the many public school supervisors in the United States and Canada (superintendents, central office directors, principals, lead teachers, department heads) who worked with me in practicums, workshops, and courses to field test, refine, and revise much of what follows. Many individual schools and school systems allowed me to see first hand the reality of successful and unsuccessful supervisory practice.

This book is intended for use as a textbook for graduate students in introductory educational supervision courses. It takes a broad field approach to the multiple skills, techniques, and tasks of supervision. Instructors in beginning courses such as "Supervision of Instruction," "Supervision of Schools," and "Introduction to Supervision" will find this book interesting and valuable. Practicing supervisors, even without the benefit of taking a course, also will find in this book practical applications to their real world of schools. They can use particular chapters to help them plan and implement direct assistance to teachers, in-service education, program evaluation, and the like. Some of the more traditional content found in supervision textbooks, such as organizational arrangements, role descriptions, and history of supervision, has been compressed in order to keep this book focused on the relationship of supervision to teacher and adult development. I believe the key to successful supervision is thoughtful practice based on viewing teachers as developing adults.

This book is a straightforward presentation of positions, ideas, and practices, supported by research and theory *only* as it applies to the practical world of school. The concrete tools, techniques, and actions proposed in these chapters are not recipes to be followed blindly. The supervisor, as a professional with intelligence, knowledge, and awareness of his or her own situation, is asked to choose, revise, and adjust proposed actions according to his or her own judgment about the local school setting. There is no way I can know your situation, your staff, your relationship with your superiors, or the outside constraints on your activities. I can write about what I believe will be successful, and you must screen that information accordingly. I cannot offer one correct action to be taken in a given situation but, rather, can suggest viable alternatives that are likely to succeed when adjusted to local conditions.

Jerome Bruner, the noted education psychologist who spearheaded the curriculum reform movement in the mid-1950s, recently made a cogent remark about education (Hechinger 1981). He stated that what exist in education are *predicaments,* not *problems.* Problems can be solved through correct solutions; in contrast, predicaments can be managed or improved on but cannot be solved once and for all. Predicaments, not problems, are the core of supervision. Improving a teacher's or a school's level of instruction is not a problem to which a single solution can be applied. It is a predicament that needs to be addressed in many ways. Ultimately, the job of supervision is to ensure that we find some of those ways.

Acknowledgments

Those who have contributed to the development of this book have my heartfelt appreciation. Many doctoral students, such as David Sinha, Rose Ann Knowlton, Katherine Ginkel, Karen Konke, and Barbara Clinton, made substantial research contributions. In particular I wish to single out graduate assistant Steve Gordon, who wrote exercises, searched references, and conducted his own research. Additionally, I was aided by numerous students in graduate classes in supervision who used and critiqued various drafts of the manuscript. Practicing supervisors in Georgia, Florida, Virginia, Ohio, California, Pennsylvania, New York, and Saskatchewan willingly provided settings for field testing my developmental propositions about supervision. My colleagues at the University of Georgia have continued to stimulate and encourage me. Professors Ray Bruce, Elmer Ellis, Charles Franzen, Edith Grimsley, Virginia Macagnoni, Jack Newfield, Ed Pajak, Dave Payne, Tony Pellegrini, and Lutian Wootton filled in considerable knowledge gaps of mine (not that I still don't have a few, but oh, how they tried!). The members of the Council of Professors of Instructional Supervision (COPIS) have provided me with resources and a forum for considering theory, research, and practice in supervision.

Special mention needs to be made of Murray Tillman, acting head of the Department of Curriculum and Supervision, and Gerald Firth, acting dean of the College of Education at the University of Georgia for their support during the three years I spent developing this manuscript. Furthermore, Professor John Krumboltz and Dean Myron Atkin of Stanford University graciously provided me the opportunity to be a visiting scholar at their university, where the initial plans for this book materialized.

The work of the staff of my department at Georgia has been terrific. This book was revised three times; the bulk of the typing, editing, and diagramming fell to Donna Bell, who was ably assisted by Ann Keenan, Anita Shannon, and Joan Towns. Putting up with my torrential requests was a demanding job unto itself, one they endured with patience, tolerance, and humor.

My thanks to the staff of Allyn and Bacon and editors Hiram Howard and Susanne Canavan, who have been my friends and supporters since 1977 when they took a chance on my first book. I'm grateful to the reviewers for Allyn and Bacon, professors David Champagne, Lee Goldsberry, Leroy Olsen, and Harold Turner. They held me to needed standards of precision.

I know there are others I have unwittingly left out, and for that, I am sorry. Those who have helped me are not responsible for any faults and limitations of this book. Any errors are mine alone. Many have extended my vision about supervision and human development: To all of you—past, present, and future—thank you.

Finally, I wish to acknowledge my spouse and best friend, Sara, and my children, Jennifer and Rachel. They need no reason for acknowledgment other than that they are special to me.

REFERENCES

An open letter to the American people. 1983. A nation at risk: The imperative for educational reform by the National Commission on Excellence in Education. *Education Week* 2(31): 12–16.

Goodlad, J. I. 1983. What some schools and classrooms teach. *Edu cational Leadership* 40(7): 8–19.

Hechinger, F. M. 1981. Psychologist sees a key to learning in managing unsolvable problems. *The New York Times,* August 18.

Tanner, O. 1984. The American high school at the crossroads. *Educational Leadership* 41(6): 4–13.

To the Instructor

At the end of each chapter you will find exercises that might be assigned to your graduate students. My colleagues and I have used the text with several supervision classes and, based on that experience, would like to offer some suggestions. The nineteen chapters correspond roughly to the weeks of an academic semester: The first three chapters are relatively brief and can be read as one assignment. Students then can complete one chapter and one exercise for each subsequent week. For those who teach on a quarter system, it is recommended that the first three chapters be assigned the first week, Chapter Four the second week, and two chapters each subsequent week.

When reading more than one chapter at a time, the student should choose to do one exercise from any of the assigned chapters. Exercises are categorized as academic, field, and developmental. *Academic exercises* are those done primarily through library research, reading, writing, and constructing. *Field exercises* are those done in practice within school settings and with other professionals. Academic exercises are suitable for graduate students who do not hold supervisory positions and/or are seeking more knowledge of theory and research. Field exercises are suitable for practitioners who wish to make immediate improvements in their professional situations. Whether or not students are in supervisory positions, we suggest that a student do both field and academic exercises at a ratio of approximately 2 to 1 weighted toward their interest, situation, and needs. We suggest a short sharing session at the beginning of each class to give students an opportunity to discuss the results of their exercises.

Developmental exercises are done as sustained projects that can be used as a term or extra-credit project. Developmental exercises are written with the purpose of encouraging students to continue their professional growth. If used as a term assignment, please allow students during the first week of classes to scan *all* the developmental activities in each chapter before asking them to make a choice for the academic term.

TO THE INSTRUCTOR

The exercises (academic, field, and developmental) are numerous and provide students a wide arena of choice. Likewise, I encourage the instructor to make his or her own choices according to his or her own expertise and experience. The sequence of chapters is consistent with the proposed model of supervision, but an individual instructor might find another order more suitable. Similarly, the instructor might wish to adapt, revise, or discard suggestions for using chapter exercises. My purpose in writing this book was to increase supervisory success in schools. However an instructor can use this book to bring about such success will make my efforts worthwhile.

PART I

Introduction

CHAPTER ONE

Supervision for Successful Schools

Take a walk with me. First, let's step into Finnie Tyler High School, with a student body of twelve hundred, in a lower- to middle-class urban neighborhood. A sign by the entrance tells all visitors to report to the office. In the halls we see students milling around, boys and girls talking in groups, couples holding hands, one couple intertwined romantically in a corner. The bell rings and students scurry to the next class. We find the school office and introduce ourselves to the secretary and school principal, who are expecting our visit. They welcome us and assure us that we may move around the school and talk to students, teachers, and other staff. The school population have been notified of our visit and understand that we have come to see how Tyler High School operates. The principal tells us we will find Tyler a pleasant place. Equipped with a floor plan of classrooms and other facilities, we continue on our way.

The principal's description is accurate: Students seem happy and uninhibited, socializing easily with each other even during instruction time. Teachers joke with students. In the faculty lounge we hear laughter that rises, falls, and then rises again. Several teachers have told us about the traditional Friday after-school gatherings at the local pizza parlor, where teachers and administrators socialize over a drink.

Classrooms vary considerably from each other; teachers tell us they can teach however they wish. Most teachers stand at the front of the room, lecturing, asking questions, and assigning seat work. Some, however, take a less structured approach, allowing students to work alone or in small groups. There is an unhurried atmosphere. Students move at a leisurely pace, and classes seldom start on time. Teachers of the same subjects use the same text-books but otherwise seem to have discretion to function as they please. As one seven-year veteran teacher at this school sums it up: "We have an ideal situation. We like each other and the administration leaves us alone. I am observed once a year. I have one faculty meeting a month to attend. I love the other teachers and we have a great time together. The kids are fine, not as academic as they should be, but this school is a nice place for them. I wouldn't want to teach any place else."

Now let's drive across town to Germando Elementary School, with six hundred students, located in a wealthy, suburban part of the city. Again, we follow the sign to the office. A few students are standing with their noses against the wall by their classroom doors. Otherwise the halls are vacant and still; all classroom doors are shut. In the principal's office sit two students with tears in their eyes, obviously fearful of their impending conference with the principal. The principal welcomes us and hands us a preplanned schedule of times to visit particular teachers. She tells us not to visit any classroom during instructional time. "I think you will find that I run a tight ship," she says. "Teachers and students know exactly what is expected of them and what the consequences are for ignoring those expectations. Teachers are here to teach, and I see to it that it happens."

Moving down the halls, we are struck by the similarity of the classrooms. The desks are in rows; the teacher is in front; the school rules are posted on the right of the chalkboard. At the first recess time the students seem to erupt onto the playground. Expecting to find a group of teachers in the faculty lounge, we are surprised to find only two people. One is knitting, the other preparing a cup of coffee. All the other teachers have remained in the classrooms, either alone or with one other teacher.

Continuing our observation after recess, we find that teachers at each grade level not only work with the same textbooks but are on the same pages as well. When we ask about this, one teacher tells us the principal has standardized the entire curriculum and knows what is being taught in every classroom at each moment of the day. At the first faculty meeting in August, the principal lays out materials, schedules, and time lines developed by the central office. We ask how the principal can enforce such procedures, and the teacher replies, "She asks for weekly lesson plans, visits my room at least once every two weeks, and has other central office personnel visit and report back to her."

In the classrooms we visit, students are generally quiet but restless. They appear attentive; those who are not are disciplined. Teachers are mostly businesslike; some show warmth toward their students, others do not. We conclude our visit with three separate interviews of teachers. It seems that teaching in Germando is perceived as a job to do. Whether one likes them or not, the principal's rules are to be followed. Teachers mention that when they have attempted to make modest changes in their instruction, they have been told to drop the changes and return to the school plan. All three mention the teacher last year who refused to follow the reading textbook and subsequently was forced to resign.

Finnie Tyler High School and Germando Elementary School are examples of real schools. Which is the successful school? Which has better attendance, attitudes, and achievement? *Neither does!* Both are ineffective, mediocre schools. The effective schools in the same system are quite different from either. Our first conclusion might be that these schools are very different. Tyler High School appears to have little supervision of instruction, whereas Germando has too much. According to the definition of instructional supervision presented in this book, however, *neither* school has effective instructional supervision. It also might appear that Tyler meets teachers' individual needs, whereas Germando meets organizational goals set by the principal. In effective schools, however, individual needs are fulfilled only through organizational goals. In these two schools *neither* need is being met. Finally, the working environments in these two schools only appear to be dissimilar; soon we will see how similar they really are.

Supervisory Glue as a Metaphor for Success

We can think of supervision as the *glue* of a successful school. Supervision is the function in schools that draws together the discrete elements of instructional effectiveness into whole-school action. Research shows that those schools that link their instruction, classroom management, and discipline with in-service education, direct assistance to teachers, curriculum development, group development, and action research under a common purpose *achieve their objectives* (MacKenzie 1983). In other words, when teachers accept common goals for students and therefore complement each other's teaching, and when supervisors work with teachers in a manner consistent with the way teachers are expected to work with students, then—and only then—does the school reach its goals. Regardless of a school's grade span, socioeconomic setting, or physical characteristics, effective schools have a common glue that keeps a faculty together and creates consistency between a school's various elements. The glue is the process by which some person or group of people is responsible for providing a link between individual teacher needs and organizational goals so that individuals within the school can work in harmony toward their vision of what the school *should* be.

This harmony does not happen by chance; those schools or systems that do not assign the responsibility for applying the glue to specific persons through job descriptions and allocations of time simply do not achieve. Unfortunately, there are more "glueless" than "glued" schools. Research findings on the effectiveness of schools paint a dismal picture. Most schools simply do not make much difference in their students' lives. Research that has focused on those rare schools that do make a difference, however, has much to tell us about how all schools could be changed for the better.

Thus the primary function of effective supervision is to take responsibility for putting more "glue" into the school. But before you run down to the nearest hardware store for buckets of glue to spill on your school floors and corridors (which, it's true, might cut down on student discipline problems and teacher absenteeism, particularly if the glue hardened during a recess period or between classes), let's caution that the adhesive under discussion is of a particular nature.

Effective supervision requires knowledge, interpersonal skills, and technical skills. These are applied through the supervisory tasks of direct assistance to teachers, curriculum development, inservice group development, and action research. This adhesive pulls together organizational goals and teacher needs, and provides for improved learning.

James McDonald (1981) talks about understanding a person's world view by the language and, particularly, the metaphors he or she uses. *Glue* is a good metaphor for effective, fully functioning school supervision. Glue is not glamorous; neither is supervision. When glue is doing its work properly—for example, by keeping a chair together—it goes largely unnoticed; so does supervision, when a school is functioning well. Glue does get attention when the legs of a chair collapse, just as supervision does when a school fragments and fails. With success, both glue and supervision are taken for granted; with failure they are both held responsible. This is as it should be: Teachers are in the forefront of successful instruction; supervision is in the background, providing the support, knowledge, and skills that enable teachers to succeed. When improved instruction and school success do not materialize, supervision should shoulder the responsibility for not permitting teachers to be successful.

Who Is Responsible for Supervision?

Any one with direct responsibility for improving classroom and school instruction is referred to as a supervisor. Typical supervisors are school principals, assistant principals, instructional lead teachers, department heads, master teachers, program directors, central office consultants and coordinators, and associate or assistant superintendents. Supervision is viewed as a process and a function, not a particular position or person. Research on effective schools documents that such schools have in common staff members who attend to the function of improving instruction. The formal titles vary from school to school, however (Schneider 1982–1983; Purkey and Smith 1982). Therefore, what is crucial is not a person's title but rather his or her responsibilities. Ben Harris (1975) clarifies the supervisor's role further by stating that supervision is related directly to helping teachers with instruction but only indirectly to instructing students. Supervision is not the act of instructing students—that is, teaching—but, rather, the actions that enable teachers to improve instruction for students.

The reason we emphasize the process and function of supervision rather than the title or position is that the titles *supervisor* and *administrator* are used indiscriminately in public schools. For example, a school system may have science supervisors, elementary supervisors, or high school supervisors who function mainly as record keepers, inventory clerks, and proposal writers and who do not work directly to improve instruction. Despite the title of supervisor, they do not function in the realm of supervision. On the other hand, persons with titles such as principal, lead teacher, or superintendent may be heavily involved in supervision through direct assistance to teachers, curriculum development, in-service education, group development, and action research. Of course, some titled supervisors do function in supervision; but the point is that what a person does in his or her job is the only key to whether or not he or she is involved in supervision. In this book the term *supervisor* will refer to any person involved with supervision, not to a particular title or position.

Schools vary with respect to who carries out supervisory responsibilities. Some schools assign responsibilities to department heads, assistant principals, guidance counselors, lead teachers, or central office personnel; in such schools the principal focuses on overall administration—the budget, community matters, schedules and reports, and physical plant. In other schools the principal might be largely responsible for supervision, with others attending to administrative matters. Again, a characteristic of effective schools is that someone, somewhere is responsible for and committed to the process, function, and tasks of supervision. Behind every successful school is an effective supervision program.

Organization of This Book

Figure 1–1 demonstrates the scope and organization of this book. For those in supervisory roles, the challenge to improving student learning is to apply certain knowledge, interpersonal skills, and technical skills to the tasks of direct assistance, curriculum development, in-service education, group development, and action research that will enable teachers to teach in a collective, purposeful manner uniting organizational goals and teacher needs. As the supervisor allows teachers to take greater control over their own professional lives, a school becomes a dynamic setting for learning.

To facilitate such collective instructional improvement, those responsible for supervision must have certain prerequisites. The first is a *knowledge* base. Supervisors need to understand the exception—what teachers and schools can be—in contrast to the norm—what teachers and schools typically are. They need to understand how knowledge of adult and teacher development and alternative supervisory practices can help break the norm of mediocrity found in typical schools. Second, there is an *interpersonal skills* base. Supervisors must know how their own interpersonal behaviors affect individuals as well as groups of teachers and then study ranges of interpersonal behaviors that might be used to promote more positive and change-oriented relationships. Third, the supervisor must have *technical skills* in observing, planning, assessing, and evaluating instructional improvement. Knowledge, interpersonal skills, and technical competence are three complementary aspects of supervision as a developmental function.

Supervisors have certain educational tasks at their disposal that enable teachers to evaluate and modify their instruction. In planning each task, the supervisor needs to plan specific ways of giving teachers a greater sense of professional power to teach students successfully. Those supervisory tasks that have such potential to affect teacher development are direct assistance, curriculum development, in-service education, group development, and action research. Direct assistance (A) is the provision of personal, ongoing contact with the individual teacher to observe and assist in classroom instruction. Curriculum development (B) is the revision and modification of the content, plans, and materials of classroom in-

FIGURE 1–1   Supervision for Successful Schools

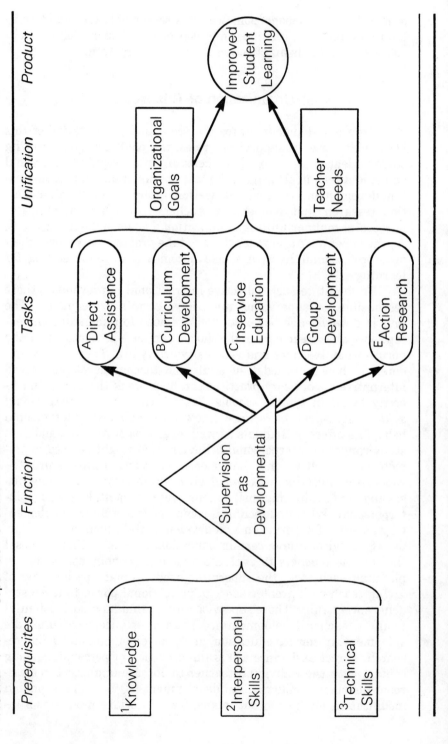

| Prerequisites | Function | Tasks | Unification | Product |

struction. In-service education (C) includes the legally sanctioned and supported learning opportunities provided to faculty by the school and school system. Group development (D) is the gathering together of teachers to make decisions on mutual instructional concerns. Action research (E) is the systematic study by a faculty of what is happening in the classroom and school with the aim of improving learning.

By understanding how teachers grow optimally in a supportive and challenging environment, the supervisor can plan the tasks of supervision to bring together organizational goals and teacher needs into a single fluid entity. The unification of individual teacher needs with organizational goals in "a cause beyond oneself" has been demonstrated to promote powerful instruction and improved student learning.

Figure 1–1, therefore, presents the organization of this textbook in a nutshell. Part II will be devoted to essential knowledge. Part III will deal with interpersonal skills. Part IV will explain technical skills the supervisor needs, and Part V will discuss the application of such knowledge and skills to the tasks of supervision. Finally, Part VI will suggest ways of applying knowledge, skills, and tasks to integrate individual needs with organizational goals to achieve instructional success.

EXERCISES

ACADEMIC

1. Compare this chapter's definition of *educational supervision* with at least four definitions of educational supervision found in other supervision texts.

2. This chapter lists five tasks of educational supervision. Rank these tasks according to what you consider their order of importance. Write a rationale for your ranking.

3. Several recent national studies have cited shortcomings in U.S. public education and have called for educational reforms. After reviewing one of these studies, discuss the major educational problems the study cites and the major reforms it recommends.

4. This chapter describes two schools, Finnie Tyler High School and Germando Elementary School. For both schools, discuss at least three instructional problems likely to result from the type of supervision practiced by the respective principals. For each probable instructional problem, discuss how such a problem could be avoided or better managed through more appropriate supervision.

5. Review three journal articles that deal with the tasks, roles, and responsibilities of educational supervision. Write a summary of each article.

FIELD

1 Prepare five questions to be asked during an interview with a school supervisor, focusing on problems the supervisor confronts in his or her attempts to facilitate instructional improvement and how he or she attempts to manage such problems. Conduct the interview and write a brief report on the supervisor's responses.

2. Arrange to visit a school with which you are not familiar. If possible, include visits to the school office, a few classrooms, the teachers' lounge, the cafeteria, and the school playground. Write a description of the learning climate of the school, including examples of how the type of supervision present in the school affects the learning climate.

3. Ask three supervisors and three teachers to list what they consider the five most important tasks of educational supervision. Write a report comparing supervisors' perceptions with teachers' perceptions with the five tasks of supervision outlined in Chapter 1.

4. Ask two supervisors, two teachers, two students, and two parents to write one or two paragraphs on "What Makes an Effective School." After reviewing the responses, write a report discussing and comparing the respondents' perceptions.

5. Arrange a panel interview of four persons on the topic "What Makes an Effective School." The panel might include supervisors, teachers, parents, students, and perhaps business and community leaders. Record the discussion on a tape recorder.

11

References

DEVELOPMENTAL

1. Write down any questions concerning educational supervision that you have raised while reading Chapter 1. Refer to these questions as you read appropriate chapters in the remainder of this book.

2. Review Figure 1–1 and the model of educational supervision it implies. As you continue to explore this book and other readings in supervision, begin to formulate your own proposed model of educational supervision.

3. Begin a file (to be kept throughout your reading of this book) on knowledge, skills, and procedures gained from the text and related activities that can be used by you as a supervisor—either now or in the future—to help teachers improve their instructional performance.

REFERENCES

2
Harris, B. M. 1975. *Supervisory behavior in education,* 2nd ed. Englewood Cliffs, N.J.: Prentice Hall.

MacKenzie, D. E. 1983. Research for school improvement: An appraisal of some recent trends. *Educational Researcher 12*(4):8.

McDonald, J. 1981. Hermeneutics and curriculum, Address to a meeting on curriculum development, Athens, Ga., May.

Purkey, S. C., and Smith, M. S. 1982. Too soon to cheer? Synthesis of research on effective schools. *Educational Leadership 40*-(3):64–69.

Schneider, E. J. 1982–1983. Stop the bandwagon, we want to get off. *Educational R & D Report 5*(1):7–11.

PART II

Knowledge

Introduction

Part II examines the prerequisite knowledge for supervision. Chapter Two will explain the optimistic news found in school research on characteristics of effective schools, with particular attention to those work environment factors within the province of supervision. Chapter Three will consider the pessimistic news—why schools typically are ineffective. The causes of ineffectiveness will be traced to the teaching career, the school environment, and some characteristics of teachers. Chapter Four will explain how optimal adult development contrasts with the teaching career. Chapter Five will look at how supervisory practices might respond to helping teachers develop and eliminate the causes of ineffectiveness. While moving from optimism to pessimism to realism, the reader will be riding through highly explosive grounds. Reactions of delight, anger, chagrin, hope, and disagreement are to be expected as current research challenges us to rethink current supervisory practices.

CHAPTER TWO

The Exception: What Schools Can Be

Background to School Effectiveness Studies

What makes schools effective? Asking what makes schools *ineffective* will help us answer this question. The research of the late 1960s and 1970s reported that most schools are not effective. James Coleman's assessment of equality in 1966 was the second-largest school study done in the United States. He and his staff canvassed schools across the country in rural, urban, and suburban settings. He considered the contributions to school quality of a wide range of characteristics—teacher academic credentials, district per-pupil expenditures, instructional materials, socioeconomic background of students, racial mix of students, structure and age of physical plant, and size of school. He found that most school variables had little or no relationship to student achievement. Performance on standardized tests was not affected by teacher credentials, per-pupil cost, materials, or curriculum. Instead, the variable that had the greatest relationship with student achievement was the composition of the student population. Students from low-income populations did significantly better when they attended schools where a majority of students came from middle- or upper-income populations. When school composition was mostly low-income, students did not perform as well. Coleman concluded that the strongest variable accounting for student achievement was parents' socioeconomic class. He observed further that this variable was beyond the control of the school. Children of middle- or upper-income families entered schools substantially ahead of students of low-income families; as they continued in school, the achievement gap between socioeconomic levels grew larger. Wealthy students stayed ahead, and poor students fell further behind. Regardless of the school's physical plant, teachers, materials, or finances, the gap enlarged. Most interpretations of Coleman's study indicate that schools made no difference in student achievement.

In 1968 Christopher Jencks and colleagues reanalyzed Coleman's data and issued a report entitled *Inequality: A Reassessment of the Effect of Family and Schooling in America.* Instead of using achievement test results to measure school effectiveness, Jencks looked at employment that students secured after leaving public school. He studied factors that contributed to students going into different careers or vocations, such as higher education, white-collar or blue-collar work, and those who remained unemployed. First, the reassessment of Coleman's data reaffirmed that school success was largely a result of socioeconomic status and not of teachers or schools. Second, a student's job success in terms of status and pay was similar to the parents' occupational status. Those who obtained high-status jobs were children of parents with high-status jobs. Finding a specific job was a matter of chance and included being at the right place at the right time. It was socioeconomic background, however, that influenced students to use behavior, language, and manners appropriate for specific job opportunities. Students of low-income parents usually mirrored the conditions of their parents and either secured low-status and low-paying jobs or went onto the unemployment and welfare rolls. Jencks concluded that public schools not only did not help alleviate inequality in the United States but, in fact, contributed to such inequality. He concluded that the solutions to equal opportunity in adult life were not to be found in the schools but, instead, in the redistribution of wealth in the larger society.

During the time of these studies, another distinguished researcher was moving across the country, visiting schools to observe classrooms and to interview teachers, principals, and administrators. He and his staff were studying classroom practices and what students were learning. In his 1971 book, *Crisis in the Classroom,* Charles Silberman concluded from his lengthy studies that schools were not only ineffective but mindless as well. When he asked teachers and principals to articulate the reasons they organized their schools or classes in certain ways, used particular instructional materials, or grouped their students as they did, the reply was more often than not an incredulous "I don't know, we've always done it this way." When he sought to establish the priorities or objectives of each school, Silberman found little consistency between the response and what actually transpired in the classrooms. He found schools were operating in a confused manner without specific purpose, commitment, understanding, or shared belief.

Silberman's study, together with those of Coleman and

Jencks, left a haze over the landscape of public education—one that has yet to lift. Popular books on education such as Jonathan Kozol's *Death at an Early Age* and Ivan Illich's *Deschooling Society* have weakened confidence further in school effectiveness. The media have focused on declining achievement scores and the continued erosion of public confidence. The National Commission on Excellence in Education in its "Open Letter to the American People" (1983) reported that U.S. students rank considerably below those of other nations on achievement tests, that twenty-three million Americans are functionally illiterate, that average achievement scores of students are lower than those of twenty-six years ago, that only 20 percent of seventeen-year-olds can write a persuasive essay, and that only a third can solve multistep problems in mathematics.

The concern with the lack of effectiveness of public education, whether fair or not, has continued to grow. For the first time in the history of U.S. public education, there is a serious move to provide federal aid to private schools in the form of tuition tax credits to parents who send their children to private schools. At the same time, the federal government has cut its expenditures to public schools. Such action is a dramatic display of the perceived failure of public education (Glickman and Bruce 1982). In the midst of all this gloom, however, a ray of light has appeared. In the last few years some research has proved that not all public schools deserve such pessimism.

What Makes Schools Effective?

Researchers including Edmonds, Brookover, Rutter, and Goodlad are proving that there *are* effective schools and school systems. The large normative studies of the mid-1960s and early 1970s were concerned with schools as monolithic institutions. A researcher who pulls together data from many schools looks for the overall influences schools have on students. If the overwhelming majority of schools are ineffective, the group results would wash out those individual schools that might have results to the contrary. The research of the mid-1970s and 1980s has focused on individual schools that are exceptional, that consistently achieve results with students far superior to those of schools in general. In composition of student body, location, socioeconomic setting, and per-pupil expenditure these schools do not differ from schools in general. Yet whether they are in poor urban areas or in wealthy suburbs, they succeed while others fail.

Ronald Edmonds, after discovering that results of his own research were consistent with those of other independent investigations, has been confident enough to predict that *all schools could be effective*. In his words (1979, p. 22):

> It seems to me, therefore, that what is left of this discussion are three declarative statements: (a) We can, whenever and wherever we choose, successfully teach all children whose schooling is of interest to us; (b) We already know more than we need to do that; and (c) Whether or not we do it must finally depend on how we feel about the fact that we haven't so far.

How can one make such bold statements? What are these findings that so contradict the gloomy assessments of Coleman, Jencks, Silberman, and the National Commission on Excellence in Education? Effective schools have faculties with a clear, collective purpose toward which they work. They believe in "a cause beyond oneself." This is the author's phrase, but let's look at how such a phrase has been derived from the research. Edmonds conducted three different studies. His first study was of two inner-city schools in Detroit; the second was of fifty-five effective schools in the Northeast (discovered by reanalyzing the Coleman study); and the third included twenty schools in inner-city New York. He found that effective schools were distinguished by the presence of:

- Strong leadership.

- A climate of expectation.

- An orderly but not rigid atmosphere.

- Communication to students of the school's priority on learning the basics.

- Diversion of school energy and resources when necessary to maintain priorities.

- Means of monitoring student (and teacher) achievement (Edmonds 1979).

Brookover's research on six improving Michigan elementary schools as contrasted with two declining schools contained similar results. Improving schools were distinguished by:

- An emphasis on academics

- Teachers' belief that students could master the subjects and

- Less satisfaction on the part of teachers in the effective
  schools with their instruction (Brookover et al. 1979).

Fifteen Thousand Hours by Rutter et al. (1979) is a study of
twelve inner-city London high schools. Effective schools were defined by high levels of student achievement, attitudes, and attendance, and low rates of delinquency. Some of their findings were as
follows:

> the teachers in the schools which were more suc-
> cessful . . . were much less likely to report that they had
> absolute freedom in planning their course [1979, p. 112].

> . . . children's behavior is most likely to be good in school
> when there is an agreed discipline approach, but not too
> much actual use of punishment [1979, p. 122].

> It was striking, however, that in the less successful
> schools teachers were often left completely alone to plan
> what to teach, with little guidance or supervision from
> their senior colleagues and little coordination with other
> teachers to ensure a coherent course from year to year
> [1979, p. 136].

"A Study of Schooling" by John Goodlad and associates was
concluded in December, 1981, and the final results recently have
been released (Goodlad 1983a, 1983b, 1983c, 1984). Goodlad studied thirteen triples (a *triple* consists of an elementary, middle, and
senior high school that pass the same students on to each other).
The triples, selected as a representative sample of schools in the
United States, were taken from seven regions. After surveying
1,350 teachers; 18,000 students; 8,600 parents; and all the principals, superintendents, and school board members in these
schools—and after 5,000 classroom observations—Goodlad (1982)
drew several strong conclusions:

- The greatest predictor of school success was goal congruence
  between teachers, administrators, students, and parents.

- The staff in effective schools had little concern about violence,
  discipline, and management; instead, their concern was with
  the school's educational priorities.

- Effective schools were perceived as workplaces that provided
  autonomy as well as involvement in educational decisions.

- Teachers in effective schools spent more time on instruction,
  and students spent more time on learning tasks.

■ There was little difference in actual techniques and methods of teaching between effective and ineffective schools.

The findings of the various studies of school effectiveness differ somewhat, but there is also a remarkable central tendency. In terms of instruction within the classroom, effective schools are marked by:

■ A particular instructional focus.

■ Student time spent on work corresponding to that instructional focus.

■ Continual monitoring and checking of students' work by teachers.

■ Teacher time spent on instruction rather than peripheral duties.

■ Consistent classroom rules.

■ Teacher reinforcement of correct behavior and avoidance of punishment.

■ Teacher expectations that students will succeed.

■ Homework assigned and corrected daily by teachers.

A Cause Beyond Oneself

Later chapters on observation, direct assistance, in-service education, and curriculum development will explain how a supervisor can use the research on effective classroom practice with teachers. For now, however, the outside-the-classroom but within-the-school factors that correlate with or predict school effectiveness provide the more significant issue. All the research on effective schools has cited a particular type of social organization, which Edmonds referred to as a "climate of expectation." Brookover called it "teacher belief that students could learn and not being satisfied with less," and Goodlad cited it as "goal participation and agreement." Rutter et al. (1979, p. 184) identified this social organization as a "concept of ethos . . . the well-nigh universal tendency for individuals in common circumstances to form social groups with their own rules, values and standards of behavior." Where ethos was developed around a clear educational purpose, an effective school emerged:

It should be emphasized that the more successful schools were not unduly regimented. Rather, good morale and the routine of people working harmoniously together as part of an efficient system meant that both supervision and support were available to teachers in a way which was absent in less successful schools [Rutter et al. 1979, p. 184].

Every major research study on effective schools has noted the organizational phenomenon of collective action, agreed-on purpose, and belief in attainment (Pratzner 1984). On the other hand, every major research study on ineffective schools has noted an absence of such purpose. Effective schools do not happen by accident: Supervision is the force that shapes the organization into a productive unit.

Clearly, one characteristic of effective schools is that each teacher has what the author refers to as "a cause beyond oneself." Teachers do not view their work as simply what they carry out within their own four walls. Instead, in successful schools, teachers see themselves as part of the larger enterprise of complementing and working with each other to educate students. For successful schools, education is a collective and not individual enterprise.

Chapter One introduced two schools, Finnie Tyler High School and Germando Elementary School. Neither was a successful school because both lacked "a cause beyond oneself." Teachers in one school, forced to do as they were told, therefore did not participate in formulating or working toward a common cause. In the other school teachers could do whatever they liked, and therefore they also did not participate in a common cause. Unless the individual needs of staff members are linked with collective school goals, a school cannot be successful.

Effective schools are characterized by teachers who enjoy working with each other *as* they accomplish school tasks. In many schools teachers enjoy being with each other, but the task dimension is missing. They laugh, they party, but they don't get anything done. In other schools, accomplishing tasks (writing curriculum, revising schedules, filling out forms, following the text) predominates over individual and social needs. People are busy; but their tension is evident in gossip, sidelong glances, and frowns. As a result, tasks are accomplished in a forced, hurried manner; the participants feel neither kinship with each other nor commitment to each other in carrying out the tasks. They may even resist carrying out the tasks because of the impersonal manner in which these tasks are chosen. Neither type of school is truly professional or effective. An effective school balances both dimensions so that people enjoy each other's company when they are accomplishing school goals.

What to Do with School Effectiveness Research: Some Propositions

Based on effective-school research, certain propositions can be made concerning the attitude, confidence, awareness, stimulation, and thoughtfulness of teachers that can be promoted via supervision.

- Proposition 1: *Supervision can enhance teacher belief in a cause beyond oneself.* Teachers can see themselves not just as individuals separated by classroom walls, but as a body of people complementing and strengthening each other.

- Proposition 2: *Supervision can promote teachers' sense of efficacy.* Teachers can see themselves as being able to instruct students successfully, regardless of influences outside of school. Within the school they can learn to believe they do have control over management and instruction. They have power to reach students.

- Proposition 3: *Supervision can make teachers aware of how they complement each other in striving for common goals.* Teachers can observe each other at work, share materials, pick up techniques from each other, and learn how to support each other.

- Proposition 4: *Supervision can stimulate teachers to plan common purpose and actions.* Teachers can be given responsibilities to guide and assist others, to make decisions about schoolwide instruction, to plan in-service training, to develop curriculum, and to engage in action research. Such involvement shows respect and trust in teachers and strengthens collective action.

- Proposition 5: *Supervision can challenge teachers to think abstractly about their work.* Teachers can be given feedback, questioned, and confronted to appraise, reflect, and adapt their current practices to future instruction. More varied and abstract thinking is the result.

In summary, supervision must be viewed as developmental if schools are to become more successful. Supervision must not only respond to current teacher performance but also encourage greater involvement, autonomous thinking, and collective action by teachers. The first order of business for a supervisor is to build the staff into a team. In order to improve school instruction, a supervisor has to work with staff to create a professional togetherness. They must share a common purpose for their instruction. They must have confidence that their collective action will make a difference in their students' lives.

Gaining knowledge of effective schools and effective classrooms is only the first step in improving schools. Using such knowledge in one's own school demands skill and practice. Skill and practice flow from knowledge. We have seen that the research on school effectiveness converges on the concept of a cause beyond oneself or a belief in collective action. To use that knowledge, a supervisor needs further understanding about teaching and the teaching profession to understand why such a cause beyond oneself does not occur naturally in schools.

EXERCISES

ACADEMIC

1. Write a personal reaction to this chapter's summary of the Coleman study in which you support or criticize its major conclusions. Base your reaction on your own experience and/or observation of public education.

2. The chapter summarizes the results of several studies of effective schools, but also suggests the majority of schools are not effective. Prepare a report expressing your agreement or disagreement.

3. Review three journal articles that deal with research on effective schools. Based on these readings and your reading of the text, compile a composite list of probable characteristics of an effective school.

4. Read single chapters dealing with the same topic from two books listed as references for Chapter Two. Write a paper comparing and contrasting the two authors' conclusions concerning the chosen topic.

5.   For each of the chapter's five propositions based on effective-school research, write a description of a related supervisory activity that you believe could improve the effectiveness of teachers in a typical school setting. Write rationales to support the relationship between each proposition and corresponding supervisory activity.

FIELD

1.   The chapter asserts that effective supervision must provide for both completing tasks and meeting individual and social needs. Observe an administrator or supervisor who is able to balance task and human needs effectively. Write a report on your observations, including a description of the knowledge, skills, and procedures the supervisor draws on in meeting both organizational goals and teacher needs.

2.   Present the chapter's five propositions based on effective-school research to a group of educators. The group may include teachers, supervisors, or both. After presenting each proposition, ask for reactions from the educators, including their opinions as to whether each proposition is or can become a reality in their own educational setting. Record the interviews in writing or on audiotape.

3.   Prepare a slide or transparency presentation on a summary of effective-school research. Make your presentation to a group of educators. Ask for and record reactions to your presentation.

4.   Visit a school that is perceived to be an effective school by both educators and community members. Seek and observe examples of effective leadership, communication, instruction, and other factors that researchers have found to be present in effective schools. Take photographs representative of the effective characteristics observed. Mount selected photographs on poster board along with brief written descriptions of how the scene in each photograph relates to effective education. Display your photo essay to interested parties.

5.   Conduct an interview with a supervisor or administrator in a business, industrial, government, or military setting, focusing on how he or she attempts to integrate organizational goals (task emphasis) with employees' individual and social needs (human emphasis). Write a summary of his or her attitudes, strategies, and methods and your opinion about whether they can be applied to a school setting.

DEVELOPMENTAL

1. Maintain an ongoing review of prominent educational journals for reports on future effective-school research. With each new research study, look for (a) findings not already indicated in the review of research in Chapter Two, and (b) any findings that tend to contradict the research cited in Chapter Two.

2. Monitor any major changes in leadership style, curriculum, in-service education, or instruction within a local school system over the next few months. Examine such changes to determine which are at least partially based on recent research on effective schools.

3. Examine statements made by prominent educational, political, and civic leaders over the next few months that include proposals for educational reform. To what extent do such proposals reflect what we have learned from research on effective schools?

REFERENCES

Brookover, W.; Beady, C.; Flood, P.; Schweiter, J.; and Wisenbaker, J. 1979. School social systems and students achievement. *Schools can make a difference*. New York: Praeger.

Coleman, J. S.; Campbell, E. Q.; Hobson, C. J.; McPartland, J.; Mood, A. M.; Weinfield, F. D.; and York, R. L. 1966. *Equality of educational opportunity*. Washington, D.C.: U.S. Government Printing Office.

Edmonds, R. 1979. Effective schools for the urban poor. *Educational Leadership 37*(1):15–24.

Glickman, C. D., and Bruce, R. E. 1982. Restructuring the role of the American public school. *Educational Forum 47*(2):151–159.

Goodlad, J. I. 1982. A study of schooling. Paper presented to the Stanford Teacher Education Project, Stanford, Calif., January 28.

———. 1983a. A study of schooling: Some findings and hypotheses. *Phi Delta Kappan 64*(7):465–470.

————. 1983b. A study of schooling: Some implications for school improvement. *Phi Delta Kappan 64*(18):552–558.

————. 1983c. What some schools and classrooms teach. *Educational Leadership 40*(7):8–19.

————. 1984. *A place called schools: Prospects for the future.* New York: McGraw-Hill.

Illich, I. D. 1972. *Deschooling society.* New York: Harrow Books.

Jencks, C. 1972. *Inequality: A reassessment of the effect of family and schooling in America.* New York: Basic Books.

Kozol, J. 1967. *Death at an early age.* Boston: Houghton-Mifflin.

National Commission on Education. 1983. An open letter to the American people, a nation at risk: The imperative for educational reform by the National Commission on Excellence in Education. *Education Week 2*(31):12.

Pratzner, F. C. 1984. Quality of school life: Foundations for improvement. *Educational Researcher 13*(3):20–25.

Rutter, M.; Maughan, B.; Mortimore, P.; Ouston, J.; and Smith, A. 1979. *Fifteen thousand hours: Secondary schools and their effects on children.* Cambridge, Mass.: Harvard University Press.

Silberman, C. E. 1971. *Crisis in the classroom: The remakings of American education.* New York: Random House.

CHAPTER THREE

The Norm: Why Schools Are as They Are

This chapter will consider why the five propositions about supervision and effective schools presented in Chapter 2 do not happen by chance but instead must be carefully planned and deliberately carried out over time by a person or persons who conceptualize the supervisory function as described in this book. Let's begin by looking at the teaching profession from three perspectives. First, we will examine the teaching career. Second, we will look at the work environment of schools. Third, we will read about the population of those who choose to teach. Finally, we will argue that supervision must intervene to change the norms of most schools if they are to become more successful.

The Teaching Career

A body of research describing the teaching profession has emerged from sociology. Sociologists have used observations, surveys, and interviews to analyze the teaching career, the work environment, and the people who enter and remain in the teaching profession. What they have found is important for supervisors who wish to promote strongly motivated career teachers. At times, it is not a pretty picture.

Dan Lortie's *School Teacher* (1975) is the seminal work about the teaching career. His findings were based on personal interviews of public school teachers in six school systems, five near Boston, Massachusetts, and one in southern Florida. He also used the data from the National Education Association (NEA) survey on the status of the American public school teacher. The following are some of his insights.

Honorable but Menial

Teaching in America began as an honored, yet poorly paid and often menial job. Teachers were second to the town minister in prestige, and much of their instruction was tied to religious matters. They were paid a subsistence allowance for their spiritual endeavors and were expected to sweep the classroom, maintain the building, and keep the stove filled with wood. From its beginnings in America, teaching has been perceived as a profession both honorable and menial—never as a high-status profession.

Preparation of Teachers

Teacher preparation has been less rigorous than training for high-status professions. Teaching has allowed relative ease of entry into its ranks. Traditionally, requirements for teachers majoring in education have been lower than for those majoring in liberal arts, language, engineering, medicine, or science. Course work within the major often is regarded by students as easy and trivial (Mickey Mouse is the common term). Education students only rarely fail courses or are removed from their preparation program. There are no required internship periods for teachers outside of undergraduate field experiences and student teaching.

Unstaged Career

A beginning teacher moves from undergraduate college to a school job with the same responsibilities as—if not more than— those of teachers who have been in the field a year, or thirty-five years. More prestigious professions avoid such an abrupt transition from student to full professional. Physicians, lawyers, engineers, and scientists all experience several transition years of apprenticeship, internship, and junior membership on the job before they qualify for full rights and responsibilities in the profession.

This set of circumstances leads to the negative characteristic of the teaching profession that perhaps most significantly differentiates it from others—an unstaged career ladder. More prestigious occupations have rigorous undergraduate screening and requirements. Furthermore, they have a transitional or proving-ground stage; only when an aspirant has endured and been judged competent by senior members does the junior member step into the next stage of the career, which provides high visibility, a substantial increase in salary, and responsibility for monitoring and judging the next wave of junior members. For example, a law school graduate must pass the bar exam and then serve as a clerk to a judge, as a legal aide, or as a junior member of a law firm. He or she works behind the scenes on writing and research that are credited to his or her superior. After proving competence over time, however, the lawyer then becomes a partner in a firm, a public prosecuter or defender, or an independent lawyer. This movement brings visibility and stature in the profession and the right to have one's own apprentices to do the less exciting work.

This apprenticeship period has persisted because aides, interns, or assistants are willing to endure the long hours and hard work in view of the ultimate benefits. It is not unusual for the salary of a legal assistant, a medical intern, a junior engineer, or a graduate assistant to double upon promotion to full membership in the profession. The public appears to recognize and applaud this long, arduous, and selective process as a requirement for membership in a high-status profession.

Teaching, on the other hand, is unstaged from entry to exit. Education majors do not have to be as academically gifted as their peers who choose other majors. Neither must they persevere through the trials, tribulations, and transitions to becoming full members of their profession. They simply take courses, spend time in schools, perform as student teachers, and then graduate from college into their own classrooms as teachers. *After that, no matter how many years they continue to teach, they do not move into another stage.* The twenty-year veteran teacher has the same classroom space, number of students, and requirements as the first-year teacher. Furthermore, for each year of experience a teacher realizes a salary increase identical to that received by all others of comparable experience.

Easy In, Easy Out

Lortie labels teaching an "easy in, easy out" profession. A teacher can teach one or two years, return five years later, and still have virtually the same job as the teacher who has continued for seven years. The same is not true of a medical doctor, dentist, lawyer, or scientist. After interrupting their careers for five years, they simply cannot return without specialized training to update knowledge and practice. When such professionals do return, their colleagues will have advanced significantly in professional responsibilities and economic benefits.

Lortie's critics say his characterization of teaching is not true in today's age of teacher surplus. The critics state that in fact a teacher who leaves may not be able to return. This point is valid but it misses Lortie's point that if, for example, I returned to teaching the sixth-grade class at Unity Grammar School in Maine, where I taught more than ten years ago, I would be able to teach much as I did in 1972. Furthermore, I would be assigned substantially the same responsibilities as the other intermediate-grade teacher, Mrs. Hawes, who would be starting her twenty-fifth consecutive year.

To summarize, Lortie has pointed out that teaching differs from more prestigious professions. First, it has a history of being both honorable and menial. Second, requirements for entry into it are neither strict nor selective. Third, the career has no internship period; it is unstaged and not future-directed. Fourth, it is an easy in, easy out profession in that responsibilities or stature do not change according to the tenure of the teacher

The Work Environment of Teachers

We can add to Lortie's research the works of Phil Jackson—*Life in Classrooms* (1968), Seymour Sarason—*The Culture of the School and the Problem of Change* (1971), and Robert Dreeben—"The School as a Workplace" (1973). Teachers have described their work environment as routinized, isolated, characterized by multiple psychological encounters and perpetual tension. What do they mean?

Routine

The routine of the teaching day is imposed by administrative fiat, school board policy, and state guidelines. Every classroom teacher is required to be at school before students enter and to remain until they have departed. In primary or elementary schools, a teacher has specific times for recess and lunch and approximate time allocations for teaching a given subject (for example, forty-five minutes for reading, thirty minutes for mathematics, thirty minutes twice a week for social studies). The teacher is assigned a certain number of students and has responsibility for these students for the entire day and school year. He or she is expected to remain physically in the assigned classroom for the entire school day, with the exception of recess, lunch, or special classes. Outside the classroom, teachers also have scheduled responsibilities for lunch, recess, and dismissal. In middle or junior high and senior high schools, the school day is different from that of elementary schools but still has a set routine. A secondary teacher will have four to seven different classes of students meeting at specific times each day for an extended period (eleven, eighteen, or thirty-six weeks). Again, the teacher begins and dismisses each class at a prescribed time and has regular duties outside the classroom (for example, monitoring the lunchroom, halls, or bathrooms).

Regardless of grade level, teachers do not schedule their own time or determine the number or type of students. Unlike more autonomous professionals, teachers do not put up a shingle on the door, ask clients to arrange for appointments, or take Wednesday mornings off. Teachers do not have the right to make changes in their schedule. Imagine a teacher asking the school secretary to clear his or her schedule for several hours so he or she can attend to other business. School goes on; students keep coming, the bells keep ringing; and teachers cannot make individual readjustments of their professional time.

Of course, elementary and secondary teachers often do make readjustments *within* the assigned time, *within* their four walls, *with* their assigned students, and *with* instruction. School time, however, is imposed. Starting and ending times, numbers of students, physical locations for teaching, and extra duties are set for the duration, and a teacher has little control. The routines the school as a workplace imposes are more like those of the factory than like those of high-status professions. The punch-in, punch-out clock may not be visible in the entering hallway of the school, but nonetheless it exists.

Psychological Dilemma

The teacher's work environment is marked by incessant psychological encounters. In just a few minutes of observation, one might see a teacher ask a question, reply with a smile to a student's answer, frown at an inattentive student, ask a student to be quiet, put a hand on a student's shoulder, and begin to lecture. Teachers have thousands of such psychological encounters in a normal school day (Jackson 1968). A look, a shrug, a word—all have intended meanings between teacher and students.

Each day an elementary teacher meets with twenty-five to thirty-five students for six and one-half hours. A secondary teacher meets with a hundred to a hundred and fifty students for five to seven fifty-minute periods. All this human interaction takes place in a nine-hundred-square-foot room, where a teacher must instruct, manage, discipline, reinforce, socialize, and attend to multiple student occurrences. This crowded professional life makes teachers wish for smaller classes to reduce the psychological demand of constant decision making. Sarason described this incessant demand as a psychological dilemma:

> ... the teacher feels, and is made to feel, that her worth as a teacher will be judged by how much her class learns in a given period of time. The strong feeling that teachers have about the complexity of their tasks stems from the awareness that they are expected to bring their children (if not all, most) to a certain academic level by a time criterion in regard to which they have no say. Faced with numbers and diversity of children *and* the pressure to adhere to a time schedule presents the teacher not with a difficult task but an impossible one. *I say impossible because I have never met a teacher who was not aware of and disturbed by the fact that she had not the time to give to some children in the class the kind of help they needed* [p. 152; emphasis in original].

To maintain their own sanity in the face of an overload of psychological encounters and an inability to attend to the psychological needs of each student in a confined and regulated work place, teachers often cope by routinizing classroom activity. The classroom routine for students becomes similar to the outside routine for teachers. For example, a science teacher might have students listen to a twenty-minute presentation, followed by a ten-minute question and answer period and then by twenty minutes of seat work. An elementary teacher might have three reading groups who rotate to him or her for fifteen minutes each; each group reads aloud, responds to teacher questions, and then works on worksheets. By routinizing what happens within the classroom, a teacher avoids making hundreds of decisions. The routinization of teaching allows the teacher to avoid the inherent conflict between being overwhelmed psychologically by the responsibility for teaching a large number of students, and being aware of neglecting the personal needs of individual students. In interpersonal terms, teaching closely resembles clinical psychology; yet it takes place in an environment more like that of factory production.

Isolation

Teachers shoulder these psychological demands and dilemmas alone. The isolation and individuality of teachers has been observed in all major studies of their work environment. As an example of this isolation, Dreeben (1973) has noted:

perhaps the most important single property of classrooms, viewed from a school-wide perspective is their
spatial scattering and isolation throughout school buildings; and because teachers work in different places at
the same time, they do not observe each other working . . . the implications of this spatial isolation are far
reaching [p. 468].

He further wrote:

Unlike hospitals and law firms, for example, where new
recruits to medicine and law learn their trade as apprentices by performing work tasks of gradually increasing
difficulty under close supervision, schools provide a less
adequate setting—the classroom—for work and training
activities to occur simultaneously [p. 470].

As Dreeben points out, structurally, classrooms are set up so
that teachers are difficult to supervise, do not receive feedback
from others, and cannot engage in work collaboratively. During a
typical work day a teacher will talk to only a few other adults—on
the way to the classroom in the morning, for twenty minutes or so
at lunch and recess, and at the end of the day on the way out of the
building. This lack of professional contact has been documented by
a study of the modal duration of professional discussions between
teachers during a school day. DeSanctis and Blumberg (1979)
found the duration was less than two minutes.

What about committee, department, and faculty meetings that
bring teachers together? Unfortunately, such meetings often are
only for disseminating information, not for purposes of discussion.

While teaching, teachers in most schools are invisible to each
other and lack any concrete knowledge of what other teachers are
doing in the classroom. To see just how strong this tradition of
classroom isolation is, think of schools built in the 1970s according
to an open-space design. Within a few years, in almost every
school, portable partitions were erected to wall off each classroom.
The one-room schoolhouses of pioneer days are still with us. Today,
however, the one-room schoolhouses are found every few yards
along a school corridor. Little wonder, then, that most school faculties do not work well together. They do not talk with each other
about professional matters, and they seldom see what others are
doing.

Suppose members of a surgical staff were given separate cubi-
cles to perform their specific but common function of saving the
patient. The patient would be wheeled first into the anesthesiolo-

gist's cubicle for drugs, then into the technician's room for monitoring of vital signs, then to the surgeon's room for the first incision, back to the technician's room for monitoring vital signs, to the surgeon's assistant's room for cleaning the incision, to the surgeon's room for the second incision. . . . An absurd notion of how to save the patient! This is the work environment of teaching—more comparable to that of a garment piecework operation, where no one except top management needs to know what each person is doing. In high-status professions, by contrast, success depends on professionals working together to combine, review, and share their knowledge, skills, and practices.

The preceding description of teaching gives some understanding of the situation supervisors must work with to help teachers bring about instructional improvement. Observations of the work environment form general and consistent patterns. As John Goodlad points out in his recent study of schooling, waves of educational reform have not made much of a dent in the unstaged nature of the teaching career or in the psychological dilemma or the loneliness of public school teaching (Goodlad, 1983).

Those Who Teach

Much of what is to follow is a description of teachers (myself included) that even at its most uncomplimentary must be understood. Keep in mind that the discussion is about groups, not individuals. Currently, the teaching profession systematically pulls out competent people and sometimes locks in individuals who would rather be elsewhere. A National Education Association (NEA) survey (UPI 1978) found that 80 percent of teachers who had taught more than five years would not choose teaching as a profession again if given the chance. A more recent study by Lowther, Stark, Austin, Chapman, and Hutcheson (1981) found that ". . . career teachers are characterized by a strong sense of being locked into their current job and negative view of their prospects." In economically distressed times, they do not have the mobility to move to another school system or a different career. Career teachers are, by and large, not happy with their fate.

There is evidence that the caliber of teachers entering the profession is considerably lower than in the past (Schlechty and Vance 1981). Members of the teaching profession are generally of low to moderate intelligence, with personalities that tend toward conformity and modest career or personal ambitions (see Lacey 1977)

Unblocking Career Aspirations

As a result of the laxity with which prospective teachers in colleges of education are screened, education majors rank significantly below other professional majors on measures of scholastic achievement, intelligence, and grades. For example, biology and physics majors in colleges score significantly higher than science education majors; English majors score significantly higher than English education majors. Lortie found that for many education students, the choice represented a blocked aspiration to major in another field. According to Lortie (1975, p. 49), "Teaching had a distinct advantage in competing for the secondary allegiance of those who could not pursue their primary goals. . . ." Those who realized that their desire to be a medical doctor, business entrepreneur, engineer, or professional athlete was not to be fulfilled could find a respectable and closely aligned second choice in teaching science, business, industrial arts, or physical education. Blocked aspirations are the result of competition among many candidates for only a few positions, deficient academic grades and test scores, lack of financial resources for additional graduate schooling, or disillusionment with initial work in the desired occupation.

Ironically, the steady decline in the achievement and intelligence test scores of those entering and remaining in the teaching profession over the last decade is one result of the unblocking of first aspirations for previously denied minority populations. In the past, racial and ethnic minorities and women were discriminated against and discouraged from entering prestigious, high paying, and visible professions. Public school teaching was a profession that was more accessible to minorities. For example, an able minority person and/or woman would be counseled not to pursue an executive-level position in law, business, science, or medicine. Instead the person would be counseled into teaching, as a secondary but respectable substitute for the blocked aspiration. Since the passage of the Equal Opportunity Act, more minority persons and/or women who excel academically have had the opportunity to enter those professions previously denied. Thus many of those who would have chosen education as a major ten years ago do not do so now. Furthermore, many of those academically able persons who have been in public school teaching for a number of years now have the chance to pursue their original aspirations in a more influential, remunerative, and prestigious profession.

One female first-grade teacher comes to mind as an example of what has been happening to the teaching profession. This teacher was superb—quick-witted, articulate, imaginative, and compassionate. Students loved her and were eager to learn. At the end of her third year, however, the teacher submitted her resignation after having been accepted as a student in a major law school. Six years later she is a lawyer specializing in international matters, dividing her time between offices in London and New York. She is probably as effective a lawyer as she was a teacher. Ten or fifteen years ago she would have remained a primary school teacher, continuing to illuminate children's lives with the excitement of learning. Today, the opportunity for her to excel in a profession other than teaching is a story of both delight and despair—delight for this teacher turned lawyer, despair for public education.

Academic Ability of Teachers

Although the unblocking of aspirations is a commendable change in society, it has had major consequences for the teaching profession. A longitudinal seven-year study of teachers in North Carolina has shown a considerable drop in National Teacher Exam scores (NTE) and in measured academic ability of entering teachers. Schlechty and Vance (1981) wrote:

> There is considerable evidence that those who choose to major in teacher education are, as a group, less academically able than most other college majors. There is some strong evidence that graduates of teacher education institutions are not as academically proficient as most other categories of college graduates [p. 106].

The conclusion of their study of characteristics of teachers who remain in the profession compared with those who decide to leave the profession was:

> There is a strong negative relationship between measured academic ability and retention in teaching.... Year after year, those North Carolina teachers who scored highest on a test of academic ability (the NTE) are the most likely to leave education [pp. 110, 112].

My own study of teachers in the state of Georgia has uncovered findings similar to those of Schlechty and Vance (Glickman and Tamashiro 1982). Results have shown that entering teachers score significantly lower on the Graduate Record Exam (GRE) and the NTE than do those who began teaching five years earlier. Furthermore, the group scores of the population of teachers who remain in the profession drops each year. This may be a state or regional phenomenon; but in September, 1981, Milton Goldberg, director of the National Institute of Education, after reviewing national statistics about teachers, reported to the U.S. House Subcommittee on Post Secondary Education that those entering teaching are not terribly promising and that those leaving are among the best in the profession. Teaching seems to be attracting, in his words, "the least academically able students" (Rosenau 1981).

One could argue that academic achievement scores are not indicators of teaching ability, but the issue remains that those who can compete academically for entry into other professions consistently do not choose to teach.

Emulation as a Career Factor

To review, teaching is honorable but menial; requirements and entry are lax; the career is unstaged; it is an easy in, easy out career. The work environment of teaching is marked by routinization, multiple psychological encounters, and isolation. These characteristics have been enduring elements of school. Those people who aspire to become teachers as a result of positive identification with their own teachers and satisfaction as students in such a setting are, according to Lacey, ". . . committed to teaching *per se,* that is, committed to a career in the classroom and the school." They choose to teach in schools because they like the profession and occupation *as it is.* They desire, perhaps unconsciously, the unstagedness, the routine, the psychological dilemma, and the isolation.

To reinforce this point, let's cite three different research findings. Studies done on the personality of teachers finds them to be largely conforming individuals (Oja 1980; Glickman and Tamashiro 1982; Harvey 1970). Teachers as a rule seek external structure to their lives, accept the conditions under which they work, and are not autonomous or agents of change. Most teachers choose to teach in part because of, not in spite of, the conditions of their profession. There are some who choose the teaching career in spite of its conditions. These persons intend to change conditions, and they also tend to be the people who drop out (Chapman and Hutcheson 1982). According to Lacey, their original choice of teaching career arises from a wish to address societal and educational inequities by using the school to reach students. The choice of the public school setting is secondary to the educational and social reforms they wish to bring about. Lacey refers to these teachers as having a "radical commitment" to social change; the school represents a means to that end. These persons do not desire to teach school in itself and do not accept the status, routine, and isolation. Not surprisingly, Lacey found that a higher proportion of the radical-commitment teachers leave the profession because "so far as teaching proves an ineffective means, it will be deserted for other, more effective means either in education or outside" (1977, p. 121).

To Qualify, Summarize, and Propose

Viewed from a sociological perspective, teaching does not appear to appeal to the brightest of the college population. The work environment of schools sanctions conforming, unobtrusive behavior on the part of teachers. The career ladder does not depend on teachers' curiosity, resourcefulness, or competence. This overall effect leads to the following propositions as obstacles to supervision.

■ Proposition 1: *Supervision cannot rely on the teaching career to provide motivation for continual instructional improvement.* Since the teaching career has moderate status, easy requirements for preparation, unstagedness, and an easy in, easy out quality, teachers do not need to improve their instruction to continue in the profession.

■ Proposition 2: *Supervision cannot rely on the existing work environment of schools to stimulate instructional improvement.* Since the work environments of schools are routinized, isolated, and psychologically tense, teachers become private and regulated in their work rather than open to improvement.

■ Proposition 3: *Supervisors cannot assume that teachers are reflective, autonomous, and responsible for their own development.* Since teachers as a group are of moderate academic ability and may be conforming by nature, change will not normally occur solely through teacher initiative.

These three bold propositions have a basis in research but nonetheless need further qualifications. We are writing about teachers as a group, but even teachers working in adjoining classrooms of a school are not the same. How much less can we accept generalizations about the two million plus teachers in public schools across the country. There are many academically gifted, autonomous, and change-oriented teachers who are seeking answers to what their classrooms and schools can become. In fact, that is the very point of this book. *It is the schools whose staff members knowingly combat the inertia of their profession and envi-*

ronment that are most effective. In the most effective schools, supervision works to break up the routine, unstagedness, and isolation of teaching and to promote intelligent, autonomous, and collective reason in order to establish a cause beyond oneself and to become a purposeful and productive body of professionals achieving common goals for students.

There are a few signs that we may have begun to turn the corner on attracting and retaining bright, creative persons in teaching. State legislatures are passing laws to increase scholarships for prospective teachers, to increase teachers' salaries and to provide for substantial career ladders (see Pipho 1984). Two recent studies (Ginkel 1983 and Konke 1984) have shown teachers to be at higher levels of conceptual thought than teachers who have been studied in the past. Such encouraging signs provide even more of a reason to understand past and present conditions in the occupation and press further for work environment reforms. As we attract and hope to retain a new corps of bright and able teachers, we must professionalize their working lives.

The next chapter will contrast research on optimal adult development and life span transitions with what is known about teacher and occupational development. The discrepancies will provide several more propositions about the information needed for successful supervision.

EXERCISES

ACADEMIC

1. Choose a period of American history (for example, colonial period, early twentieth century) and research the state of teaching as a profession during that era. Prepare a report comparing the role, functions, working conditions, and status of teachers in the selected era and the current era.

2. Research the state of teaching as a profession in an industrialized nation other then the United States. Prepare a report comparing the role, functions, working conditions, and status of teachers from the selected nation with those of U.S. public school teachers.

3. The chapter lists routine, psychological dilemma, and isolation as three factors associated with the work environment of

teachers. Interview a supervisor about the work environment of teachers in his or her school. How does he or she attempt to improve conditions? Write a summary of your interview.

4. In most public school systems a teacher's career is unstaged. Outline a plan for a staged teaching career. Include recommended entry requirements, screening methods, description of an apprenticeship period (other than student teaching), and suggested requirements and rewards for promotion to full membership in the teaching profession. Suggest ways in which teachers who have attained full professional status can be presented with new challenges and rewarded for meeting such challenges.

5. Write an autobiographical essay in which you discuss your experiences with the daily routine, psychological encounters, and isolation you have confronted as a teacher or observed as a visitor in a public school.

FIELD

1. Interview three public school teachers of various experience levels about why they chose teaching as a career. Write a report including a brief description of each teacher, a summary of his or her reasons for becoming an educator, and comparison of the various teacher responses.

2. Conduct interviews with a veteran and a first-year public school teacher in which you ask them to compare their written job descriptions with the duties they actually carry out. During both interviews, write out a list of duties the teacher carries out that are not listed on the formal job description. Prepare a report summarizing your findings and drawing conclusions.

3. Interview a member of a graded profession (physician, attorney, college professor, scientist, engineer, and the like) who has reached full professional status. Ask the professional about the stages and challenges he or she had to pass through to attain such status, the extent to which having to pass through these grades increased his or her professional performance, and the rewards of reaching full professional status. Prepare a report summarizing the interviewer's responses and giving your opinion of whether aspects of such a graded career could be adapted to the teaching profession.

4. Interview a veteran instructor or supervisor in a teacher preparation program. Ask him or her to compare students who are preparing for a career in education today with teacher candidates of ten years ago in terms of academic preparation, performance, and commitment to a teaching career. If the interviewee perceives significant differences between present and past teacher candidates, ask for his or her perceptions of why such differences exist and how they are likely to affect the future of public education. Prepare a report summarizing the interview and drawing your own conclusions.

5. Interview an individual who was a teacher for at least five years and voluntarily left teaching for a new career. Request (a) his or her reasons for entering the teaching field, (b) his or her reasons for leaving teaching, and (c) a comparison of the teaching profession with his or her present career. Prepare a written report on the interview.

DEVELOPMENTAL

1. Refer to this book's propositions on obstacles to supervision as you read the remainder of the book. Examine the remaining chapters for proposals for dealing with instructional problems implicit in the propositions.

2. Begin a diary of how the major characteristics of your work environment affect your job performance over a period of time.

3. Begin a notebook of ideas for breaking up the inertia of the teaching profession and environment. Over time, add your own ideas and also record the ideas and actions of both teachers and supervisors you observe attempting to counter the routine, psychological dilemma, and isolation of the teaching environment. Include in your notebook ideas for promoting teacher autonomy and encouraging teachers and supervisors to focus on a cause beyond oneself.

REFERENCES

Chapman, D. W., and Hutcheson, S. M. 1982. Attrition from teaching careers: A discriminant analysis. *American Educational Research Journal* 19(1):93–105.

41

References

DeSanctis, M., and Blumberg, A. 1979. An exploratory study into the nature of teacher interactions with other adults in the schools. Paper presented at the annual meeting of the American Educational Research Association, San Francisco, April.

Dreeben, R. 1973. The school as a workplace. In R. M. Travers, ed., *Second handbook of research on teaching*. Chicago: Rand McNally, pp. 450–473.

Ginkel, K. 1983. An overview of a study which examined the relationship between elementary school teachers' preference for supervisory conferencing approach and conceptual level of development. Paper presented at the annual meeting of the American Educational Research Association, Montreal, April.

Glickman, C. D., and Tamashiro, R. T. 1982. A comparison of first year, fifth year, and former teachers on efficacy, ego development and problem solving. *Psychology in the Schools 19-*(4):558–562.

Goodlad, J. I. 1983. A study of schooling: Some findings and hypotheses. *Phi Delta Kappan 64*(7):465–470.

Harvey, O. J. 1970. Beliefs and behavior: Some implications for education. *The Science Teacher 37*(December):10–14, 73.

Jackson, P. W. 1968. *Life in classrooms*. New York: Holt, Rinehart & Winston.

Konke, K. 1984. A study of the relationship of teacher conceptual level with perceptions of teachers in regard to staff development, curriculum development, and instructional improvement. Paper presented at the annual meeting of the American Educational Research Association, New Orleans, April.

Lacey, C. 1977. *The socialization of teachers: Contemporary sociology of the school*. London: Methuen

Lortie, D. C. 1975. *School teacher: A sociological inquiry*. Chicago: University of Chicago Press.

Lowther, M. A.; Gill, S. J.; and Coppard, L. C. 1981. The quality of teachers' worklife. Unpublished manuscript, University of Michigan.

Lowther, M. A.; Stark, J. S.; Austin, A. E., Chapman, D. W.; and Hutcheson, S. M. 1981. Career lock-in as a factor in teachers' perceptions of occupational and life satisfaction. Paper presented at the annual meeting of the American Educational Research Association, Los Angeles, April.

Oja, S. N. 1980. Adult development is implicit in staff development. *Journal of Staff Development,* October, pp. 7–56.

Pipho, C. 1984. Stateline: Governors provide leadership for education. *Phi Delta Kappan 65*(7):445–446.

Rosenau, F. S. 1981. Washington report: House subcommittee hears testimony on quality of U. S. teacher training 1981, December, pp. 119–230.

Sarason, S. 1971. *The culture of the school and the problem of change.* Boston: Allyn and Bacon.

Schlechty, P. C., and Vance, V. S. 1981. Do academically able teachers leave education? The North Carolina case. *Phi Delta Kappan,* October, pp. 106–112.

United Press International (UPI). 1978. Stress, fear, frustration causing teaching dropouts. *The Delaware (Ohio) Gazette,* July 6, p. 20.

CHAPTER FOUR

Contrasting Optimal Adult Development with Actual Teacher Development: Clues for Supervisory Practice

This chapter will serve as a core for thinking and practicing supervision in a developmental framework. We have looked at effective and ineffective schools and have defined "a cause beyond oneself" as a demarcation between the collective, thoughtful, autonomous, and effective staffs of successful schools and the isolated, unreflective, and powerless staffs of unsuccessful schools. Knowledge of how teachers can grow as competent adults is the guiding principle for supervisors in finding ways to return wisdom, power, and control to both the individuals and the collective staff in order for them to become true professionals. With understanding of how teachers change, the supervisor can plan direct assistance, in-service education, curriculum development, group development, and action research at an appropriate level to stimulate professional growth and instructional improvement.

The research on adult development has been prolific (Loevinger 1976; Levinson 1977; Harvey, Hunt, and Schroeder 1961; Neugarten 1977), and the research in teacher development is advancing (McNergney and Carrier 1981; Sprinthall and Thies-Sprinthall 1982; Oja 1979; Burden 1982; Christensen, Burke, and Fessler 1983). I have attempted to distill the knowledge of adult and teacher development that has direct applications for supervision and supervisors. Readers who desire more detail should refer to the suggested references at the end of the chapter. The use of such readily available and potentially rich knowledge about human growth can be extremely valuable to those who work with adults. In order for schools to be successful, supervision must respond to teachers as changing adults.

What Is Known about Adult Development

What is known about adults, of course, cannot be summarized in a few pages, an entire book, or even a number of books. Instead it can only be hoped that this section will provide an abbreviated outline of what is known about adults in reference to hierarchies of thought and occupational transitions. The distinction between research on adult development and research on life span transitions needs to be made. Adult development is the study of adults' capabilities to improve over time. Research on life span transitions focuses on typical events and experiences that people encounter as they age.

Adult development studies have built on some of the findings of research on children. Adults change in predictable ways according to age, individual characteristics, and the demands of the environment. One major finding of adult research is that cognitive, social, and language development do not solidify at adolescence or early adulthood but continue throughout life. In childhood, changes are dramatic, as when a child changes from uttering sounds to speaking in full sentences or, within two years, goes from lying on his or her back to crawling, to walking, to running. Changes in adults usually are not so dramatic or so rapid. An adult's thinking, attitudes toward work, and social relationships change in subtle ways; differences become apparent only after many years. Keeping gradual change in mind, however, the principles of development uncovered for children appear to apply equally to adults:

1. There are common stages of growth through which all humans are capable of passing.

2. The stages are in order in that one stage precedes the next.

3. The rate of passage from one stage to the next varies from individual to individual.

In considering stage theory, some caution is necessary. Life is a complex mix of person and environment, and not all of life is growth-oriented. For example, an individual's neurological and visual capacities become less responsive over time. Each of us knows firsthand that we cannot sustain physical activity or react as quickly to stimuli as we were able to do in younger years. On the other hand, decision making, information processing, and understanding can improve with age. In some ways individuals have the capability to improve; in other ways they begin to degenerate. Research on adult development focuses on the improvement, and school supervisors can apply such knowledge to help educators improve.

Cognitive, Conceptual, and Personality Development

The areas of research in adult development most applicable to educational supervision are cognition, conceptual attainment, and personality. Havighurst (1980, p. 6), in his review of life span counseling, wrote about findings in cognition, "Research studies of the relation of aging to learning during the past 20 years have found that there are two brands or categories of intelligence, one which increased during adulthood, while the other decreases." The work of Horn and Cattell (1967), Long and Mirza (1980), and others has labeled these two categories of learning *fluid* and *crystallized*. Fluid learning depends on physiological and neurological capacities. Given similar tasks in inductive reasoning, figure matching, memory span, and perceptual speed, those below the age of thirty consistently outperform those over thirty. The decline of the nervous system accounts for the slowing of abilities to handle instant and visual information. Yet the reverse appears to be true for crystallized learning, which is predicated on relations between experiences. Older people naturally have more experience and knowledge to draw on in processing new information and solving familiar tasks. Experiments show that performance on tasks of verbal comprehension, mechanical knowledge, arithmetic ability, fluency of ideas, experiential evaluation, and general information continues to improve throughout much of the life span. The rate of increase gradually slows and, for inactive persons over sixty, eventually comes to a halt. To generalize, intelligence or the ability to solve new problems becomes a slower but more thorough process with age. An older person cannot respond as quickly but can relate more experience to understanding new problems.

In the field of conceptual development, the same type of movement is apparent. *Concept formation* might be defined as the acquisition of symbols or abstractions that accommodate particular events into an integrated, larger category. For example, the concept of *justice* is formed on the basis of multiple discrete events such as stealing, punishment, rewards, courts, trials, laws, and punishment. The research of Kohlberg and Turiel (1971) demonstrates a hierarchy of concepts related to morality. People in stage 1 of moral reasoning think that morality (reasoning what is right or wrong) is based on whether the individual is caught and punished. If he or she is going to be caught, then a person shouldn't steal. If he or she won't be caught, then it's all right. Stage 1 is called *punishment and obedience orientation*. In stage 2 people reason according to parental and societal rules. Something is judged as right or wrong according to external standards determined by authority. This is labeled the *good boy/good girl orientation*. However, persons in the highest stage (stage 6), decide what is right or wrong according to universal criteria. They consider the consequences of the act of stealing on the basis of the best interest of all people, not according to prescribed law. This orientation is labeled *individual principles of conscience*. Kohlberg found that moral reasoning is age-related and that the majority of persons do not move beyond stage 4, *conventional reasoning according to rules of authority*.

David Hunt's (1966) work on how people form concepts parallels Kohlberg's studies. According to Hunt, the normal course of conceptual development "leads to more orientations towards the environment and the interpersonal world" (Sullivan, McCullough, and Stager 1970). Stage 1 is characterized by concepts based on learning the rules or cultural standards of one's group. Stage 2 is marked by learning how the individual is distinct from the cultural standards of the group. In stage 3 one learns to empathize with others. Stage 4 is characterized by learning to see oneself both apart from and in relation to others. Concept development, as moral and crystallized learning, is the natural tendency to acquire more information about oneself, one's situation, and one's relationship with others before making judgments.

Jane Loevinger's research at the Institute for Social Science has been concerned with ego or personality development, which she defines as broader than concept or moral development. The scheme accounts for four domains: (1) impulse control or character development, (2) interpersonal style, (3) conscious preoccupations, and (4) cognitive style (Witherell and Erickson 1978). Her research on adults has resulted in definitions of ten stages and transitional levels the adult uses to make sense out of the complexity of life. Her developmental theory moves from *symbiotic* and *impulsive* thinking, where the individual is dependent on others deciding for him or her; to *conformist* levels, where thinking is conceptually simple, conforming to socially approved codes with little awareness of inner choice; to *autonomous* thinking, where a person is a "synthesizer—able to integrate conceptually ideas that appear unrelated or even oppositional to those at lower stages" (Witherell and Erikson 1978, p. 231).

Cognitive, moral, conceptual, and ego development research and theory are of use to the practicing supervisor who needs to be able to determine teacher levels when planning for direct assistance, in-service education, curriculum development, group development, and action research. Let's conclude with the statement that the findings of adult research reinforce the child development research findings of Piaget (1955) and Bruner (1960) in underscoring human development from simplistic, concrete thinking to multi-informational and abstract thinking. Soon we will look at what schools and supervisors can do to support or negate such thinking among teachers.

Life Transition

The last area of adult studies to be discussed is research on life span transitions or critical events in adults' lives. These studies are drawn from the pioneering work of Charlotte Buhler (1956) and Erik Erikson (1950). They have been refined by the work of Bernice L. Neugarten (1977) in her studies of men and women between the ages of forty and seventy; by Daniel Levinson's study (1977) of forty men of various occupational levels from their mid-thirties to mid-forties; and by Blum and Meyer's (1981) study of twenty-five heart attack patients ranging in age from thirty-one to seventy-two.

Some conclusions about life adaptations and transitions can be made. Buhler found that adults between the ages of eighteen and twenty-five are dominated by the issue of occupation and life dreams. For the next twenty years, from twenty-five to forty-five, the adult is concerned with "creative expansion" and realization of possibilities in regard to occupation, marriage, and home. The years from forty-five to sixty-five are characterized by the "establishment of inner order," with a reassessment of priorities.

Neugarten studied the timing of events such as childbearing, occupational advancement and peaking, children leaving home, retirement, personal illness, and death of a spouse or close friend. Many of these events are common to all adults; the time of their occurrence, according to Neugarten, influences how the person responds and continues with life. For example, the Blum and Meyer (1981) study of the recovery of adult men from severe heart attacks highlights the difference in timing of critical events. Young men were bitter and hostile toward their heart attack and couldn't wait to resume their previous lives. Middle-aged men were reflective about the heart attack and seriously weighed whether they wanted to continue to live as they had before. They contemplated changes in family relations, job, and living environments. Older men were accepting and grateful that the heart attack had left them alive with the opportunity to finish some of their desired retirement plans. As one can see, the same event—a heart attack—resulted in quite different reactions depending on the time and age of the adult.

Levinson's work (1977) is a coherent treatment of changes in a person's life but has limitations in that the subjects were all male, middle-class, and white-collar. However, his findings suggest some commonalities with other men and women in various occupations and might be particularly helpful in understanding the life transitions of teachers. The beginning years of adulthood are marked by active mastery of the outer world. As one approaches mid-life, the issue of making it becomes important. One sees advancement to higher status and responsibility as important not only in itself but also as a sign of how high one might aspire. If promotion or advancement does not occur, younger people move ahead while the individual remains on a plateau. With such an occurrence, the person can either accept the plateau, move to another organization within the same profession, or attempt to change careers. Becker (1971) has singled out a critical element in career success within the same organization and profession: Conforming to the social norms of the organization is imperative for career success. Advancing in a career is often tied to one's degree of assimilation to the conventions, standards, and rules of the organization. Levinson mentions that a young adult has an advantage in an organization if he or she finds a mentor. A senior executive or other established person takes the young adult under his or her wing and cautions, advises, and protects. Through the mentor, the young adult learns how to behave for later success.

Young adulthood is often a time of feelings of omnipotence, when all one's dreams are attainable. Middle adulthood is ushered in by a loss of such feelings of omnipotence with the realization of one's limitations. It occasions a period of reexamination of self and a revision of plans. The mentor relationship becomes less important as the young adult continues to move toward his or her goals and the middle-aged mentor no longer appears so exalted or wise. On the one hand, the middle-aged adult becomes more autonomous in deciding his or her priorities; on the other hand, he or she confronts the limits to what he or she can ultimately hope to accomplish. This dilemma often results in so-called mid-life crisis—a groping to find a consistent meaning to one's life. In older age people accept their life and affiliations, and focus on concluding important activities.

Human reactions to crucial life events can be extremely complex and idiosyncratic. We have already seen how the timing of an event such as a heart attack can alter a person's response. Besides timing, there are other influences on a person's choices. Let's take an example. Based on our temperament, intelligence, attractiveness, and based on the environment in which we grew up (cold, friendly, lonely, secure, aggressive, or warm), we may have chosen very different careers and life-styles. For example, from the age of twenty-five to thirty, we both thought about making a career move in education. Because of my own limited intelligence and the perceived attractiveness and friendliness of a rural environment, I decided to become a teacher, writer and self-styled farmer. You, because of your higher intelligence and the excitement of living in a city, aspired to be a school principal or director in an urban, sophisticated area. Now I spend my Sunday mornings chasing escaped cows; you (ah! the road not taken) spend yours reading the *Times,* listening to baroque music, and dining on smoked salmon and French pastries. In young adulthood we both passed through a stage of sorting out aspirations, but our choices differed. Adult life span research focuses on common or predictable experiences rather than the variety of ways individuals respond to those experiences.

Placing Adult Development with Life Transition

We now can summarize and relate the two areas of adult studies. In adult development there is an improvement of thinking, concept formation, and ego development that is characterized as crystallized (using more information), complex, and autonomous. Also, it has been shown that adult transitions encompass a life span moving developmentally through initial feelings of omnipotence, greater reflection and reordering of reality, and finally consolidation and acceptance of life. The interaction of crucial life events and individual characteristics influences the scope and intensity of transitions.

Adult development does *not* mean that *all* people become more autonomous, abstract, and accepting. Folklore says the opposite: "You can't teach an old dog new tricks." There's probably some truth to this adage, but research on adult development suggests that adults *are* capable of learning new tricks and becoming more flexible. The capacity to improve and become a more integrative problem solver exists in humans. Its occurrence or failure to occur is a significant matter—one which is fundamental to successful or unsuccessful instructional supervision.

Figure 4–1 shows the relation of adult development and life transitions. The young adult is marked by limited experience, simple standards of reasoning about concepts, egocentricity, and dependence on authority during a period of unbounded dreams and feelings of omnipotence. The middle-aged adult has had a variety of experiences, has developed the ability to draw relationships between self and others, and possesses an awareness of his or her own abilities. This happens during a period of reflection, reordering of priorities, and setting of limited goals. Finally, the older adult has had many experiences, can understand more easily the plight of others, and can make decisions that take into account more of the total situation. This is done during a time of acceptance, consolidation, and planning for future tasks.

Critical influences on development are individual traits, environmental characteristics, timing of life events, and the interpersonal mentor-disciple relationship. The next section will juxtapose what is known about optimal adult development with what is known about teacher development.

FIGURE 4–1   Adult Development and Life Transitions

Age	*21*	*40*	*65*
Crystallized intelligence	⟶ New information more easily related to old ⟶		
Concept formation	⟶More comparisons and relations between self⟶ and others		
Ego state	⟶ More autonomous and integrated outlook ⟶		
Life transitions	Omnipotence; aspirations for family, occupation, and life-styles	Reflection; reordering of priorities	Acceptance; consolidating; finalizing

Teachers Are Adults

The apparently self-evident statement that teachers are adults takes on new meaning when knowledge of the adult as learner is contrasted with the treatment of teachers. Supervisors treat teachers as if they were all the same, rather than individuals in various stages of adult growth. In most schools, teachers receive the same in-service workshops, the same observations, and the same assessments. It is as if teachers were stamped out of teacher-training institutes as identical and thereafter have no further need to be viewed as individual learners. The research on adults shows the lack of wisdom of such assumptions. A discussion of how stages of adult development apply to teacher development and how life transitions apply to teaching transitions will follow.

Results of research on stages of ego, conceptual, and moral development of teachers are similar to findings of the population of all adults. Most teachers have been found to be in the conformist to conscientious stages of Loevinger's ego development scale (Oja and Pine 1981; Glickman and Tamashiro 1982). According to Oja and Pine (1981, p. 112):

These levels indicate ego stages which are characterized by conformist behavior to external standards, little self-awareness ... *Conventional moral adjustments* based upon often unquestioned conformity to peer, social, and legal norms, with few self evaluated standards ... and *conceptual levels* indicating thinking in terms of stereotypes and cliches with dawning recognition of individual differences ... [emphasis in original].

On conceptual development, according to Harvey (1970), teachers were found to be mostly in stage 1 of a four-stage system—that is, in the unilateral-dependence state. Unilateral dependence describes a stage in which concepts are undifferentiated and do not account for ambiguity. Thought is absolute and concrete, with dependence on authority. Harvey's (1970) study shows that a higher proportion of undergraduate education majors than of liberal arts majors are in lower stages of conceptual thinking. Furthermore, there are more practicing or experienced teachers than preservice teachers in the lower stages of conceptual thinking.

Research on moral reasoning of teachers is consistent with ego and conceptual studies of teachers. Wilkins (1980), in comparing Australian preservice teachers with U.S. preservice teachers, concluded that the majority of teachers were in the conventional-reasoning stage. Morality in that stage is governed by adherence to external rules of a group.

The majority of teachers appear to be in relatively low stages of ego, conceptual, and moral development—stages characterized by dependence, simplicity, and concreteness. The larger question about the results that show low levels of teacher development is: So what? What difference does it make that many teachers are not complex or autonomous? Perhaps one does not need higher-ordered thinking to teach? One could argue that if teaching is a simple enterprise with no need for decision making, then it would make little difference. In fact, if most teachers were autonomous and abstract, then trying to do a simple job would create great tension, resentment, and noncompliance. If teaching is a simple activity, schools need people who can reason simply. If teaching is complex and ever-changing, however, then higher levels of reasoning are necessary. A simple thinker in a dynamic and difficult enterprise would be subjected to overwhelming pressures.

Sociologists have documented the environmental demands posed by making thousands of decisions daily, by constant psychological pressure, and by expectations that the teacher must do the job alone—unwatched and unaided. A teacher daily faces up to 150 students of various backgrounds, abilities, and interests, some of whom succeed while others fail. Concrete, rigid thinking on the part of the teacher cannot possibly improve instruction. Teacher improvement can only come from abstract, multi-informational thought that can generate new responses toward new situations. Glassberg's (1979) review of research on teachers' cognitive development as related to instructional improvement concluded:

> in summary these studies suggest that high stage teachers tend to be adaptive in teaching style, flexibile, and tolerant, and able to employ a wide range of teaching models . . . effective teaching in almost any view is a most complex form of human behavior. Teachers at higher, more complex stages of human development appear as more effective in classrooms than their peers at lower stages.

The problem with the need for high-stage teachers is that, although the work by its nature demands autonomous and flexible thinking, teachers in most schools are not supported in ways to improve their thinking. *The only alternative for a teacher in a complex environment who cannot adjust to multiple demands and is not being helped to acquire the abilities to think abstractly and autonomously is to simplify and deaden the instructional environment.* Teachers make the environment less complex by disregarding differences between students, by establishing routines and instructional practices that remain the same day after day and year after year. Research on effective instruction (Rutter et al. 1979; Berman and McLaughlin 1975) indicate that effective instruction is based on adaptation of curriculum and materials to local settings. In other words, effective teachers think about what they currently are doing, assess the results of their practice, and explore with each other new possibilities for teaching students. *Successful teachers are thoughtful teachers.*

Evidence of the relationship between high-stage attainment of conceptual and ego development and effective instructional practice can be found in several research studies. Harvey (1967) found high-concept teachers to have students with higher achievement, less nurturance, more cooperation, and more involvement in their work than low-concept teachers. Hunt and Joyce (1967) found correlations between teacher conceptual level and ability to use learners' needs as a basis for planning and evaluation. High-concept teachers used a greater range of learning environments and teaching methods. Murphy and Brown (1970) found that high-stage teachers could help students theorize and express, could ask precise questions, and could encourage exploration and group involvement significantly more effectively than low-stage teachers. Parkay (1979), in a study of inner-city high school teachers, found that high-concept teachers stimulated positive student attitudes and student achievement gains and were less susceptible to professional stress. Witherell and Erickson (1978, p. 232) found in case studies of teachers that the teachers of highest levels of ego development demonstrated

> greater complexity and commitment to the individual [student] in the following areas: (a) analytic self-reflection and "explanatory power" . . . (b) philosophy of education . . . (c) constructs relating to children and the capacity to take the child's perspective, (d) the generation and use of varieties of data in teaching, and (e) understandings and practices relating to rules, authority, and moral development. . . .

Thies-Sprinthall's study of teachers showed that as teachers acquired higher conceptual levels, their indirect teaching increased. Indirect teaching (the use of less lecture, more praise, and more acceptance of student ideas) has been positively associated with pupil achievement gain (Gage 1978).

The works of Thies-Sprinthall (1980), Sprinthall and Thies-Sprinthall (1982), Oja (1981), and Parker (1983) are particularly important because they suggest that teachers, when provided with a stimulating and supportive environment, can increase their levels of cognitive complexity. Research on adults shows that crystallized learning does increase over time. However, some studies on teachers (Schlechty and Vance 1981; Glickman and Tamashiro 1982) indicate that teachers' capacity to integrate new information related to previous experience does not increase.

Why, if optimal adult learning suggests a continued capability to learn, are teachers characterized by a lack of such cognitive growth? Sociologists have even suggested that problem-solving ability of teachers *decreases* over time. Philip Jackson in *Life in Classrooms* has noted the common pattern of nontechnical language and regulated responses among teachers. Judith Little, on the other hand, found that teachers in successful schools used precise, technical language in discussing instructional concerns (Little 1982). Teachers in effective schools do continue to think and are challenged to extend the use of their mental abilities. If a supervisor could promote thinking among the school staff, school effectiveness might not be far behind. Thinking improves when people interact with each other, when they break routine by experimenting, when they observe others at work, and when they assess and revise their own actions. A cause beyond oneself becomes the norm, and the school becomes successful.

Teachers who are isolated in their classrooms, receive no systematic feedback, attend monthly faculty meetings only to listen to monologues of announcements, and spend a few minutes each day chatting idly in the lounge may be viewed as remarkable specimens of survival. Such teachers, however, are not contributors to a successful school.

Life Transitions of Teachers

Recent research has shown that the third year of teaching is a crucial transition time. It is known that two-thirds of beginning teachers in one southeastern state leave before their third year, and at least one state director of teacher recruitment claims the problem is nationwide (Scott 1979). His assertion about the first three years is supported by two different longitudinal studies of teachers, conducted by Adams, Hutchinson, and Martray (1980) in Kentucky and by Ayers (1980) in Tennessee. Both studies found that ratings of teacher effectiveness, as measured by principal evaluation, student surveys, and classroom observations, rose for the first three years of teaching and then dramatically dropped off. Why do teachers continue to improve their instruction for the first three years but not afterwards? Ayers, addressing this point, speculated that:

1. At the end of the third year of teaching, individuals receive tenure in the schools. It was felt that many teachers after this point may relax their teaching style since they feel that the pressure to achieve a stable position has been eased.
2. Initially, most individuals who enter the teaching profession have high ideals and expectations. It was felt that after several years, these ideals and expectations give way to an attitude that reflects the climate of the school. Acceptance of the norms of the school becomes more commonplace and the level of teaching may be reduced.
3. After several years of teaching it was felt that subjects may be losing enthusiasm for the profession. ... [p. 31]

The loss of enthusiasm mentioned by Adams also has been studied by Nathalie Gehrke (1979) with teachers in Arizona. She wrote that "most teachers do not become aware of feelings of boredom and waning enthusiasm until they have taught at least two years. First year teachers seldom remark about the repetitive nature of the job, with good reason. First year teachers are overwhelmed by new experiences." In the third year, however, teachers perceive the job as basically unchanging. They grow bored as a result of "inflexible scheduling and housekeeping duties, the relatively unchanging nature of the content they taught, or the shallowness of the peers or students with whom they worked" (p. 190).

Teaching becomes largely a personal issue of making it through the day. Since there exists little uncertainty or challenge in the work itself (the materials, the classroom, the loneliness, and the schedule), only the students are unusual. Therefore, many of those who remain in teaching appear to establish their procedures in the first three years and then resign themselves to a monotonous existence. Many who leave simply cannot endure the sameness of existence (Scriven 1979; Ellison 1981; Kotulaw 1978).

It may be an oversimplification to depict teaching as a rush of excitement for three years followed by increased boredom and dissatisfaction. Many experienced teachers continue to find excitement in their work, to vary their environment, and to seek out new challenges. Some continue to improve for over thirty years. On the other hand, many teachers leave the profession within the first three years, others never show improvement, and still others finally begin to improve after ten years of repetitive teaching. The exceptions point out the wonderful complexities of human behavior, but too often the general course of teaching is characterized as initial excitement and growth followed by a leveling off into a monotony of procedures by those who choose to remain, or by abandonment of the profession by those who seek more varied work.

Occupational development of teachers appears to run counter to the needs of adults in critical transition times. The work of Levinson (1977), and Neugarten (1977) points to early adulthood as a period of bravado, romance, and the pursuit of dreams. The young adult aged twenty to thirty-five is on an exciting search for status, comfort, and happiness in work, family, and friends. The middle years, thirty-five to fifty-five, provide a transition into some disillusionment, reflection, and reordering of priorities according to a reassessment of one's capabilities and opportunities. In teaching, however, the young adulthood period, which should be one of romance, quickly becomes one of disillusionment. The young person of twenty-four or twenty-five who has entered teaching to pursue his or her dreams often finds after three years that work life is going nowhere. The job does not excite; the advancements do not exist; and the variety of work is nonexistent. The result can be intense boredom, leading to resignation—either *from* the job or *on* the job. What does it mean to education when a young teacher's natural inclination toward excitement and idealism is bound by a straitjacket of repetition?

Let's ask the next question. What happens when the natural inclination of the middle-aged teacher to reflect and reorder his or her teaching priorities confronts the same six periods of thirty students that he or she has faced for the past twenty years? One might expect a further despair of any impulse to change and to improve. Finally, what about the older teacher who is perceived by many as an anomaly, a relic who has remained in teaching because of inability to advance into administration or supervision. The acquisition of thirty years of experience coincides with the natural time for consolidating achievements and identifying one's remaining career objectives. Instead, there is only the same job—the same job as that of the new teacher down the hall, who might be the age of the older teacher's grandchild. Where is the sense of responsibility, generativity, and accomplishment in seniority? Old and new teachers are treated the same, accorded the same status, expected to conform to the same routines.

Teaching appears to be a topsy-turvy occupation, running against the needs of life transition periods. Those who continue to make lasting improvement and enhance their students' educational lives should have our utmost respect. If not fortunate enough to be in a school that responds and supports change in teachers according to principles of adult learning and transitions, the effective teacher truly transcends the system and educates in spite of, not because of, the school.

Optimal Teacher Development

In describing optimal development, we are discussing what the individual is capable of becoming. There are mitigating factors that impede the growth of adults and teachers. To study how outstanding teachers change may give us guidance for altering conditions for those teachers who are not improving. We have already seen how teachers judged outstanding on measures of flexibility, adaptability, and improvements in student achievement and attitudes have in common the ability to think at high abstract levels.

Abstraction

The normal development of thinking moves from concrete to abstract (see Figure 4–2). Learners' initial interaction with objects is determined by the singular physical dimension of the objects being present. With development, however, a learner's interaction is independent of the objects' presence. The learner can hold a mental image of the object and categorize its dimensions in multiple ways (Piaget 1955; Flavell 1977). The vehicle for movement of a person's thinking toward greater abstraction is provision of a concrete learner with familiar experiences and information that are embedded in the actual physical context. Gradually, unfamiliar experiences are provided by introducing uncommon or novel information that asks the learner to hold onto a mental image. At the end of the continuum, the abstract learner can seek unfamiliar experiences by mentally imagining novel information and thus thinking of truly new ways of acting.

Abstract thought is the ability to determine relationships, to make comparisons and contrasts between information and experience to be used to generate multiple possibilities in formulating a decision. Therefore, as experience (with objects and persons) increases from the familiar to the unfamiliar, so does abstract thought.

Teachers (like any learner) can be helped to think more abstractly by providing information and experience that are slightly novel. If we begin to assess teachers on a continuum of abstract

FIGURE 4–2   Development of Abstract Thought

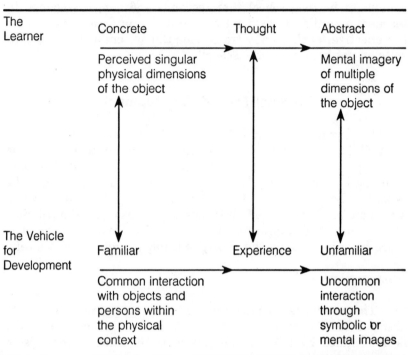

thinking, clues to the type and delivery of information and experience emerge. As in Table 4–1 (Glickman 1981), we can classify the abstract thinking of teachers as low, moderate, or high.

Teachers with low levels of abstract thinking have difficulty in determining whether changes in their classroom are necessary. Often they do not see the relationship of their own behavior to the problem; they may say, "The students are lazy," or "The parents don't care." If they do perceive a need for changes, they often expect someone else to tell them exactly what to do. Left to themselves, they often respond to a dilemma by making a decision that is either habitual ("Whenever a student misbehaves, I give him more homework") or impulsive ("I changed the assignments because I felt like it").

Teachers with moderate levels of abstract thinking realize that improvement is needed but have difficulty deciding what actions to take or what the consequences of certain actions would be. They believe that when students are failing or misbehaving, it relates in some way to what the teacher is doing. However, they are limited in determining the relationships between their teaching practice, materials, organization, and student needs. They often choose a change in the curriculum, grouping, or instruction that contains unexpected consequences, which in turn create further problems. Inadequate definition of the problem often leads to further difficulties.

Highly abstract teachers can use a rational process of problem solving by incorporating several sources of information and applying their own knowledge and experience. For example, a particular student's learning difficulty will be considered against knowledge of the student's previous work, her peers, her work with other teachers in other situations, her family and out-of-school time, current instruction, materials, student level of achievement, and student attitude toward work. This is all considered *before* the teacher generates possible changes such as regrouping, changing materials, holding a conference with the student, or setting rewards. This might appear to be a lengthy process but highly abstract teachers can think and respond to a problem rapidly and decisively (Parker 1983).

Concern

Francis Fuller in the 1960s and early 1970s conducted pioneer studies of teacher concerns. In analyzing both her own studies and six others, she found that the responses by hundreds of teachers at various stages of experience showed different concerns. Beginning

TABLE 4-1   Levels of Abstract Thinking

Low	Moderate	High
Confusion about situation	Can define situation by focusing on one dimenion	Can define the situation by drawing relationships between several sources of information
Doesn't know what can be done	Can think of several responses	Can relate the information to change in classroom practice
Asks to be shown	Has difficulty in thinking of consequences of changing the situation	Can generate many alternative responses
Has habitual responses to varying situations		Can evaluate the consequences of each response and choose the one most likely to succeed

teachers were concerned mainly about their own survival. They wanted to know how the school principal, other supervisors, and other teachers perceived them—how adequate they were and whether they could maintain control over the classroom. Older teachers identified as superior were not concerned with mere adequacy but instead with the impact that they were having on students. In Fuller's words (1969, p. 221), "When concerns are 'mature,' i.e., characteristic of experienced teachers, concerns seem to focus on pupil gain and self evaluation as opposed to personal gain and evaluation by others." Superior teachers, as identified by principals and fellow teachers, were distinct from other teachers in that pupil progress was of overriding importance. On the other hand, many experienced teachers *not* identified as superior had concerns about their own adequacy, similar to those of beginners. Later work on teachers' concerns by Hall and Loucks (1978), Adams and Martray (1981), Demarte and Mahood (1981), and others has refined Fuller's work into three developmental substages of concerns: (1) self concerns, (2) task concerns, and (3) impact concerns. The general direction of concerns has remained consistent from study to study. I believe the trend from self (or egocentric) to student (or altruistic) concerns is similar to the ego-development progression of Loevinger and the moral reasoning stages of Kohlberg (see Figure 4–3).

Beginning teachers are concerned with their own survival— whether or not they can make it as teachers. Their concern corresponds to the ego state of fearfulness and the moral state of avoidance of punishment. They want to know if they can avoid being driven out by students, ostracized by peers, or fired by superiors. Such concerns can be classified as an *egocentric motivation to teaching;* they revolve around the person's survival and security. With survival and security assured, teachers think less of their own needs and begin to address the tasks of teaching. They begin to think about altering or enriching the classroom schedule, the teaching materials, and their instructional methodology. The beginning teacher is concerned with learning *any* system that will enable him or her to survive. The more experienced teacher, assured that his or her teaching practice is adequate for survival, still doubts its adequacy for all students. The experienced teacher is concerned with *adapting* the instructional system to improve learning for students. Note that the shift in the nature of teachers' concerns corresponds to the shift in moral reasoning based on learning other conventional practices that are avilable and accepted in the school and that will improve teaching tasks. The teacher is now concerned about his or her class as a group, and thus can be identified as having progressed to the teacher development pattern of *group motivation*. The concern of superior teachers for individual student impact is correlated with the ego state of autonomy and the moral state of principled reasoning. Superior teachers mature beyond the group and conventional orientation to teaching; they seek help for individual students that may be outside the accepted norms of the school. The autonomous teacher wants to succeed with every student, even at the risk of being different. His or her thinking is altruistic in that actions are motivated by the needs of others and not of self. The autonomous teacher is willing to help other teachers, to work on school wide change, and to address larger issues of education and the profession. When a teacher's underlying concern is with improving education for all, that teacher has progressed to the development pattern of *altruistic motivation*. The unfolding of teacher concerns occurs on a continuum beginning with *I* concerns to concern for *my group* to concerns for *all students*.

FIGURE 4–3   Development of Teacher Concerns, Ego, and Moral Development

Concerns (Fuller 1969)			
	Self-adequacy	Task impact	Student impact
Ego (Loevinger 1969)			
	Fearful	Conforming	Autonomous
Moral reasoning (Kohlberg 1969)			
	Punishment	Conventional	Principled
Unfolding pattern of teacher development (Glickman 1981)			
	Egocentric motivation	Group motivation	Altruistic motivation

This characterization of teachers' concerns does not mean that certain specific types of instructional practice are superior—for example, "The best teachers have individualized classrooms." It is not the particular classroom practice but the reasoning *behind* the teacher's practice that marks the level of maturity of the teacher. An autonomous teacher might teach in a very traditional manner as a response to the individual needs of students.

Finally, if we accept that there is optimal teacher development, which moves from egocentric to altruistic motivation and that there is optimal teacher thinking, which moves from concrete to abstract, then we can begin to assess teachers as developing adults. The lack of such movement becomes apparent and ultimately may be traced to conditions of the work environment and the occupation.

Plotting Teacher Abstraction and Motivation

Development of thought and motivation can be plotted in graph form for individual teachers (see Figure 4–4). If thinking and motivation developed together, then we would have only three classifications of teachers, found in boxes Ia, IIb, and IIIc. Box Ia would represent teachers with concrete thinking and egocentric concerns. They would be attempting to keep their jobs without the abstract ability to identify instructional problems or to plan for improvement. They would be restricted to a single, and repetitive approach, to teaching at a minimum maintenance level. They might be seen as resistant to change, satisfied with keeping their job without purpose or reason. Box IIb would represent the next level of teachers, concerned about improving teaching tasks within their classrooms and able to think in a restricted manner. They would be able to identify the instructional needs of their classroom,

FIGURE 4–4   Thought and Motivation of Teachers

	Concrete Thought	Restricted Thought	Abstract Thought
Egocentric Motivation	Ia (resistant)	Ib	Ic
Group Motivation	IIa	IIb (willing)	IIc
Altruistic Motivation	IIIa	IIIb	IIIc (capable)

at least in part, but would lack the experience and knowledge to propose varied solutions or to choose among them. They might be seen as willing, well-intentioned, but often confused. Box IIIc would characterize teachers at the highest level of motivation and thinking. These teachers would be self-motivated to adjust instruction to the individual needs of students, and their altruism would place them in a helping relationship to people outside their classes, other students, teachers, parents, and administrators. They would have not only the desire to affect all persons but also the cognitive ability to weigh carefully and choose realistically among proposals for change. These teachers would be willing to take risks after carefully considering the consequences. They might be referred to as capable and competent teachers and change agents.

Sullivan, McCullough, and Stager (1970) have shown the positive but not perfect correlation between concern, conceptual thinking, and moral reasoning. Loevinger has pointed out that all development, by definition, must be interrelated. Yet those who work with adults know of the impossibility of a classification system accounting for the entire range of human behavior. Cell Ia (*resistant*), cell IIb (*willing*), and cell IIIc (*capable*) identify many teachers in a school setting, but the three cells do not account for all teachers. Furthermore, the same teacher can be identified in different cells according to the situation. In a previous work (Glickman 1981), I identifed four teacher types to provide help for practicing supervisors in determining approaches to clinical supervision. Such a typology, however, simply does not account for the large variability in teacher behavior that needs to be considered for implementing all the tasks of supervision. The nine-category system, as shown in Figure 4–4, is an attempt to account for more variation but still must be seen as presenting approximate guideposts, not clear lines of demarcation.

Cell Ib: Teachers would have egocentric motivation and restricted thought. They might be seen as acting in a routine manner, doing the things necessary to keep their job yet aware of some changes needed to improve their teaching.

Cell Ic: Teachers would have the abstract ability to propose worthwhile improvement for themselves, their students, and others, but would lack the motivation to do so.

Cell IIa: Teachers would have the motivation to improve instruction for their group but without help would be unable to think of realistic and appropriate improvements.

Cell IIc: Teachers would be capable of deciding for themselves about classroom changes, but their range of solutions would be confined to those already in use and traditionally sanctioned by the administration and school.

Cell IIIa: Teachers would be willing to try almost anything that might be helpful but would be unable to make their own decisions. Instead, they would be indiscriminate followers of others.

Cell IIIb: Teachers would be able to consider problems and solutions for themselves and would be willing to implement possible solutions, but would become confused by unanticipated occurrences during implementation.

Expanding the category system from three or four types of teachers to nine permits distinctions between shades of difference, which are important in determining appropriate supervisory strategies for working with individuals or groups of teachers. Type I (Ia, Ib, Ic) teachers are motivated by job security and are largely unconcerned with their students. The a, b, c classifications pertain to their degree of awareness of changes that *could* be made to improve instruction. In all type I cases, however, the individual teacher will not initiate a change independently.

Type II teachers (IIa, IIb, IIc) are motivated by the learning needs of their students as a group. They desire change to improve group learning. The a, b, c classifications pertain to their degree of knowledge and experience in proposing answers to classroom change. Authority and school norms limit the type of conceivable change. Change will occur within the limits of conventional practice, with the need for external direction depending on the teacher's level of abstract thinking.

Type III teachers (IIIa, IIIb, IIIc) are concerned with all aspects of education and are motivated by the needs of the individual, small group, class, other classes, other teachers, the school, and the profession as a whole. They willingly work at all levels of education and will consider practices that are in opposition to established norms. The a, b, c classifications pertain to their ability to generate ideas and practices to improve all aspects of education.

Considering Teacher Development within the Context of the School

One theme of this book is that teacher development, according to levels of motivation and levels of thought, is crucial for deciding approaches and skills to help teachers become more abstract and altruistic. The ideal teacher is committed to the needs of all students and has the cognitive skills to improve his or her own instruction. In helping teachers grow, supervisors must consider characteristics of the teacher as a client. For example, one would not work with a type Ia (resistant) teacher in the same way as with type IIIc (capable) teacher. The approaches and skills used in direct assistance, staff development, curriculum development, group development, and action research will differ according to the level of motivation and level of thought of teachers. A supervisor must be able to choose those skills and techniques that will enable teachers to develop individually and collectively to create a cause beyond oneself. A commitment to that cause is essential for school success.

This chapter has been intentionally theoretical and research-based. It provides the basis for choosing supervisory skills and strategies for working with individuals or groups of teachers. We can view teacher development against the background of adult development, life transitions, the work environment of the school, and characteristics of the teaching profession. The context of teacher development is illustrated in Figure 4–5. Imagine a large

FIGURE 4–5   The Context of Teacher Development

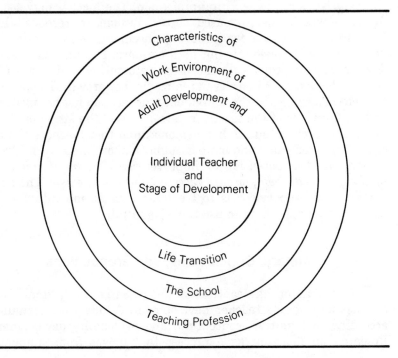

felt board representing the context of a teacher's life. At the center is the individual with his or her unique development and life transitions embedded into the work environment of the school, which is in turn embedded into characteristics of the teaching profession. When viewing a teacher's growth (or lack of growth), we must consider both the characteristics of the individual and the influences of the work environment and the teaching profession. For example, a type Ia teacher may be resistant because of previous negative experiences within the work environment of the school. Perhaps at one time the teacher was concerned with improving her class and used abstract thought to implement a new classroom design. Perhaps other teachers or a supervisor frowned on such experimentation and threatened the teacher with the loss of her job. This teacher, needing to keep the job for financial reasons, therefore gave up trying to change. She retreated from improvement because of adverse pressure. This teacher might now be resistant, but she still has the ability to improve. Improvement will not occur, however, until changes occur in her immediate work environment. Another example might be a type IIb (willing) teacher who has found a satisfactory, maintenance level of group instruction and can live comfortably with the school norms. The reasons he does not demonstrate further improvement might be traced to characteristics of the teaching profession. The teacher may see no future prospects for increased status, income, or responsibility. Without any prospects for career advancement, he may rationally decide to remain adequate but nothing more. The supervisor must develop ways to provide advancement, recognition, and/or status in this teacher's career in order to realize further growth. The point is that characteristics of the individual teacher may not be fixed but, rather, functions of the teacher's perceptions of the larger environment. Research on adults has demonstrated that teachers can become more motivated and more thoughtful about their work. Every person has the potential to improve: *Such potential might be blocked, slowed down, or even reversed, but it still exists.* The challenge for the supervisor is to treat teachers as individual adult learners to enable them to use their potential.

Summary, Conclusions, and Propositions

This chapter has contrasted the research on optimal adult development versus teacher development. Adults were examined according to cognitive, conceptual, and personality development. Research on learning as a process that moves from simplistic, concrete thinking to multi-informational, abstract thinking was cited. Critical life transitions of adults were shown—from the young adult's feelings of omnipotence to the middle-aged person's need to reflect and reorder, to the older adult's needs to accept and consolidate. When comparing research on teachers versus optimal development of adults, it becomes apparent that teachers' thinking does not automatically become more abstract. Furthermore, the teaching career does not coincide appropriately with adult life transitions. Teaching responsibilities are not increased, mentor relationships are not provided, and—usually after the third year of teaching—there is a general loss of enthusiasm for the occupation. Propositions for supervision that emerge from the contrasting of adult and teacher development are as follows:

- Proposition 1: *Supervision, to be effective, must be a function that responds to the developmental stages of teachers.* Teachers are not all alike in their thinking or their motivation for teaching. They should not be treated as a homogeneous group.

- Proposition 2: *Supervision, to be effective, must be a function that responds to adult life transitions of teachers.* Initial enthusiasm should be encouraged by gradually increasing responsibilities through mid-career. Late in their careers, teachers should be given reduced responsibilities so they may pursue their remaining educational goals.

These two propositions provide the general developmental *principles of action* that will serve as the core of supervisory thought and practice. The supervisory goal is to improve classroom and school instruction by enabling teachers to become more adaptive, more thoughtful, and more cohesive in their work. In the last chapter, on prerequisite knowledge for developmental supervision, a supervisor's present platform of practice will be examined to determine its fit in the developmental framework.

EXERCISES

ACADEMIC

1. Review the theories of a major author on adult development or adult life span transitions as found in the list of suggested

additional readings. Write a paper summarizing the author's theories and any research on which those theories are based.

2. Review the research of a prominent investigator of teacher development or teacher life span transitions as found in the list of suggested additional readings. Write a paper summarizing the major conclusions the researcher has drawn from his or her studies.

3. Review literature and/or research on adult learning. On the basis of your review, list at least eight generally accepted principles of adult learning. For each principle, infer and list an implication for educational supervision.

4. Review three research studies and write a report summarizing general research findings on any one of the following:

   a. adult cognitive development

   b. adult conceptual development

   c. adult ego development

   d. adult moral development

5. The chapter reports that teachers' enthusiasm and performance appear to improve for the first three years of teaching but not afterward. Possible reasons for the dropoff are cited. Write a reaction in which you (a) put forward your own proposal of why enthusiasm appears to wane and (b) offer possible solutions to the problem.

FIELD

1. Visit the classrooms of a teacher you perceive to be a highly abstract thinker and one you perceive to be a highly concrete thinker. Write a report comparing the teachers in terms of teaching methods, interaction with students, classroom management, attention to individual student needs, and general teaching effectiveness (use fictitious names in your report).

2. On the basis of observations of leader-teacher, teacher-teacher, and teacher-student interactions; faculty meeting activities; posted communications; and the like, infer a group of *social norms* that prevail at a selected school. Write a paper stating your perceptions of the school's social norms and your opinion of whether those norms are positive or negative influences on teachers' conceptual development.

3. Interview a veteran teacher who is nearing retirement. Ask the teacher to discuss the major transitions that have taken place during his or her career. Summarize the interview in writing.

4. Reflect on your own career and the major transitions that have taken place during your career. Choose an artifact that symbolizes each major transition. Prepare a display of your artifacts and a verbal or written report explaining the relationship between your career transitions and these artifacts.

5. Ask a first-year teacher, a third-year teacher, and a teacher with at least ten years of teaching experience to list their concerns about teaching. Prepare a report comparing the various responses and drawing relevant conclusions.

DEVELOPMENTAL

1. List your major career concerns in writing. Review your list in one year to see if your career concerns have changed.

2. Begin a career scrapbook with the purpose of documenting your own professional development.

3. Begin an in-depth study of a major topic discussed in Chapter 4 (for example, adult life span transitions, adult cognitive development, adult conceptual development, adult ego development, adult moral reasoning, adult learning).

REFERENCES

Adams, R. D.; Hutchinson, S.; and Martray, C. 1980. A developmental study of teacher concerns across time. Paper presented at the annual meeting of the American Educational Research Association, Boston, Massachusetts, April.

Adams, R. D., and Martray, C. 1981. Teacher development: A study of factors related to teacher concerns for pre, beginning, and experienced teachers. Paper presented at the annual meeting of the American Educational Research Association, Los Angeles, California, April.

OPTIMAL ADULT DEVELOPMENT VS. ACTUAL TEACHER DEVELOPMENT

Ayers, J. B. 1980. A longitudinal study of teachers. Paper presented at the annual meeting of the American Educational Research Association, Boston, Massachusetts, April.

Becker, H. S. 1971. Personal change in adult life. In H. S. Becker, ed., *Sociological work: Method and substance.* London: Allen Lane.

Berman, P. J., and McLaughlin, M. W. 1975. *Federal programs supporting educational change,* Vol. 4. *The Finding in Review.* Santa Monica, Calif.: Rand Corporation.

Blum, L. S., and Meyer, R. 1981. Developmental implications of myocardial infarction for mid-life adults. Paper presented at the annual meeting of the American Educational Research Association, Los Angeles, California, April.

Bruner, J. S. 1960. *The process of education.* Cambridge, Mass.: Harvard University Press.

Buhler, C. 1956. *From childhood to maturity.* London: Rutledge and K. Paul.

Burden, P. R. 1982. Developmental supervision: Reducing teacher stress at different career stages. Paper presented at the annual conference of the Association of Teacher Educators, Phoenix, Ariz., February.

Christensen, J.; Burke, P.; and Fessler, R. 1983. Teacher life-span development: A summary and synthesis of the literature. Paper presented at the annual meeting of American Educational Research Association, Montreal, April.

Demarte, P. J., and Mahood, R. W. 1981. The concerns of teachers in rural, urban, and suburban school settings. Paper presented at the Annual Meeting of the American Educational Research Association, Los Angeles, April.

Ellison, E. 1981. Survey here cites high teacher stress. *The Atlanta (Georgia) Constitution,* February 26, p. 8B.

Erikson, E. L. 1950. *Childhood and society.* New York: Norton.

Flavell, J. H. 1977. *Cognitive development.* Englewood Cliffs, N.J.: Prentice-Hall.

Fuller, F. F. 1969. Concerns of teachers: A developmental conceptualization. *American Educational Research Journal* 6-(2):207–266.

Gage, N. L. 1978. *The scientific basis of the art of teaching.* New York: Teachers College Press.

Gehrke, N. J. 1979. Renewing teacher enthusiasm: A professional dilemma. *Theory into Practice 18*(3):188–193.

Glassberg, S. 1979. Developing models of teacher development. ERIC document ED 171 685, March.

Glickman, D. D. 1981. *Developmental supervision: Alternative approaches for helping teachers to improve instruction.* Alexandria, Va.: Association for Supervision and Curriculum Development.

Glickman, D. D., and Tamashiro, R. T. 1982. A comparison of first year, fifth year, and former teachers on efficacy, ego development and problem solving. *Psychology in the Schools 19*(4):558–562.

Hall, G. E., and Loucks, S. 1978. Teacher concerns as a basis for facilitating and personalizing staff development. *Teachers College Record 80*(September):36–53.

Harvey, O. J. 1967. Conceptual systems and attitude change. In C. Sherif and M. Sheif, eds., *Attitude, ego involvement and change.* New York: Wiley.

———. 1970. Beliefs and behavior: Some implications for education. *The Science Teacher 37*(December):10–14, 73.

Harvey, O. J.: Hunt, D. E.; and Schroeder, H. M. 1961. *Conceptual systems and personality organization.* New York: Wiley.

Havighurst, R. J. 1980. Life-span developmental psychology and education. *Educational Researcher,* November, pp. 3–8.

Horn, J. L., and Cattell, R. B. 1967. Age differences in fluid and crystallized intelligence. *Acta Psychologica 26*:107–129.

Hunt, D. E. 1966. A conceptual systems change model and its application to education. In O. J. Harvey, ed., *Experience, structure, and adaptability.* New York: Springer-Verlag, pp. 277–302.

Hunt, D. E., and Joyce, B. R. 1967. Teacher trainee personality and initial teaching style. *American Educational Research Journal 4*(3):253–255.

Hunt, D. E., and Sullivan, E. 1974. *Between psychology and education.* New York: McGraw-Hill.

Jackson, P. 1968. *Life in classrooms*. New York: Holt, Rinehart and Winston.

Kohlberg, L., and Turiel, E. 1971. Moral development and moral education. In G. Lessor, ed., *Psychology and educational practice*. Chicago: Scott Foresman.

Kotulaw, R. 1978. Combat neurosis taking higher toll of teachers. *Buffalo (New York) News 197*(12):1.

Levinson, D. J. 1977. *The seasons in a man's life*. New York: Knopf.

Little, J. W. 1982. Norms of collegiality and experimentation: Workplace conditions of school success. *American Educational Research Journal 19*(3):325–340.

Loevinger, J. 1976. *Ego development*. San Francisco: Jossey-Bass.

Long, H. B., and Mirza, M. S. 1980. Some qualitative performance characteristics of adults at the formal operations stage. *Journal of Research and Development in Education 13*(3):21–24.

McNergney, R. F., and Carrier, C. A. 1981. *Teacher development*. New York: Macmillan.

Murphy, P., and Brown, M. 1970. Conceptual systems and teaching styles. *American Educational Research Journal 7*(November):529–540.

Neugarten, B. L. 1977. Personality and aging. In J. E. Birren and K. W. Schaie, eds., *Handbook of the psychology of aging*. New York: Van Nostrand Reinhold.

Oja, S. N. 1979. A cognitive-structural approach to adult ego, moral, and conceptual development through in-service education. Paper presented at the annual meeting of the American Educational Research Association, San Francisco, April.

———. 1981. Deriving teacher educational objectives from cognitive-developmental theories and applying them to the practice of teacher education. Paper presented at the annual meeting of the American Educational Research Association, Los Angeles, April.

Oja, S. N., and Pine, G. J. 1981. Toward a theory of staff development. Paper presented at the annual meeting of the American Educational Research Association, Los Angeles, April.

References

Parkay, F. W. 1979. Inner-city high school teachers: The relationship of personality traits and teaching style to environmental stress. Paper presented to the Southwest Educational Research Association, Houston.

Parker, W. C. 1983. The effect of guided reflection and role-taking on the interactive decision making of teachers. Paper presented at the annual meeting of the American Educational Research Association, Montreal, April.

Piaget, J. 1955. *The language and thought of the child.* New York: World Publishing.

Rutter, M.; Maughan, B.; Mortimore, P.; Ouston, J; and Smith, A. 1979. Fifteen thousand hours. *Secondary schools and their effects on children.* Cambridge, Mass.: Harvard University Press.

Schlechty, P. C., and Vance, V. S. 1981. Do academically able teachers leave education? The North Carolina case. *Phi Delta Kappan,* October, pp. 106–112.

Scott, P. 1979. Few teachers stay past their third year. *Atlanta (Georgia) Journal,* September 25.

Scriven, R. 1979. The big click. *Today's Education 68*(4):34–36.

Sprinthall, N. A., and Thies-Sprinthall, L. 1982. Career development of teachers: A cognitive developmental perspective. In H. Mitzel, *Encyclopedia of educational research,* 5th ed. New York: Free Press.

Sullivan, E. V.; McCullough, G.; and Stager, M. A. 1970. Developmental study of the relationship between conceptual, ego, and moral development. *Child Development 41:*399–411.

Thies-Sprinthall, L. 1980. Promoting the conceptual and principled thinking level of the supervising teacher. Unpublished research report, St. Cloud State University (Minnesota).

Wilkins, R. A. 1980. If the moral reasoning of teachers is deficient, what hope for pupils. *Phi Delta Kappan,* April, pp. 548–549.

Witherell, C. S., and Erickson, V. L. 1978. Teacher education as adult development. *Theory into Practice 17*(June):229–238.

CHAPTER FIVE

Supervisory Beliefs and Reflections on Practice

As we seek ways to improve school and classroom instruction, we need to understand how present thinking, beliefs, and practice in the field of supervision interact with teacher development. This chapter will show how supervisory beliefs are related to a particular educational philosophy or platform and will then provide an instrument to help clarify the reader's own supervisory belief. Next we will discuss how one's own supervisory belief fits along a developmental continuum. Finally, some propositions about supervisory belief and consequences for teacher development will be made.

Sergiovanni and Starrat (1983, pp. 226–227) note the importance of understanding one's own supervisory beliefs:

> What is needed is some firm footing in principle. Some have called our often unexpressed constellation of principles a platform. Just as a political party is supposed to base its decisions and actions on a party platform upon which it seeks election, so, too, supervisory personnel need a platform upon which, and in the light of which, they can carry on their work. With a clearly defined platform, they can begin to take a position relative to educational practices, looking beyond the surface behavior to probe for the real consequences of a variety of school practices.

Knowing oneself as a supervisor is necessary before considering alternative practices and procedures. To move from a platform we must first know where we are standing. Teachers appear to be able to detect a supervisor's philosophy. Let's look at four descriptions of central office supervisors as described by teachers (Glickman 1983):

The supervisor is viewed as a detached person who has little concern with the everyday problems of teachers in the field. His main concern is with "numbers." Are the teachers meeting their goals? As long as goals are being met and no individuals are causing problems, not many teachers will hear from the supervisor.

(From a rehabilitation counselor)

The supervisor is viewed as exceptionally competent. His ability to get teachers to strive for excellence stems from their recognition that he accepts nothing less from himself and treats teachers as professionally able and willing to do their very best. He seeks the assistance of teachers and values their opinions and ideas.

(From a high school teacher)

The typical supervisor is a vivacious, interested person who periodically observes my teaching. She gives positive feedback. She takes the initiative to organize after school meetings within our school system of all elementary physical education teachers for us to share problems and ideas for solution. She has limited knowledge of our field and gives us much freedom.

(From an elementary physical education teacher)

The supervisor is good at politicking and P.R. words. She knows how to say the right things and knows whose a–– to kiss.

(From a high school teacher)

From the four descriptions of central office supervisors, underlying philosophies can be surmised. In description 1 the supervisor might be seen to have an *essentialist* philosophy, concerned with monitoring imposed results. In description 2 the supervisor has an *experimentalist* philosophy, concerned with shared participation. In description 3 the supervisor might be said to have an *existentialist* philosophy, concerned with human freedom. In description 4 the supervisor probably has no philosophy; *expediency* is the goal. The reader might think about or write a description that teachers would use to describe oneself as a supervisor. The next section deals with the development and implications of each philosophy.

Supervisory Platform as Related to Educational Philosophy

Most supervisors, naturally, are former teachers. As a result, their views about learning, the nature of the learner, knowledge, and the role of the teacher in the classroom influence their view of supervision. After all, supervision is in many respects analogous to teaching. Teachers wish to improve students' behavior, achievement, and attitudes. Supervisors similarly wish to improve teachers' behavior, achievement, and attitudes. A definition of *improvement* merges teaching and supervision. (Scratch the surface of a supervisor, and underneath one is likely to find a teacher.)

Many different philosophies exist. Some, such as idealism and realism, date back to ancient times. Others, such as pragmatism and behaviorism, have been developed within the last century. Even more recent has been the emergence of progressivism, reconstructionism, and existentialism. Philosophies are numerous and overlapping, and many have historical roots in each other. To unravel the major philosophical trends in education, one must decipher how philosophies differ from each other and then build overriding conceptual categories. Each conceptual category or superphilosophy is created by grouping various philosophies that have central agreement on the type and scope of education. In other words, there may be disagreement on the specific nature of knowledge, truth, and reality; yet they hang together as a general educational philosophy because they are in agreement on the purpose and treatment of education.[1]

With educational application in mind, divergent philosophies can be simplified and classified. Three major educational superphilosophies have direct relevance to supervision. These categories have been labeled, according to Johnson et al. (1973), as essentialism, progressivism, and existentialism. We would like to substitute for progressivism the more general term *experimentalism,* as described by Van Cleve Morris (1961).

Essentialism

Essentialism as a philosophy is derived from idealism and realism. *Idealism,* which dates back to Plato, espouses a belief in absolutes: The world we live in is merely a reflection of reality. Reality, truth, and standards of morality exist beyond our common ways of knowing. Only by training the mind do we glimpse the ultimates. Yet training the mind is not sufficient in itself; it only brings the mind nearer to grasping reality. Divine revelation, insight, and faith are the necessary elements for ultimate knowledge of what exists. Therefore, idealism emphasizes truth and reality existing outside of people. It is absolute and unchanging. Realism, developed at the onset of the industrial age, places a similar emphasis on truth and reality being outside of people. Yet, instead of humankind and the outer environment being separated from each other, realism espouses that humanity is part and parcel of that environment. The world is a preordained, mechanistic reality. All of existence operates according to scientific, cause-and-effect relations. It is as if existence is a clock that always runs according to mechanical principles governing levers, gauges, and gears. Humans have no existence apart from this clock. They are a part of that predetermined machine. Knowledge is learning how that machine works. Truths are the scientific laws of regulation. Nothing exists outside the principles of nature. The purpose of education is to condition the mind to think in a natural, logical way. The mind should be trained to become consciously aware of the predeterminism of the world.

Essentialism, created by William L. Bagley in 1938, encompassed the educational philosophies of idealism and realism. He took the ideas of knowledge being eternal and outside of humankind (idealism—absolutes, realism—natural laws) to form pedagogy. Essentialists emphasize that there is a body of timeless knowledge, both historical and contemporary, that is of value to the living.

Essentialism in terms of supervision emphasizes the supervisor as the person who teaches truths about teaching to teachers. Supervisors are those most knowledgeable about those absolute standards. Teachers are then worked with mechanistically to systematize and feed content to students. As teachers digest these teaching truths, they move closer to being good teachers.

Experimentalism

As Western society became more industrialized, optimism and confidence in human ability to control nature emerged. The philosophy of pragmatism developed by Charles S. Pierce and William James emphasized what people can do to nature rather than what nature does to humankind. John Dewey, circa 1920, further expanded on the writings of James by putting the individual squarely in the context of society. Humans can both reform and be reformed by society. Dewey's philosophy is, of course, the well-known school of progressive thought. Reconstructionism is a further offshoot of both pragmatism and progressivism. Richard Pratte (1971) cites the pamphlet *Dare the Schools Build a New*

Social Order, written by George S. Counts in 1932 as a guiding document for the then-radical notion that schools and students were the reformers of society.

Experimentalism emerges from the philosophies of pragmatism, progressivism, and reconstructionism. They hold in common a historical break from the more traditional philosophies of realism and idealism. The essentialist idea that knowledge, truth, and morality exist as absolute and outside of humans was rejected. The emerging faith in the scientific method; the fact that humans could create their own laws, principles, and machines; and that such man-made inventions would work for them demanded an accompanying philosophy. Experimentalism provided that philosophy.

Reality was what worked. If a person could form a hypothesis, test it, and find it to work, then it was regarded as tentatively true. On repeated experimentation with the same results, it became real. Yet experimentalists never would claim an absolute truth. The human environment was believed to be constantly changing, so that what one can do and prove today may not be probable tomorrow. A new situation and a different approach may alter yesterday's reality. Experimentalists point to the historical evidence of Newton's law of gravity as a past truth that has given way to Einstein's theory of relativity; they believe that in time a new theory will replace Einstein's.

Morality is also viewed in relation to what works for humanity and human society. Morality is that behavior which promotes one's working with the group to achieve greater ends. To be wise is to understand how the environment (of things and people) affects oneself and how one might affect it. Whether action is moral or not is determined by the degree of progress that has been achieved by the group. The use of trial and error in a laboratory setting is the key to evaluating the outcome of action. Therefore, experimentalists do not view knowledge as absolute or external to human capabilities. Rather, knowledge is a result of the interaction between the scientific person and the environment.

The educational application of experimentalist thinking to supervision is well documented in the writing of Dewey. Teachers (as students) need to learn what are the truths of their time, but they should not rest content with that parcel of knowledge. Supervisors view schools as laboratories for working with teachers to test old hypotheses and to try new ones. Supervisors work democratically with teachers to achieve collective ends that will help everyone. Supervisors are not solely conveyors of age-old wisdom, they are both the conveyors of the rudimentary knowledge of the time and the guiders of trial-and-error, exploratory learning.

Existentialism

Existentialism as a school of thought is derived from the rejection of the other philosophies encompassed in essentialism and experimentalism. As such, it is a large category for many diverse philosophers. They have in common a scorn for rational, empirical, and systematic thinking as the way of knowing reality. As you recall, the essentialists believe in rational thinking to help elevate the mind to uncover the absolutes of the universe. Experimentalists believe in rational, scientific thinking to explore and frame the relevant knowledge of the times. However, the existentialists believe that this same rational thinking restricts humans from discovering existence, and therefore keeps them ignorant.

This philosophy has roots in the writings of Sören Kierkegaard in the mid-nineteenth century. It has been popularized in drama and literature by such exponents as Albert Camus and Jean-Paul Sartre. The current popular cults of transcendental thinking, meditation, and introspection (knowing oneself) have a kinship with existentialism. The basic tenet of the philosophy is that the individual is the source of all reality. All that exists in the world is the meaning the individual puts on his or her own experiences. There is no absolute knowledge, no mechanical working of the universe, and no preordained logic. Rather, to believe in such inventions is merely the narrow, incorrect way humans interpret their own experiences.

Beyond the individual exists only chaos. The only reality that exists is one's own existence. Only by looking within oneself can one discern the truth of the outside disorder. Humanity is paramount. Human dignity and worth is of greatest importance. They are the source and dispenser of all truth. With this realization one acquires a profound respect for all human beings and their uniqueness. Human relations become very important, affirming individual worth and protecting the individual's right to discover his or her own truth. Morality is the process of knowing oneself and allowing others the freedom to do likewise. Faith, intuition, mysticism, imagery, and transcendental experiences are all acceptable ways of discovery. Humans are totally free, not shaped by others, not restricted by the flux of the times. They hold within themselves the capacity to form their own destiny.

This philosophy of education, applied to supervision, means a full commitment to individual teacher choice. The supervisor provides an environment that enables the teacher to explore his or her own physical and mental capabilities. Teachers must learn for themselves. The supervisor does not dispense information and shies away from intrusively guiding a teacher. Supervisors help when needed, protect the rights of others to self-discovery, and encounter the teacher as a person of full importance.

Checking Your Own Educational Philosophy and Supervisory Beliefs

Here are two instruments to test whether or not your supervisory beliefs have a relationship to your educational philosophy. The first, developed by Patricia D. Jersin and entitled "What is Your Educational Philosophy?" is found in Appendix A. The second, developed by Glickman and Tamashiro (1981) and entitled "Determining One's Beliefs Regarding Teacher Supervision," helps the reader look at supervisor practices in school settings as reflective of three predominate systems. Those belief systems correspond to the philosophies of essentialism, experimentalism, and existentialism, and are labeled *directive* supervision, *collaborative* supervision, and *nondirective* supervision. Glickman and Tamashiro (1980) wrote:

> *Directive Supervision* is an approach based on the belief that teaching consists of technical skills with known standards and competencies for all teachers to be effective. The supervisor's role is to inform, direct, model, and assess those competencies.
> *Collaborative Supervision* is based on the belief that teaching is primarily problem solving, whereby two or more persons jointly pose hypotheses to a problem, experiment, and implement those teaching strategies that appear to be most relevant in their own surroundings. The supervisor's role is to guide the problem-solving process, be an active member of the interaction, and keep the teacher(s) focused on their common problems.
> *Non-Directive Supervision* has as its premise that learning is primarily a private experience in which individuals must come up with their own solutions to improving the classroom experience for students. The supervisor's role is to listen, be nonjudgmental, and provide self-awareness and clarification experiences for teachers [p. 76].

The inventory is as follows.

Checking Your Own Educational Philosophy and Supervisory Beliefs

The Supervisor Beliefs Inventory

This inventory is designed for supervisors to assess their own beliefs about teacher supervision and staff development. The inventory assumes that supervisors believe and act according to all three of the orientations of supervision, but that one usually dominates. The inventory is designed to be self-administered and self-scored. Supervisors are asked to choose one of two options. A scoring key follows.

Instructions: Circle either A or B for each item. You may not completely agree with either choice, but choose the one that is closest to how you feel.

1. A. Supervisors should give teachers a large degree of autonomy and initiative within broadly defined limits.
   B. Supervisors should give teachers directions about methods that will help them improve their teaching.

2. A. It is important for teachers to set their own goals and objectives for professional growth.
   B. It is important for supervisors to help teachers reconcile their personalities and teaching styles with the philosophy and direction of the school.

3. A. Teachers are likely to feel uncomfortable and anxious if the objectives on which they will be evaluated are not clearly defined by the supervisor.
   B. Evaluations of teachers are meaningless if teachers are not able to define with their supervisors the objectives for evaluation.

4. A. An open, trusting, warm, and personal relationship with teachers is the most important ingredient in supervising teachers.
   B. A supervisor who is too intimate with teachers risks being less effective and less respected than a supervisor who keeps a certain degree of professional distance from teachers.

5. A. My role during supervisory conferences is to make the interaction positive, to share realistic information, and to help teachers plan their own solutions to problems.
   B. The methods and strategies I use with teachers in a conference are aimed at our reaching agreement over the needs for future improvement.

SUPERVISORY BELIEFS AND REFLECTIONS ON PRACTICE

6. In the initial phase of working with a teacher:
   A. I develop objectives with each teacher that will help accomplish school goals.
   B. I try to identify the talents and goals of individual teachers so they can work on their own improvement.

7. When several teachers have a similar classroom problem, I prefer to:
   A. Have the teachers form an ad hoc group and help them work together to solve the problem.
   B. Help teachers on an individual basis find their strengths, abilities, and resources so that each one finds his or her own solution to the problem.

8. The most important clue that an in-service workshop is needed occurs when:
   A. The supervisor perceives that several teachers lack knowledge or skill in a specific area, which is resulting in low morale, undue stress, and less effective teaching.
   B. Several teachers perceive the need to strengthen their abilities in the same instructional area.

9. A. The supervisory staff should decide the objectives of an in-service workshop since they have a broad perspective on the teachers' abilities and the school's needs.
   B. Teachers and supervisory staff should reach consensus about the objectives of an in-service workshop before the workshop is held.

10. A. Teachers who feel they are growing personally will be more effective than teachers who are not experiencing personal growth.
    B. The knowledge and ability of teaching strategies and methods that have been proved over the years should be taught and practiced by all teachers to be effective in their classrooms.

11. When I perceive that a teacher might be scolding a student unnecessarily:
    A. I explain, during a conference with the teacher, why the scolding was excessive.
    B. I ask the teacher about the incident, but do not interject my judgments.

12. A. One effective way to improve teacher performance is to formulate clear behavioral objectives and create meaningful incentives for achieving them.
    B. Behavioral objectives are rewarding and helpful to some teachers but stifling to others; some teachers benefit from behavioral objectives in some situations but not in others.

13. During a preobservation conference:
    A. I suggest to the teacher what I could observe, but I let the teacher make the final decision about the objectives and methods of observation.

B. The teacher and I mutually decide the objectives and methods of observation.

14. A. Improvement occurs very slowly if teachers are left on their own; but when a group of teachers work together on a specific problem, they learn rapidly and their morale remains high.

B. Group activities may be enjoyable, but I find that individual, open discussion with a teacher about a problem and its possible solutions leads to more sustained results.

15. When an in-service or staff development workshop is scheduled:

A. All teachers who participated in the decision to hold the workshop should be expected to attend it.

B. Teachers, regardless of their role in forming a workshop, should be able to decide if the workshop is relevant to their personal or professional growth and, if not, should not be expected to attend.

Scoring Key

Step 1. Circle your answer from Part II of the inventory in the following columns:

Column I	Column II	Column III
1B	1A	
	2B	2A
3A	3B	
4B		4A
	5B	5A
6A		6B
	7A	7B
8A		8B
9A	9B	
10B		10A
11A		11B
12A	12B	
	13B	13A
14B	14A	
	15A	15B

Step 2. Tally the number of circled items in each column and multiply by 6.7.

2.1 Total response in column I _____ × 6.7 = _____

2.2 Total response in column II ＿＿＿＿＿ × 6.7 = ＿＿＿＿＿

2.3 Total response in column III ＿＿＿＿＿ × 6.7 = ＿＿＿＿＿

Step 3. Intepretation: The product you obtained in step 2.1 is an approximate percentage of how often you take a directive approach to supervision, rather than either of the other two approaches. The product you obtained in step 2.2 is an approximate percentage of how often you take a collaborative approach, and that in step 2.3 an approximate percentage of how often you take a nondirective approach.

What Does Your Belief Mean in Terms of Teacher Control?

Beliefs about supervision and educational philosophy can be thought of in terms of control (see Table 5–1). An essentialist philosophy is premised on the supervisor being the expert on instruction and, therefore, having major control over the teacher. A situation of high supervisor control and low teacher control is labeled *directive supervision.* An experimentalist philosophy is premised on the supervisor and teachers being equal partners in instructional improvement; equal supervisor and teacher control is labeled *collaborative supervision.* Existentialist philosophy is premised on teachers discovering their own capacities for instructional improvement. Low supervisor control and high teacher control is labeled *nondirective supervision.* As we clarify our own educational philosophy and supervisory beliefs, we rarely find a pure ideological position. Therefore, Sergiovanni's idea of a supervisory platform becomes helpful. What combination of various philosophies and beliefs do we consider important? Perhaps our beliefs are mainly essential-

TABLE 5–1   Relationship of Philosophy, Control, and Supervisory Belief

Educational Philosophy	Control	Supervisory Belief
Essentialism	Supervisor high, teacher low	Directive
Experimentalism	Supervisor equal, teacher equal supervisor low	Collaborative
Existentialism	Supervisor low, teacher high	Nondirective

list and directive, yet contain parts of experimentalism and collaboration; or perhaps we have another combination of beliefs. A particular platform is not right or wrong, but is instead an assessment of the bits and pieces we use to create the floor we stand on.

Developmental Supervision

My own supervisory platform is based on the premise that human development is the aim of education. Therefore, supervision should be *eclectic* in practice, directed toward the goal of nondirective, existentialist supervision. My goal as a supervisor is eventually to return control to the teaching faculty to decide on collective, instructional improvements. Such an ideal cannot be achieved suddenly, if at all. Instead, the supervisor at times might use behaviors that come from an essentialist-directive belief structure as a point of entry, or might use behaviors that come from an experimentalist-collaborative belief structure as another point of entry. Regardless of the entry point, the supervisor should always strive to shift control to teachers. The supervisor may never allow total autonomy, but moving in that direction is worth the effort. My platform is, therefore, one of collaborative experimentalism striving toward nondirective existentialism.

Here are some examples of why I believe a purposeful, developmental supervision can be substantiated for the improvement of instruction. Research on reading effectiveness shows the merits of different supervisory orientations when matched to the particular characteristics of the teaching staff. Reading effectiveness occurred in previously failure-prone schools and classrooms when teachers with little experience, competency, or desire to improve their instruction were monitored, evaluated, and directed by the supervisor (principal) to use a new, systematic reading program (Vanezky 1982). The results speak clearly for a directive orientation when the teaching force is unskilled and unmotivated. In still other schools, which had had several years of successful reading improvement, researchers noted frequent group problem-solving meetings and mutual adaptation of the curriculum (Humphries 1981; McLaughlin and Marsh 1978). For a staff that has successfully developed competency and motivation, a collaborative approach to future improvement appears to be in order Finally, a staff with extensive background, competency, and motivation, who know how to work both together and alone, should find ways to improve student performance informally and independently. A nondirective orientation is most appropriate here.

Summary, Conclusion, and Propositions

We have examined the relationship of educational philosophy to supervisory belief and practice. The reader was asked to determine his or her own supervisory platform by responding to two instruments. I revealed my platform of supervision as collaborative experimentalism striving toward nondirective existentialism within a developmental framework. I believe teachers will become collectively purposeful as they gain greater control over decisions for instructional improvement.

The following propositions about supervision that will enhance collective teacher actions are now possible:

■ Proposition 1: *Supervisors should use a variety of practices that emanate from various philosophies and belief structures with developmental directionality in mind.* Directive, collaborative, and nondirective supervisory approaches are all valid as long as they aim to increase teacher self-control.

■ Proposition 2: *As supervisors gradually increase teacher choice and control over instructional improvement, teachers will become more abstract and committed to improvement, and a sense of ethos or of a cause beyond oneself will emerge.*

Allowing for gradual choice will increase teacher abstraction and autonomy and lead to more altruistic, collective faculty action.

EXERCISES

ACADEMIC

1. Write your own educational platform. Your platform need not exclusively reflect any of the three major philosophies discussed in the chapter.

2. Design a chart comparing the three major philosophies discussed in the chapter in terms of what each philosophy assumes about:

   a. Human nature.

   b. What constitutes reality.

    c.   The human relationship to the environment.

    d.   The human relationship to fellow humans.

Design a second chart comparing *implications* of the three philosophies in terms of:

    a.   How people best learn.

    b.   The proper goal(s) of education.

    c.   The appropriate role of the teacher.

    d.   The appropriate role of the educational supervisor.

3.   Prepare a report in which you identify one of the three major philosophies discussed in the chapter (essentialism, experimentalism, existentialism) as the one most clearly reflected in U.S. public education today. Provide a rationale for your choice.

4.   Read at least one chapter from another text on educational supervision. Prepare a report identifying one of three major philosophies discussed in the text (essentialism, experimentalism, existentialism) as having the greatest influence on the author. Include quotations from the text that support your position.

5.   Write a reaction to the author's supervisory platform. Include your perceptions of problems that might be encountered by a supervisor attempting to make the author's platform a reality within a public school setting.

FIELD

1.   Ask five teachers from different school districts for single-paragraph descriptions of central office supervisors. Assuming each teacher has given an accurate description of at least one central office supervisor, classify each described supervisor according to his or her probable philosophy (experimentalist, essentialist, existentialist, or other). Summarize your study and conclusions in writing. (Supervisors and school districts should remain anonymous in the teacher descriptions; responding teachers should remain anonymous in your written summary.)

2.   Ask five adults to list improvements that should be made in U.S. public education. On the basis of the lists, attempt to

relate each respondent to one of the major philosophies described in the chapter (essentialism, experimentalism, existentialism). Summarize your study and conclusions in writing.

3. Ask five teachers each to write one or two paragraphs on "What Makes an Effective Supervisor." On the basis of the teachers' responses, predict which supervisory approach each teacher would prefer during classroom supervision or staff development activities.

4. Ask five students to write one or two paragraphs on "What Makes a Good School?" Attempt to relate each student response to one of the three major philosophies described in the chapter (essentialism, experimentalism, existentialism). Write a report reviewing the students' responses and showing whether and/or how each response relates to one of the three philosophies.

5. Visit or recall the organization and climate of a selected school. On the basis of your observations or recollections, which of the three major philosophies described in the chapter (essentialism, experimentalism, existentialism) does the school's organization and climate most clearly reflect? Prepare a report discussing the school's organizational and climate characteristics and supporting your philosophical classification of the school.

DEVELOPMENTAL

1. Begin an in-depth study of one of the philosophies described in Chapter 5. As you carry out the study, continue to relate your inquiry to education and educational supervision.

2. Plan to retake the Supervisory Beliefs Inventory after finishing this book in order to detect and interpret any changes in your attitude toward supervision.

3. Begin a review of the works of popular authors who present what they consider successful approaches to management, leadership, or interpersonal communication. For each author, consider whether his or her recommended approach or system most nearly resembles a directive, collaborative, nondirective, or eclectic approach. Make a personal evaluation of each author's proposals.

Note

1. The descriptions of philosophy in Chapter 5 are taken from C. D. Glickman and J. P. Esposito, *Leadership Guide for Elementary School Improvement: Procedures for Assessment and Change* (Boston: Allyn and Bacon, 1979), p. 20.

REFERENCES

Gates, P. E.; Blanchard, K. H.; and Hersey, P. 1976. Diagnosing educational leadership problems. *Educational Leadership* *33*(February):348–354.

Glickman, C. D. 1981a. *Developmental supervision: Alternative practices for helping teachers improve instruction.* Alexandria, Va.: Association for Supervision and Curriculum Development.

Glickman, C. D. 1981b. Play and the school curriculum: The historical context. *Journal of Research and Development 14*(3):1–10.

Glickman, C. D. 1983. An informal study of teachers' perceptions of typical central office supervisors. In progress, descriptions collected in 1983.

Glickman, C. D., and Esposito, J. P. 1979. *Leadership guide for elementary school improvement: Procedures for assessment and change.* Boston: Allyn and Bacon.

Glickman, C. D., and Tamashiro, R. T. 1980. Determining one's beliefs regarding teacher supervision. *Bulletin 64*(440):74–81.

———. 1981. The supervisory beliefs inventory. In C. D. Glickman, *Developmental supervision: Alternative practices for helping teachers to improve instruction.* Alexandria, Va.: Association for Supervision and Curriculum Development, pp. 12–16.

Humprhies, J. D. 1981. Factors affecting the impact of curriculum innovation on classroom practice. Unpublished Ph.D. diss., University of Georgia.

Johnson, J. A.; Collins, H. W.; Dupuis, V. L.; and Johansen, J. H. 1973. *Foundations of American education.* Boston: Allyn and Bacon.

McLaughlin, M. W., and Marsh, D. D. 1978. Staff development and school change. *Teacher College Record 80*(1):69–74.

Morris. V. C. 1961. *Philosophy and the American school.* Boston: Houghton Mifflin.

Pratte, R. 1971. *Contemporary theories of education.* Scranton, Pa.: T. Y. Crowell.

Sergiovanni, T. J., and Starrat, R. J. 1983. *Supervision: Human perspectives,* 3rd ed. New York: McGraw-Hill, pp. 226–227.

Vanezky, R. L. 1982. Effective schools for reading instruction. Address to the California (Calfee) reading project, Stanford Univerity, January 22.

SUGGESTIONS FOR ADDITIONAL READING

Bobbitt, F. 1918. *The curriculum.* Boston: Houghton Mifflin.

Butler, D. J. 1968. *Four philosophies and their practice in education and religion.* New York: Harper and Row.

Cremin, L. A. 1964. *The transformation of the school.* New York: Vintage Books.

Cubberly, E. P. 1969. *Public adminstration.* Boston: Houghton Mifflin.

Hanson, K. 1960. *Philosophy for American education.* Englewood Cliffs, N.J.: Prentice-Hall.

Johnson, J. A.; Collins, H. W.; Dupuis, V. L.; and Johansen, J. H. 1973. *Foundations of American education.* Boston: Allyn and Bacon.

Kilpatrick, W. H. 1963. *Philosophy of education.* New York: Macmillan.

Marler, C. D. 1975. *Philosophy and schooling.* Boston: Allyn and Bacon.

Marshall, J. P. 1973. *The teacher and his philosophy.* Lincoln, Neb.: Professional Educators Publications.

Morris, V. C. 1961. *Philosophy and the American school.* Boston: Houghton Mifflin.

References

Peters, R. S., ed. 1967. *The concept of education.* London: Humanities Press.

Pratte, R. 1971. *Contemporary theories of education.* Scranton, Pa.: T. Y. Crowell.

Tanner, D., and Tanner, L. 1975. *Curriculum development: Theory into practice.* New York: Macmillan.

Taylor, F. W. 1911. *The principles of scientific management.* New York: Harper.

PART II

Conclusion

Part II reviewed the prerequisite knowledge for supervision as the developmental function for effective schools. We read about "The Exception: What Schools Can Be" (Chapter Two); "The Norm: Why Schools Are As They Are" (Chapter Three); "Contrasting Optimal Adult Development With Actual Teacher Development: Some Clues for Supervisory Practices" (Chapter Four); and "Supervisory Beliefs and Reflections on Practice" (Chapter Five). A number of propositions were constructed from each chapter to set the framework for supervision being viewed as a developmental function.

Those propositions are placed together as general, guiding principles to review

What Can Be

- Proposition 1: Supervision can strengthen teachers' belief in a cause beyond oneself.
- Proposition 2: Supervision can promote teachers' sense of efficacy.
- Proposition 3: Supervision can make teachers aware of how they complement each other in striving for common goals.
- Proposition 4: Supervision can stimulate teachers to appraise, reflect, and adapt their instruction.
- Proposition 5: Supervision can challenge teachers toward more varied, abstract thought.

What Is

- Proposition 1: Supervision cannot rely on the teaching career to provide motivation for continual instructional improvement.
- Proposition 2: Supervision cannot rely on the existing work environment of schools to stimulate instructional improvement.
- Proposition 3: Supervisors cannot assume that teachers are reflective, autonomous, and responsible for their own development.

Implications of Contrasting Adult and Teacher Development

- Proposition 1: Supervision, to be effective, must be a function that responds to the developmental stage of teachers.

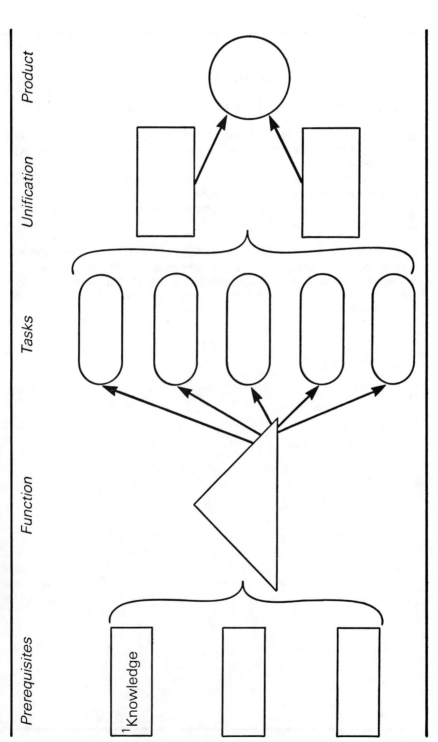

FIGURE II–1 Supervision for Successful Schools

Prerequisites *Function* *Tasks* *Unification* *Product*

[1]Knowledge

■ Proposition 2: Supervision, to be effective, must be a function that responds to the adult life transitions of teachers.

Supervisory Belief to Move from What Is to What Can Be

■ Proposition 1: Supervisors should use a variety of practices that emanate from various philosophical and belief structures with a developmental directionality in mind.
■ Proposition 2: As supervisors gradually increase teacher choice and control over instructional improvement, teachers will become more abstract and committed to improvement, and a sense of ethos or cause beyond oneself will emerge.

At the end of each section, the reader will be reminded of the organization of effective supervision as a developmental function. See Figure II–1, where we can see the knowledge prerequisite attained with many more geometric figures to go. The next section will deal with the prerequisite of interpersonal skills.

PART III

Interpersonal Skills

Introduction

The organization of this book was outlined in Figure 1–1, Chapter One. The prerequisites for supervision as a developmental function are knowledge, interpersonal skills, and technical skills. In Part II, Chapters Two through Five, we examined the critical knowledge base. In Part III we will describe interpersonal skills. Chapter Six will introduce the supervisory behavior continuum, Chapter Seven will detail the use of nondirective behaviors, Chapter Eight will detail the use of collaborative behaviors, and Chapter Nine will detail the use of directive behaviors. Chapter Ten will discuss application of alternative interpersonal skills according to characteristics of individuals and groups of teachers.

Knowledge of what needs to be done to promote teacher growth and school effectiveness is the base dimension of a triangle for supervisory action (see Figure III–1). Knowledge needs to be accompanied by interpersonal skills for communicating with teachers and technical skills for planning, assessing, observing, and evaluating instructional improvement. We will now turn to the interpersonal skill dimension.

FIGURE III–1   Prerequisite Dimensions for a Supervisor

Knowledge

CHAPTER SIX

Supervisory Behavior Continuum: Know Thyself

This chapter looks at the range of interpersonal behaviors available to a supervisor who is working with individuals and groups of teachers. It will assess how supervisors typically behave with staff in school settings and then determine other behaviors that might be used skillfully and effectively. Later chapters will provide training in each of three clusters of interpersonal skills.

What are the categories of behaviors? After many years of collecting supervisors' observations in meetings with individuals and groups of teachers for purposes of making classroom or school decisions, broad categories of supervisory behaviors have been derived (Glickman 1981; Wolfgang and Glickman 1980). These categories encompass almost all observed supervisor behaviors that are deemed purposeful. A *purposeful* behavior is defined as one that contributes to the decision being made at the conference or meeting. The derived categories of supervisory behaviors are listening, clarifying, encouraging, reflecting, presenting, problem solving, negotiating, directing, standardizing, and reinforcing. Definitions of each category are as follows:

> *Listening:* The supervisor sits and looks at the speaker and nods his or her head to show understanding. Gutteral utterances ("uh-hu", "umm . . .") also indicate listening.
>
> *Clarifying:* The supervisor asks questions and statements to clarify the speaker's point of view: "Do you mean that?" "Would you explain this further?" "I'm confused about this." "I lost you on . . ."
>
> *Encouraging:* The supervisor provides acknowledgment responses that help the speaker continue to explain his or her

positions: "Yes, I'm following you." "Continue on." "Ah, I see what you're saying; tell me more."

Reflecting: The supervisor summarizes and paraphrases the speaker's message for verification of accuracy: "I understand that you mean..." "So, the issue is..." "I hear you saying..."

Presenting: The supervisor gives his or her own ideas about the issue being discussed: "This is how I see it." "What can be done is..." "I'd like us to consider..." "I believe that..."

Problem Solving: The supervisor takes the initiative, usually after a preliminary discussion of the issue or problem, in pressing all those involved to generate a list of possible solutions. This is usually done by statements such as "Let's stop and each write down what can be done." "What ideas do we have to solve this problem?" "Let's think of all possible actions we can take."

Negotiating: The supervisor moves the discussion from possible to probable solutions by discussing the consequences of each proposed action, exploring conflict or priorities, and narrowing down choices with questions such as "Where do we agree?" "How can we change that action to be acceptable to all?" "Can we find a compromise that will give each of us part of what we want?"

Directing: The supervisor tells the participant(s) what is to be done: "I've decided that we will do..." "I want you to do..." "The policy will be..." "This is how it is going to be." "We will then proceed as follows."

Standardizing: The supervisor sets the expected criteria and time for the decision to be implemented. Target objectives are set. Expectations are conveyed with words, such as: "By next Monday, we want to see..." "Report back to me on this change by..." "Have the first two activities carried out by..." "I want an improvement of 25 percent involvement by the next meeting." "We have agreed that all tasks will be done before the next observation."

Reinforcing: The supervisor strengthens the directive and the criteria to be met by telling of possible consequences. Possible consequences can be positive, in the form of praise: "I know you can do it!" "I have confidence in your ability!" "I want to show others what you've done!" Consequences also can be negative: "If it's not done on time, we'll lose the support of . . ." or "It must be understood that failure to get this done on time will result in . . ."

The foregoing categories of interpersonal supervisory behaviors move participants toward a decision. Some supervisory behaviors place more responsibility on the teacher(s) to make the decision, others place more responsibility on the supervisor to make the decision, and still others indicate a shared responsibility for decision making. The categories of behaviors are listed in a sequence on the supervisor behavior continuum (Figure 6–1) to reflect the scale of control or power.

When a supervisor *listens* to the teacher, *clarifies* what the teacher says, *encourages* the teacher to speak more about the concern, and *reflects* by verifying the teacher's perceptions, then clearly it is the teacher who is in control. The supervisor's role is that of an active prober or sounding board for the teacher to make his or her own decision. The teacher has high control and the supervisor low control over the actual decision (big *T*, small *s*). This is seen as a *nondirective interpersonal approach*.

When a supervisor uses nondirective behaviors to understand the teacher's point of view but then participates in the discussion by *presenting* his or her own ideas, *problem solving* by asking all parties to propose possible actions, and then *negotiating* to find a common course of action satisfactory to teacher and supervisor, then the control over the decision is shared by all. This is viewed as a *collaborative interpersonal approach*.

Finally, when a supervisor *directs* the teacher in what will be done, *standardizes* the time and criteria of expected results, and *reinforces* the consequences of action or inaction, then the supervisor has taken responsibility for the decision (small *t*, big *S*). The supervisor is clearly determining the actions for the teacher to follow. These behaviors are called a *directive interpersonal approach*.

Your Own Interpersonal Behavior Approach

Chapter Five dealt with supervisory beliefs and practicing beliefs. Now let's step back and watch ourselves at work. First watch how we act with individual teachers and then with groups. Read the Supervisory Interpersonal Behavior Questionnaire for Working with Individuals, and select the approach you most often take.

FIGURE 6–1   The Supervisory Behavior Continuum

	1	2	3	4	5	6	7	8	9	10	
						Problem					
T	Listening	Clarifying	Encouraging	Reflecting	Presenting	Solving	Negotiating	Directing	Standardizing	Reinforcing	t
s											S

Clusters
of
Behaviors:

           Nondirective   Collaborative   Directive

Key: T = Maximum teacher responsibility   *S* = Maximum supervisor responsibility
     t = Minimum teacher responsibility   *s* = Minimum supervisor responsibility

Source: From Carl D. Glickman, *Developmental Supervision: Alternative Practices for Helping Teachers Improve Instruction*. Reprinted with permission of the Association for Supervision and Curriculum Development, Alexandria, Va. Copyright © 1981 by the Association for Supervision and Curriculum Development. All rights reserved.

Supervisory Interpersonal Behavior Questionnaire for Working with Individuals: A Scenario*

The school day has just ended for students at Whichway School. Just as the teacher sits down at the desk, you the supervisor appear at the door and the teacher invites you in. "How is everything going?" you ask. Looking at the large stack of papers to correct, the teacher predicts a number of them will reflect that the students did not understand the work. "It's very frustrating working with this class. They have such a wide range of ability!" Then the teacher mentions another source of frustration: "Some of the students are discipline problems and their behavior results in class disruption."

After further discussion, the teacher and you agree that you will come into the classroom to observe what is going on, followed by a conference to discuss the classroom visit.

A few days later, after you have observed in the classroom and carefully analyzed the collected information, you begin to plan for the conference. You consider a number of approaches to use in the conference to help the teacher.

Approach A

Present what you saw in the classroom and ask for the teacher's perceptions. Listen to each other's responses. After clarifying the problem, each of you can propose ideas. Finally, you will agree on what is to be done in the classroom. You will mutually identify an objective and agree to an action plan that both of you will work together to carry out. The plan is for both of you to make.

Approach B

Listen to the teacher discuss what is going on in the classroom. If asked, offer your perceptions regarding what you observed. Encourage the teacher to analyze the problem further, and ask questions to make sure the teacher is clear about his or her view of the problem. If the teacher requests your views on how to proceed, respond, but only if asked. Finally, ask the teacher to determine and detail the actions he or she will take and find out if you might be of further help. The plan is the teacher's to make.

Approach C

Present your beliefs about the situation and ask the teacher to confirm or revise the interpretation. After identifying the problem, offer directions to the teacher on what should be done and how to proceed. You can go into the classroom to demonstrate what you are telling the teacher to do, or tell the

*Adapted from an instrument developed by Katherine C. Ginkel, 1982. "An Overview of a Study Which Examined the Relationship between Elementary School Teachers' Preference for Supervisory Conferencing Approach and Conceptual Level of Development," a paper presented at the annual meeting of the American Educational Research Association, Montreal, April. Used with permission of Katherine C. Ginkel.

teacher to observe another teacher who does well in this particular area. Praise and reward the teacher for following the given assignment. The plan is for you the supervisor to make.

Response

Most often, I use Approach _____.

Interpretation

Approach A: A cluster of *collaborative behaviors* in which the supervisor and teacher share the decision making about future improvement.

Approach B: A cluster of *nondirective behaviors* in which the supervisor helps the teacher formulate his or her own decision about future improvement.

Approach C: A cluster of *directive behaviors* in which the supervisor makes the decision for the teacher.

Next take a look at the interpersonal behaviors you typically use when meeting with groups of teachers. Please respond to the Supervisory Interpersonal Behavior Questionnaire for Working with Groups.

The Supervisory Interpersonal Behavior Questionnaire for Working with Groups

You have just called upon the science teachers to decide on a policy for allowing students to use laboratory equipment after school. Many students have complained about not having enough class time for doing their experiments. The issue is how and when to free up more laboratory time for students (before school, at lunchtime, during study hall, after school) under the supervision of certified teachers. How would you work with the science teachers to make a decision?

Approach A

Meet with the staff and explain that they need to decide what to do about this issue. Present the information you have about the problem and ask for clarification. Paraphrase what they say and, once the teachers verify your summary, ask them to decide among themselves what they are going to do. Remain in the meeting, helping to move the discussion along by calling on people, asking questions, and paraphrasing, but do not become involved in making your own position known or influencing the outcome in any conscious way.

Approach B

Meet with the staff by first explaining that you have to make a decision that will meet the needs of students, teachers, and supervisor. Either by consensus or, if not, then by majority vote, make a decision. You should listen, encourage, clarify, and reflect on each staff member's perception. Afterwards, ask each member including yourself to suggest possible solutions. Discuss each solution; prioritize the list; and, if no consensus emerges, call for a vote. Argue for your own solution, but go along with the group's decision.

Approach C

Meet with the staff and tell them you want their feedback before you make a decision about the issue. Make it clear that the staff's involvement is to be advisory. Ask for their suggestions, listen, encourage, clarify, and paraphrase their ideas. After everyone has had a chance to speak, decide what changes should be made. Tell them what you are going to do, when the changes will be made, and that you expect them to carry out the plan.

Response

Most often, I would use Approach _____.

Interpretation

Approach A: A cluster of *nondirective behaviors* in which the supervisor assists the group to make its own decision.

Approach B: A cluster of *collaborative behaviors* in which the supervisor works as part of the group in making a group decision.

Approach C: A cluster of *directive behaviors* in which the supervisor makes the decision for the group.

Valid Assessment of Self

After assessing our own approach to individuals and groups, we need to make sure that how we perceive ourselves is consistent with how others perceive us. For example, if we checked that we typically use a collaborative approach with individuals and a nondirective approach with groups, then we need further information to know whether that is true. If not, then later in this chapter we might recommend a continuation, refinement, or discontinuation with a cluster of behaviors that simply do not exist in anyone's mind but our own. As an example, let me give a personal instance of erroneous self-perception.

As a school principal in New Hampshire, I regarded myself as operating a successful school and being accessible to teachers. I could document my success by external evidence—state and national recognitions the school had received, complimentary letters from numerous visitors. I documented my accessibility through casual discussions with teachers in the lounge and by having an open-office policy for every staff member who wished to speak with me. In my third year as a principal at this particular school, the superintendent asked all principals in the school system to allow teachers to evaluate principal performance. One item on the evaluation form was "Ability to Listen to Others," followed by a numerical scale of responses from 1 ("rarely listens") to 7 ("almost always listens"). Before giving the form to teachers, I filled out the same evaluation form according to my own perception of my performance. I confidently circled the number 7 on "ability to listen." Once the teachers' responses were collected and results were received, I was amazed to find that the lowest teacher rating on the entire survey was on that very item on which I had rated myself highest. To my chagrin, there was an obvious discrepancy between my own perception of performance and staff perceptions. We'll refer to this painful recollection as we look at perceptions of supervisory behavior.

Johari Window

The Johari window (Luft 1970) provides a graphic way to look at what we know and do not know about our behavior (see Figure 6–2). Visualize a window with four windowpanes. In this scheme there are four windowpanes of the self in which behaviors are either known or not known by self (the supervisor) and others (the teachers). In windowpane I there are behaviors that both supervisor and teachers know the supervisor uses. This is the *public self*. For example, the supervisor knows that when he or she is anxious, speech will become halting and hesitant; teachers are also aware of what such speech indicates.

In windowpane II is the *blind self*—behaviors the supervisor practices that are unknown to the self but are known to teachers. For example, as a school principal I was displaying behaviors toward teachers that I thought were listening behaviors, but teachers saw the same behaviors as a failure to listen. Of course, once one becomes aware of teachers' perceptions of those behaviors, the blind self becomes the public self.

In windowpane III is the *private self*—behaviors the supervisor has knowledge about but that teachers do not know. For instance, in new situations a supervisor might mask his or her unsureness by being extroverted in greeting others. Only the supervisor knows that her behavior is covering up insecurity. Once the supervisor discloses this perception to others, the private self becomes public.

Finally, there is windowpane IV, the *unknown self.* There are actions a supervisor takes of which both supervisors and teachers are unaware. From time to time the supervisor might rapidly shift his legs while speaking behind a table. Neither supervisor or teachers are aware of this leg movement. Perhaps a supervisor becomes irritated while a certain teacher is speaking. The supervisor may not know why she is irritated or even that she feels this way, and the teacher may not know either. The unknown self is unconscious to all; it becomes private, blind, or public only by circumstances that create a new awareness.

What does the Johari window have to do with supervision? We cannot become more effective as supervisors unless we know what we are doing. We may, at our discretion, decide to keep parts of ourselves private (for example, we may not want teachers to know all the details of our life and personality). Yet we need to understand that by remaining largely private and not sharing the experiences that bind us as humans, we are creating a distance when we work with teachers. We may prefer formality and distance and may be able to document that such privateness accomplishes certain results. On the other hand, we must also accept that our privateness will be reciprocal, and that staff may not

FIGURE 6–2   Adaptation of Johari Window

	Known to Supervisor	Not Known to Supervisor
Known to Teachers	1. Public self	2. Blind self
Not Known to Teachers	3. Private self	4. Unknown self

Source: Adapted from Joseph Luft, *Group Processes: An Introduction to Group Dynamics* (New York: National Press Books, 1970).

easily discuss personal situations that may affect teaching performance. First we must be aware of how private or public we are with our staff and determine if we desire teachers to be the same way with us. Second, as supervisors, we cannot afford to be blind to our own behaviors and the effect of those behaviors on others. We can improve only what we know; to believe only our own self-perceptions is to court disaster.

My perception of my listening behavior as a principal is a case in point. As long as I saw myself as a wonderful, accessible listener, it did not seem probable that teachers were not coming to me with instructional problems. However, I discovered that on two different occasions teachers had gone to the superintendent about instructional problems of which I was unaware. After the superintendent had told me that teachers were going over my head, I angrily confronted the teachers with their "unprofessional" behavior. It did not occur to me that I might have been the one at fault. After the staff evaluations, I could no longer delude myself. Many teachers were not telling me their concerns because they did not believe that I would really listen. I had to face the fact that the staff did not see me as accessible. I might have avoided collecting such information, continued with my euphoric self-perception, and then been devastated as the school fell apart.

We need to check the validity of our own perceptions. Try this: Photocopy the Supervision Belief Inventory (Chapter Five), the Supervisory Interpersonal Behavior Questionnaire for Working with Individuals, and the Supervisory Interpersonal Behavior Questionnaire for Working with Groups. Give the copies to a staff member who is trusted by the other teachers to distribute and collect the inventories and questionnaires. Instructions to teachers should be that no names are to be written on the pages; only circles or checks need to be made on the response sheets. Confidentiality will increase the honesty of the responses. Teachers should know that only summarized results prepared by the designated teacher will be given to the supervisor. Therefore a teacher's individual responses cannot be identified or used against him or her. The supervisor can see which of his or her supervisory beliefs and practices are public (consistent between one's own perception and others') and which are blind (inconsistent between one's own perception and others'). With such information the supervisor can determine which are valid perceptions and which are invalid. With the invalid perceptions we can attempt to move from the blind to the public self via a program of behavior change.

Cognitive Dissonance

Invalidity of perceptions creates *cognitive dissonance* according to a theory of motivation by psychologist Leon Festinger (1957). The theory is based on the premise that a person cannot live with contradictory psychological evidence—that is, thinking of herself in one way while other sources of information indicate that she is different. When my perception of my listening abilities were contradicted by teacher perceptions, then mental turmoil or cognitive dissonance was created. For example, if you believe that you are a collaborative supervisor and then you receive feedback from teachers that you are a directive supervisor, this will cause cognitive dissonance. We must wrestle with disparent perceptions and reconcile them. If not, the two differing sources of information will continue to bother us. This mental anguish strives to resolve the question of what is it that we really do. The resolution can come about in three alternative ways (Hyman 1975).

First, we can dismiss the source of contrary evidence as biased and untrue. For example, the principal might rationalize, "I really am a good listener; teachers marked me low because they didn't like the way I scheduled bus duties." Or the supervisor might think he or she really is collaborative: "Teachers simply don't understand what is collaboration." By dismissing the other source of information as erroneous, we can continue to believe that we are what we originally thought. No further change is necessary.

Second, we can change our own self-perception to conform to the other source of information and can then live with the new perception of ourselves. We accept that they are right and we are wrong; thus our perception will now be theirs. For example, "I really was wrong about my listening abilities, and I now reconcile myself to being a poor listener," or, "The supervisor is really not collaborative but instead is, as the teachers say, directive." Accepting the other source of information makes dissonance vanish so that no further change is necessary.

Third, we can accept our original self-perception as how we wish to be perceived, use the other source of information as an indicator of how we are currently perceived, and then change our behaviors to be more similar to our wish. In other words, our perception was not accurate, but it still represents what we want to be. I thought I was a good listener, but others say that I was not; so I attempt to change my listening behaviors in order to become a good listener. The supervisor thought he or she was collaborative but others say that he or she was directive; so he or she changes behavior to become more collaborative.

The third alternative to resolving cognitive dissonance creates behavioral change. Whenever we have an idea of how we desire to be matched against the reality of how others see us, there exist conditions for individual change. The acknowledged gap between what is and what should be becomes a powerful stimulus to change.

We change our behaviors and gather feedback from others to determine whether others are forming new perceptions of us and more positive results are forthcoming.

Summary, Conclusions, and Preview

This chapter outlined the supervisory behavior continuum and the clustering of interpersonal behaviors into nondirective, collaborative, and directive approaches. Several assessment instruments were provided. A discourse on the Johari window and cognitive dissonance was given so that we might check the perception of our own beliefs and behaviors by those who are recipients of our behaviors. To assess our own perceptions, supervisory beliefs, and interpersonal behavior with those of teachers is believed to be important in refining and changing behaviors.

What information do we have from those we supervise to confirm or reject our perceptions? What if we find inconsistency in the ways we believe, the ways we work with individuals, and the ways we work with groups? In fact, in real life we may not be consistent in the ways we work with one individual as opposed to another individual, or with one group and another. Neither consistency nor inconsistency is being advocated here. A particular approach is not necessarily better than others. However, there is research evidence that the effectiveness of different supervisory behaviors and approaches is dependent on characteristics of individuals and groups of teachers. In the last chapter of this section, we will discuss how one might vary his or her approach according to those characteristics to help staff become more self-reliant and cohesive. For now, however, the reader should assess his or her own beliefs and practices as predominantly nondirective, collaborative, directive, or some combination thereof. We will next explain and practice the skills of each supervisory approach in terms of actual conferencing and meeting behaviors. Understanding how we behave as supervisors and then refining our present behaviors are the first steps toward acquiring new interpersonal behaviors.

Each of the next three chapters begins with a scenario of an idealized conference followed by a discussion of the supervisory responses. These chapters are meant for practical skill building in each of the three approaches. As a result, involvement and role playing are expected of the reader.

EXERCISES

ACADEMIC

1. After reviewing the ten categories of supervision defined in the chapter, list specific behaviors your supervisor has exhibited while supervising you. For each example, write a brief description of your feelings toward the supervisor while he or she was using the given behavior, as well as your behavioral response to the situation. What does a review of your feelings and responses tell you about the supervisory approach you most prefer? Least prefer?

2. The chapter proposes three possible ways of resolving the mental conflict brought about by cognitive dissonance. Prepare a report in which you cite examples of cognitive dissonance you have personally experienced and your reaction to each resulting dilemma. Based on your recollections, which of the three possible responses to cognitive dissonance has been your typical mode of resolution?

3. Label the left-hand column of a sheet of paper "Public Self" and the right-hand column "Private Self." Think of personality or other characteristics that you intentionally disguise in your work setting. For each characteristic, describe in a few words the image you consciously present to others (left-hand column) and the real you that your public behavior conceals (right-hand column).

4. Locate a research study on the effectiveness of one or more of the following supervisor approaches to supervisor-teacher conferences: (1) directive, (2) collaborative, (3) nondirective. Summarize the purpose, methods, results, and conclusions of the study in writing.

5. Chapter 6 relates an experience in which a discrepancy between my blind self and public self led to communication

problems with subordinates. Discuss in writing three other situations in which conflicts between a supervisor's blind self and public self might eventually lead to leadership problems.

FIELD

1. Arrange to visit a teacher's class for a postobservation conference with that teacher. The postobservation conference should include an analysis of the teacher's instructional performance, setting of instructional improvement goals, and planning a strategy for meeting those goals. Record the postobservation on audiotape. Refer to the categories of supervisor behavior in this book as you listen to the tape. Write a paper in which you state whether you used a primarily directive, collaborative, or nondirective approach during the postobservation conference. Cite examples of specific behaviors you exhibited during the postobservation conference. Compare those behaviors with your results on the Supervisor Beliefs Inventory and the Supervisory Interpersonal Behavior Questionnaire for Working with Individuals.

2. Carry out the exercise suggested in the chapter. Prepare a written report on the results of the exercise and your reaction to those results.

3. Rewrite the Supervisory Interpersonal Behavior Questionnaire for Working with Individuals or the Supervisory Interpersonal Behavior Questionnaire for Working with Groups so that the rewritten instrument asks *teachers* which type of interpersonal behavior they would prefer a supervisor to exhibit during supervisor-teacher interaction relative to the situation described in the chosen questionnaire. Report on your collected data and conclusions in writing.

4. Put yourself in the shoes of an individual you supervise or have supervised (even those not in formal supervisory roles have at one time or another been responsible for supervising others). Write a description of your supervisory style, (be careful to describe your supervisory style as the other person would, not as you would). Compare this description of your supervisory style with your results on the Supervisor Beliefs Inventory, the Supervisory Interpersonal Behavior Questionnaire for Working with Individuals, and the Supervisory Interpersonal Behavior Questionnaire for Working with Groups.

5. Draw a two-frame cartoon for each of the following titles: (1) public self–private self, (2) my message–their perception, (3) cognitive dissonance. Base your cartoons on personal experiences or observations in a school setting.

DEVELOPMENTAL

1. Begin to make mental notes on behaviors you use when supervising others. Look for patterns of behavior that can be related to an orientation toward supervision (directive, collaborative, nondirective, eclectic) of which you may not now be conscious.

2. Informally observe others in leadership roles. Do their behaviors tend to cluster toward a directive, collaborative, or nondirective approach?

3. Begin to examine discrepancies between your public self and your private self, and consider possible reasons for such discrepancies.

REFERENCES

Festinger, L. 1957. *A theory of cognitive dissonance.* Stanford, Calif.: Stanford University Press.

Ginkel, K. 1983. An overview of a study which examined the relationship between elementary school teachers' preference for supervisory conferencing approach and conceptual level of development. Paper presented at the annual meeting of the American Educational Research Association, Montreal, April.

Glickman, C. D. 1981. *Developmental supervision: Alternative practices for helping teachers improve instruction.* Alexandria, Va.: Association for Supervision and Curriculum Development.

Hyman, R. T. 1975. *School administrator's handbook of teacher supervision and evaluation methods.* Englewood Cliffs, N.J.: Prentice-Hall, pp. 46–47.

Luft, J. 1970. *Group processes: An introduction to group dynamics.* New York: National Press Books.

Wolfgang, C. H., and Glickman, C. D. 1980. *Solving discipline problems: Alternative strategies for teachers.* Boston: Allyn and Bacon.

CHAPTER SEVEN

Nondirective Behaviors

Teacher (barging into supervisor's office): This damn place is a zoo! I can't stand it any longer. These kids are a bunch of ingrates! I've had it.

Supervisor (looking at the teacher): Wow, you are angry! Tell me what's going on? Have a seat.

Teacher (refusing to sit): I get no help around here from you or the administration. The students know that they can act any way they damn please and get away with it. I'm not going to put up with it anymore.

Supervisor: What have they been doing?

Teacher: Just now, I went back into the class after being called out for a message and they were jumping all over the place, running around, throwing papers and being totally obnoxious. I can't leave them for a minute.

Supervisor: What did you do?

Teacher: What do you think? I screamed my bloody head off at them and after it all, Terence had the nerve to laugh at me.

Supervisor: Terence laughed at you?

Teacher: Yeah, that little snot! He always has the last word. He's so defiant it drives me mad!

Supervisor: Is he always like that?

Teacher: He sure is. Terence is my number one problem; if I could get him to behave and learn, the rest of the class would be no problem.

Supervisor: So the main problem is Terence. What do you do when he misbehaves?

Teacher: I've been sending him out of the room but that doesn't work. He could care less about school and will only work when forced to. He really gets to me.

Supervisor: He's a lot to handle.

Teacher: He sure is! That kid is a bundle of jumping nerves. He doesn't pay any attention to what goes on in class.

Supervisor: He must really keep you hopping! Does Terence do anything right in class?

Teacher: Hardly! He's just not excited about anything in school. If he could live in a world of rock videos and football games, he'd be just fine.

Supervisor: (joking): Well, maybe we need a flashing movie room of video and football highlights to keep him entertained!

Teacher: (laughing and calming down): Oh, I don't know. He just drives me nuts. He's not a bad kid.

Supervisor: Could we capitalize on his interests to improve his classroom behavior?

Teacher: I need to sit down with him and talk to him one on one. I really want to find something in class that would interest him and keep him out of my hair.

Supervisor: What might that be?

Teacher: Students get to do special history projects in class. Maybe I could tie his love for music or sports into a history project, or maybe make a contract with him about his good behavior so that he could earn time to listen to music? Let me talk to him.

Supervisor: Sorry about your class today. It sounds to me as if Terence is the key and you have some ideas. Are there ways that I could help?

Nondirective Behaviors with Individuals

Nondirective supervision is based on the assumption that an individual teacher knows best what instructional changes need to be made and has the ability to think and act on his or her own. The decision belongs to the teacher. The role of the supervisor is to assist the teacher in the process of thinking through his or her actions.

As the foregoing hypothetical script shows, the supervisor behaves in ways that keep the teacher's thinking focused on observation, interpretation, problem identification, and problem solutions. Notice how in the example the nondirective approach allowed the teacher to move from an angry outburst about the entire class to an analytical focus on Terence's behavior. Rarely will a teacher move this rapidly from anger to reflection, but the pattern of supervisor helping teacher come to his or her own conclusions is characteristic of a nondirective approach. The supervisor does not interject his or her own ideas into the discussion unless specifically asked. All verbalizations by the supervisor are intended as feedback or to extend the teacher's thinking; they do not influence the actual design.

Refer to the supervisory behavior continuum to understand how nondirective behaviors are used. Read carefully, because the misuse of listening, clarifying, encouraging, reflecting, problem-solving, and presenting behaviors can result in a decision that is not really the teacher's.

Figure 7–1 shows a typical pattern of supervisory interpersonal behaviors used in a nondirective conference. They begin with listening and end with asking the teacher to present his or her decision. The sequence of behaviors between start and finish can vary, but the end should be the same—a noninfluenced teacher decision.

1. Listening: *Wait until the teacher's initial statement is made.* Face and look at the teacher; concentrate on what is being said. Avoid thinking about how you see the problem or what you think should be done. It is not easy to restrain your mind from galloping ahead, but your job is to understand what the teacher initially has said.

2. Reflecting: *Verbalize your understanding of the initial problem.* Include in your statement the teacher's feelings and perceived situation: "You're angry because students don't pay attention." Wait for an acknowledgment of accuracy from the teacher: "Yes, I am, but . . ." Do not offer your own opinion; your job is to capture what the teacher is saying.

3. Clarifying: *Probe for underlying problem and/or additional information.* You now ask the teacher to look at the problem in some different ways and to consider new information that might be contributing to the problem. Clarifying is done to help the teacher further identify, not solve, the problem. Questions such as "Do you mean that you are really fed up with school?" "Is it a particular student who is getting to you?" or "When has this happened before?" are appropriate information-seeking questions. Avoid ques-

FIGURE 7-1   The Supervisory Behavior Continuum: Nondirective Behaviors

	1	2	3	4	5	6	7	8	9	10	
T	Listening	Clarifying	Encouraging	Reflecting	Presenting	Problem Solving	Negotiating	Directing	Standardizing	Reinforcing	t
s											s

1. Wait until the immediate message is finished

2. Verbalize initial problem— feeling and situation

3. Probe for underlying problem and/ or additional information

4. Show willingness to listen further

5. Constantly paraphrase understanding of teacher's message

6. Ask teacher to think of possible actions

7. Ask teacher to consider consequences of various actions

8. Ask teacher for commitment to a decision

9. Ask teacher to set time and criteria for action

10. Restate the teacher's plan

Key: T = Maximum teacher responsibility S = Maximum supervisor responsibility
t = Minimum teacher responsibility s = Minimum supervisor responsibility

tions that are really solutions in disguise. Such questions as "Have you thought about taking up yoga to relax?" or "Maybe you could suspend that student for a few days, what do you think?" are inappropriate. Such leading or suggestive questions are attempts to influence the teacher's final decision.

4. Encouraging: *Show willingness to listen further as the teacher begins to identify the real problems.* Show that you will continue to assist and not leave the discussion incomplete. Statements such as "I'm following what you're saying, continue on," or "Run that by me again," or "I'm following you" are correct. Saying, "I like that idea," "Yes, that will work," "Ah, I agree with that," are, even unintentionally, influencing behaviors. A teacher, like any other person, cannot help but be influenced by the judgments a supervisor is making on what they say. Encouraging keeps the teacher thinking; praise, on the other hand, influences the final decision.

5. Reflecting: *Constantly paraphrase understanding of teacher's message.* Throughout the discussion, check on the accuracy of what you understand the teacher to be saying. When the teacher adds more information to the perceived problem, or explains different sources of the problem, considers the possible actions, and finally makes a decision, the supervisor should paraphrase. First, whenever you are uncertain of what the teacher is saying, you should paraphrase with statements such as "I think you're saying . . ." or "I'm not sure but do you mean . . ." Then you can sit back and allow the teacher to affirm or reject your understanding. Second, when the teacher has come to a halt in thinking about the problem, the paraphrase should be used to jog the teacher's mind to reflect on what has already been said and what more needs to be done. For example, after a considerable pause in the teacher's talk, the supervisor might say, "Well, let me see if I can summarize what has been said so far . . ." or "So this is where you are—you're angry because . . ." Comprehensive summarizing allows the teacher to rest, mentally stand off from his or her self, and think about what has been said. Usually such paraphrasing will stimulate the teacher to interject, add, and continue. Reflecting should not become mechanical or artificial, with the supervisor paraphrasing every teacher statement. Instead it should be used judiciously when the supervisor is not completely clear about what has been said or when there is a long pause in the conversation. Incessant interjections of "I hear you saying . . ." without aim or purpose make teachers skeptical about the supervisor's concern.

6. Problem solving: *Ask teacher to think of possible actions.* After the teacher has finished identifying the problem and you are

clear about his or her perception of the problem, your responsibility shifts to helping the teacher generate possible solutions. You can do this by asking straightforward questions: "What can you do about this?" "What else could be done?" "Think hard of actions that might help." "Let me see if you can come up with four to six possible solutions." It is helpful to allow the teacher to think for a minute or two about possible actions before verbalizing them. After actions have been proposed, you should reflect on the proposals, check on their accuracy, and probe for others. Regardless of whether the teacher proposes only a few or many possibilities, if further probing is not successful, then you should move the conference on.

7. Problem solving: *Ask teacher to consider consequences of various actions.* The moment of truth is almost at hand. Your emphasis is on having the teacher move from possible to probable solutions. Taking each solution in order, ask: "What would happen if you did . . . ?" "Would it work?" "What problems would be associated with it?" Finally, after having the teacher explore the advantages and disadvantages of each action, he or she should be asked to compare the various actions: "Which would work best?" "Why do you think so?" "How would that be better than the others?"

8. Presenting: *Ask teacher for commitment to a decision.* After you have explored possible actions and the teacher has compared their likelihood of success, you must emphasize that the teacher should select actions that are within his or her resources (*do-able*), can be implemented in a short period of time (*feasible*), and are concrete (*accountable*). A simple question—"Well, what will you do now that is likely to improve the situation?"—should cut quickly to the heart of the matter.

9. Standardizing: *Ask teacher to set time and criteria for action.* The teacher is assisted in monitoring his or her own decision about future improvement by specifying the time period during which the action will be implemented, when various parts of the plan will be done, what resources are needed, and how the teacher will know the decision is working. A further series of supervisor questions to accomplish this purpose would be "Now tell me what you are going to do" "What will be done first, next, last?" "What do you need in order to do it?" "How will you know it's working?" "When will it be done?" After the teacher can answer these questions, the conference is near completion.

10. Reflecting: *Restate the teacher's plan.* Before leaving, repeat the teacher's entire plan with "So you're going to do . . ." After the teacher verifies the restated plan, the session is over.

Nondirective Behaviors with Groups

It would be redundant to explain step by step each behavior a supervisor should use in being nondirective in a meeting with a group. As noted in the scenario presented in Figure 7–2, whether the meeting is about bus schedules or textbook adoptions, the supervisory behaviors and sequence of steps are comparable to those of an individual conference. The supervisor would begin such a meeting by asking and *listening* to group members discuss their perceptions of the group issue. The supervisor would encourage all the members to express themselves and would constantly *clarify* and *reflect* on what they were saying. Once the problem had been discussed, the supervisor would ask the group to *problem solve* by asking each member to propose possible new actions. After compiling a list of possible actions generated by the group, she would ask members to discuss the consequences of each action on the list. She would see that each proposed action was understood by the group. If not, then she would ask for further clarification and then paraphrase the meaning so that the proposer of the action could verify accuracy. After the list of actions was understood, the supervisor would ask for a discussion of the merits of each proposed action and then ask for a comparison of actions most likely to succeed. After problem solving, the supervisor would ask if there was a consensus of action to be taken. If not, she would ask for further discussion and then ask the group to determine how to resolve the deadlock. The supervisor would not be part of the decision. After the decision was made, the supervisor would ask the group to detail the decision by *standardizing* the criteria. She would ask for a time line, specific activities each group member would take, resources needed by the group, and indications of success. If there was no clear consensus on details of standardizing the plan, the supervisor again would ask the group for further discussion.

Please note that the supervisor using nondirective behaviors is in the role of expediter of the group making its own decision. The supervisor is not a participant in the decision. She does not offer her own ideas and does not influence the choices. The supervisor's role is to keep the group focused on steps for making its own decision.

Issues with Nondirective Supervision

Based on numerous skill-training sessions that I have conducted with school leaders on employing nondirective behaviors, some common issues and practical questions have arisen:

FIGURE 7–2   Scenario: Nondirective Supervision

During fifth period planning time, Supervisor Eldredge sits down with the sixth-grade middle school team of Mrs. Murdock, English teacher; Mr. Holtz, social studies teacher; Ms. Elright, mathematics teacher; and Mrs. Patrick, science teacher. The supervisor begins by asking, "Well, what's on your minds this week?" Mrs. Murdock replies: "I have a real problem with Mr. Handwright the custodian. Twice in the last week, I've sent kids on errands and he has stopped them and started yelling at them for not being in the classroom."

Supervisor Eldredge listens until Mrs. Murdock finishes her account and then asks the team, "Has this occurred often with Mr. Handwright?" Mrs. Patrick replies, "Yes, it has, his voice just booms all over and he scares the kids to death." Mr. Holtz adds: "He's even yelled at students when they have been seated in my classroom. He talks through the open door and tells them not to scuff the floors or drop papers. I don't think it's right."

The supervisor responds: "Let me summarize; you are finding that Mr. Handwright is disciplining students in a loud and abusive way for things that they have not done or for things that are not his responsibility. You believe it is not the custodian's job to discipline?" Ms. Elright answers: "Yes, that's right! His job is to clean, our job is to discipline. He's putting his nose into things that are none of his business. He's upsetting our students and us."

Supervisor Eldredge now presses the team, "O.K., I understand the problem; now what do you think should be done?" "That's easy," says Mrs. Patrick. "Someone needs to tell him what is and what is not his job. The principal should do that." "I disagree," says Mr. Holtz. "I think that before we report him to the principal, we should talk with him. Maybe we are being remiss in cleaning up or we are doing some things that are bothering him."

Supervisor Eldredge listens to the discussion and asks Mrs. Patrick, "What do you think of Mr. Holtz's suggestion?" Mrs. Patrick replies to Mr. Holtz: "I don't object; let's sit down with Mr. Handwright and straighten this out. Should we do it as a team or as individuals?" Ms. Elright says: "It would be less threatening if only one of us talked to him. John [Holtz], since you know him best, could you?" Mr. Holtz replies, "Sure I'll talk to him this afternoon."

The supervisor interjects: "You've agreed to talk to the custodian this afternoon, and John will be the representative. What should the topics be, and when will he report back?" Mr. Holtz answers: "I'm going to tell him that we don't want him to yell at students. If there's a problem, he's to come to the teacher and the teacher will handle discipline. I'm also going to see if there are ways that we can make his job easier. I'll give a progress report to all of you tomorrow morning. . . ."

NONDIRECTIVE BEHAVIORS

1. Can a supervisor really remain nonjudgmental and not influ-ence the teacher's or group's decision?

2. What happens if the teacher or group desires the supervisor's input?

3. What does a supervisor do with a teacher or group who are reluctant or not capable of generating solutions?

4. How exact or variable is the sequence of nondirective behav-iors?

5. In what circumstances should nondirective behaviors be used?

Whether or not a supervisor can really remain nonjudgmental is a legitimate concern. Even when one is consciously avoiding praise, not interjecting one's own ideas, and not offering solutions in the guise of questions, some influencing probably will take place. Studies by Mears, Shannon, and Pepinsky (1979) analyzing the tapes of counseling sessions conducted by the most renowned expert on nondirectiveness, psychologist Carl Rogers, revealed a definite pattern to his interrupting the patient and to which state-ments he selected to paraphrase. It is apparent that any interac-tion between humans is bound to be influential. Frequency of eye contact, timing of questions, facial expressions, and ways of para-phrasing can always be interpreted by a teacher as approving or disapproving. There is no way to avoid influencing through uncon-scious supervisory responses. The best one can do is to minimize those behaviors that knowingly influence. One should not know-ingly offer ideas, praise, or directions that will influence the teacher's decision.

What if the teacher or group ask for the supervisor's sugges-tions? The answer to this question revolves around timing. If the suggestions are asked for and given in the initial stages of a con-ference or meeting before the teacher or group have been required to think through the issue, then such feedback will structure the stream of subsequent thought and heavily influence the decision. If the suggestions are given after the teacher or group have already narrowed their own choices of actions, however, a supervisor's answer will not be as influential. Ideally, it is better to refrain completely from giving one's own ideas. If asked, the supervisor might respond: "I'm sorry, but I don't want to answer that. Instead, I want you to think through what can be done. Only you know your own situation. Therefore, what *I* think is not as important as what *you* think." If the teacher or group will not make a decision with-out knowing the supervisor's ideas, then one might as well give up being nondirective and move into a more collaborative mode, which will be explained in the next chapter.

Being nondirective with an individual or group who are reluctant or not capable of generating solutions is tricky. Reluctance and capability are not necessarily inversely related. If the teacher is reluctant but capable, the worst possible response would be for the supervisor to take over decision making for the teacher. Such a move might reinforce the teacher's reluctance to speak his or her own mind. Reluctance usually stems from a disbelief that one will be listened to or allowed to act on one's own initiative. The supervisor must be patient, give constant encouragement, and be persistent. Patience is shown by listening and waiting, encouragement by accepting what the teacher says, and persistence by not allowing the teacher to rest without making a decision. A supervisor can be persistent by asking questions, by taking breaks from the conference, and by giving the teacher time for further reflections.

Capability is a different matter. What if a teacher or group are incapable of making a decision? If they continually insist they do not know what the problem is or have no ideas about what could be done, and if every supervisory prompt is met by vacant stares and shrugs of shoulders, then patience, encouragement, and persistence on the part of the supervisor will create further frustration and perhaps antagonism. If they simply don't know, no matter how nondirective the supervisor is, no decisions will be forthcoming. Obviously, if lack of capability is the source of nonresponsiveness, then the nondirective approach is an unwise choice of supervisory behaviors.

Finally, there is the question of sequence of nondirective behaviors. How precise is the order? The description of nondirective behaviors presented a prototype of ten steps within the supervisory behavior continuum (Figure 7–1). The behaviors are: (1) listening-waiting, (2) reflecting-verbalizing, (3) clarifying-probing, (4) encouraging-willing, (5) reflecting-paraphrasing, (6) problem solving—asking for possible actions, (7) problem solving—asking for probable consequences, (8) presenting—asking for a commitment, (9) standardizing—asking for criteria, and (10) reflecting—restating the plan. One might visualize these steps as analogous to playing the left-hand side of a piano keyboard. The supervisor-pianist begins the musical score with the furthest left-hand note (listening-waiting) and will end the score at note 10 (reflecting-restating). During the score (conference or meeting) the adept player will strike the notes (behaviors) back and forth between one and ten, pounding on some notes, lightly touching on others, returning, and swelling the underlying tone of the teacher or group voice. The score ends on note 10—reflecting and restating the teacher's or group's decision. The behaviors are not a prescription of fixed steps but rather a directionality of movements with a definite beginning and end.

When to Use Nondirective Behaviors

When and with whom should nondirective behaviors be used? To satisfy the reader's curiosity, let us lay out some quick criteria for using nondirective behaviors. Chapter 10 will take an in-depth look at this question after detailing all three supervisory approaches. For now, a supervisor should consider using a nondirective approach:

1. When the teacher or group possess most of the knowledge and expertise about the issue and the supervisor's knowledge and expertise are minimal: "If you don't know anything about it and they do, let them solve it."

2. When the teacher or group have full responsibility for carrying out the decision and the supervisor has little involvement: "If they are going to be accountable for it and you aren't, let them solve it."

3. When the teacher or group care about solving the problem but the problem doesn't matter to the supervisor: "If they want to act and you couldn't care less, let them decide."

The criteria of (1) expertise, (2) responsibility, and (3) care appear to be straightforward. Chapter 10 will show the greater complexity of this criteria and the critical role of supervisor judgment.

Practicing Nondirective Behaviors

Up to now we have explored nondirective behaviors as an exercise in reading. To understand nondirective behaviors fully demands real life practice. Even if you think you already are proficient in these skills, it would be valuable to try out the exercise in Appendix B (skill practice in nondirective behaviors) and intentionally practice being nondirective in some school situations.

Summary

Supervisors can use nondirective behaviors in helping teachers determine their own plans. Such supervisory behaviors consist of listening, reflecting, clarifying, encouraging, and problem solving. When individuals and groups of teachers possess greater expertise, commitment, and responsibility for a particular decision than the supervisor does, then a nondirective approach is appropriate. Important considerations for a supervisor when using nondirectiveness are attempting to be nonjudgmental, hesitating in response to teachers' wishes for more supervisor input, and adjusting one's behavior when teachers demonstrate reluctance to generate solutions. The purpose of nondirective supervision is to provide an active sounding board for thoughtful professionals.

EXERCISES

ACADEMIC

1. Write an imaginary dialogue between a supervisor and teacher during a conference in which the supervisor successfully uses a nondirective approach. Be sure to include examples of each of the ten nondirective behaviors discussed in Chapter 7.

2. The chapter explains a sequence of ten nondirective behaviors that take place during a nondirective conference. Think of a situation in which a successful nondirective conference would start with the first suggested behavior (listening-waiting) and end with the tenth (reflecting-restating the plan), but would have a *different sequence* of eight intermediate behaviors. Describe the situation and modified sequence of nondirective behaviors in writing. Include a rationale for the suggested sequence.

3. Write an imaginary dialogue between a supervisor and a teacher in which the supervisor implements nondirective procedures with mechanical precision but still fails to be truly nondirective.

4. Write a paper comparing the nondirective approach as described in this book with the version of nondirective assistance espoused by an author cited in the Suggestions for Additional Readings.

5. Assume you have just listened to a talk by a school administrator in which he or she argued against the use of nondirec-

tive behaviors by educational supervisors with *any* teacher. The thrust of the administrator's argument was that such an approach is essentially laissez-faire and allows complete deference to a teacher's decision, even when such decisions are clearly in error and are likely to result in harm to the teacher's instructional performance or to the students. The administrator further argued that for a supervisor to withhold his or her observations, perceptions, and suggestions unless they are requested by the teacher is counterproductive to the supervisory process. You have been asked to prepare a reply to the administrator to be presented at an upcoming seminar. Write a paper in which you argue for the use of nondirective behavior with certain teachers. Address the administrator's objections in your paper.

FIELD

1. Use a nondirective approach by either using the simulation activity found in Appendix B or conducting an actual postobservation conference with a teacher. Prepare a written report in which you (a) evaluate your success in displaying nondirective behaviors, (b) summarize the problems discussed and decisions made during the conference, (c) give your perceptions of the "teacher's" responses to your nondirective efforts, and (d) judge the conference in terms of overall success.

2. Observe an educational supervisor or other leader whom you know to possess a nondirective orientation. Based on your observations and interview with the leader, write a paper describing both successes and failures that he or she has experienced while using nondirective behaviors. Include possible reasons for the nondirective leader's greater success in some situations than in others.

3. Observe three teachers or staff members who clearly respond positively to nondirective supervision. Prepare a report examining personal and social characteristics of these individuals that may account for their positive response to a nondirective approach.

4. Prepare a picture album entitled "Self-Direction for Instructional Improvement." Each picture should be accompanied by a written explanation of how that entry relates to the album theme.

5. Videotape or audiotape a conference or staff development activity in which the supervisor is using a nondirective approach. As you review the tape, compare the recorded activities with the sequence of behaviors that, according to the author, exemplifies the nondirective approach of a supervisor during a decision-making process. Prepare a report on your findings.

DEVELOPMENTAL

1. Through interaction with various individuals in a variety of situations, begin to establish a set of personal guidelines that will indicate when the nondirective approach is most appropriate in carrying out present or anticipated leadership functions.

2. Begin an in-depth study of the writings of a prominent humanistic educator or psychologist. Relate that author's ideas to the concepts of nondirective supervision discussed in this chapter.

3. Record a simulated or actual supervisor-teacher conference in which you, as supervisor, attempt to display nondirective behaviors. Review the tape for analysis of your performance. Over the next four weeks, attempt to practice nondirective leadership whenever appropriate opportunities arise. Record another simulated or actual conference in four weeks. Review both tapes to discover any improvement in terms of successfully displaying nondirective behaviors.

REFERENCE

Mears, N. M.; Shannon, J. W.; and Pepinsky, H. B. 1979. Comparison of the stylistic complexity of the language of counselor and client across three theoretical orientations. *Journal of Counseling Psychology 26* (3): 181–189.

SUGGESTIONS FOR ADDITIONAL READINGS

Carkhuff, R. R. 1969. *Helping and human relations: A primer for lay and professional helpers,* vol. 2: *Practice and Research.* New York: Holt, Rinehart and Winston.

Combs, A.; Avila, D. L.; and Purkey, W. H. 1979. *Helping relationships: Basic concepts for the helping professions,* 2nd ed. Boston: Allyn and Bacon.

Gazda, G. M.; Asbury, R. R.; Balzer, F. J.; Childers, W. C.; and Walters, R. P. 1977. *Human relations development: Second edition, a manual for educators.* Boston: Allyn and Bacon.

Mosher, R. L., and Purpel, D. E. 1972. *Supervision: The reluctant profession.* Boston: Houghton-Mifflin. See Chapter 6.

Rogers, C. R. 1951. *Client-centered therapy: Its current practice, implications, and theory.* Boston: Houghton-Mifflin.

CHAPTER EIGHT

Collaborative Behaviors

Teacher: I refuse to have Steve sent out of my class.

Supervisor: Don't you think being hit by him and being bruised is the last straw?

Teacher: No, I don't. It's my body and I don't think Steve meant it. He was angry and didn't know what he was doing.

Supervisor: Listen, he's been in fights with other students since the first day of school, and the latest episode of striking could have resulted in serious damage. He has to come out.

Teacher: I know that you're thinking about my own welfare, but that kid is making progress. He's beginning to do some assignments and has been behaving better. The hitting incident was an accident. He's not bothering the other students too much.

Supervisor: I think you're wrong. Let's put him into a special classroom.

Teacher: No, he stays with me.

Supervisor: You know that whatever is done, we will both agree to do. You don't want him to leave and I think, for his own good, he should be given special attention. Steve is dangerous to you and the other students.

Teacher: I don't have anything against special attention. It's just that we've come so far and I hate to see him cut off from me and the class. He has a better chance to make it in our class than to begin all over in another class.

Supervisor: Then you would be receptive to having him receive special attention as long as he stays in your class?

Teacher: Yeah, I think so. I have no problem with a qualified person working with him in my classroom or even for a small part of the day outside of the classroom.

Supervisor: That seems reasonable, I think that we are getting somewhere. . . .

Collaborative Behaviors with Individuals

The foregoing script, based on a real conference, highlights collaborative supervisory behaviors. The supervisor wishes to resolve a problem that is shared equally with the teacher. The supervisor encourages the teacher to present his or her own perceptions and ideas. Yet the supervisor also honestly gives his or her own views. The result is a frank exchange of ideas. Both participants know they will both have to agree on any course of action. In fact, when the disagreement becomes obvious, the supervisor restates the disagreement and reassures the teacher that they will have to find a mutual solution. Disagreement is encouraged, not suppressed. As the conversation continues, some openings for possible agreements become apparent, and the supervisor steers the conversation toward those ends. Finally, they will either agree to an action or wind up stalemated. A stalemate will mean further negotiating, rethinking, and even the possible use of a third-party mediator or arbitrator.

Figure 8–1 shows a prototype of collaborative behaviors according to the supervisory behavior continuum. A conference between supervisor and teacher begins with an understanding of each other's identification of the problem and concludes with mutual agreement on the final plan. Again, the reader should think of the supervisory behaviors as a piano keyboard, with the musician beginning by hitting the keys on the left, then playing the keys back and forth, and culminating by hitting the middle key—negotiating.

1. Clarifying: *Identifying the problem as seen by the teacher.* First, ask the teacher about the immediate problem or concern: "Please tell me what is bothering you" or "Explain to me what you see as the greatest concern."

2. Listening: *Understanding the teacher's perception.* You the supervisor want to have as much information about the problem as possible before thinking about action. Therefore, when the teacher narrates his or her perceptions, the full range of nondirective behaviors should be used (eye contact, paraphrasing, asking probing questions, and being willing to allow the teacher to continue talking): "Tell me more." "Uh huh, I'm following you." "Do you mean . . . ?"

3. Reflecting: *Verifying the teacher's perception.* When the teacher has completed his or her description of the problem, check

for accuracy by summarizing the teacher's statements and asking if the summary is accurate: "I understand that you see the problem as . . . . Is this accurate?"

4. Presenting: *Providing supervisor's point of view.* Until this point, we have seen an abbreviated nondirective conference. Instead of asking the teacher to begin thinking of his or her own possible actions, however, you now move in and become part of the decision-making process. Give your own point of view about the current difficulty and fill in any information about the situation of which the teacher might be unaware: "I see the situation in this way" or "The problem, as I see it, is . . ." (To minimize influencing the teacher's position, it is better for you to give your perceptions only after the teacher has given his or hers.)

5. Clarifying: *Seeking teacher's understanding of supervisor's perception of problem.* In the same way that you paraphrased the teacher's statement of the problem and asked for verification, you now ask the teacher to do likewise: "Could you repeat what you think I'm trying to say?" Once you feel confident that the teacher understands your views, problem solving can begin.

6. Problem solving: *Exchanging suggestions of options.* If you and the teacher are familiar with each other and have worked collaboratively before, you can simply ask for a list of suggestions: "Let's both think about what might be done to improve this situation." Then listen to each other's ideas. If the teacher is not familiar with you or with the collaborative process, however, he or she may feel apprehensive about suggesting an idea that is different from the supervisor's. It might be better to stop the conference for a few minutes and have both supervisor and teacher write down possible actions before speaking: "So that we don't influence each other on possible solutions, let's take the next few minutes and write down what actions might be taken and then read each other's list." Obviously, once actions are in writing, they will not change according to what the other person has written. You the supervisor, therefore, have promoted a spectrum of personal ideas that are ready to be shared and discussed.

7. Encouraging: *Accepting conflict.* To keep the conference from turning into a competitive struggle, you need to reassure the teacher that disagreement is acceptable and that there will be no winners or losers: "It appears that we have some different ideas on how to handle this situation. By disagreeing we will find the best solution. Remember our agreement, we both have to agree with the solution before it will take place." You must genuinely believe that conflict between two caring professionals is productive for finding the best solution.

FIGURE 8–1 The Supervisory Behavior Continuum: Collaborative Behaviors

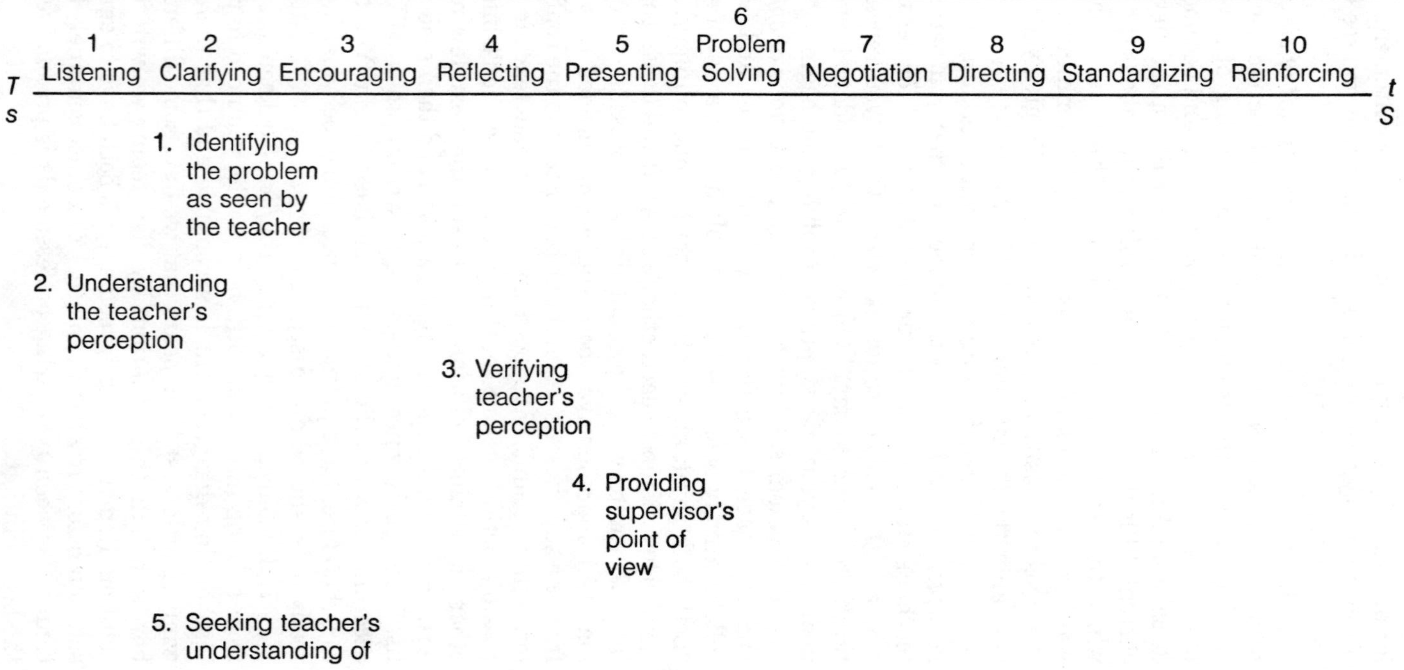

T	1	2	3	4	5	6	7	8	9	10	t
s	Listening	Clarifying	Encouraging	Reflecting	Presenting	Problem Solving	Negotiation	Directing	Standardizing	Reinforcing	s

1. Identifying the problem as seen by the teacher

2. Understanding the teacher's perception

3. Verifying teacher's perception

4. Providing supervisor's point of view

5. Seeking teacher's understanding of

supervisor's
perception of
problem

6. Exchanging
   suggestions
   of options

7. Accepting
   conflict

8. Finding an
   acceptable
   action

9. Agreeing on
   details of
   plan

10. Agreeing
    to a final
    plan

Key: *T* = Maximum teacher responsibility   *S* = Maximum supervisor responsibility
     t = Minimum teacher responsibility   *s* = Minimum supervisor responsibility

8. Problem solving: *Finding an acceptable solution.* After sharing and discussing, ask if there are suggestions common to both—"Where do we agree?"—and if there are suggestions markedly different—"Where do we differ?" If you find agreement, then the conference proceeds. But if there is a vast difference in suggestions, then you can take four sequential actions. First, check to see if the differences are as vast as they appear by having both yourself and the teacher explain thoroughly what is meant by your respective suggestions. Second, if the disagreement is still real, then find out how convinced each of you is that your suggestion be chosen: "How important is it to you that we do it your way?" If the importance of one person's suggestion is far greater than that of the other person's suggestion, then the question becomes whether one can give up his or her idea and live with the other's. Third, if grounds for agreement are not reached, you can consider a compromise: "How about if I give up this part of my suggestion and if you give up . . ." Or see if a totally new idea can be found: "Since we can't agree, let's drop our top choices for solutions and see if we can find another one." Fourth, if there is still no movement and a true stalemate remains, then you can either call for a period of time for both parties to reflect on the issue before meeting again—"Look, we're not getting anywhere. Let's sit on this matter and meet again tomorrow"—or ask for a third person to play the role of a mediator or arbitrator: "We can't agree; how about if we call someone that we both respect to help us resolve this?" or "Since we can't agree, how about calling someone we both have confidence in to solve this for us?" A mediator or arbitrator is an extreme option for most conferences between a supervisor and teacher and should remain a last resort. However, the teacher must know that the procedures of collaboration ensure that he or she does not have to go along with a plan that he or she disagrees with. There are other options available.

9. Standardizing: *Agreeing on details of plan.* Once agreement on an acceptable action has been reached, the supervisor needs to attend to the details of time and place. When will the plan be implemented? Where will it take place? Who will help? What resources are needed? These details need to be discussed and agreed to so there will be a clarity and precision to the final plan.

10. Negotiating: *Agreeing to a final plan.* The supervisor concludes the conference by checking that both parties agree to the action and details. The supervisor might do this verbally—"Could you repeat what you understand the plan to be and then I'll repeat my understanding"—or in writing: "Let's write this down together so that we are clear on what we've agreed to do."

Collaborative Behaviors with Groups

After meeting for the fourth time in the past month, most of the members of the school science textbook adoption committee have reviewed all the new commercial textbook series and have made up their own minds about which they prefer. It is 5:30 on Wednesday afternoon, and the meeting is in its second hour. The science supervisor, Roger Loren, is uneasy; he believes that some people have not said what's on their minds. He asks, "Do we wish to discuss the science programs anymore before voting?" Ten of the eleven members shake their heads.

The supervisor, seeing that Phyllis Moonale has not joined with the others, asks, "Phyllis, do you think we need more time before deciding?" Phyllis says quietly: "Yes, I do. From what I've been hearing from the other members, they already made up their minds to keep the old science program before we even started. That old program is ridiculously out of date. Just because we might have to change our lesson plans, bulletin board displays, and exam questions—that's no reason to keep the same series. Let's think about the students! They're not learning anything at all about recent science issues such as test tube babies or acid rain. We can't ignore these real science topics for the convenience of keeping our old lesson plans intact!"

The supervisor, after listening carefully, believes that what Phyllis has said is right. The supervisor says: "I agree, we shouldn't keep the old textbook; there are at least three others that would be an improvement over what we have now. I'd go along with any of those three texts."

Fred Willopt, who has been an adamant spokesperson for the old textbook series, speaks: "Come on, let's get on with it! We agreed that this was going to be a group decision; if we couldn't agree unanimously then we would take a majority vote. It's not bad to keep an old program—we do right well by it! Phyllis, why don't you teach those other radical topics all you want, but don't keep us from doing what we want. You and Roger are in the minority. It's time to vote!"

The supervisor responds, "O.K., Fred, you're right—we did agree that this would be a group decision. I don't want that old series. Maybe others don't either. We'll vote on it." Roger calls for a vote: "How many want to keep the old series?" Ten hands go up. "How many want a new series?" Phyllis and Roger raise their hands. Roger looks at Phyllis and can't help feeling disappointed. He says, "All right, we keep the old series. I don't agree, but we'll go along with what the group has decided. The meeting is over."

The supervisor has tried to convince the group of his prefer-ence. When it comes to the final decision, however, his vote has no more weight than that of any other member. Furthermore, the group knows that the procedures for making the decision, ex-plained at the first meeting, have been adhered to and that the final decision will be upheld.

A supervisor using a collaborative cluster of behaviors leads the members to a group decision. In the meeting described here, the collaborative supervisor did not exercise a veto when the decision was not turning out the way he preferred. The supervi-sor's responsibility is to ensure that the full range of ideas and feelings are discussed, including his or her own, before making the final decision. The example given was of a group meeting where collaborative supervision resulted in a decision by majority vote. Obviously, when collaboration is used in an individual conference with a single teacher, the final decision must be made by consen-sus. Both supervisor and teacher have equal say; if they disagree, no decision can be made. Further discussion about a compromise or alternative solution would be necessary to find a decision satisfac-tory to both persons. In a group meeting the same principle for resolving lack of consensus can be used with a majority vote. Col-laborative supervisory behaviors, whether with an individual teacher or with a group of teachers, results in a mutually shared decision whereby the one-vote, one-person rule holds regardless of the status, title, or power of any individual.

The sequence of collaborative behaviors a supervisor uses in reaching a group decision are similar to those used in meeting with an individual. The main difference is that more time is needed for each member of the group to identify the problem and discuss everyone's suggestions. The supervisor needs to be sensitive to whether the meeting drags—for example, if the same issues are being discussed and positions are not being changed. The supervi-sor is both an advocate of his or her own position and an expeditor of group movement toward a final decision. Let's quickly review collaborative supervisor behaviors in a group meeting.

The supervisor calls the meeting to order. Preliminary to dis-cussion, he *clarifies* the task and procedures for making the deci-sion. He states that they are meeting on a certain issue (selecting next year's textbook) and that the procedures will be collaborative (one vote for each person, with the final decision being made either by consensus or by majority vote). As he initiates the discussion, he asks each group member to *clarify* what he or she sees as the current needs in looking for a textbook. After soliciting group members' opinions, he *reflects* his understanding of what they have been saying. He then *presents* his own opinion. He clarifies his position by asking the group to paraphrase his statements, and asks for questions. The next step is *problem solving*—asking the group to suggest possible actions to solve the identified problem. This is handled by allowing each individual to present his or her own suggestions. The supervisor might write down all suggestions coming from the group. The supervisor, as an equal member, offers his own suggestion. All group members are *encouraged* to offer their ideas, no matter how improbable or different from others'. When no more suggestions are forthcoming, the supervisor calls for the group to narrow down the list of possibilities to the two or three best ideas. If consensus about the best ideas is not apparent, the supervisor can ask members to rank all ideas and keep the three ideas with the highest scores. The group further whittles down the list to a single choice as the supervisor asks members to discuss the merits and demerits of each idea. Again, the supervisor leads the discussion by probing for agreements and negotiating between conflicting positions to find a common path. If agreement on a course of action is not emerging, he looks for ways to synthesize or compromise disparate ideas. Finally, if the choices of group members remain distant and there is no consensus, a majority vote can be taken. The winning idea is *standardized* by the group according to time, place, and persons to be involved in carrying out the plan. The supervisor must then *renegotiate* the final plan by consensus or majority vote on the final standardized and detailed plan.

Issues in Collaborative Supervision

My work with collaboration has shown that it is a deceptively simple set of behaviors for supervisors to understand. The reason is that collaboration appears to be the democratic way of doing things. Most of us have been schooled in equality and democracy, and collaboration appears to be democracy in action. Therefore, it seems apparent that we should ask others for input and that decisions should be made by the majority. However, collaboration with an individual or a group involves more than democratic procedures. It is an attitude of acceptance and a practice of being equal. Therefore, it is not always the mechanical procedures of democracy that demonstrate whether or not collaboration is in use. What appears to be nondemocratic might indeed be collaborative, and what appears to be democratic might not be collaborative. For example, two people can agree as equals that one is better qualified to make a particular decision; the less qualified person might ask the more qualified person to decide for both of them. Here, one person making the decision for both persons appears undemocratic, but it is collaborative. On the other hand, two people can appear to make a collaborative decision; but if one person has discreetly let the other know of his or her power—for example, a personal acquaintanceship with the superintendent of schools—the less powerful person might profess agreement with the more powerful person even though inwardly he or she did not agree. On the surface, the agreement appears to be collaborative; but in reality one person has knuckled under to the power of the other. The purpose of collaboration is to solve problems through a meeting of minds of equals. True equality is the core of collaboration.

One difficulty in working collaboratively occurs when the teacher (or group) believes a supervisor is manipulating the decision when in fact he or she is not. The teacher appears to concur with the supervisor's ideas and suggestions not because of their merit but because the teacher believes the supervisor is really giving a directive. The underlying message the teacher perceives is: "This is my supervisor telling me what she thinks I should do. Even though she says we are making a joint decision, I know I had better do what she says." How does the supervisor know whether a teacher's agreement is sincere or mere compliance? The supervisor might confront the issue by asking the teacher whether he or she is agreeing or only pretending to agree with the supervisor's idea. Acknowledging that the supervisor suspects something is amiss brings the issue out into the open. A teacher who responds, "I don't believe you really are going to let me have equal say" can be dealt with more easily than is possible when a supervisor guesses at the teacher's hidden feelings.

Teachers who refuse to disclose their feelings probably have a history of being mistreated by supervisors. Until the supervisor can demonstrate consistently that she really means to be collaborative, no progress will be made. The teacher is not going to believe the supervisor is being collaborative until he or she sees proof. True intent can be demonstrated by refusing to allow decisions to be made without teacher feedback. With nonresponsive and readily acquiescing teachers, a supervisor might say: "I don't know if you're agreeing with me because you like the idea or because of some power I hold over you. We won't carry out any action unless we both agree with that action. I want to be collaborative because I believe you have as much expertise on this matter as I do. Together we can make a better decision than separately. I'm uncertain why you are agreeing with me. Please tell me what you think." A supervisor cannot find out what a teacher thinks unless she asks. As they continue to meet, the supervisor should begin by encouraging teachers to offer their own thoughts about the problem and suggestions for action. The supervisor should try to withhold any ideas of her own. Once the teacher's ideas are forthcoming, the supervisor can offer her own. When negotiating a final decision, the supervisor should let teachers take the lead. If teachers continue to be unresponsive or overly compliant with the supervisor after she has confronted the issue of perception and encouraged teacher initiative, then, after several unsuccessful attempts, the supervisor might consider another approach.

The collaborative group process appears to be predicated on the use of consensus or majority vote. However, a supervisor can work collaboratively with a group by using other decision-making procedures such as averaging, frequency ranking, the nominal method, the Delphi technique, or even minority or expert decision. We will explain these procedures in Chapter Seventeen on group development.

Collaboration is defined as working jointly with others in an intellectual endeavor (Webster 1973). The work is done jointly, but one person can participate more than another. The test of collaboration in supervision is whether the agreed-on decision to improve instruction was satisfactory to all participants. Therefore, although the degree of involvement may vary, the end results are equally determined. With such a definition, we are intentionally allowing for times when a supervisor, teacher, or individual member of a group might convince others of the value of his or her own ideas because of his or her persuasiveness, expertise, and creditability. If ideas are judged on the basis of their merits and not of the power of the individual, than collaboration is at work.

The issues of collaboration are complex. First a supervisor must differentiate democratic procedure from collaboration. Second, he must differentiate between acquiescence to power and agreement with ideas. When acquiescence is suspected, the supervisor should bring the issue out into the open. Third, the supervisor needs to keep in mind that some teachers have a history of mistrusting supervisors and must be shown over a period of time that the supervisor truly intends to be collaborative.

It would be nice to say we can lay these issues to rest, but we cannot. Unless the supervisor remains conscious of the complexity of collaboration, he can mistakenly allow collaborative behaviors to become something other than they appear. For practice in collaborative behaviors, the reader might wish to do the activity found in Appendix C (Skill Practice in Collaborative Behaviors).

When to Use Collaborative Behaviors

There are circumstances in which a supervisor definitely should use collaborative behaviors. We will leave more detailed instructions for Chapter Ten, but, for now, collaboration should be used:

1. When the teacher(s) and supervisor have approximately the same degree of expertise on the issue. If the supervisor knows part of the problem and teachers know the other part, the collaborative approach should be used.
2. When the teacher(s) and supervisor will both be involved in carrying out the decision. If teacher(s) and supervisor will be held accountable for showing results to someone else (say, parents or the superintendent), then the collaborative approach should be used.
3. When the teacher(s) and supervisor both intensely care about the problem. If teachers want to be involved, and if leaving them out will lead to low morale and distrust, then the collaborative approach should be used.

Summary

Collaborative supervision is premised on participation by equals in making instructional decisions. Its outcome is a mutual plan of action. Collaborative behaviors consist of clarifying, listening, reflecting, presenting, problem solving, negotiating, and standardizing. Collaboration is appropriate when teachers and supervisors have similar levels of expertise, involvement, and concern with a problem. The key consideration for a supervisor is the fact that collaboration is both an attitude and a repertoire of behaviors. Unless teachers have the attitude that they are equal, collaborative behaviors can be used to undermine true equality.

EXERCISES

ACADEMIC

1. Write an imaginary dialogue between a supervisor and teacher during a conference in which the supervisor successfully

makes use of a collaborative approach. Be sure to include examples of each of the ten collaborative behaviors discussed in Chapter Eight.

2. The chapter suggests that a sequence of ten collaborative behaviors takes place during a collaborative conference. Think of a situation in which a successful collaborative conference would start with the first suggested behavior (identifying the problem as seen by the teacher) and end with the tenth (agreeing to final plan), but would have a *different sequence* of eight intermediate behaviors. Describe the situation and modified sequence of collaborative behaviors in writing. Include a rationale for the suggested sequence.

3. Write an imaginary dialogue between a supervisor and a teacher in which the supervisor implements apparently collaborative procedures with mechanical precision but fails to be collaborative in an effective sense.

4. Prepare a report comparing the collaborative approach as described in this book with the version of collaboration espoused by an author cited in the Suggestions for Additional Readings.

5. Listening, clarifying, encouraging, reflecting, presenting, problem solving, and standardizing are categories of behavior the chapter uses when describing the nondirective as well as the collaborative approach to supervision. Write a paper explaining how each of these seven categories actually refers to different behaviors, depending on whether the nondirective or the collaborative approach is being used. For each of the seven behavior categories, give a specific behavior that might be displayed by a nondirective supervisor and a specific behavior that might be displayed by a collaborative supervisor.

FIELD

1. Assume the role of a supervisor using a collaborative approach by either using the simulation activity found in Appendix C or conducting an actual postobservation conference with a teacher. Prepare a written report in which you (a) evaluate your success in displaying collaborative behaviors, (b) summarize the problems discussed and decisions made during the conference, (c) give your perceptions of the "teacher's" responses to your collaborative efforts, and (d) judge the conference in terms of overall success.

2. Participate in a group conference that results in a collaborative contract, with some type of instructional improvement as the anticipated result of contract fulfillment. Prepare a report on how the meeting was conducted, any problems that arose, and how the group reached decisions.

3. Observe an educational supervisor or other leader whom you know to have a collaborative orientation in dealing with individuals and/or groups. On the basis of your observations and/ or an interview with the leader, prepare a report describing both successes and failures the selected leader has experienced while using collaborative behaviors. Include possible reasons that the collaborative leader was more successful in some situations than in others.

4. Prepare a photo album entitled "Collaboration for Instructional Improvement." Each photograph should be accompanied by a written explanation of how that entry relates to the album theme.

5. Videotape or audiotape a collaborative conference or staff development activity. As you review the tape, compare the recorded activities with the sequence of behaviors that, according to the chapter, exemplifies the nominal collaborative decision-making process. Prepare a written report on your findings.

DEVELOPMENT

1. Through interaction with various individuals in a variety of situations, begin to establish a set of personal guidelines that will indicate when the collaborative approach is most appropriate for your own use in carrying out present or anticipated leadership functions.

2. Initiate an in-depth study of Japanese-style management. As you proceed with your study, compare and contrast this style of management with the collaborative approach to supervision discussed in this chapter.

3. Record a simulated or actual supervisor-teacher conference in which you, as supervisor, attempt to display collaborative behaviors. Review the tape for analysis of your performance. Over the next four weeks, attempt to practice collaborative leadership whenever appropriate opportunities arise. Record another simulated or actual supervisor-teacher conference, and determine what changes you have made.

REFERENCE

Webster's New Collegiate Dictionary. 1973. Springfield, Mass.: G. & C. Merriam Company, p. 219.

SUGGESTIONS FOR ADDITIONAL READING

Blumberg, A. 1980. *Supervisors and teachers: A private cold war,* 2nd ed. Berkeley, Calif.: McCutchan.

Cogan, M. 1973. *Clinical supervision.* Boston: Houghton-Mifflin.

Gordon, T. 1977. *Leader Effectiveness Training, L.E.T.: The no-lose way to release the productive potential of people.* New York: Wyden Books.

Harris, T. 1967. *I'm OK—you're OK: Practical guide to transactional analysis.* New York: Harper & Row, Chapters 3 and 4.

Wagner, A. 1981. *Transactional manager: How to solve people problems with transactional analysis.* Englewood Cliffs, N.J.: Prentice-Hall.

Wiles, K. 1967. *Supervision for better schools,* 3rd ed. Englewood Cliffs, N.J.: Prentice-Hall.

CHAPTER NINE
Directive Behaviors

Supervisor: Have you been using the microcomputers yet? I haven't seen any students at the desks.

Teacher: Well, I really don't think computers are such an important topic for seventh-grade mathematics. The students need training in basic geometry, not in how to play games with a computer.

Supervisor: As you know, part of a geometry curriculum is on a computer disk. It's not just fun and games. They could be learning geometry as they become familiar with operating the computer.

Teacher: All this computer emphasis is ridiculous! It's another educational fad that's going to solve all our problems! I have enough trouble getting kids to learn what's in the book.

Supervisor: I understand your reservations about using the computer, but our school curriculum states that microcomputers are to be used in seventh grade mathematics. We're committed to doing so, particularly after spending so much money on the equipment and software.

Teacher: I think it's ridiculous.

Supervisor: That's beside the point. I want to see your kids using them.

Teacher: I'd rather not. Couldn't they teach computers in science class? After all, computers are science.

Supervisor: We're probably going to see computer use in every subject before long, but for now it's to go on in mathematics. I'd like to see at least one-third of your class begin the software program on plotting graphs by next Friday.

Teacher: Who's going to show them how to operate the program? I don't know how to.

Supervisor: Mrs. Techno, you were a participant in the computer class last summer. You know how to do it.

Teacher: I didn't understand the foggiest bit of it. Professor Wallenwood was a terrible teacher. He just paid attention to all those teachers who already had a computer background.

Supervisor: Well, I wasn't aware that you were unsure of how to use the microcomputer in class. I'll call Fred Tirtial, director of media, to come into your class next week to demonstrate how to use the equipment. I'll see to it that he gets the program started in your class, and then you continue with it.

Teacher: Any help would be appreciated.

Supervisor: You keep me posted, and we'll shoot for at least one group of your students working on the graphing program by a week from Friday.

Directive Behaviors with Individuals

The foregoing scenario shows a supervisor using directive behaviors to assist a teacher in improving instruction. The obvious question is what happens if the teacher responds to such directiveness with a firm refusal: "I am not going to meet with you or follow through with your plans." If the supervisor has a position of conferred authority over teachers, he can pull rank by restating the directive and telling the teacher to comply or suffer the consequences. If the supervisor does not have such authority—which, with the exception of school principals, is often the case—then the supervisor can direct only by convincing the teacher his plan is correct. Regardless of a line or staff relationship, the supervisor uses directive behavior with teachers when there is an assumption that the supervisor has greater knowledge and expertise about the issue at hand. In other words, the belief behind directive behaviors is that the supervisor knows better than the teacher what needs to be done to improve instruction.

It is evident in the scenario that the supervisor has taken over the teacher's problem. At first the supervisor identified the problem by gathering information from his own observations and discussing his information with the teacher. Next he told the teacher what to do and provided an explanation of why his suggestion would work.

He concluded by reviewing the proposed action and reiterating his expectations for the teacher. The teacher was left with a concrete understanding of what she was expected to do. As we look at a typical sequence of behaviors along the supervisory behavior continuum (Figure 9–1), keep in mind that the sequence and frequency of behaviors will vary, especially in the beginning of the conference, but the directive approach will end with the supervisor either making the final decisions for the teacher or clearly suggesting a final decision that the supervisor wishes the teacher to consider. This chapter will accentuate directive behaviors that control teacher actions. The next chapter will distinguish between directive controlling behaviors and directive informational behaviors.

1. Listening: *Identifying the problem.* The supervisor begins with a general idea of what the needs and difficulties are. He has used observations and gathered information from other sources before he tells the teacher what he sees as the problem: "I understand that there is a problem with . . ."

2. Clarifying: *Asking teacher for input into the problem.* The supervisor wants to gather direct information from the teacher about the problem prior to the solution stage. She does this by using the teacher in an advisory capacity, asking the teacher such questions as, "How do you see the problem . . ." and "Why do you think these conditions exist."

3. Listening: *Understanding the teacher's point of view.* To gather maximum information in the shortest amount of time, the supervisor must attend carefully to what the teacher says. He listens both to the surface messages—"Computers are a waste of time"—and to underlying messages—"I don't know how to use them"—in formulating a complete problem.

4. Problem solving: *Mentally determining the best solution.* The supervisor processes the information and thinks, "What can be done?" After considering various possibilities, she selects the needed actions. She should be confident that she does indeed have a good, manageable solution to the problem before conveying it to the teacher.

5. Directing: *Telling expectations for teachers.* The supervisor tells the teacher in a matter-of-fact way what needs to be done: "I want to see you do the following . . ." The phrasing of the directive is important. Avoid timid, circular expectations: "Well, maybe you might consider doing . . ." or "Don't you think it would be a good idea to . . ." The supervisor is not asking or pleading with the teacher, but *telling.* On the other hand, directing does not mean being vindictive, overbearing, condescending, or insulting. Avoid personal slights or paternalistic references: "I don't know why you

can't figure out what needs to be done." "Why can't you get it right in the first place?" "Now listen, honey, I'm going to help you by . . ." A supervisor should state actions as *I* statements, not as what others think. Tell the teacher what *I* want to happen, not what parents, other teachers, or the superintendent would want to see. A statement such as, "If the superintendent saw this, he would tell you to do . . ." is hiding behind someone else's authority. The supervisor needs to make statements based on her own position, credibility, and authority.

6. Clarifying: *Asking teacher for input into the expectations.* Possible difficulties with the supervisor's directive should be known before the teacher leaves the conference. For example, if circumstances exist that make teacher compliance with the directive impossible, it is better to adjust to those circumstances during the conference than to find out two weeks later why the plan failed. Therefore, after telling the teacher what is expected—"I want one-third of your students using the computers"—the supervisor needs to ask such questions as, "Tell me what you need to carry out this plan?" or "How can I help you carry out the plan?"

7. Standardizing: *Detailing and modifying expectations.* After considering the teacher's reactions to the directive, the supervisor solidifies the plan by building in the necessary assistance, resources, time lines, and criteria for expected success. The teacher then is told the revisions: "I can rearrange the visit time to. . . ," "I will find those materials for you," "I will arrange for you to attend. . . ," "I will change the time to three weeks."

8. Reinforcing: *Repeating and following up on expectations.* The supervisor reviews the entire plan and establishes times for checking on progress. The supervisor closes the meeting by asking if the teacher clearly understands the plan: "Do you understand what you're to do?" or "Tell me what it is you're now going to do."

Directive Behaviors with Groups

The seven Physical Education Department members meet with their supervisor. The supervisor addresses them.

Supervisor: I've been noticing that our physical education classes have not been starting on time. They are to begin at five minutes past the hour and end at fifteen minutes before the next hour. We're supposed to get in a full forty minutes of physical education. Some classes are being dismissed early, some late, and the other teachers in the school are complaining. They say

FIGURE 9–1 The Supervisory Behavior Continuum: Directive Behaviors

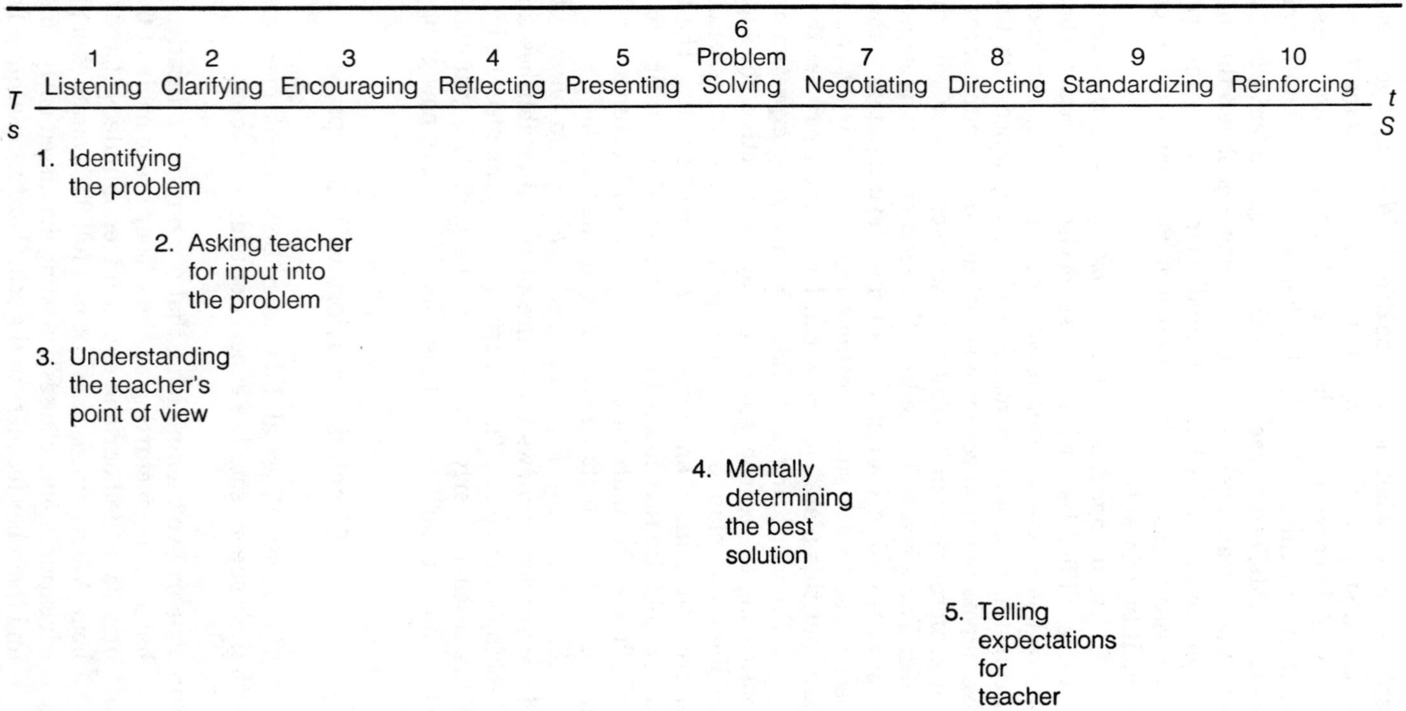

```
 T
 s
     1         2          3            4           5          6         7           8          9            10          t
 Listening  Clarifying  Encouraging  Reflecting  Presenting  Problem  Negotiating  Directing  Standardizing  Reinforcing  s
                                                             Solving
```

1. Identifying
   the problem

2. Asking teacher
   for input into
   the problem

3. Understanding
   the teacher's
   point of view

4. Mentally
   determining
   the best
   solution

5. Telling
   expectations
   for
   teacher

6. Asking teacher
for input into
the expectations

7. Detailing and
modifying
expectations

8. Repeating
and following
up on expecta-
tions

Key: *T* = Maximum teacher responsibility   *S* = Maximum supervisor responsibility
t = Minimum teacher responsibility   *s* = Minimum supervisor responsibility

our sloppiness is causing other problems—students loitering in the halls, looking into class windows, and straggling in late. We need to begin and end on time. Why is this happening?

Fred Soccerman: Those regular classroom teachers are fine ones to talk! They send the kids to us at all times of the day.

Supervisor: Is that true of all of you? [The other members all nod their heads in agreement.] Are there other problems, Shirley?

Shirley Dancercise: I don't intend to dismiss my students early or late, but I don't think the clocks in the lunchroom are synchronized with the classroom clocks.

Supervisor: I'll check on that. Are there other reasons?

Fred Soccerman: The students get a full period in my class; I don't think this is a real issue.

Supervisor: Maybe not, but I'm going to emphasize that we all begin class at five past and dismiss at quarter of. In the meantime, I'll check with the custodians about seeing that the clocks are synchronized, and at the faculty meeting I'll mention our concerns about other teachers sending their students to us at the wrong time. Does everyone understand what I expect of you? Walt?

Walt: I hope some of us are not intentionally letting the students out early. By gosh, we have enough to accomplish with the little time we have.

Supervisor: I'm not implying that we are shortening our instructional time. I'm simply stating that from now on we're going to have a full, consistent forty minutes of instruction for every teacher and every class. If need be, I'll be coming around to see that we are doing it.

Fred: Let's not make this such a big deal. We'll get it done. Now can we talk about the new aerobic exercise elective that we're supposed to be planning?

Although the issue of starting time at the supervisor's meeting might appear to be of relative unimportance to staff members, it was important to the supervisor. Instead of letting the issue pass and risk further complications with other teachers, she decided to meet the issue head on. In the supervisor's role of leader, expert, and possessor of a larger view, she judged that the staff needed to know of her concern and that they would be expected to comply with her directive. At the same time, she was willing to listen to their reactions and to use their information to remedy the situation. It was clear from the outset that the supervisor was making the decision and that the staff was being used in an advisory, not a decision-making, capacity.

In group meetings a supervisor uses directive behaviors to give a clear message about what changes are expected. The supervisor states her understanding of the problem (*presenting*), asks group members if they have more to add (*clarifying*), listens to their input (*listening*), and then mentally reassesses the problem and possible solutions (*problem solving*). She proceeds to state what is to be done (*directing*), asks for input (*clarifying*), lays out the actual actions (*standardizing*), and monitors the expected performance (*reinforcing*).

Issues in Directiveness

Two of three major issues with using directive behaviors have already been mentioned. One has to do with being forthright, the other with source of authority. The third issue is a consideration of time.

A supervisor who needs a teacher to do something has to tell the teacher exactly and honestly what it is. The precision and frankness of a message can be misconstrued or lost in a conference or meeting. Most of us find it difficult to look another person squarely in the eye and say, "I want you to do this." Instead, we often attempt to soften the message by equivocating. It is the difference between telling a person, "Maybe you could try to be more prompt in starting and ending your class" and telling him, "Starting tomorrow I want your class to begin at 8:05 A.M. and end at 8:45 A.M." "Be more prompt" is open to interpretation; "beginning tomorrow at 8:05" means just that. Being direct takes the ambiguity out of the expectations. I'll illustrate this with a personal example. An elementary supervisor I know would become angry at teachers for not doing what he expected of them, only to realize later that the teachers never understood what he meant. He learned a trick that helped him become clearer in giving such messages. He would write down word for word the critical statement he wanted to tell the teacher or group. He would keep the written statement in front of him during the conference or meeting. Thus there was no guesswork involved in giving the message. After a meeting he could look at the written statement and know whether he had delivered it or not.

DIRECTIVE BEHAVIORS

To many of us, directiveness connotes an adversary relationship. It conjures up an image of the pushy, authoritarian boss at work. This is a stereotyped connotation, however. Being directive basically involves letting the other person know (1) what the supervisor is convinced will improve the teacher's instruction *and* (2) that the supervisor is willing to assume complete responsibility for that decision. A teacher might welcome knowing the depth and clarity of the supervisor's expectations. It is better to be up front about the directive than to pretend that teachers have decision-making power over issues that in reality they do not control. Some supervisors avoid being directive by going through the collaborative or nondirective behaviors of involving staff when they've already made the decision. One might be able to succeed with such manipulation temporarily; but once staff become aware that their involvement was of no signficance, they will be resistant to further involvement with the supervisor. With each issue, it is best to let teachers know the degree of their involvement, ranging from full involvement to none, rather than being nebulous. Anyone would prefer to work in a place where the game is *on,* not *under,* the table. Directiveness should be viewed as being informative, decisive, and clear about what teachers have little control over. It also means listening and being willing to modify one's expectations according to reactions from teachers that point out the error of one's directives.

The other major issue raised by directive behavior concerns power and authority. Unless a supervisor holds formal line authority over teachers, he cannot enforce his directives: He can't make the teacher do what he wants. Instead, a supervisor with a staff relationship can expect teachers to follow his plans only if they respect him and trust his judgment. The supervisor must demonstrate and convince the teachers of his superior expertise. If the supervisor has line authority over teachers, however, it is more difficult to separate teacher compliance due to respect for the supervisor from that due to a perceived threat to job security. The line supervisor might believe teachers are following his orders because of his superior knowledge, but the teachers might actually believe the supervisor is an ignoramus. Because of such ambiguity, a line supervisor must be extremely careful when being directive.

Directiveness should be a measure of last resort when an immediate decision is needed. Other nondirective or collaborative approaches normally will ensure greater receptivity by teachers and greater likelihood of successful implementation of a decision, but decisions will take longer to make. Inevitably, when there are many people involved in a decision, discussion, conflict, and resolution will take more time than when only one person is deciding. However, not every instructional problem needs to be addressed at length; a supervisor using directiveness judiciously might actually save time for those decisions most important to staff. There are matters (such as scheduling or budgeting) in which teachers may not desire involvement. A supervisor who attempts to involve people in decisions they view as a waste of time is just as inept as one who does not involve people in decisions about which they care intensely. At times a supervisor does better by being directive and making the decision.

The issue of time includes the need for directiveness in response to emergencies. When the flow of school life is interrupted by irate parents, student defiance, malfunctioning heaters, or media investigations, the supervisor may have to be unilaterally decisive. She simply will not have time to meet with teachers before responding. For example, a middle school principal was called at home by a newspaper reporter who sought her reaction to a fire marshal's report about unsafe cardboard partitions in a classroom of her school. The principal, totally unaware of the marshal's visit, refused comment and called the fire marshal to confirm the report. The marshal told her that all cardboard in classrooms was to be removed by the following morning. Deciding not to fight the fire marshal's orders and thus to avoid further newspaper attention, the principal told each teacher arriving at school the next morning of the fire marshal's report and told them to have their rooms cleared of all cardboard partitions before ten o'clock. She also informed them that they would meet later that afternoon to discuss the fire marshal's ruling and determine if they wanted to appeal it. For the moment, she had used her own judgment. Later, when there was time to review the matter, she and the staff decided collaboratively to meet with the marshal about a proposal to reinstall cardboard partitions covered with fire-resistant plastic. This example shows that at a time of emergency a supervisor, whether ultimately right or wrong, will have to be directive.

When to Use Directive Behaviors

Since directive behaviors raise issues of power, respect, expertise, and line and staff relationships, the following guidelines are given with caution. Directive behaviors should be employed:

1.   When teacher(s) do not have much knowledge about an issue but the supervisor does have such knowledge. If the supervi-

sor knows what the problem is and teachers do not, then most likely the directive approach should be used.

2. When the teacher(s) will have no involvement and the supervisor will be involved in carrying out the decision. If the supervisor will be held totally accountable and the teachers will not, then most likely the directive approach should be used.

3. When the supervisor cares intensely about the issue and the teachers do not. When decisions do not concern teachers and they prefer the supervisor to make the decision, most likely the directive approach should be used.

4. In an emergency, when the supervisor does not have time to meet with teachers, the directive approach should be used.

Further practice in using directive behaviors can be found in Appendix D.

Summary

Directive supervision is used to transmit supervisor expectations to teachers clearly. Supervisors in a line position *over* teachers can use directive controlling language—"I want you to do"—whereas supervisors in a staff position *with* teachers can use directive informational language: "You might do." Directive supervision consists of behaviors of presenting, clarifying, listening, problem solving, directing, standardizing, and reinforcing (with line authority). The source of presenting, problem solving, and directing is mostly from supervisor to teacher. Directive behaviors are useful in limited circumstances when teachers possess little expertise, involvement, or interest with respect to an instructional problem and time is short. In these circumstances, directiveness is not an adversarial or capricious set of behaviors, but an honest approach with teachers to an emergency.

EXERCISES

ACADEMIC

1. Write an imaginary dialogue between a supervisor and teacher during a conference in which the supervisor success-

fully uses a directive approach. Be sure to include examples of each of the eight behaviors discussed in Chapter Nine.

2. The chapter suggests that a sequence of eight directive behaviors takes place during a directive conference. Think of a situation in which a successful directive conference would start with the first suggested behavior (identifying the problem) and end with the eighth (repeating and following up on expectations), but have a *different sequence* of six intermediate behaviors. Describe the situation and modified sequence of directive behaviors in writing. Include a rationale for the suggested sequence.

3. Write an imaginary dialogue between a supervisor and a teacher in which the supervisor implements directive procedures with mechanical precision but fails to be directive in an effective sense.

4. Write a paper comparing the directive approach as described in this book with the version of directive behavior espoused by an author cited in the Suggestions for Additional Readings.

5. Assume you have recently attended a seminar at which a university professor argued against educational supervisors using the directive approach with any teacher. The professor proposed that the supervisor should play the role of a helper, not attempt to control a teacher's behavior. The speaker argued that successful change cannot be brought about unless the teacher perceives the need for change and has had a part in deciding how to bring about the needed change. He concluded that a directive supervisory approach will only alienate teachers and make supervisors unwelcome in many classrooms. You have been asked to reply to the professor's arguments at an upcoming seminar. Write a paper in which you present an argument for using directive behaviors with some teachers and under some circumstances. Address the professor's arguments against directive supervision.

FIELD

1. Assume the role of a supervisor using a directive approach by either using the simulated activity in Appendix D or conducting an actual postobservation conference with a teacher. Prepare a written report in which you (a) evaluate your success in displaying directive behaviors, (b) summarize the problems

discussed and decisions made during the conference, (c) give your perceptions of the "teacher's" responses to your directive efforts, and (d) judge the conference in terms of overall success.

2. Observe an educational supervisor or other leader whom you know to possess a directive orientation in dealing with individuals and/or groups. On the basis of your observations and/or an interview with the leader, write a paper describing both successes and failures the selected leader has experienced while using directive behaviors. Include possible reasons that the directive leader has been more successful in some situations than in others.

3. Observe three teachers or staff members who clearly respond positively to directive supervision. Write a paper examining personal and social characteristics of these individuals that may account for their positive response to a directive approach.

4. Prepare a photo album entitled "Supervisory Direction for Instructional Improvement." Each photograph should be accompanied by a written explanation of how it relates to the album theme.

5. Videotape or audiotape a conference or staff development activity led by a supervisor who typically uses a directive approach. As you review the tape, compare the recorded activities with the sequence of behaviors that, according to the chapter, exemplify the directive process. Prepare a report on your findings.

DEVELOPMENTAL

1. Through interaction with various individuals in a variety of situations, begin to establish a set of personal guidelines that will indicate when the directive approach is most appropriate for your own use in carrying out present or anticipated leadership functions.

2. Begin an in-depth study of assertiveness/assertion training. As you progress through your study, note how training in assertiveness can be used by supervisors when they find themselves with teachers or in situations requiring a direct approach.

3. Record a simulated or actual supervisor-teacher conference in which you, as supervisor, attempt to display directive behav-

iors. Review the tape for analysis of your performance. Over the next four weeks, attempt to practice directive leadership whenever appropriate opportunities arise. Record another simulated or actual conference in four weeks. Review both tapes to discover any improvement in terms of successfully displaying behaviors the chapter describes as directive.

SUGGESTIONS FOR ADDITIONAL READING

Supervision

Lucio, W. H., and McNeil, J. D. 1979. *Supervision: A synthesis of thought and action,* 3rd ed. New York: McGraw-Hill.

Setting Criteria

Mager, R. F., and Pipe, P. 1970. *Analyzing performance problems or "You really oughta wanna."* Belmont, Calif.: Fearon.

Assertiveness

Alberti, R. E., and Emmons, M. L. 1974. *Your perfect right: A guide to assertive behavior.* San Luis Obispo, Calif.: Impact.

Smith, M. 1975. *When I say no, I feel guilty.* New York: Dial Press.

CHAPTER TEN

Applying Interpersonal Skills to Characteristics of Individuals and Groups

Now that we know about the various supervisory behaviors and the three approaches (nondirective, collaborative, and directive), how do we determine which skills and approaches to use? The chapters explaining each approach provided some simple guidelines. Basically, when an individual teacher or group of teachers have expertise on an issue, have a strong commitment to its solution, and will be held accountable for the subsequent plan of action, then the supervisor might best work in a nondirective manner. On the other hand, when an individual or group of teachers have little expertise, little commitment, and no accountability, then the supervisor might best work in a directive manner. When the individual or group have some expertise, a moderate degree of commitment, and some accountability, then the supervisor might best work in a collaborative manner. Furthermore, when an individual or group fluctuate from characteristic to characteristic—for example, have moderate expertise, low commitment, and high accountability—then a supervisor might best handle the situation with a collaborative approach.

As a rule of thumb, the collaborative approach should be the most successful with most individuals and groups of experienced teachers. Recent research bears this out. When a stratified sample of 210 K-12 teachers were asked for their preferred supervisory approach, 63 (30 percent) preferred a supervisor to work with them nondirectively; 141 (67 percent) preferred a supervisor to work with them collaboratively, and only 6 (3 percent) preferred a supervisor to work with them directly (Ginkel 1983). Blumberg also surveyed experienced teachers about supervisory behaviors they perceived to be most positive. As with the Ginkel study, experienced teachers split primarily into two groups. One group perceived collaborative supervisory behaviors—listening to the teacher as well as presenting the supervisor's own views—as most positive. The other group saw nondirective supervisory behaviors—primarily listening, reflecting, and asking the teacher—as most positive. Experienced teachers did not view directive behaviors as positive (Blumberg and Weber 1968; Blumberg 1980).

Student or neophyte teachers prefer a different supervisory approach. Various studies of preservice teachers have been conducted by Zonca (1973); Vudovich (1976); Copeland (1978, 1980); and Lorch (1981). The findings were consistent in that most preservice teachers preferred a directive supervisory approach. Most of them wanted a supervisor to tell them precisely what changes they were expected to make to improve instruction.

Three tentative conclusions can be drawn from these studies of experienced and preservice teachers:

1. Experienced teachers vary in their preference of supervisory behaviors between nondirective and collaborative. Between the two, collaborative supervisory behaviors are preferred by the majority of teachers.

2. Directive supervisory behaviors are preferred by only a small minority of experienced teachers.

3. Neophyte teachers (student and beginning teachers) initially prefer a directive approach by their supervisors.

There are explanations for these differences in supervisory preference among teachers with various levels of experience. Human development theory and teacher development theory might help the supervisor make judgments about which behaviors and approaches to use with certain individuals and groups. First, some important cautions: Rigorously controlled, experimental, and school-based studies on matching supervisory approaches to developmental characteristics of teachers have not been performed. Although we can make a substantial case for why certain supervisory approaches are more appropriate for certain teachers, we cannot prove it empirically. No one has taken a random sample of teachers; divided them into four groups; trained supervisors in each of the three approaches; applied a directive approach to one group, a collaborative approach to another group, a nondirective approach to the third group, and no treatment to the fourth group; and then compared class performance changes across all four groups. Although a few scaled-down studies are in progress (Wilsey and Killion 1982; Rossicone, in press; Gordon, in press) it is unlikely that a fully controlled study within a school or school system will ever be done. The difficulty in conducting such research is that concerned administrators and supervisors will not knowingly allow an experiment to continue that is improving the performance of one group of teachers over that of another group. This is an understandable ethical dilemma, typical of most education research that requires a treatment. In reading the remainder of the chapter, remember that the case for different approaches is built on theory, related research, logic, and common sense—not on proven, generalizable experiments.

The Need for Structure: More and Then Less

"As long as you have rules, you have a chance for freedom" (Suzuki 1970).

Let's again briefly review the research of Francis Fuller, described in Chapter Four on teacher concerns. What a teacher is concerned about in the beginning of his first year is usually quite different from his concerns in the second, fifth, or tenth year. Fuller (1969; Fuller et al. 1974) conducted several studies with groups of teachers of various degrees of experience, from beginning teachers to teachers with many years of experience. She and her staff surveyed hundreds of these teachers with the question, "When you think about teaching, what are you concerned about?" She isolated a group of experienced and superior teachers (determined by administrator and peer ranking of teachers within each school). In these studies she found a consistent developmental pattern between beginning, experienced and superior teachers. Beginning teachers were mostly concerned about their own adequacy or survival. They were worried about whether they could measure up as teachers. They wondered if their students would run away with the classroom, if the principal would judge them to be competent, and if other teachers in the school would accept them as real members of the staff. Beginning teachers were concerned with simply surviving from one day or week to the next. Experienced teachers were less concerned with their own survival and more concerned about their students. They worried more about helping individual students and improving classroom instruction. They wanted to do more to help students learn. Once a teacher became confident of his own survival, concern shifted to the survival of his students. The quality of classroom life became paramount.

The third group of superior and experienced teachers also showed concern with their impact on students, but in addition they were concerned with helping other students, other classrooms, the school as a whole, and the teaching profession. Their concern went beyond their own classroom to a desire to improve education for all participants. Fuller's studies of teacher concerns have been repli-cated in many geographic areas in diverse socioeconomic, rural, urban, and suburban communities with largely the same results (Adams and Martray 1981).

Figure 10–1 is a generalized scheme for viewing teacher con-cerns as related to the developmental principles of moral reasoning as uncovered by Piaget (1965) and Kohlberg (1969). Stages of moral reasoning move from a preconventional, egocentric stage to a con-ventional, law-and-order stage to a postconventional, altruistic stage. There is a developmental pattern of stages of moral reasoning related to levels of teacher concerns. Teacher concerns with self-sur-vival can be related to egocentric moral reasoning; teacher concerns with instructional impact on classroom students can be related to conventional law-and-order reasoning; and teacher concerns with students and teachers beyond one's immediate classroom can be related to postconventional, altruistic reasoning. In Figure 10–1, note that levels of concern and stages of reasoning do not vanish when new levels and stages have been acquired. Instead, former levels and stages remain, but the new ones predominate.

Developmental theory is based on research that shows marked stages of thought, movement, language, and socialization that are structurally different from each other and loosely related to age. High stages of reasoning and concerns are acquired by relatively few persons, and usually those are older and more ex-perienced teachers. There are exceptions to this rule because the rate of passage through stages can vary from individual to individ-ual. Therefore, some first-year teachers might reason in ways char-acteristic of the highest stage. Some exceptional teachers might resolve their survival concerns with the first month of school and proceed rapidly to concerns with instructional impact and educa-tional improvement by the end of the first year. On the other hand, there might be individual teachers in their fortieth year of teach-ing who remain in the self-survival stage, without thinking beyond the immediate needs of keeping one's job. Stage theory character-izes movement of *groups* of beginning and experienced teachers, not individuals. Also keep in mind that few teachers reason in the highest or lowest stages and that reasoning and concerns can vary from one situation to another as well as regress to lower stages. A teacher might reason at the highest level in one school and, on being transferred to another school, reason at a lower stage. A teacher might have self-survival concerns with playground super-

FIGURE 10–1   Relationship of Teacher Concerns to Moral Reasoning

	Beginning Teachers	*Experienced Teachers*	*"Superior" Teachers*
Concerns (Fuller 1969)	Self-survival ("Will I make it as a teacher?")	Impact on classroom students ("What can I do to make students learn?")	Impact beyond my own classroom ("What can I do to make education better for all?")
Moral Reasoning (Kohlberg 1969)	Preconventional egocentric ("Will I get caught?")	Conventional law and order ("What are the rules?")	Postconventional altruistic ("What is in the best interest of all people?")

vision but go beyond classroom concerns with teaching English literature, human and situational variability needs always to be considered when thinking about development.

Maslow and Herzberg: Theories of Motivation

Stages of teacher concerns and moral reasoning can be seen in relation to human needs. Abraham Maslow developed a classical framework for understanding human motivation (Maslow 1954). Maslow's premise was that there exists a hierarchy of needs that motivate humans to act, in the following order.

Physiological Needs

The initial motivation for humans is to satisfy biological demands for food, oxygen, water, sleep, and exercise. Unless these needs are satisfied, a human is motivated by nothing else. An individual who is starving is not interested in security, money, or companionship. She will exert all her energy to find food. The same is true of any unmet physiological need.

Safety

After physiological needs are satisfied, the individual is motivated to attend to the niceties of human life. He seeks a comfortable, regulated environment. Security, stability, dependency, and rules all eliminate anxiety and fear of the unknown. An individual is motivated to seek a shelter in a familiar location with a secure source of income.

Belonging and Love

After safety needs are satisfied and the individual has established a home in the broadest sense, she begins to seek involvement with others as a group member and as a partner. She desires affectionate relationships with friends and acceptance as a member of a group—signified by affiliations in informal and formal clubs, associations, and teams. Her identity becomes merged with other people in religious, social, civic, and/or informal groups.

Esteem

Once needs for belonging and love have been satisfied, the individual's motivation changes from gaining acceptance within a group to becoming a contributing and leading member of the group. It is no longer adequate to be one of the gang; he wants to be an admired and visible member. The individual takes a role of initiating actions, assuming leadership and helping others so that they will see him as important. The attainment of status and prestige affirms his competence and value to the group.

Self-Actualization

The culminating human need comes after the acquisition of self-esteem and confidence in one's ability to be successful in the eyes of others. Motivation in the previous stage was based on being liked and admired by others. Now the motivation becomes to act and achieve according to one's own standards. The individual follows what he believes is best, regardless of what others might think. Being true to one's own inclinations becomes the mark of self-actualization or, as Maslow defined it, "What a man *can* be, he *must* be" (1954, p. 46).

Let's put Maslow's theory of human motivation into common language. An individual who is hungry does not care about shelter. A person who is no longer hungry begins to think about a roof to keep out the rain and four walls to ward off the cold. He desires order and regulation in life. Once a person is secure in his environment, he cares about belonging and participating with others. After he has affiliated and feels comfortable as a member of a group, he then desires to be regarded as an important member of the group. Finally, with confidence in the regard others hold for him, the individual turns inward to what he wishes to become.

Maslow's theory of human motivation is developmental. The needs of a lower stage must be satisfied before a person is motivated by needs of the next higher stage. The stages are hierarchical. Each person moves through them in the same sequence, from physiological needs to safety needs, to belonging and love needs, to esteem needs, to self-actualization needs. The rate of passage varies from individual to individual. Finally, retreat can occur when the individual's situation is dramatically altered. For example, a person might have acquired self-esteem in her present job; but when she is hired to fill a new position, suddenly she may be groping for safety, routine, and security in the work environment. Initially she is concerned with how to get a parking permit, how to fill out voucher forms, and where to apply for medical insurance. The furthest thought from her mind is leading the group or being self-actualized. All she wants to know is where is her territory, what are the rules, and what is she expected to do.

This retreat and recapitulation of needs is exactly what happens with teacher concerns and reasoning. It is not that a beginning teacher has been in an egocentric self-survival stage all of his life. Any person thrown into a new environment, regardless of his previous functioning, will go through a transition period of floundering and feeling insecure before feeling safe and ready to contribute to the world outside himself.

Herzberg's research on human motivation supports Maslow's hierarchy of needs. Herzberg, Mausner, and Snyderman (1959), in their study of engineers and accountants, were originally concerned with what business and service employees perceived as positive or "satisfiers" and negative or "dissatisfiers" about their jobs. To Herzberg's surprise, satisfiers and dissatisfiers were quite distinct from each other. Negative factors or dissatisfiers most often cited were

- Organizational policy and administration.
- Technical supervision.
- Salary.
- Working conditions.
- Status.
- Job security.
- Effects on personal life.
- Interpersonal relations.

On the other hand, positive incidents most cited were

- Work itself.
- Achievement.
- Possibility of growth.
- Responsibility.
- Advancement.

Herzberg found that elimination of dissatisfiers did not improve an individual's performance. Dissatisfiers were maintenance or hygiene factors. In other words, if a person's major dissatisfaction with her job is poor working conditions (poor lighting or inadequate facilities), it will remain a source of irritation and might make her work less hard but, if corrected, will not make her work harder. If the lighting is fixed, she will no longer be dissatisfied, but it will not increase her productivity. Rather, she will accept the correction as the way it should have been in the first place.

The positive factors that Herzberg called satisfiers did motivate individuals to work harder. When an employee found the work itself exciting, when she had a sense of achievement, when she saw future growth in her career, when she was given responsibility or advancement—then she improved performance. If a teacher is given increased responsibility for making decisions about materials to use in his classroom and is encouraged to modify his teaching lessons to add more topics or projects that he believes to be exciting and valuable, then he will tend to put more time and energy into changing and improving his performance. In other words, if a teacher is given increased responsibility to make decisions, he will work harder to see that he succeeds. Herzberg, therefore, cited satisfiers as the key motivators to improving work performance. Since these original studies, there have been replications of Herzberg's research in other businesses (Herzberg 1966; King 1970; Hoy and Miskel 1982) and in education (Sergiovanni 1966; Schmidt 1976). Studies that have used Herzberg's research methodology have found the same distinctions between negative, or hygiene, and positive, or motivating, factors. For example, a study by Sergiovanni (1966) consisted of interviews of teachers. He found the same loadings of factors as Herzberg except that work itself and advancement were less often cited by teachers as motivators. This was probably attributable to the nature of the teaching career, which offered little change in the work itself and almost no possibility of advancement (Lortie 1975).

Cawelti (1976) and Drucker (1973) have pointed out the link between Maslow's theory of motivation and Herzberg's research on hygiene and motivators. We might view this relationship by placing Herzberg's factors side by side with Maslow's stages (Figure 10–2).

Without forcing a perfect one-to-one correspondence, it is apparent that Herzberg's hygiene factors, which maintain performance, corresponds to Maslow's lower-level needs—physiological, safety, and love and belonging. This interaction between hygiene and lower-level needs characterizes the teacher's working to "find one's niche." The individual is learning to perform in an acceptable manner that is officially sanctioned by one's peers, technical supervisors (evaluators), and the formal organization.

Herzberg's motivation factors likewise correspond with Maslow's higher stages. This interaction between motivation and higher-level needs defines an area in which the teacher is "going beyond competence." The individual knows performance is acceptable and now strives for excellence. Notice the small overlapping area in Figure 10–2 between "finding one's niche" and "going beyond competence" called "choice." This is the critical area in which a teacher can choose either to remain minimally competent or to grow in new ways. The choice becomes available when hygiene factors and lower-stage needs have been met and when there is encouragement to go beyond competence by providing a sense of achievement, responsibility, recognition, and advancement so that teachers can choose to improve their instruction. The administrative function of a school should provide for the hygiene factors that enable teachers to reach the plateau from which supervision for improvement of instruction can proceed.

FIGURE 10–2   Interacting Areas of Herzberg's Factors with Maslow's Stages

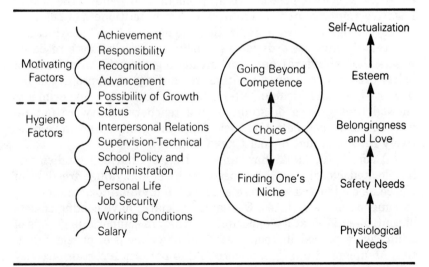

Sources: F. Herzberg, B. Mausner, and B. Snyderman, *The Motivation to Work* (New York: Wiley, 1959); and A. H. Maslow, *Motivation and Personality* (New York: Harper & Row, 1954).

deCharms and Deci on Motivation

The reader might believe the preceding explanation of teacher motivation was based on outdated theory and research. After all, Maslow wrote in 1954, Herzberg in 1966. What does current research say about human motivation? Since 1973 there have been over seventy studies on the undermining effect of control versus individual choice (Morgan 1984). The research led by deCharms (1968, 1976) and Deci (1975, 1982) not only validates the work of Maslow and Herzberg but also adds to our understanding of why the interacting area of "choice" is the critical determinant in teacher improvement.

deCharms conducted studies whose findings contradicted motivation theories based on external stimulus. The most prevalent practices in industry and schools are based on the premise that individuals will change and increase their production if reinforced by rewards, bribes, or coercion (Ouchi 1981). Extrinsic-motivation theory posits that one motivates others by either positive means—praising, rewarding, and providing salary incentive—or negative means—threatening job security, withholding pay, or criticizing. Such motivation is based on behavioral, stimulus-response psychology identified with B. F. Skinner (1971) that humans are conditioned by external forces. Pure behaviorists consistently advocate positive reinforcement and believe the use of negative reinforcement is ineffective. Yet practitioners of behavioral psychology in most organizations do not make such distinctions and readily mix rewards with punishments. deCharms's research upsets the behavioral applecart in finding that the most basic of behavioral propositions—positive rewarding of appropriate behavior—has undesirable after-effects. deCharms's experiments showed that groups of students and teachers who were not rewarded performed *better* on tasks than did groups who were positively rewarded (deCharms 1968, Chap. 10).

Deci (1975, 1982) has amplified on deCharms's studies and has looked closely at the consequences of individual freedom of choice as contrasted with reinforcing an individual to act according to someone else's dictates. Deci and associates have conducted sets of controlled laboratory experiments wherein comparable groups of adults were placed in rooms with an assortment of puzzle activities. Members of one group were told to perform a certain activity and that they would be paid for completing that activity. The other group were told they could choose from any of the activities and could work as long as they pleased. No reinforcement was provided to the second group. The first study found that the rewarded subjects spent less time with the assigned activity and were less satisfied with doing the activity than were the subjects who had free choice. In the second study the same groups of subjects returned to the activity room and were told to work as they pleased. The previously rewarded group showed decreased attention and performance. The previously rewarded group avoided the activity they had been paid to do previously, whereas the free-choice group tended to return to the activity they had worked on before. The attitude and commitment of the previously unrewarded group was significantly higher than that of the rewarded group. Thus Deci, like deCharms before him, concluded that there are indirect and undesirable consequences of using external reinforcement to motivate humans.

The Issue of Choice

Deci, as a laboratory researcher, is convinced—and as a field-based educator I concur—that reinforcement or extrinsic motivation is not the way to promote professional and personal growth. External reinforcement is necessary in an organization as a way of satisfying Maslow's low-stage needs—physiological, safety, and belongingness—and the hygiene factors of salary, work conditions and job security, to maintain minimal competence. Once the person is minimally competent, then external reinforcements, even positive ones, are not growth-inducing.

Any type of organization must control employee behaviors within broad limits (a school cannot have teachers of moral education deal drugs any more than a crime syndicate can have drug peddlers who are moral educators). The nature of the organization limits the behaviors of its employees. Hence any organization must have control; which is an administrative function. Control means that some person representing the governance of the organization has the job of getting employees to comply with those limits (the ringleader of the drug syndicate must tell the moral educator among the drug peddlers to stop preaching or get out). With compliance inevitably comes some form of resistance. Although a person will do what he is told to do if the reward or sanction is great enough, the controller knows there will be an indirect consequence of resistance. If resistance were not inevitable, there would be no reason to control. The employee will perform, but he also might resent the controller, do the task begrudgingly, or even do the opposite of what the controller wants when the controller is not present. A study by Brown (1975) found that teachers, when ordered by a supervisor to perform in a prescribed manner, often did the opposite of the orders. This type of resistance can be seen when teachers are told to use certain textbooks they do not like as part of school policy. They will bring out the books when the controller (principal or superintendent) is there. When the controller is not there, however, they will use the books halfheartedly (as a part of their lesson) or not at all (to keep the door open or for short students to sit on). An experienced school administrator or teacher is well aware that control leads to immediate compliance and subsequent resistance.

Many issues that arise in schools with teachers are issues of control. As part of the school organization, teachers simply must behave in certain ways. As the controls are articulated clearly, a teacher becomes familiar with the norms and minimum expectations of the organization. *But let's not confuse controlling behavior with improving instruction.* Ultimately the individual teacher always has a choice, even when the choice is "Do what I say or get out!" Yet the narrowing of choice is not motivating; rather, it is the expansion of choice or the opportunity to decide that motivates a teacher to go beyond competence.

Controlling versus Informational Environments

Deci distinguishes between working with people in controlling as opposed to informational environments. *Controlling* environments, as already mentioned, restrict individual choice, gain compliance, and create resistance. *Informational* environments expand individual choice, promote autonomy, and encourage commitment to improvement. An informational environment is one in which the individual considers alternative sources of feedback on her performance, thinks through consequences of her actions, and freely chooses according to her own interests and curiosity. The premise of an informational environment is that humans are innately curious and desire to follow their own inclinations. deCharms calls this drive to be powerful, independent, and active the quality of being an "origin." Persons who have been conditioned by a controlling environment to feel powerless, dependent, and passive he calls "pawns." When the professional environment matches the individual's need to be an initiator, then—and only then—does enduring improvement occur. Pajak and Seyfarth (1983) clarify the distinction between controlling and informational environments by referring to supervisory language. According to them, it is the difference between a supervisor working with a teacher in a "must" manner as opposed to working with a teacher in a "can" manner. Words such as *must, should, ought to,* and *need to* connote supervisor control and lack of teacher choice. Words such as *can, could, consider,* and *might* connote supervisor information and teacher choice. Anyone in a formal supervisory position might consider using the *must* context only when control is the paramount issue and using the *can* context when information and improvement are of greatest importance. A recent study has shown that teachers are extremely sensitive to the differences between controlling and informational language used by a supervisor (Pajak and Glickman 1984). Woe to the person who mistakenly uses *must* to mean *can,* or *consider* to mean *should.* We have trouble enough communicating our true intent to others without compounding the problem by unwittingly using control words when we mean to use informational ones or vice versa.

Finally, this discussion of human motivation in a supervisory context brings us back to the use of the delineated interpersonal approaches—directive, collaborative, and nondirective. For a supervisor working with individual teachers and group members, there are two environments that must be considered when using various approaches. These two environments are depicted in Table 10–1.

In an informational environment, the supervisor allows the teacher to make her own choice. Yet the supervisor varies the source and amount of information depending on the teacher's expertise and competence in problem solving. The directive, informational approach (cell A) in which the supervisor tells the teacher what can be done to improve instruction ("I think student attention would be greater if you had smaller groups") is predicated on

TABLE 10–1   Supervisory Environment and Approach

	Approaches		
Environments	*Directive*	*Collaborative*	*Nondirective*
Informational	[A]Supervisor's information for teacher to consider	[B]Sharing information for both to consider	[C]Actively listening to teacher's information
Controlling	[D]Supervisor telling teacher what to do	[E]Guise of involvement: Make teacher believe he/she shared in decision	[F]Manipulating teacher to think he/she is making own decision

supervisor knowledge of possibilities and teacher lack of such knowledge. The collaborative informational approach (cell B) is premised on both supervisor and teacher having helpful information ("This is what you think can be done. . . . This is what I think. . . .") The nondirective informational approach (cell C) is premised on teacher expertise and supervisor's facilitation of teacher knowledge ("How do you see your classroom?") When we move into controlling environments, we are responding to beginning and/or insecure teachers' needs for safety, structure, and security. If the supervisor does possess formal authority, she can use the directive controlling approach (cell D) in emergency or survival situations ("You *must* stop using corporal punishment, it is against school policy"). The collaborative, controlling approach (cell E) and the nondirective, controlling approach (cell F) have no place in schools. To use collaborative skills to manipulate teachers to do what the supervisor had wanted all along or to use nondirective skills to subtly reinforce compliance with a supervisor's demand is dishonest and unethical. Besides the questionable ethics of such behavior, once the game is known the supervisor will reap the undesirable consequence of resistance from teachers.

A supervisor should use directive control as an initial resort or in an emergency. She could use directive information, collaborative information, and nondirective information in her everyday work. The choice can be governed by the expertise and competence of the teacher or group. A supervisor can use criteria about an individual's or group's ability to solve problems as an indication of which approach to use first.

Teacher Problem Solving as Cueing Information for Deciding Supervisory Approach

Expertise refers to the body of knowledge, or know-how, an individual or a group possesses for improving instruction. *Competence* refers to the performance of an individual or group of teachers in achieving desired learning results with students. Therefore, expertise is the knowledge (training and experience) that one brings to instructional problems; competence is one's on-the-feet performance with students. The process of problem solving is an integration of expertise and competence. One puts knowledge into action via decision making. We will outline the rational decision-making method as providing cues to the supervisor in deciding which approach to use when working with a teacher. The rational decision-making method will be explained rather than a more intuitive method because teachers' rational decision making has been correlated with some measures of teacher effectiveness (Clark and Joyce 1976; Hunt and Sullivan 1974; Riley 1980). Keep in mind that there are exceptions to the rules. Some teachers appear to be more intuitive and spontaneous, yet run exceptionally fine classrooms. Therefore, not all good rational problem solvers are good teachers, nor are all poor rational problem solvers poor teachers. More good teachers display rational problem-solving abilities than not, but the ultimate criterion must be whether teachers are achieving desired individual and collective goals of student learning.

Rational problem solving can be viewed as a five-step procedure with two major components.

1. Problem awareness.

2. Identifying causes of problem.   *Identify*

3. Alternative solutions.

4. Selecting solution.   *Solve*

5. Testing.

Steps 1 and 2 *identify* the problem; steps 3, 4, and 5 *solve* the problem. Obviously it is difficult to solve a problem that has not been identified correctly. One study has shown that when supervisors were given problem scenarios and asked to identify problems, over 80 percent of their responses were solutions (Clinton, Glickman, and Payne 1982). In other words, most of us tend to leap before we look. Rational problem-solving skills are important for supervisors as well as for teachers. A supervisor might use the five-step problem-solving procedure when deciding which interpersonal approach is appropriate with which teacher(s). We first use our own expertise or knowledge about interpersonal skills and our own competence to perform the interpersonal skills. We then look at the teacher's problem-solving abilities, gather information about teacher proficiency, generate alternative approaches toward working with the teacher, choose one, and try it out. Asking ourselves the following questions when assessing an individual teacher can help.

1. Is the teacher aware of improvements that can be made in the classroom? Can the teacher identify those needs?

2. Has the teacher considered possible causes of the instructional needs? Does the teacher gather information from multiple sources about the instructional needs?

3.　Can the teacher generate several possible solutions? How carefully does the teacher weigh the merits of each solution? Does the teacher consider what he or she can do about the problem without looking unrealistically for outside help?

4.　Can the teacher be decisive in choosing a course of action? Does the teacher commit him- or herself to an implementation procedure?

5.　Does the teacher do what he or she says?

These are some questions to answer in determining the necessary degree of intervention with nondirective, collaborative, or directive approaches. A teacher who shows no inclination to improve and is considered less than competent by those with responsibilities for formal teacher evaluation is appropriately matched with a controlling directive approach. A teacher who desires to improve his or her performance but is at a loss for what to do is appropriately matched with an informational directive approach. A teacher who is aware of potential areas for improvement and can think of possible actions is appropriately matched with a collaborative approach. A teacher who is aware, knowledgeable, and decisive about instructional improvement is appropriately matched with a nondirective approach. Further amplification on appropriate matching with individuals will be found in Chapter Fourteen on direct human assistance.

Situational Leadership for Groups

Hersey and Blanchard's (1977) famous model of situational leadership of groups has been applied to education by Gates, Blanchard, and Hersey (1976) and Cawelti (1976). It is a generalized approach to leadership styles. They suggest that a leader consider the maturity level of a group before deciding on the type of leadership style to use. They define leadership in terms of relationship and task behaviors. *Relationship* behaviors consist of those behaviors that consider the feelings of group members (praise, encouragement, humor). *Task* behaviors are those that focus on accomplishing the task of the meeting (setting time limits, asking specific questions, proposing answers). Group maturity is determined by

1.　*Achievement* or motivation of the group.

2.　*Responsibility:* Is there a willingness on the part of the group to assume leadership?

3. *Education* or experience: Does the group have the background to accomplish the task?

Figure 10–3 depicts the Hersey/Blanchard Situational Leadership Model.

If the group is rated high on all three characteristics (achievement, responsibility, and education) then they are considered a highly mature group—M4. If they score some combination of high on two of the three characteristics, they are considered a moderately high mature group—M3. If they score some combination of low on two of the three characteristics, they are considered a mod-

FIGURE 10–3   The Hersey/Blanchard Situational-Leadership Model

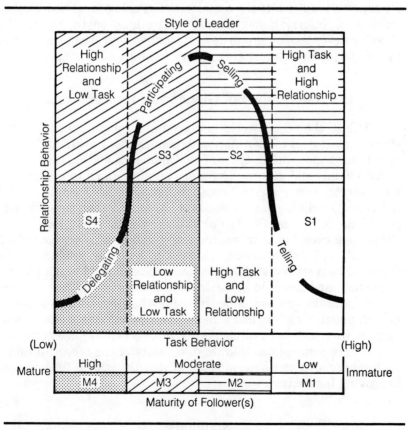

Source: For a complete discussion of the Hersey/Blanchard situational-leadership model, see Paul Hersey and Kenneth H. Blanchard, *Management of Organizational Behavior: Utilizing Human Resources,* 3rd Ed. © 1977, p. 169. Reprinted by permission of Prentice-Hall, Inc., Englewood Cliffs, N.J.

erately low mature group—M2. If they score low on all three, they are considered a low mature group—M1. According to Hersey and Blanchard, an immature group (M1) is best matched with a leadership of high task, low relationships, or a *telling* posture (S1). A moderately low mature group (M2) is best matched with a leadership of high task and high relationship, a *selling* posture (S2). A moderately high group (M3) is best matched with a leadership of high relationship and low task, a *participating* posture (S3). Finally, a highly mature group (M4) is best matched with a leadership of low relationship and low task, a *delegating* posture (S4).

My own supervisory behavior continuum, alternative supervisory approaches, and matching with characteristics of individuals and groups of teachers have been influenced by Hersey and Blanchard's theory. Hersey and Blanchard have provided the framework for my own studies into the complexities of using supervisory behaviors and informational versus controlling environments. In Chapter Seventeen on group development we will speak more of the use of Hersey and Blanchard's theory to group situations.

Not Algorithms but Guideposts for Decisions

Life in the school world is ragged and complex. This chapter offers a great deal of information to ponder about available behaviors, human motivation, types of environments, and characteristics of individuals and groups. There are no algorithms to provide exactly correct responses to human behavior. Such formulas as "if individual exhibits characteristics *A, B,* and *C,* then supervisor *Y* should do *D, F,* and *G*" do not and should not exist. Such algorithms are useful only in mechanically and technically controlled systems (such as computer operations, assembly production, or chemical alterations). Algorithms work in technical but not human endeavors, and it would be misleading to suggest that such supervision formulas are available. Instead, what is available is information about ourselves and others than can serve as guideposts to suggest what *might* be of use. Such developmental guideposts can help reduce some of the infinite complexity of the school world so that supervision can be a purposeful and thoughtful function for improving instruction.

Summary

This chapter explored the application of interpersonal skills to characteristics of individuals and groups. I cited research showing that most beginning teachers appear to prefer a directive approach, whereas a large majority of experienced teachers prefer the collaborative and nondirective approaches. We explained this preference according to stage theory. Human motivation, according to Maslow, Herzberg, deCharms, and Deci, explains why information environments that provide choice for teachers are more likely to sustain instructional improvements than are control environments that limit choice. Steps in teachers' rational problem solving can be clues used by supervisors for determining the degree of supervisory intervention. The supervisor needs to use his or her own problem-solving abilities to identify, choose, and determine the most appropriate interpersonal approaches to use with his or her staff.

EXERCISES

ACADEMIC

1. Prepare written composite profiles of (a) a teacher who would benefit most from nondirective supervision, (b) a teacher who would benefit most from collaborative supervision, and (c) a teacher who would benefit most from directive supervision.

2. Write an essay comparing Maslow's four highest human need categories to your own development within a work or social organization. Evaluate Maslow's theory of motivation in terms of whether it is relevant to your own needs, experiences, and growth in progressing from a novice to an experienced member of the selected organization.

3. Create a written list of six motivating (intrinsic) factors and six hygiene (extrinsic) factors related to teaching within a public school setting. Categorize each of Herzberg's twelve related factors according to one of Maslow's stages by placing an A (self-actualization), E (esteem), B (belongingness), S (safety), or P (physiological) after each factor. Give a brief rationale for each Herzberg and Maslow related classification you decide on.

4. Describe a situation in which a supervisor would be required to use directive control, and explain what specific behaviors you as a supervisor would exhibit in that situation. Describe

a second set of circumstances in which directive information would be more appropriate, and explain specific behaviors you would display if you were the supervisor in that second situation.

5. Describe an instructional problem that is typically dealt with by a supervisor working with a group of teachers. Using that same problem for each of four descriptions, describe how a supervisor following the Hersey/Blanchard Situational Leadership Model would interact with teacher groups, charged with solving the problem, that are of (a) low maturity, (b) moderately low maturity, (c) moderately high maturity, and (d) high maturity.

FIELD

1. Ask five teachers each to write a paragraph or two on the topic "What Motivates Me to Improve My Teaching." Write a paper comparing the teachers' responses with the research findings of deCharms and Deci.

2. Share a description of an actual classroom problem with a small group (the teacher and/or students involved in the classroom problem should remain anonymous). Simulate a problem-solving session in which the group (a) identifies causes of the problem, (b) proposes and considers alternative solutions to the problem, (c) chooses the most promising alternative, and (d) selects an appropriate method of testing the agreed-on solution. Write a report summarizing the problem-solving session and evaluating the quality of the problem-solving behaviors displayed by the group.

3. Observe an educational supervisor using what Hersey and Blanchard refer to as a "telling," "selling," "participating," or "delegating" leadership style with a group of teachers. Write a report in which you evaluate (a) the appropriateness of the leadership style in relation to the maturity level of the group and (b) the effectiveness of the observed leadership style in terms of meeting instructional improvement objectives.

4. Examine developmental characteristics of an individual for whom you have supervisory responsibility. Use the supervisory approach (nondirective, collaborative, directive) that you perceive as the best match for the selected individual. Summarize and evaluate your matched supervision.

5. Evaluate the maturity level (as defined by Hersey and Blanchard) of a group for which you have leadership responsibility. Use the leadership style (high risk and low relationship, high task and high relationship, high relationship and low task, or low relationship and low task) that you perceive as the best match for the group in question. Summarize and evaluate your matched leadership.

DEVELOPMENTAL

1. Begin an in-depth investigation of one of the following:

   a. Achievement motivation.

   b. Organizational management.

   c. Creative problem solving.

   d. Job satisfaction.

2. Continue to observe differing characteristics of beginning teachers, experienced teachers, and superior teachers. Hypothesize how supervision might be modified to accommodate such differences.

3. Begin to analyze ways in which your needs, concerns, and motivations change in relation to varying situations and changing circumstances.

REFERENCES

Adams, R. D., and Martray, C. 1981. Teacher development: A study of factors related to teacher concerns for pre, beginning and experienced teachers. Paper presented at the annual meeting of the American Educational Research Association, Los Angeles, April 13.

Blumberg, A. 1980. *Supervisors and teachers: A private cold war,* 2nd ed. Berkeley, Calif.: McCutchan.

Blumberg, A., and Weber, W. A. 1968. Teacher morale as a function of perceived supervisor behavioral style. *Journal of Educational Research 62*:109–113.

Brown, A. F. 1975. Teaching under stress. In B. M. Harris, *Supervisory behavior in education,* 2nd ed. Englewood Cliffs, N.J.: Prentice-Hall, p. 218.

Cawelti, G. 1976. Selecting appropriate leadership styles for instructional improvement—video tape. Alexandria, Va.: Association for Supervision and Curriculum Development.

Clark, C. M., and Joyce, B. R. 1976. Teacher decision making and teacher effectiveness. Paper presented at the annual meeting of the American Educational Research Association, San Francisco.

Clinton, B. C; Glickman, C. D.; and Payne, D. A. 1982. Identifying supervision problems: A guide to better solutions. *Illinois School Research and Development 9* (1).

Copeland, W. D., and Atkinson, D. R. 1978. Student teachers' perceptions of directive and non-directive supervision. *Journal of Educational Research 71:*123–127.

Copeland, W. D. 1980. Affective dispositions of teachers in training toward examples of supervisory behavior. *Journal of Educational Research 74:*37–42.

deCharms, R. 1968. *Personal causation.* New York: Academic Press.

––––––. 1976. *Enhancing motivation: Change in the classroom.* New York: Irvington.

Deci, E. L. 1975. *Intrinsic motivation.* New York: Plenum.

Deci, E. 1982. Motivation. Paper presented to the annual meeting of the Midwest Association of Teachers of Educational Psychology, Dayton, Ohio, October 30.

Drucker, P. 1973. *Management.* New York: Harper and Row, pp. 232–245.

Fuller, F. F. 1969. Concerns of teachers: A developmental conceptualization. *American Educational Research Journal 6* (March):207–226.

Fuller, F. F., and others. 1974. *Concerns of teachers: Research and reconceptualization.* ED 091 439. Austin: Research and Developmental Center for Teacher Education, Texas University.

Gates, P. E.; Blanchard, K. H.; and Hersey, P. 1976. Diagnosing educational leadership problems. *Educational Leadership 33* (February):348–354.

References

Ginkel, K. 1983. Overview of study that investigated the relationship of teachers' conceptual levels and preferences for supervisory approach. Paper presented at the annual meeting of the American Educational Research Association, Montreal, April.

Gordon, S. In press. Developmental supervision: Supervisor flexibility and the post observation conference. Unpublished Ed.D. diss., University of Georgia.

Hersey, P., and Blanchard, K. H. 1977. *Management of organizational behavior,* 3rd ed. Englewood Cliffs, N.J.: Prentice-Hall.

Herzberg, F.; Mausner, B.; and Snyderman, B. 1959. *The motivation to work.* New York: Wiley.

———. 1966. *Work and the nature of man.* New York: World, pp. 137–178.

Hoy, W. K., and Miskel, C. G. 1982. *Educational administration theory, research and practice,* 2nd ed. New York: Random House.

Hunt, D. E., and Sullivan, E. V. 1974. *Between psychology and education.* Hinsdale, Ill.: Dryden Press.

King, N. 1970. Clarification and evaluation of the two-factor theory of job satisfaction. *Psychological Bulletin* 74:18–31.

Kohlberg, L. 1969. Stage and sequence: The cognitive-developmental approach to socialization. In D. Goslin, ed., *Handbook of socialization theory and research.* Chicago: Rand McNally.

Lorch, N. 1981. Teaching assistant training: The effects of directive and non-directive supervision. Unpublished Ed.D. diss., University of California, Santa Barbara.

Lortie, D. C. 1975. *Schoolteacher: A sociological study.* Chicago: University of Chicago Press.

Maslow, A. H. 1954. *Motivation and personality.* New York: Harper & Row.

Morgan, M. 1984. Reward-induced decrements and increments in intrinsic motivation. *Review of Educational Research 54*(1): 5–30.

Ouchi, W. G. 1981. *Theory 2: How American business can meet the Japanese challenge.* Reading, Mass.: Addison-Wesley.

Pajak, E. F., and Glickman, C. D. 1984. Teachers' perceptions of supervisory communication: Control versus information. Paper presented at the annual meeting of the American Educational Research Association, New Orleans, April.

Pajak, E. F., and Seyfarth, J. J. 1983. Authentic supervision reconciles the irreconcilables. *Educational Leadership 40*(8): 20–23.

Piaget, J. 1965. *The moral judgement of the child*. New York: Free Press–Macmillan.

Riley, J. F. 1980. Creative problem solving and cognitive monitoring as instructional variables for teaching training in classroom problem solving. Unpublished Ed.D. diss. University of Georgia.

Rossicone, G. In press. Investigation of individual variables which affect supervisory approach. Unpublished Ed.D. diss., St. John University.

Schmidt, G. L. 1976. Job satisfaction among secondary school administrators. *Educational Administration Quarterly 12:* 68–85.

Sergiovanni, T. 1966. Factors which affect satisfaction and dissatisfaction of teachers. *Journal of Educational Administration 5:* 66–82.

Silver, P. F. 1982. Synthesis of research on teacher motivation. *Educational Leadership 39*(3):551–555.

Skinner, B. F. 1971. *Beyond freedom and dignity*. New York: Knopf.

Suzuki, S. 1970. *Zen mind, beginner's mind*. New York: Weather Hill.

Vudovich, D. 1976. The effects of four specific supervision procedures on the development of self-evaluation skills in preservice teachers. Paper presented at the annual meeting of the American Educational Research Association. ERIC Reproduction No. ED 146-224.

Wilsey, L., and Killion, J. 1982. Making staff development programs work. *Educational Leadership 40*(1):36–43.

Zonca, P. H. 1973. A case study exploring the effects of an intern teacher of the condition of openness in a clinical supervisory relationship. Unpublished Ph.D. diss., University of Pittsburgh, 1973. *Dissertation Abstracts International 33:* 658–59A.

PART III

CONCLUSION

Critical vocabulary words in Part III included *supervisor behaviors; non-directive, collaborative,* and *directive approaches; skill practice;* issues of *control* versus *information; motivation* and *choice;* and human variation, development, and complexity. The purpose of Part III was to equip the supervisor with the interpersonal skills and behaviors needed to assist individual and groups of teachers to develop their own thinking capacities. The question behind Part III was not how a supervisor motivates teachers to improve instruction but, rather, how the supervisor provides choice to teachers to motivate themselves. The matching of interpersonal behaviors and approaches to teachers' developmental levels is one skill base for doing this. Having gained knowledge and interpersonal skills, we can now turn to the third dimension of supervision as a developmental function: the technical skill dimension.

Figure III–2 shows us where we've been and where we are going. We have concluded our discussion of the second dimension of interpersonal skills. One more prerequisite dimension remains before we apply the function of supervision to the five task areas.

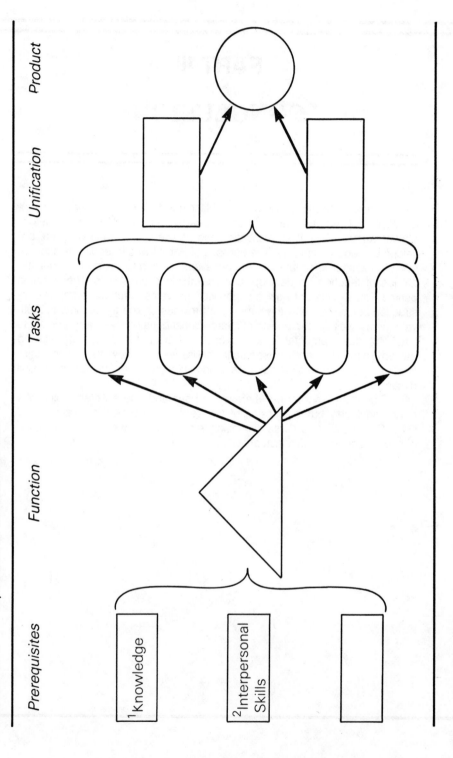

FIGURE III-2 Supervision for Successful Schools

Prerequisites Function Tasks Unification Product

¹Knowledge

²Interpersonal Skills

PART IV

Technical Skills

INTRODUCTION

The supervisor who knows about characteristics of successful schools, the norms that mediate against success, and the ways teacher development contrasts with optimal adult development can begin to formulate a supervisory belief system that becomes a reality when interpersonal and technical skills of supervision are applied in practice.

The previous section matched nondirective, collaborative, and directive interpersonal skills in working with developmental levels of individuals and groups of teachers. Part IV deals with the technical supervisory skills needed in working with teachers to assess, plan, observe, research, and evaluate the instructional program. Understanding schools and relating well to teachers are necessary components, but technical skills are equally important for accomplishing the tasks of supervision.

CHAPTER ELEVEN

Assessing and Planning Skills

This chapter deals with technical skills of assessing and planning. Assessing and planning skills are useful to a supervisor in setting goals and activities for herself as well as for others. The chapter begins with personal organization of time—assessing one's current use of professional time and then planning and managing the use of future time. It goes on to focus on techniques for organizational planning for the improvement of instruction. Whether the changes to be made are in curriculum development, in-service education, or direct assistance to teachers, a supervisor's forethought about the sequencing and organization of the program can increase the chances of successful implementation.

Assessing and planning are two sides of the same coin. *Assessing* involves determining where you and your staff have been and where you and your staff currently are. *Planning* includes deciding where you want to go and choosing the path you and your staff hope to traverse in order to reach that destination. Until you are certain of the origination and destination of your travel, a map is useless. Once you are certain, a route can be created.

Personal Plans

I recently returned from a consulting visit to a school system where I met with several first-year principals. The purpose of the consultation was for the new principals to talk to me privately about their beginning experiences and to discuss possible changes that might improve their situations.

One principal stated she was averaging three hours a day observing and participating in classrooms. Her major concern was with the amount of waiting time students were experiencing. Most of her teachers had divided their heterogeneous classrooms into numerous small groups. The principal wondered whether, if certain classes were grouped homogeneously to begin with, there might be fewer groups and less waiting time. We discussed the possible consequences of such a major change and whether less radical changes within the existing instructional program might be better. She left the session with a plan to discuss with the faculty the issue of waiting time and student grouping at the next school meeting.

The second beginning principal I met with told me his major problem was getting out of his office to visit teachers. He wanted to be with his staff but found that paperwork, phone calls, and student discipline referrals kept him trapped in the office. He could find barely an hour a day to talk with staff and visit classrooms. Furthermore, the one-hour time outside the office was often interrupted by the school secretary calling him back with urgent business. We proceeded to discuss why he was trapped in his office and what changes might be made.

After hearing about the second principal's situation, I realized the second principal had no more constraints on his time than did the first principal, who was averaging three hours a day visiting classrooms. Both had schools of comparable size in the same neighborhood. They worked for the same superintendent and had identical job responsibilities. Yet one principal was functioning as a supervisor attending to instructional improvement while the other one was only functioning minimally in the realm of supervision. It seemed that the real difference between the two principals was not their intentions to function as supervisors but their ability to assess and plan' professional time to correspond with professional intentions. Let's look at the use of professional time.

Assessing Time

To organize future time, we need to assess our current use of time. This can be done by keeping a daily log for five to ten consecutive school days. Those supervisors who keep detailed appointment books might need only to return to their books at midday and at the end of the day to add notations on what actually transpired. Those who do not operate with such planned schedules can keep a daily log to be filled out at midday and at the end of the day. The log should be simple and should require only a few minutes to fill out. It might look like this:

Monday

| 8:00– 8:50 | Walked halls, visited teachers and custodians |
| 8:50– 9:20 | Conference with parent |

ASSESSING AND PLANNING SKILLS

9:20– 9:35	Phone call from textbook salesman
9:35–10:30	Emergency, covered for sick teacher
10:30–12:00	Worked on class schedules—made 3 phone calls, received 5 phone calls
12:00–12:30	Ate in cafeteria with teachers
12:30–12:35	Wrote morning log
12:35–12:55	Met with textbook salesman
12:55– 1:30	Classroom visitation of Mr. Tadich
1:30– 2:30	Meeting at superintendent's office
2:30– 3:00	Helped supervise school dismissal
3:00– 3:15	Talked with parents
3:15– 4:00	Faculty meeting
4:00– 4:15	Talked with teachers informally
4:15– 4:50	Answered mail
4:50– 5:00	Wrote afternoon log

After at least five days (preferably ten) the supervisor can analyze his or her current use of time by subsuming daily events in the log under large categories of time consumption. Figure 11–1 shows a sample categorical scheme.

Before transferring the daily log entries onto the supervisor time consumption chart, the supervisor should look at his or her job description and determine how his or her time *should* be spent according to job priorities. Which categories of supervisory involvement ought to receive the most attention? The supervisor can indicate approximate percentages according to this ideal use of time. After making an ideal list of time use, he or she can then write in actual time on the consumption charts, add up total time for each category, and then find the actual percentage of time being consumed for each category. He or she then has a comparison between preferred and actual consumption of time. The comparison might look like this:

Preferred Time	*Actual Time*
Paperwork—10%	25%
Phone calls—5%	6%

FIGURE 11-1 Supervisor Time Consumption Chart

	Monday	Tuesday	Wednesday	Thursday	Friday	Total	%
Paperwork							
Phone calls							
Private conference							
students							
parents & community							
faculty							
auxiliary personnel							
central office							
others							
Group meetings							
students							
parents & community							
faculty							
auxiliary personnel							
central office							
others							
Classroom visits							
School hall and ground visits							
Private time for thinking							
Miscellaneous: emergencies							

Private conferences—25%	25%
Students—5%	10%
Parents—3%	5%
Faculty—10%	5%
Auxiliary—3%	1%
Central office—1%	1%
Others—3%	3%
Group meetings—25%	28%
Students—2%	5%
Parents—5%	2%
Faculty—15%	7%
Auxiliary—1%	6%
Central office—1%	8%
Others—1%	0%
Classroom visits—25%	10%
School hall and ground visits—5%	2%
Private time for thinking—3%	1%
Miscellaneous visits—2%	3%

This comparison of time was that of the second principal, who complained about the inability to get out of his office. The comparison showed that he was indeed spending much more time in the office (10% perferred, 25% actual) and much less time on classroom visits (25% perferred, 10% actual). Further discrepancies were noted in considerably more time spent in private conferences with students (5% preferred, 10% actual) and group meetings with central office (1% preferred, 8% actual).

Changing Time Allocations: Planning

With this information on preferred and actual time use in front of the supervisor, he or she can decide what changes realistically can be made to attain the goal of increasing visitation time with teachers. The supervisor can consider a range of options to increase teacher visitation time. Some possibilities might be:

Paperwork: Delegate more clerical work to secretary, aides, or assistants. Schedule paperwork for uninterrupted hours after school.

Private conferences: Spend less time disciplining students by setting more stringent procedures for teacher referrals of students to office.

Group meetings: See if central office meetings could be short-ened or scheduled after school hours.

Classroom visits: Increase classroom visits from one to two periods a day. Set up backup system with secretary to cover all but real emergencies when in the classroom. Schedule visits for a set time each day.

Naturally, the supervisor cannot hope to achieve exact con-gruence between preferred and actual time use, but he can come closer to his preference. Some time constraints, such as the time of central office meetings, probably are not under the principal's con-trol. There are other factors over which he has direct control: when he will meet parents, accept phone calls, do paperwork, and accept student referrals. The key to future planning of time use is to accept the limitations that exist and work on those time periods that can be altered.

The first part of a plan to make actual use of time closer to preferred time use is to answer the question: "What is the objec-tive?" A sample response might be, "To double classroom visitation time." The second part of the plan is to answer the question, "What actions need to be taken?" A sample response might be: "(a) Sched-ule set times each day for two classroom observations; (b) schedule uninterrupted paperwork in two two-hour blocks of time after school." The third part of the plan is to answer the question, "When will these activities be done"? Sample responses might be: "(a) Classroom visits from 9 to 11 A.M. Monday and Wednesday and 1:00 to 2:30 P.M. Tuesday and Thursday; (b) paperwork scheduled for Monday and Friday 3:00 to 5:00 P.M." The fourth part of the plan is to answer the question, "What resources will be needed to imple-ment the activities"? Sample responses might be: "(a) Explain to secretary the need to protect uninterrupted times; (b) discuss with faculty the change and rationale behind my new schedule and ar-range classroom visitation schedule." The fifth and final part of the plan is to answer the question, "How will the success of the goal be evaluated?" A sample response might be, "Check whether the new schedule was followed and, after two weeks, review daily log to see if time in classrooms has doubled."

We could become more elaborate in our planning techniques by developing a flow chart (see Figure 11–2). Although flow charts look impressive, they are not necessary for simple plans. When we look at more complex planning, however, keep flow charts in mind. As long as we can answer the five questions dealing with (1) objec-tive, (2) activities, (3) time deadlines, (4) resources, and (5) evalua-

ASSESSING AND PLANNING SKILLS

tion, then implementation can proceed. If we cannot answer any of the five questions, however, then the plan is incomplete. For example, if we know our objective but don't know what activities, resources, or evaluation to use, then we are still not sure of what to do. On the other hand, if we know our objective, activities, and resources, but don't know how to evaluate our success, we will be acting without any knowledge of results.

As we move from assessment and planning of personal change to assessment and planning of faculty improvement, the elements to be considered become more complex and planning becomes more detailed. Other techniques for planning may be necessary. Let's use a "wild" analogy. When a naturalist is tracking a single large elephant, she can basically track the beast by herself; but when the

FIGURE 11–2   Flow Chart for Increasing Classroom Visits

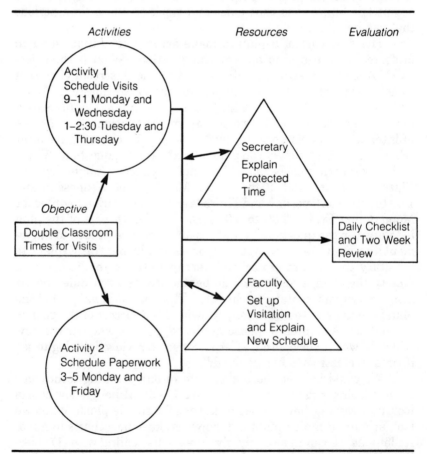

naturalist's task expands to tracking three herds of forty-five elephants each, then she needs other people; more equipment (radios, binoculars, cameras, jeeps, and helicopters); and an awareness of multiple potential obstacles (ill staff workers, malfunctioning equipment, rough terrain). This analogy can be extended only so far, as supervisors are not naturalists nor are teaching faculties herds of elephants but the point is that the larger the organizational effort, the more carefully one needs to account for the sequence and the relationships of activities, resources, and evaluation to overall objectives.

Assessing and Planning within the Organization

The five steps of assessing and planning are the same for both personal and organizational plans. Only the complexity and specificity differ. We might think of assessing and planning as a recipe (Bruce and Grimsley 1979). A plan for direct assistance, staff development, curriculum development, or group development has the same elements as a cooking recipe. *We decide our objective:* "to bake sweet potato souffle" (thanks to Ms. Donna Bell for providing this culinary example). Knowing our family's previous history of food preferences, we are confident that if we cook the souffle correctly, they will enjoy it and we will be held in positive regard for at least ten minutes. Next, *we determine the activities and when they will take place.*

Activity 1: Mash 6 cups of cooked sweet potatoes.

Activity 2: Beat into the mashed potatoes: 4 eggs, 1 cup butter, 2 cups sugar, 1 cup milk, 1 teaspoon vanilla.

Activity 3: Spread out in unbuttered pan.

Activity 4: Mix in a separate bowl: 1 cup brown sugar, ⅔ cup flour, 1 cup butter, 1 cup chopped pecans.

Activity 5: Spread this mix (Activity 4) evenly over the potatoes (Activity 3).

Activity 6: Bake at 350° for 1 hour.

With the activities and times determined, *we need to identify resources.* Equipment resources are: an oven, measuring cups, measuring spoons, a large bowl, a pan, a mixing fork, and a spreading knife. Food resources are: potatoes, eggs, butter, sugar, vanilla, brown sugar, flour, pecans, and milk.

Finally, *we will evaluate the success* of our cooking endeavor by the following criteria: Everyone in our family will eat the sweet potato souffle (even Rachel). At least two of the three members (Sara, Jennifer, and Rachel) will ask for seconds. All of them will tell us we're wonderful cooks, and they will volunteer to wash the dishes.

If the supervisor might think of himself as a gourmet of instructional cookery and plan recipes for success, than all staff members will delight in the souffle of instructional improvement. The food analogy has run its course (by now, the reader is probably heading for the refrigerator), and we can turn to assessing and planning within the school context. For purposes of illustration, let's take an example of an elementary reading supervisor who is responsible for developing revised curriculum guides in reading.

Ways of Assessing Need

The first question for the reading supervisor is, "What do we hope to accomplish with a new curriculum guide?" To answer this question, we need to collect information about the past and present state of reading instruction. The supervisor can use multiple ways of assessing need. We will discuss in order: (1) eyes and ears, (2) official records, (3) third-party review, (4) written open-ended survey, (5) check and ranking list surveys, and (6) the Delphi technique.

Eyes and Ears

Talk to teachers, administrators, aides, and anyone else who works directly with the task under consideration. In this case, the supervisor would want to ask teachers and aides individually and in small groups what they believe are the strengths and weaknesses of the curriculum guide. How is it being used? Is it helpful, and in what ways? Where does it break down? When is it not useful?

Official Records

Look at any documents that indicate the current use and effect of the task under consideration. In this case, what do reading achievement test scores show? How about diagnostic reading tests? Are students mastering reading skills, or are there certain areas (comprehension, fluency, vocabulary) that are consistently out of line with others? What about the curriculum guide itself? When was it last revised? What recent knowledge about writing curriculum guides, instructional approaches to readings, and reading topics are not reflected in the current curriculum.

Third-Party Review

Having a neutral outside person review the task area can be helpful. The supervisor might contact a university or central office consultant, a graduate doctoral student, or some other person with expertise to do an investigation and write a report. The third-party person should be provided a clear description of the task (to look at the strengths and weaknesses of the reading curriculum guides), and care should be taken not to bias the third-party person's judgment. The report can then serve as an additional source of objective knowledge, not tied to any special interest in the forthcoming project.

Written Open-Ended Survey

To document and add to the information already received through eyes and ears and official records, a written survey can be administered. Send out a brief questionnaire that asks teachers, aides, administrators, and parents what they think about the current reading curriculum. Keep the survey brief, and word the questions simply without education jargon. Again, an example of a survey is found in Figure 11–3.

Check and Ranking List

After gathering ideas of the strengths and weaknesses of the task at hand from many sources, the supervisor can ask staff to rank the ideas. The supervisor can then compile a group frequency and numerical priority for each idea previously mentioned. For example, if—through eyes and ears, official documents, and open-ended surveys—the supervisor has collected a list of ideas about perceived weakness of the current reading program, she then could disseminate the list back to teachers, aides, and others. The disseminated form might be as shown in figure 11–4. The supervisor can meet with the staff and show the frequency of numbers assigned to each idea and the average score for each item. Those items receiving frequent low scores and/or with the lowest average scores would be the first to focus on when discussing curriculum revisions. The ranking list can be further refined by having the participants do two separate rankings—first, to see how all the ideas rank, and then to rerank a shortened list of prioritized ideas.

FIGURE 11–3   Survey of Reading Curriculum

Explanation: As you may know, this year we are determining changes to be made in our reading curriculum. Would you please take a few minutes to respond to the following questions. Please be frank! We will use the information to rewrite our curriculum guides.

Question 1.   What do you think about the current reading curriculum?

Question 2.   What are the strengths of the current reading curriculum?

Question 3.   What are the weaknesses of the current reading curriculum?

Question 4.   What changes do you believe would improve the reading curriculum?

FIGURE 11–4   Ranking Ideas for Improving Reading Curriculum Guides

---

Directions: The following are the ideas for possible changes that you have suggested. Please prioritize this list by placing the number 1 next to the idea needing the greatest attention, number 2 next to the item needing the next most attention, and so on, until all items are ranked.

_____   Format of the guides.
_____   Readability of the guides.
_____   Activities to go with curriculum objectives.
_____   Objectives and units dealing with reading newspapers.
_____   Objectives and units dealing with reading in other subject areas.
_____   More phonic and word recognition objectives.
_____   Cross-reference units with materials in the classrooms.
_____   Cross-reference objects with fourth-grade competency-based reading test.

Delphi Technique

Another written way to prioritize needs is the Delphi technique developed by the Rand Corporation (Hostrop 1975; Weaver 1971). The technique, originally intended to forecast future trends, is often used for needs assessment. It is a combination of open-ended survey and ranking. The supervisor sends around a problem statement to staff: "We are looking at revisions in the reading curriculum. Write down what you believe needs to be done." The supervisor retrieves the written comments, reproduces everyone's comments, and returns all the comments to the participants. They read the comments and then individually write a synthesis of the various ideas. The supervisor then collects everyone's synthesis and makes a new list of all synthesized ideas. The new list goes back to the participants for ranking. The supervisor collects and computes average and frequency of ratings and then returns the tallies to participants to rerank. This procedure continues until clear priorities emerge.

Planning

After assessing needs and prioritizing ideas, planning proceeds. The steps of operationalizing include objectives, activities, time lines, resources, and evaluation. Techniques of planning include management by objectives (MBO), Gant charts, flow charting, program evaluation and review techniques (PERT), and program planning and budgeting systems (PPBS).

Management by Objectives (MBO)

Most teachers are familiar with classroom performance objectives used in lesson planning. Management by objectives basically involves setting performance objectives for organizational planning (Knezevich 1972). Management objectives make explicit how the goal is to be accomplished. The objective has four elements:

1.   What will be performed?

2.   When will it be performed?

3.   Who will do it?

4.   What will be the criteria of success?

Our example of reading curriculum revisions might contain an overall goal: "The reading faculty will update and revise curriculum guides to better meet the instructional needs of students." The goal provides general intent but does not offer the specifics of how it is to be accomplished. After conducting a needs assessment, the reading faculty might have decided on the following management objective: "By October 15, 1985, all reading teachers will be able to write daily lesson plans that incorporate objectives and activities of the new written curriculum guides."

Notice how the management objective has all four elements: what will be done ("will be able to write in daily lesson plans that incorporate objectives and activities of the new curriculum guide"); when will it be performed ("by October 15, 1985"); who will do it ("reading teachers"); what will be the criteria of success ("*all* reading teachers"). To reach this management objective, management activities are specified, such as

1. A representative teacher from each grade level will read the reading curriculum guides, write notations on changes to be made, and submit the changes to the curriculum council on October 1.

2. By December 1, the curriculum council will review five different formats for writing curriculum guides and approve a single format to be used for all grade levels.

3. The resource center director and staff will read the current guides and recommend a procedure for cross-referencing curriculum units with library and media materials to the council by February 1.

4. By April 1, the director of competency-based education and the council will decide on procedures of cross-referencing the sixth-grade competency reading exam with all lessons contained in the curriculum guides.

5. A reading consultant and four teachers will be selected by the council to do the actual rewriting and reformatting of the curriculum guides in order to have the final guides completed by August 1.

6. On August 28, the consultant, the four curriculum writing teachers, and the council will conduct a half-day in-service session for all reading teachers on the use of the new curriculum guides.

FIGURE 11–5   Revisions of Curriculum Guides

I. Management objective:
   By October 15, 1985, all reading teachers will be able to show on their written daily lesson plans the use of the new curriculum guides.

Management activity
   A. A representative teacher from each grade level will read their reading curriculum guides, write notations on changes to be made, and submit the changes to the curriculum council on October 1.

Procedures
   1. _____ Explain task at first faculty meeting.
   2. _____ Ask grade departments to elect representatives.
   3. _____ Devise questions for representative teachers to use in their notations.
   4. _____ Meet with representatives and review work to be done.
   5. _____ Check on progress of individuals.
   6. _____ Convene council meeting on October 1.

Resources: Meeting room, stipend of $50.00 for each teacher = $200.00 total, two copies of each curriculum guide, written questions mimeographed.

A comprehensive MBO system will have an identification of resources for each management activity. Figure 11–5 is an example of writing a complete management activity, including procedures and resources.

MBO provides a clear description of the system for implementing a goal. It demands that the supervisor think of the necessary steps and time lines for successful completion of the overall task. Time lines can be shown graphically by using a technique called a Gant chart.

Gant Charts

A Gant chart is simply a graph that portrays the beginning and completion dates of each activity involved in completing the overall task (Bishop 1976). As shown in Figure 11–6, the activities for revising the curriculum guides are placed on the left-hand side of the chart. The beginning and ending time for each activity is shown by a black solid line across the time line. The supervisor can refer to the chart at any time to check on the progress of the project and be reminded of what groups and what subtasks should be receiving his or her attention.

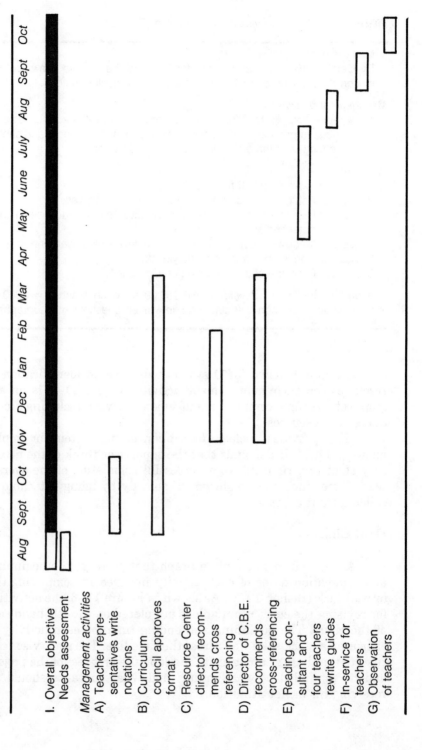

FIGURE 11–6 Gant Chart
Task: Revising Curriculum Guides

Program Evaluation and Review Technique (PERT)

PERT is another planning technique used for large projects that depend on the coordination of many individuals, groups, and subtasks. It shows the interrelationships of activities needed in a large project. It is usually found in conjunction with an MBO system and a Gant chart. The PERT flow chart was developed by the organizers of the Polaris Fleet Ballistic Missile Program in 1958. It enabled federal managers to coordinate the work of hundreds of subcontractors in completing the construction of the ballistic missile program two years ahead of original expectations. Since then it has been adapted to planning in education settings (Case 1969; Cook 1966; Anderson 1975; Bishop 1976).

The supervisor thinks of all the events and activities needed to complete the task. Then she puts those events and activities into a sequence with durations of time. The sequence and duration of events and activities are then flow charted (see Figure 11–7).

FIGURE 11–7 PERT: Revising Curriculum Guides

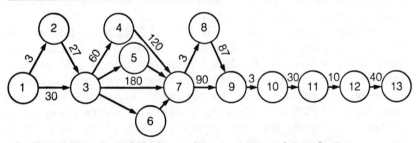

1. Need assessment of faculty, students, parents, and consultants.
2. Select grade-level representatives to write notations on current guides.
3. Curriculum council meeting to assign task of formating the guides.
4. Curriculum council proposes format.
5. Director of competency-based education proposes format.
6. Resource center director proposes format.
7. Curriculum council formalizes format.
8. Select four teachers with consultant to rewrite guides.
9. Curriculum council reviews and approves new guides.
10. Curriculum council plans inservice.
11. In-service held.
12. Council chooses, observes, and meets with teachers to explain rationale and logistics for observations.
13. Observation of teachers' lesson planning.

The circled numbers represent important points (meetings, selections, and reports) on the way to completing the task. The critical path is the straight line. (1) → (3) → (7) → (9) → (10) → (11) → (12) → (13). The circles outside the critical path are activities at work simultaneously with other activities. They must also be carried out in order for the critical decision points to be completed. Circles stand for events such as reports submitted, decisions made, and documents produced. Arrows represent activities such as individual and committee work in progress. The numbers above the arrows ($\overset{30}{\rightarrow}$) are the time (in days) needed to complete the activity.

A PERT chart provides for close monitoring of a project and a clear description of how events and activities fit together. It also displays to persons involved with the project how their own work fits into the overall scheme.

Planning, Programming, Budgeting System (PPBS)

PPBS is a financial accounting system that supplements other planning systems such as MBO and PERT (Alioto and Jungher 1971). Originally a financial planning device used by the U.S. Department of Defense under Robert J. McNamara, PPBS has been adapted to education often under the name Education Resources Management System (ERMS) and Data Based Educational Planning Systems (DEPS). The basic concept is for managers and supervisors to request funds for programs in terms of program outcomes. Traditional requests for school programs have been based on general line items for textbooks, supplies, salaries, and consultants. PPBS is a planning system that shows the cost of a particular program and the expected results of the program in producing changes in student or teacher performance. For example, if a school desires to have 80 percent of all students reach a tenth-grade mathematics achievement level before graduation, then a PPBS plan would respond to the following questions:

What changes in mathematics programs need to be made?

What would be the cost?

To reach the 80 percent objective, how much will a school system need to expend in terms of personnel, materials, facilities, and time?

What alternative plans and costs can be considered to reach the objective?

Eventually the potential grantor of the program (superintendent, federal grant office, or school board) can consider alternative plans and costs and can make a financial decision based on the expected results.

Let's return to our example of revising curriculum guides. After a needs assessment, our objective is that "*all* reading teachers will be able to show on their written daily lesson plans the use of the curriculum guides." We already have shown one plan for achieving this objective (MBO, Gant chart, and PERT flow chart). Now, what will it cost to implement this plan? Let's say it will cost $3,000 in released time, $2,000 in materials and supplies, $500 for in-service, and $500 for a consultant—a total cost of $6,000. What are alternative plans? One plan might be to involve only one representative teacher instead of four, hire no consultants, and produce only half the needed curriculum guides (with the premise that two teachers would share a guide). Making these changes would reduce the cost by $3,500. Obviously, each plan has advantages and disadvantages that need to be explained. The $6,000 expenditure will involve more staff; the $2,500 expenditure will mean that the task will be done largely by central office staff. The degree of teacher acceptance might vary according to the plan chosen. The funding agent will make a decision about monies to be allocated based on an understanding of likely outcome. "Putting your money where your mouth is" is the cliché that best summarizes the PPBS approach.

Planning: To What Extent

Keep in mind that a plan is intended to help you and your staff get where you want to go. It is a *means,* not an end in itself. Planning should not get in the way of doing. The extent of planning should depend on how much detail is needed. Frymier (1980) warns of the dangers of overplanning. Planning can be seductive; drawing circles and wording one's objectives can camouflage inactivity. Most supervisory tasks in schools do not need extensive management objectives, flow charts, graphs, or cost analysis. Providing immediate help only requires a supervisor to pause, think about what needs to be done, and then step out of the office and do it.

Extensive MBO and PERT charts are helpful when the proposed change will take place over a considerable amount of time (half a year or more) and will involve many individuals and groups. Extensive planning helps people remember the stages of a project. It also is helpful when many groups or individuals have overlapping or concurrent responsibilities; plans can help the supervisor know whom to contact, and when. Finally, extensive planning is essential when funding is contingent on such details. It is no coincidence that public school supervisors began writing plans with management objectives, time lines, and flow charts in the late 1960s, when federal funding became more available to schools. The federal government required such specifications as part of any proposal. Now most school superintendents, school boards, and state directors expect to see similar planning devices whenever a major instructional change is contemplated.

A final word about planning: Remember that plans are not ironclad, unchangeable from beginning to end. Plans provide a direction to success; when circumstances make a preplanned activity or event unnecessary or problematic, the supervisor and staff should be flexible enough to make substitutions and alterations. The final goal is to reach the objective, not to stick to a plan that is doomed.

Summary

This chapter has explained the complementary nature of assessment and planning for instructional improvement. It began with examining ways to assess and plan supervisory time. The next topic was assessing and planning organizational change. Assessment techniques discussed were: eyes and ears, official records, third-party review, written open-ended surveys, check and ranking lists, and the Delphi method. Planning techniques discussed were: management by objectives (MBO), Gant charts, program evaluation and review techniques (PERT), and program planning and budgeting systems (PPBS). The last section discussed when to use extensive written and formalized plans.

Assessing and planning skills are generic; they help us to organize our own professional life as well as organize instructional improvement programs that involve many people. Assessing and planning enable us to take stock of present conditions; analyze consequences; and choose events, activities, and resources.

EXERCISES

ACADEMIC

1. Prepare a written summary of the major suggestions of one writer on time management. Discuss how the suggestions can be applied to educational supervision.

2. Describe and compare two program assessment processes successfully used in a public school system and not discussed in this book.

3. Summarize and discuss a description, found in the educational literature, of the Delphi technique applied to an educational needs assessment.

4. Write a paper summarizing and discussing how the program evaluation and review technique (PERT) has been adapted to planning in educational settings.

5. Write a paper reviewing how the program planning and budgeting systems (PPBS) approach has been adapted for decision making in educational settings.

FIELD

1. After using the methods suggested in this chapter for assessing your work time (daily log, time consumption chart, comparison of preferred priorities to actual time spent), write out a personal plan for making actual use of time closer to preferred use. Be sure each of the five questions in a personal improvement plan is answered. Implement your plan over a period of two weeks. At the end of the implementation period, prepare a written evaluation of your plan.

2. Write out a personal work improvement objective. Prepare a flow chart as an aid for reaching your objective. Carry out the activities outlined in your flow chart; then evaluate whether your objective has been met. Write a report analyzing your improvement plan and its implementation. Include a discussion of the utility of the flow chart as part of your improvement effort.

3. Use at least one of the four ways of assessing need within an organization (eyes and ears, official records, third-party review, written open-ended survey) to determine needs within an educational program. Write a report on your assessment. Include a discussion of the assessment process and the needs that were discovered.

4. Participate in a group in which an educational improvement plan is created, using at least two of the following planning techniques: (a) management by objectives (MBO); (b) Gant charts; (c) flow charting; (d) program evaluation and review techniques (PERT); (e) program planning and budgeting systems (PPBS). Prepare a written report on the experience.

5. Interview a leader in business, industry, government, or the military who has had extensive experience with one of the planning techniques listed in the previous exercise. Prepare a report on your interview, including a description of how the technique is used in the interviewee's field and a discussion of how it might be modified for use in an educational setting.

DEVELOPMENTAL

1. Use a Gant chart to plan a long-range personal project. Carry the project through to completion.

2. Volunteer for participation in an educational planning process.

3. Begin an in-depth exploration of what prominent authors in educational supervision have to say about educational assessment and planning.

REFERENCES

Alioto, R. J., and Jungher, J. A. 1971. *Operational PPBS for education: A practical approach to effective decision making.* New York: Harper & Row.

Anderson, S. 1975. *Encyclopedia of educational evaluation.* San Francisco: Jossey-Bass, pp. 290–293.

Bishop, L. J. 1976. *Staff development and instructional improvement: Plans and procedures.* Boston: Allyn and Bacon, p. 229.

Bruce, R. E., and Grimsley, E. E. 1979. Course supplementary reading—introduction to supervision. Unpublished manuscript, University of Georgia.

Case, C. M. 1969. The application of PERT to large-scale educational and evaluation studies. *Educational Technology 9:*79–83.

Cook, D. L. 1966. PERT: *Applications in education.* Cooperative Research Monograph No. 17. Washington, D.C.: U.S. Government Printing Office.

Frymier, J. 1980. Practical principles of educational leadership. Annual Johnnye E. Cox lecture of the Georgia Association of Curriculum and Instructional Supervision, Athens, September.

Hostrop, R. W. 1975. *Managing education for results,* 2nd ed. Homewood, Calif.: ETC Publications.

Knezevich, S. J. 1972. MBO—Its meaning and application to educational administration. *Education 93:*12–21.

Weaver, W. T. 1971. The Delphi forecasting method. *Phi Delta Kappan 52:*267.

SUGGESTIONS FOR ADDITIONAL READING

Anderson, S. 1975. *Encyclopedia of educational evaluation.* San Francisco: Jossey-Bass, pp. 290–293.

Bishop, L. J. 1976. *Staff development and instructional improvement: Plans and procedures.* Boston: Allyn and Bacon, Chap. 8 (PERT).

English, F. W., and Kaufman, R. 1978. *Needs assessment: Concept and application.* Englewood Cliffs, N.J.: Educational Technology Publications.

Harris, B. M. 1975. *Supervisory behavior in education,* 2nd ed. Englewood Cliffs, N.J.: Prentice-Hall, Chap. 3 (PERT, MBO).

Johns, R. L., and Morphet, E. L. 1969. *The economics and financing of education: A systems approach,* 2nd ed. Englewood Cliffs, N.J.: Prentice-Hall (PPBS).

Kaufman, R. A. 1972. *Educational system planning*. Englewood Cliffs, N.J.: Prentice-Hall.

Koerner, T. F. 1972. *PPBS and the school: New system promotes efficiency, accountability*. Washington, D.C.: National School Public Relations Association.

Mager, R. F. 1972. *Goal analysis*. Belmont, Calif.: Fearon (MBO).

Neagley, R. L., and Evans, N. D. 1980. *Handbook for effective supervision of instruction,* 3rd ed. Englewood Cliffs, N.J.: Prentice-Hall, Chap. 12 (MBO).

Weaver, W. T. 1971. The Delphi forecasting method. *Phi Delta Kappan 52:*267.

CHAPTER TWELVE

Observing Skills

Observation seems simple. Anyone with normal vision appears to be observing every moment his or her eyes are open. Why, then, so many books, approaches, and debates about the types and uses of observation for instructional improvement (Beegle and Brandt 1973; Simon and Boyer 1967; Jones and Sherman 1980; Eisner 1981)? As Webster defines it, observation is "(1) an act or the faculty of observing, (2) an act of recognizing and noting a fact or occurrence often involving measurement with instruments . . . (3) a judgment and inference from what one has observed" (Webster 1974, p. 792). Observation is thus the act of noting and then judging. The issue of observation in educational settings has focused on questions of instruments and the basis for inferences. These are some of the issues:

1. Is there a need for an externally structured instrument to measure what is happening in a classroom, or can a supervisor instead use subjective, anecdotal methods of observation?

2. What is the basis for inferring that observed instructional practices such as student behaviors or teacher actions are good or bad?

3. Does inference need to be derived from a numerical accounting of classroom events, or can a supervisor judge effective practices from a feel for the classroom?

These are complicated questions. The purpose of this chapter is to answer them by arriving at general agreement on observation procedures, describing the various methods of observation that can be used by supervisors, and then providing criteria for choosing appropriate observation forms.

Consider the classroom shown in Figure 12–1. If you were an observer of this classroom, what would you say is happening? Of course, one illustration is not enough basis for an observation, but pretend you are seeing this episode for an entire class period. Could you say that the students are behavior problems, discipline is lax, the teacher is not responding to the students' interests, or the teacher is lecturing too much?

If your observations are similar to those listed here, then you have fallen into the *interpretation trap*, which is the downfall of most attempts to help people improve their performance. How would you respond if your evaluator—say, the superintendent of schools—observed you conducting a faculty meeting and later told you that teachers lack respect for you? Your response probably would be a combination of defensiveness ("It isn't so"), confusion ("What do you mean?"), and quiet hostility ("Who are you to say that to me"). The superintendent inadvertently has turned you against him or her, and compliance on your part will be grudging at best.

FIGURE 12–1   Classroom Picture

Observation is a two-part process—first *describing* what has been seen and then *interpreting* what it means. The mind almost simultaneously processes a visual image, integrates that image with previously stored images related to satisfactory and unsatisfactory experiences, and ascribes a value or meaning to that image. If we see a student yawn, our mind signals "boredom." If a teacher yells at students, our mind registers "losing control." A judgment derives from an image or a description of events. We must be aware of splitting that almost simultaneous process, of separating description from interpretation. When we lose the description of the event and retain only the interpretation, we create communication difficulties and obstacles to improvement.

Let's return to the superintendent's interpretation that "teachers lack respect." How much different would your response have been if the description behind the interpretation had been shared with you: "I saw that six of the fifteen teachers arrived late to your faculty meeting." You could agree that, indeed, six members did arrive late; however, you might disagree with the interpretation of lack of respect as arbitrary. You could not only accept that six members had been late, but also do something about it. You cannot do anything about lack of respect, because you don't know what needs to be changed. On the other hand, you can correct lateness and eventually improve the superintendent's interpretation of the teachers' respect. Sharing the description of events is the forerunner of professional improvement. Interpretation leads to resistance. When both parties can agree on what events occurred, they are more likely to agree on what needs to be changed.

Differentiating description from interpretation in observation is so crucial for instructional improvement that we need to refer back to our original illustration of the classroom (Figure 12–1). Look at the picture again and tell what you now see going on. You might say there are three students looking away from the teacher and talking to each other while the teacher stands in front of the room calling on a boy in the front row. Can we agree that this is happening? Probably so, and thus we can *later* judge the rightness or wrongness of the event in regard to student learning. The teacher can more readily change the events of three students talking to each other and two others looking away than he or she can change being "a poor classroom manager." Now, we can move on to alternative ways of describing and interpreting.

Ways of Describing

In describing, the goal is to eliminate any confusion about what is happening. A good check is to use the person off the street as corroborator. One can feel confident about one's description of what is happening in a classroom if a sidewalk passerby could be pulled into the classroom and no matter what his or her credentials, would in fact see what the observer is seeing. If the passerby would have to make any professional judgment—about, say, the rapidity of presentation, the responsiveness to learning style, or the permissiveness of discipline—then it would no longer be a description. If the passerby could describe such happenings as the frequency of teacher-student talk, interruptions, the arrangement of the room, the physical space used by the teacher, and what teacher and students are saying, then the person-off-the-street check has been passed and you may remove the passerby from your mind. (Please do not physically pull people from the street into the classroom—one can only take the neighborhood school concept so far.)

There are many ways to record descriptions. At the end of this chapter there are multiple references to various observation methods and instruments. An observation instrument is a tool for organizing and recording different categories of classroom life. It can be as simple as a single category or as complex as a matrix of dozens of possible coded combinations. For example, an instrument can be used to count the displays on a classroom wall, or to record the hundreds of students' and teachers' verbal and nonverbal interactions.

I have formed a strong bias from using observation instruments as a school principal and working with hundreds of administrators and supervisors. Observation instruments developed for research purposes are usually too time-consuming and cumbersome to be used by practitioners. Most of us do not have the capability or inclination to record twelve categories of behaviors every three seconds and then transcribe the check marks into appropriate columns and ratios. I do not mean to attack instruments such as those developed by Bales (1951), Flanders (1970), or Medley and Mizel (1963). These instruments have contributed immensely to research on effective teaching and have directed practitioners toward instructional practices that need to be emphasized. The instruments have been used by trained, usually paid data collectors, however, and are not as easily used by a single supervisor with thirty or more faculty members to observe. I believe there are ways to adapt the more complicated instruments so they can be used to provide valid descriptions for the nonresearch purpose of describing classroom events to a teacher. A listing and explanation of many adapted ways of observing will follow.

We will first look at quantitative observations, including

categorical instruments, physical indicator instruments, visual diagramming, and space utilization. The second section will deal with qualitative observations, including detached open-ended narrative, participant observation, focused questionnaire observation, and educational criticism.

Quantitative Observations

Quantitative observations are ways of measuring classroom events, behaviors, and objects. Definitions and categories must be precise. Eventually the observations can be used for statistical operations.

Categorical Frequency Instrument

A categorical instrument is a form that defines certain events or behaviors that can be checked off at frequency intervals and then counted. There is nothing mysterious about it. Almost any aspect of classroom life can be isolated and counted. For example, teacher behaviors can be divided into verbal and nonverbal categories. Each category can then be subdivided into countable subcategories. Verbal behaviors could be information-giving, questioning, answering, praising, direction-giving, and scolding. An instrument might look like Figure 12–2.

The observer, after clearly defining each subcategory, would listen to each teacher verbalization and move down the sheet for each different statement made. One check exists for each horizontal line. Most instruments that record teacher verbal behavior also record student verbal behavior, so that verbal interactions between teacher and student and student and student can be analyzed.

Other classroom topics can be observed with categorical instruments. For example, one can focus on student academic behavior. Academic behavior can be divided into two categories: attentive and inattentive. Furthermore, attentive behavior can then be divided into subcategories: (1) watching instructor, (2) working on assignments, and (3) talking to others about the learning task. Inattentive behavior can be broken into: (4) staring off into space, (5) not doing assignments, and (6) talking to others about nonacademic matters. The instrument would then look like Figure 12–3.

The observer would pick ten students at random and follow them throughout the period for one-minute observations at random intervals. Each one-minute observation would result in a check for what each student was seen to be doing. Therefore, each horizontal

FIGURE 12–2   Teacher Verbal Behaviors

	Information Giving	Questioning	Answering	Praising	Direction Giving	Scolding
1.		X				
2.		X				
3.	X					
4.	X					
5.	X					
6.	X					
7.			X			
8.			X			
9.	X					
10.	X					
11.			X			
12.			X			
13.	X					
14.	X					
15.	X					
16.	X					

FIGURE 12–3   Student Academic Behavior

	Attentive			Inattentive		
	1) Watching	2) Doing	3) Talking	4) Not Watching	5) Not Doing	6) Talking
1.	XXXXX		X			XX
2.	XXX	XXXX		X		X
3.		XXXX	XX	XXX	X	
4.						
5.						
6.						
7.						
8.						
9.						
10.						

FIGURE 12–4   On-Task Behavior

	Attentive to Task	Inattentive/Passive	Inattentive/Active
11:00	XXXXXX	XXX	X
11:10	XXXX	XXXX	XXX
11:20	XXXXX	XXXX	X
11:35	XXXXXXXX	X	X
11:40	XXXXXXXXX	X	

line would contain ten checks. A slightly different version of this instrument could be used to record student on-task behavior, broken into categories of attentive to task, inattentive but passive (nondisruptive), and inattentive-active (disruptive) (see Figure 12–4).

As long as the categories can be precisely defined so that the supervisor and teacher know what is to be observed, the instrument serves its purpose of providing a description of events. Every ten minutes, the observer could take a one-minute sample of the same ten students. From the foregoing sample, the observer readily could share with the teacher the changing pattern of on-task behavior and discuss the circumstances that might explain an increase in attentive behavior.

The preceding categorical frequency instruments are not suitable for research purposes unless they have been developed further for interrater reliability and validity. However, if supervisor and teacher find the information gathered useful for their purpose, then they should use the instruments.

Physical-Indicator Instruments

Physical-indicator instruments are usually of the yes/no type: Either the indicator does or does not exist. For example, an instrument focused on the physical classroom might be as shown in Figure 12–5.

A physical-indicator instrument of the classroom is simple to record. As a descriptor, it is relatively value- or interpretation-free. For example, if indicator 6 is checked no, it means there is litter on the classroom floor. In discussing this information with the teacher, the supervisor might find that litter on the floor is all right since students are assigned to cleaning up after school. On the other hand, it may not be all right if the teacher was unaware of the litter and had not noticed that students were not keeping their desk areas clean at all times. The supervisor's check, whether yes or no, should not prejudge desirability but should allow for clarification, later judgment of desirability, and teacher action when appropriate.

FIGURE   12–5   Physical Classroom

Classroom	Yes	No	Uncertain
1. Walls and floors clear of graffiti and blemishes.			
2. Student displayed materials.			
3. Teacher displayed materials.			
4. Student materials on display are less than four weeks old.			
5. Teacher materials on display are less than four weeks old.			
6. Floors clear of litter at conclusion of class.			
7. Student resource materials filed in storage area.			
8. Teacher resource materials filed in storage area.			
9. "In" and "Out" box for student papers clearly marked.			
10. Checkout system posted for classroom library.			

Performance-Indicator Instrument

A performance-indicator instrument also calls for a yes/no response, but the items focus on teacher or student actions, either observed or not. Figure 12–6 is an example of a performance indicator derived from the teacher performance assessment instrument used to assess beginning teachers by the Georgia Department of Education (Capie et al. 1979).

The observer sits in on a classroom session, reviews student and teacher work, talks with students and teachers, and then checks whether the descriptors were evident or not. Did the teacher ask learners questions to help identify learning problems? Was there evidence that progress results were used by students to determine further study for future tests? Did learners receive oral or written feedback on their unit tests? Were individual conferences conducted? Descriptors such as these provide for the occurrence but not the frequency of the occurrence. For example, an observer would check yes if individual conferences were held, regardless of whether the teacher held two or thirty conferences. Frequencies or degrees of performance can be made by changing the response from yes or no to an amount (see Figure 12–7). The change from yes/no to amount provides further precision.

Remember that descriptors for observation purposes should not imply a prejudged standard. Whether a teacher holds confer-

FIGURE 12–6   Illustration

Indicator communicates with individual learners about their needs and progress.

Item	*Response*

a. Classroom questioning is used to˙help learn-   Yes _____ No _____
ers identify learning problems.
Explanation: Many types of oral classroom
questioning techniques may be used by a
teacher. The teacher may question a student
to find out whether the student understands
or to determine areas of difficulty. Another
method of questioning is often referred to as
the Socratic approach.

> After adding 14 and 17 and getting a sum of
> 21, the child is asked how he proceeded with
> the problem.
> *Student:*   First I added 7 and 4.
> *Teacher:*   What is their sum?
> *Student:*   11.
> *Teacher:*   How many 10s is that and many 1s?
> *Student:*   It's one 10 and one 1.
> *Teacher:*   What do you do with the one 10?
> *Student:*   Oh, I see. I need to add it to the 10s.

Learning problems are difficulties encountered
during the unit of study.

b. Progress check results are used to help   Yes _____ No _____
learners identify learners' problems.
Explanation: Feedback on progress checks
is given to students during the unit.

c. Learners are given feedback on summative   Yes _____ No _____
test scores.
Explanation: Learners receive feedback on
their unit tests.

d. Conferences are conducted with individual   Yes _____ No _____
students to discuss learning or motivational
problems.
Explanation: Teacher discusses individual
problems in private conferences with the student. One-to-one discussions may occur in
or out of the classroom.

FIGURE 12-7   Frequency of Performance Indicators

	Frequency			
Performance Indicators	*10–25% of Students*	*25–50% of Students*	*50–75% of Students*	*50–100% of Students*
Learners given feedback on summative test scores				
Conferences conducted with individual students to discuss learning or motivational performance				

ences with 25 percent or 100 percent of students, it is neither good nor bad until supervisor and teacher discuss the circumstances surrounding the evidence.

Visual Diagramming

Visual diagramming is another way to portray what is occurring in a classroom. Videotaping a classroom captures the closest representative picture of actual occurrences. Without videotapes, however, there are other ways to portray observations such as verbal interactions among teachers and students and how a teacher uses space. After diagramming the occurrence, the supervisor and the teacher can view the picture and then analayze the events.

Classroom verbal interactions can be done by drawing arrows symbolizing verbal statements between members in a classroom (see Figure 12–8). The observer can use six separate sheets of this diagram and fill out one sheet for each time sample of five minutes spaced throughout the hour. Each arrow drawn on the diagram would indicate a full statement directed to another person. The arrows are numbered in the sequence of statements. After diagramming, the observer would then have information on the frequency of individual student interaction, the amount of interaction with different areas of the room, which students triggered interactions among others, and which students were excluded. For illustration purposes, if the diagram was a sample consistent with the other five samples of the classroom period, the observer would be able to state some of the following conclusions:

1.   Interaction is mainly directed toward the left aisle and front row.

2. There is almost no attention to the last two rows in the back of the room or the two rows on the right.

3. Of fourteen interactions, twelve included the teacher, two were between students.

Such diagramming is easier to follow with small groups and when students are not moving around the classroom. Class activi-

FIGURE 12–8   Diagram of Verbal Interaction, 9:10–9:15

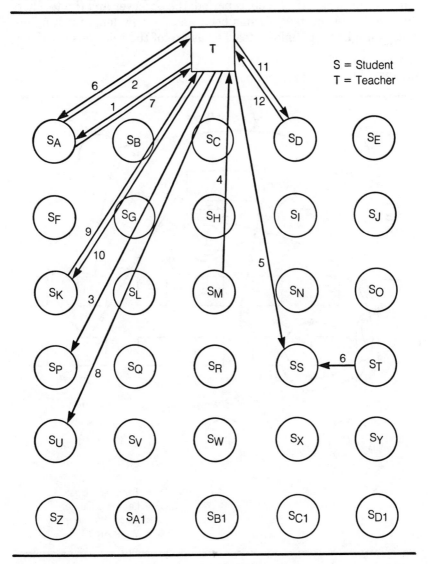

ties such as teacher lecturing interspersed with questions and answers or classroom discussions would be instructional sessions appropriate for diagramming. Another type of diagramming is flow charting teacher space utilization, which follows the teacher's movement throughout the classroom. A sketch of the physical classroom is done first; then the observer follows the teacher by using arrows on the sketch (see Figure 12–9)

Figure 12–9 illustrates a period of reading instruction. The arrow follows the teacher with each movement and is labeled with the time on the clock. After a class period, the observer and the teacher can see where the teacher has been and for how long. Such information might help make a teacher aware of the relationship of his

FIGURE 12–9   Teacher Space Utilization

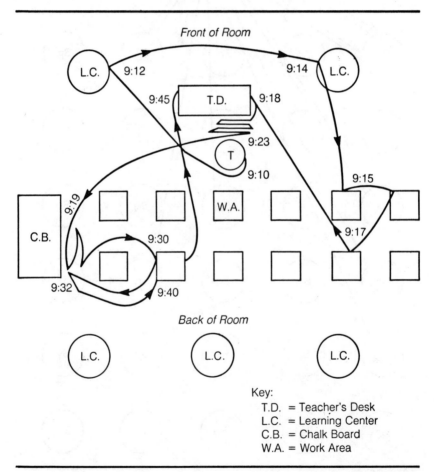

space utilization to concerns of classroom management and instruction. For example, in Figure 12–9 there is much physical presence in the front and on the left side of the classroom, with no presence at the rear learning centers or the middle work area.

Quantitative and Qualitative Instruments

Structured forms used to record categorical frequencies, physical indicators, performance indicators, and visual diagrams all measure classroom occurrences. Categorical forms can measure the amount of verbal, nonverbal, on-task, or off-task behaviors of teachers and students. One can derive percentages, ratios, and means of total and type of behaviors (total teacher talk, ratio of teacher to student talk, breakdown of amount of teacher questions, directions, answers, and so on). The performance-indicator instruments are a measure of occurrence one time (yes/no) or frequency of time. For example, a performance indicator entitled "feedback on tests" can be measured by teacher-written comments. Therefore, the observer looks for teacher-written comments on tests and possibly at the number of tests. Diagramming events in classrooms is another way to count occurrences, lengths of occurrences, and placement of occurrences. For example, the observer can record how much time a teacher spends in different areas of the classroom and the frequency with which the teacher repeats certain walking patterns. All these instruments are quantitative in that they isolate occurrences in the classroom, provide a measurement standard for compiling the amount of occurrences, and lend themselves to further statistical treatment. Structured instruments enable the observer to know precisely what she is looking for prior to entering the classroom.

There are alternative means of observing based on not knowing exactly what is to be recorded. These are called qualitative or descriptive forms of observation. The observer goes into the classroom with a general focus, or no focus at all, and records events as they occur. The events are not made to fit into a specific category, nor are they measured. Only after the recording of events does the observer rearrange her observations into themes. Such recording of observations defies the use of an instrument (an instrument is technically a measurement device). Instead, qualitative observations record the complexity of classroom life. Suppose two supervisors go into the same classroom. Supervisor A fills out a quantitative instrument on interaction; Supervisor B qualitatively describes classroom life. They both observe the teacher asking: "Why did Britain go to war in Argentina? Doesn't anyone know? What a bunch of dummies." Supervisor A listens and places two check marks in the teacher question box and another check in the teacher statement box. Supervisor B writes: "Ms. Egghart smiles and asks if anyone knows why Britain went to war. With no response she asks if anyone understands the question. She looks up, rolls her eyes, throws up her hands and says 'what a bunch of dummies.' The students smile and laugh. She laughs with them."

	Question	Statements	Directions
11	X		
12	X		
13		X	

The quantitative observation reveals the *amount* and ratios of teacher questions and statements; the qualitative instrument reveals the *nature* of teacher questions, statements, and relations. Both observations are correct. However, one observation reduces the amount of information into fixed categories; the other builds a range of description to be compiled later into common, emerging themes.

Qualitative Observations

There are several types of qualitative observations. We will look at detached open-ended narrative, participant observation, focused questionnaire observation, and educational criticism. These observations can be used by a supervisor to provide a broad and complex recording of classroom life.

Detached Open-Ended Narrative

Detached open-ended narrative occurs when the supervisor steps into a classroom and records every person, event, or material that attracts his attention. At the start the pages are empty, without questions, indicators, or categories. The heading might simply say:

```
┌─────────────────────────────────────────────────────────┐
│                                                           │
│                   Open-Ended Narrative                    │
│                                                           │
│   Observation Teacher:_____Time ____Observer_____     │
│                                                           │
└─────────────────────────────────────────────────────────┘
```

The recorder then has the task of writing, writing, writing. . . A sample of such an observation might read:

> Students begin arriving at 10:13; the teacher is at his desk correcting papers. The bell rings at 10:15 to begin third period. Students keep arriving. Mr. X gets up from his desk to begin class at 10:25. In the meantime, students have put away their school bags and are awaiting instruction, except three girls in the back corner who are talking, combing their hair, and spreading the contents of their pocketbooks on their desks. Five minutes after Mr. X begins, he talks to them and they put away combs and pocketbooks. Mr. X describes the activities for the day but then cannot find his prepared handouts. After two minutes of looking, he finds the papers in his desk drawer.
>
> The intercom comes on at 10:30 with two announcements by the principal. Mr. X gives the assignments, and the class begins to read at 10:33. Two students are reprimanded for talking, and occasional student talk can be heard as Mr. X moves around and reviews yesterday's homework with students. He talks with twelve students before asking for class attention at 10:45. He then lectures on the classification of insects. The overhead projection on the board is difficult for students in the back to read. One student asks if he can darken the lights. . . .

With practice the observer can write in shorthand to keep up with the flow of events. It is impossible to record all that could possibly be seen and heard in a classroom. The observer constantly must scan the entire classroom and decide what is significant.

Participant Open-Ended Observation

Participant open-ended observation occurs when the supervisor becomes a functioning part of the classroom (Spradley 1980). She assists in the instruction, helps students with questions, uses classroom materials, and talks with teacher and students. Being involved in the classroom gives the supervisor an inside-out view of the classroom different from that of the detached observer who tries to be invisible and keep away from students and teachers. Obviously, events cannot be written down as they occur if the supervisor is engaged in talking, moving, and assisting. Instead, she must write between pauses in the action. She carries the observation form on a clipboard so that notes can be taken on the run.

The participant observer takes sketchy notes (catch phrases and words) during classroom time so that afterward he can write in greater detail. These quick notes serve to remind the observer of the situation that he will describe more fully after the observation period is over. The following is an example of such short notes.

Teacher X directs students into study groups.

John B. does not understand the assignment. I work with him on organizing the theme of a play.

Sally T. and Ramona B. are wandering around. I ask them if they need help; they say no and leave the room (ask teacher about this).

Sondra and her group are ready to role play their theme. I listen as they read through their parts.

Steven's group is stuck; he doesn't know how to find materials on historic buildings. I suggest calling the town historic society.

Susan is not participating at all—looking at *Teen Magazine*. The rest of the group just leaves her alone (I wonder why?).

The filmstrip shown has everyone's attention.

Teacher B dismisses the class. I overhear a student say, "This class goes so quickly, I wish other [classes] were as much fun."

These are some notes from a fifty-minute classroom period. Much more happened in the classroom than is noted, but the observer picks up insights from his involvement. The supervisor can later fill in details—the two girls leaving the classroom, the specifics of John's confusion about the theme, Susan's absorption in *Teen Magazine*.

Focused Questionaire Observation

Qualitative observation can be done in a more focused manner by having general topics to use in recording events. An observer seeks information about specific questions. In order to answer the questions, the observer writes pertinent evidence. For example, Harris (1975, pp. 364–376) has developed a detached observation questionnaire that has as its topics: (1) classroom, (2) teacher, (3) pupil, and (4) lesson. Figure 12–10 are sample questions taken from each category.

An observer enters the classroom with questions in hand and looks for the answers. Some questions lend themselves to detached observations; others demand participant observations. For example, the question, "What shows that the teacher has a warm, friendly relationship with pupils?" could be answered by participant observation, such as: "Overheard three students saying how nice Ms. Y is. Noticed how Ms. Y put her hand on the shoulders of five different students when speaking to them." The question "How is the classroom made attractive?" could be answered by detached observation: "Classroom freshly painted, bulletin boards have recent work. Student art work is framed and evenly spaced." It is the task of the observer to respond to these questions with descriptions of the evidence.

Educational Criticism

Elliott Eisner (1979) has developed an approach to observation that merges detached and participant observation with description and interpretation. Observers are trained to look at the classroom as an art critic might look at a painting. Just as a person would have to accummulate the experience of viewing numerous

FIGURE 12–10   Focused Questionnaire

Topic 1: Classroom
How is the classroom made attractive?

Topic 2: Teacher
What shows that the teacher has a warm, friendly relationship with the pupils?

Topic 3: Pupil
What indicates that pupils know what they are doing and why they are doing it?

Topic 4: Lesson
How do classroom and homework assignments indicate that consideration is given to, and use made of, resources of the community and real-life situations of pupils?

---

paintings and become knowledgeable in the history and variations of particular art forms to be a critic, so must an educator become familiar with many types of classrooms and forms of instruction to be an education critic.

Eisner believes classroom observations can be done via the same procedures of criticism. He calls the needed educational expertise "connoisseurship." Just as a wine connoisseur can look at the color, viscosity, smell, and taste of a wine to form specific judgments about its overall quality, so can an educational connoisseur make judgments about the specifics of classroom events and the overall quality of classroom life.

Eisner argues that supervisors can develop educational connoisseurship by finding what the classroom *means* to the participants. The education critic attempts to take the perception of students and teachers in viewing the influence of the classroom environment, events, and interactions and then makes the hidden meaning of the classroom known to the participants to see whether they agree. Teachers and students may be so involved in the classroom that they are unaware of the meaning of what they do. The participant observer attempts to describe and interpret events through their eyes.

The following are excerpts from an observation made by an education critic (Knowlton 1984, pp. 80–82):

> The sparsely furnished, drab, grimy classroom filled with students rapidly after the bell rang. The floor of the room caught one's attention because it characterized the entire atmosphere. The faded tile covering appeared to have never been thoroughly cleaned. There was a buildup of dirt mixed with old wax all around the ends of the floor where it met the walls. Four long fluorescent tube light fixtures were suspended from the rather high ceiling. In the upper reaches of the ceiling were exposed steel beam supports and two curious thin strips of a lighter weight metal dangling, unattached at one end from the ceiling. The inevitable alphabet strip above the chalkboard behind the teacher's desk stood out as the newest addition to the environment.
>
> Rows of student desks faced the chalkboards and the teacher's desk was located front-center. On the same wall as the room's only door was a large sheet of posterboard on which was depicted a form of student progress record. There was no key included to interpret the mean-

ing of the horizontal rows of outlined and solidly filled-in boxes beside student names. A shop-worn wooden box with three sections was resting in an old chair in the back of the room. The orange enamel exterior was badly chipped and scratched alluding to heavy usage of the box. Within the three sections of the box were stacks of folders labeled with student names. Also located in the rear of the room was the only place for students to work other than their desks. This was a dilapidated wooden table with three chairs. Adding to the bleakness of the room was the wall of windows which had been painted a third way from the top with runny green paint.

In working with the first small group at the low table, the teacher stood near the door. A broken yardstick was used to point to a list of words on a chart positioned on top of the file cabinet beside the door. This was a rather awkward location for such an instructional aid. The students had to look up about four feet above their eye level at the table in order to read the chart. New words on the chart which might have spelling or pronunciation exceptions were noted by the teacher as being "sight words." Students moved fairly fast through the steps of writing, spelling aloud, and reading the words from the list. The students read the words aloud to themselves as they wrote them in their tablets at the table. They then proceeded to "proof and correct" their spelling of the words as they compared them with the list atop the file cabinet.

Notice how language is expository, nontechnical, and elaborated; "the drab, grimy, classroom," "shop-worn wooden box," "runny green paint." The writing is intended to capture the tone or feel of the room so that the observation can be used to verify the particulars ("wooden box") and the general aspects of classroom life ("adding to the bleakness . . ."). Education critics record their information by playing both roles of distant and participant observer—distant observer by being apart from the classroom and participant observer by listening to students and teachers talk with each other to uncover further insights into the participant's perceptions of the classroom.

At first glance, an education critic would seem to differ little from the observer mentioned in the beginning of this chapter. That observer failed to distinguish between interpretation and description and instead wrote what he or she liked or disliked ("the class-

room is a mess"). However, the education critic knows the difference. The critic has carefully recorded descriptions intermingled
with interpretations derived from the particpants' perspective. The
education critic has caught the atmosphere (which later will be
given to the participants to verify); the nondiscriminating evaluator is left with only his or her own judgments of events.

Types and Purposes of Observations

Figures 12–11 illustrates the types of observation available to
a supervisor. The purpose of the observation should determine the
type, method, and role of observation. The categorical-frequency
observation is a quantitative method used by a detached observer
for the purpose of counting, totaling, and statistically analyzing
behaviors. The physical-indicator observation is quantitatively
used by a detached observer for finding physical evidence. In the
same manner, a performance-indicator observation is quantitatively used by a detached observer to record evidence of human
behavior. Visual diagramming is a quantitative observation used
by a detached observer for the purpose of depicting verbal interaction. Human space utilization observation is a quantitative measure used by a detached observer for the purpose of depicting the
length and pattern of physical movement. The detached open-
ended narrative is a qualitative observation used by a detached
observer for recording events as they unfold. Participant open-
ended observation is a qualitative technique used to record how
people and events unfold to one involved in the classroom. The
focused questionnaire is another qualitative method that can be
used by a detached or participant observer for the purpose of
gathering evidence according to general questions about classroom
topics. Finally, educational criticism is a qualitative observation
conducted by a combination of detached and participant observation for the purpose of capturing the meaning of classroom life
from the teacher's and students' perspective.

Caution When Using Observations

To reiterate, the purpose of observation should determine the
type, method, and role used. No one type of observation is superior
to all others; rather, some types of observations are better for serving certain purposes. If the goal of an observation is to

FIGURE 12–11   Observation Alternatives

Type	Method		Role of Observer		Purpose
	Quantitative	Qualitative	Detached	Participant	
Categorical frequency	X		X		Count Behaviors
Physical indicator	X		X		Evident or not
Performance indicator	X		X		Evident or not
Visual diagramming	X		X		Picture verbal interaction
Space utilization	X		X		Picture movement
Detached open-ended narrative		X	X		Attention to unfolding event
Participant open-ended observation		X		X	Inside-out view
Focused questionnaire		X	X or	X	Focus on particular events
Educational criticism		X	X or	X	Meaning to participants

determine the frequency of praise, then educational criticism or open-ended narrative would be inappropriate when categorical frequencies would accomplish the goal. If the purpose of an observation is to determine those activities with greatest student interest, then a categorical- or performance-indicator instrument would be of little value and a focused questionnaire would be more useful. There is a tendency for educators to view a new method of observation as a panacea to use at every opportunity. This has been the case with categorical frequency instruments. Training programs, workshops, and courses have prepared thousands of supervisors with skills in defining and checking off categories. Hordes of prepared supervisors have run back into classrooms ticking off behaviors. In some cases it was important for future instructional improvement to know the ratio of teacher statements, questions, and directions given. In other classrooms, interaction frequencies and ratios were never a concern to begin with, and the observation was meaningless. The new techniques of educational criticism should not be used indiscriminately by every supervisor and every classroom simply because they are new. Instead, they should be used only when the supervisor and teacher share a concern about the meaning of the classroom to participants. An instrument should not become a focus for all observation because of its availability or newness. It should be used only if it is a priority concern of teachers and supervisors.

Summary

There are many ways to observe classrooms. The choice of a particular type of observation depends on the purpose and focus of the observation. Observation enables a supervisor to put a mirror of the classroom up to the teacher, who can then attend to matters previously unknown. Several studies (Brophy and Good 1974, pp. 297–328) have shown that teachers often change instructional behaviors on their own after their classrooms have been described to them by an observer. The mirror can often be the stimulus for change. The observer must be careful in using interpretations because such value judgments can actually cloud the mirror and prevent the teacher from seeing his or her own image. At all times, the observer needs to distinguish description from interpretation when recording and explaining events to the teacher.

EXERCISES

ACADEMIC

1. Review a system either developed by or adapted from Bales (1951), Flanders (1970), Medley and Mizel (1963), or Hyman (1975), designed to aid in the observation of classroom behavior. Write a paper describing the specific purpose(s) of the chosen system, procedures involved in its use, your perceptions of the utility of the system for direct assistance, and supervisory goals for which use of the system would be most appropriate.

2. Locate one example of each type of instrument listed here in outside literature on educational supervision. Describe each instrument, and discuss the specific purpose and procedures for the use of each instrument.

    (a) A categorical-frequency instrument.

    (b) A physical-indicator instrument.

    (c) A performance-indicator instrument.

3. Write a paper comparing and contrasting quantitative classroom observation with qualitative classroom observation. Cite relevant works found in the references for Chapter Twelve in your writing.

4. After reviewing relevant portions of Eisner's *The Educational Imagination* (1979), write a paper summarizing Eisner's ideas on educational connoisseurship.

5. Write an essay giving your position on each of the three issues presented at the beginning of this chapter. Support your position with citations from relevant readings listed in the references for Chapter Twelve.

FIELD

1. Use a categorical-frequency instrument. Arrange to observe a class and try out the instrument.

2. Use a performance-indicator instrument. Use the instrument during a classroom observation.

3.   Write a detached open-ended narrative during a visit to a classroom.

4.   Visit a classroom. Write a description of the classroom, learning activities, and teacher-student interactions from the teacher's perspective. Next, write the same three descriptions of the classroom, learning activities, and teacher-supervision interactions from the students' perspective.

5.   Review an instrument used by supervisors in a selected school district during classroom observations. Prepare a written evaluation of the instrument. Include your opinion on whether the instrument fulfills its stated purpose.

DEVELOPMENTAL

1.   Continue to differentiate between *descriptions* and *interpretations* of observed events by listening to others discuss observations they have made and by reviewing your own comments regarding your observations.

2.   Continue to review systems and instruments designed for use as tools for quantitative observations. Attempt to match different systems and instruments with different observation purposes and goals.

3.   Through continued readings and practice in classroom observation, especially in listening to teachers and students, begin to develop the skills of Eisner's educational critic.

REFERENCES

Bales, R. 1951. *Interaction process analysis.* Reading, Mass.: Addison-Wesley

Beegle, C., and Brandt, R. M., eds. 1973. *Observational methods in the classroom.* Washington, D.C.: Association for Supervision and Curriculum Development.

Brophy, J. E., and Good, T. L. 1974. *Teacher-student relationships: Causes and consequences.* New York: Holt, Rinehart and Winston.

References

Capie, W.; Johnson, C. E.; Anderson, S. J.; Ellet, C. D.; and Okey, J. R. 1979. *Teacher performance assessment project.* Atlanta: Georgia Department of Education.

Eisner, E. 1979. *The educational imagination.* New York: Macmillan.

———. 1981. On the differences between scientific and artistic approaches to qualitative research. *Educational Researcher* 10(1):5–9.

Flanders, N. A. 1970. *Analyzing teacher behavior.* Reading, Mass.: Addison-Wesley.

Harris, B. M. 1975. *Supervisory behavior in education,* 2nd ed. Englewood Cliffs, N.J.: Prentice-Hall.

Hyman, R. T. 1975. *School administrator's handbook of teacher supervision and eveluation methods.* Englewood Cliffs, N.J.: Prentice-Hall.

Jones, K., and Sherman, A. 1980. Two approaches to evaluation. *Educational Leadership* 37:553–557.

Knowlton, R. A. 1984. Educational criticism for assessment of program implementation. Unpublished Ed.D. diss., University of Georgia.

Medley, D. M., and Mizel, H. E. 1963. Measuring classroom behavior by systematic observation. In N. L. Gage, ed., *Handbook of research on teaching.* Skokie, Ill.: Rand McNally.

Simon, A., and Boyer, E. C. 1967. *Mirrors of behavior: An anthology of classroom observation instruments.* 6 vols. Philadelphia: Research for Better Schools.

Spradley, J. P. 1980. *Participant observation.* New York: Holt, Rinehart and Winston.

Webster's new collegiate dictionary. 1974. Springfield, Mass.: G. & C. Merriam.

CHAPTER THIRTEEN

Research and Evaluation Skills

This chapter will explain several dimensions of research and evaluation. First, it will deal with the link between classical research, school research, and school evaluation. Second, it will describe special-project evaluation and then overall instructional program evaluation. Third, it will consider the role of the supervisor in evaluation.

How do we know our instructional programs are successful? Should we continue with the same curriculum, instructional methods, scheduling, and grouping practices, or should changes be made? Evaluating is the act of making such a judgment. How does one decide whether something is good or bad? Frequently we make judgments with statements such as, "What a great reading program," "What a lousy classroom," or "What wonderful students." How do we really know if something is great, lousy, or wonderful? Wolfe (1969) offers a tongue-in-cheek classification of five typical methods by which we make such judgments:

Cosmetic Method: You examine the program, and if it looks good it is good. Does everybody look busy? The key is attractive and full bulletin boards covered with projects emanating from the project.

Cardiac Method: No matter what the data say you know in your heart that the program was a success. This is similar to the use in medical research of subclinical findings.

Colloquial Method: After a brief meeting, preferably at a local watering hole, a group of project staff members conclude that success was achieved. No one can refute a group decision.

Curricular Method: A successful program is one that can be installed with the least disruption of the ongoing school program. Programs that are truly different are to be eschewed at all costs.

Computational Method: If you have to have data, analyze it to death. Whatever the nature of the statistics, use the most sophisticated multivariate regression discontinuity procedures known to humans.

Wolfe's methods aside, let's look at reasonable, valid ways of evaluating. In the turbulence of instructional change, it is useful to know whether the new practice is going to be any better than the old. If not, then we may be investing large amounts of human and physical energy without a justifiable increase in instructional benefits to students. As discussed in Chapter Eleven on assessing and planning, if we are to make a commitment to instructional change, we also need to make a commitment to evaluating that instructional change. If not, then we truly do not know what we are doing.

How does one make a judgment of worth? In education, there are at least three components of a comprehensive evaluation:

1. Determine if the instructional program took place as planned. Did teachers and administrators carry out the intended program? This is called *fidelity* or *implementation evaluation.*

2. Determine if the instructional program achieved its instructional objectives for students. Did the program accomplish what it set out to do? This is called *product* or *outcome evaluation.*

3. Determine if unforeseen consequences to students and teachers resulted from the program. Were there any benefits or drawbacks for students as by-products of the program? This is called *serendipitous evaluation.*

These three components of evaluation, when done thoroughly, provide those with program decision responsibilities (curriculum council, superintendent, school boards, state and federal agencies) with a comprehensive report on the results of the instructional program.

This chapter will show the supervisor how to use the skills of evaluating as an aid to knowing when to revise, change, improve, continue, or discontinue an instructional program. Evaluation used to modify and improve an ongoing instructional program is called *formative* evaluation. Evaluation used to make a final judgment about the continuation (or discontinuation) of a program is called *summative* evaluation. Formative evaluation is ongoing and continuous, summative evaluation is one-time and final (Scriven 1967).

Research Design: The Classical Loop

Educational research was once considered a search for universal truths, and evaluation was thought of as the search for value of a particular situation (Popham 1975, pp. 12–13). With the recent attention given to *applied* and *action* research, however, the distinction between research and evaluation has become less clear-cut (Payne 1983). Nowadays research is often concerned with a particular situation. The main difference between research and evaluation is that researchers usually define a problem prior to a study and then use students, teachers, or classrooms as subjects for their study, whereas evaluators study what already exists in the schools. Since educational evaluation design grew out of research design, it is necessary to understand traditional research, described by Gage (1982), as the classical research loop. The research loop consists of descriptive, correlational, and experimental studies.

For illustrative purposes, let's take a topic of educational study through the classical loop. *Descriptive studies* are used to form hunches about why one phenomenon appears to differ from another. Descriptive studies are conducted by observing, talking to participants, collecting available performance results, gathering samples of work, and generally becoming familiar with the phenomena under investigation. Let's pretend we are social studies supervisors and are intrigued by the apparent motivation, interest, and achievement of students in the classrooms of four high school teachers. These classrooms appear to be exceptional. Before, during, and after class students are usually seen smiling and discussing social studies topics with each other. They volunteer to do extra projects, regularly win awards in local and regional social studies essay contests, and consistently outperform their peers in the other thirteen teachers' classrooms on social studies achievement tests.

What is it about these four teachers? We decide to visit all the high school classrooms, talk to students, interview the teachers, collect test results, and observe the classrooms to try to speculate about what the differences are. Indeeed, after looking at student scores on social studies unit tests, interviewing students about their attitude toward the subject, and counting the number of student projects completed, we see that the classrooms of those four teachers do outperform the others. We share our notes to determine if we agree about why those classrooms appear to do so well. After considerable discussion, we decide that the following are possible differences in the four exceptional teacher classrooms as contrasted with those of the other teachers.

1. The exceptional teachers appear really to love their subject. They read books, visit museums and libraries, and attend lectures about historical and social issues simply for their own enjoyment. The other twelve teachers appear to think of social studies simply as what they teach and do not pursue the subject on their own.

2. The exceptional teachers appear to give students many more independent activities apart from reading the textbook. The other twelve teachers appear to stick to the textbook and give more large-group instruction.

3. The exceptional teachers appear to ask many questions of their students, and most of their questions are open-ended. The other twelve teachers appear to ask fewer questions, and most of them simply involve recalling facts.

To check whether our hunches about the differences between these teachers are correct, we move to the next phase of our research loop by doing correlational studies. Correlational studies measure several facets or variables of a phenomena to determine if they move together over time (see Figure 13–1).

A variable is simply a factor that can be measured. In sample A, when variable A moves from low to high at the same rate that variable B moves from low to high, then there exists a perfect positive correlation, stated as a +1 correlation. For example, if variable A was student performance and variable B was teacher love for subject, and a perfect correlation existed, then as teacher love for subject increased, so would student performance. In sample B, when variable A moves from high to low at the same rate that variable B moves from low to high, then there exists a perfect negative correlation between the two variables, stated as a −1 correlation. This means that both variables move in an inverse relation to each other. For example, if variable A is student performance and variable B is the amount of teacher activities, and there is a −1 correlation, then student performance would increase at the same rate that teacher activities decreased. In sample C, when variable A remains constant while variable B moves from low to high, then there exists no correlation between the two variables; this is stated as a 0 correlation. This means that one variable moves completely independent of the other. For example, if variable A was student performance and variable B was the amount of teacher open-ended questions, and there was a 0 correlation, then this would mean that as student performance increased, the amount of teacher questions varied.

RESEARCH AND EVALUATION SKILLS

When testing for correlation of variables, one rarely finds variables correlating perfectly at $+1$, -1, or 0. Correlations such as $-.83$, $-.11$, $+.53$, or $+.77$ are more typical. Generally, any correlation above $+.70$ or below $-.70$ is an indication that a strong relationship does exist between the two measured variables. For example, think of correlating height and weight of the human popu-

FIGURE 13–1   Sample Correlations

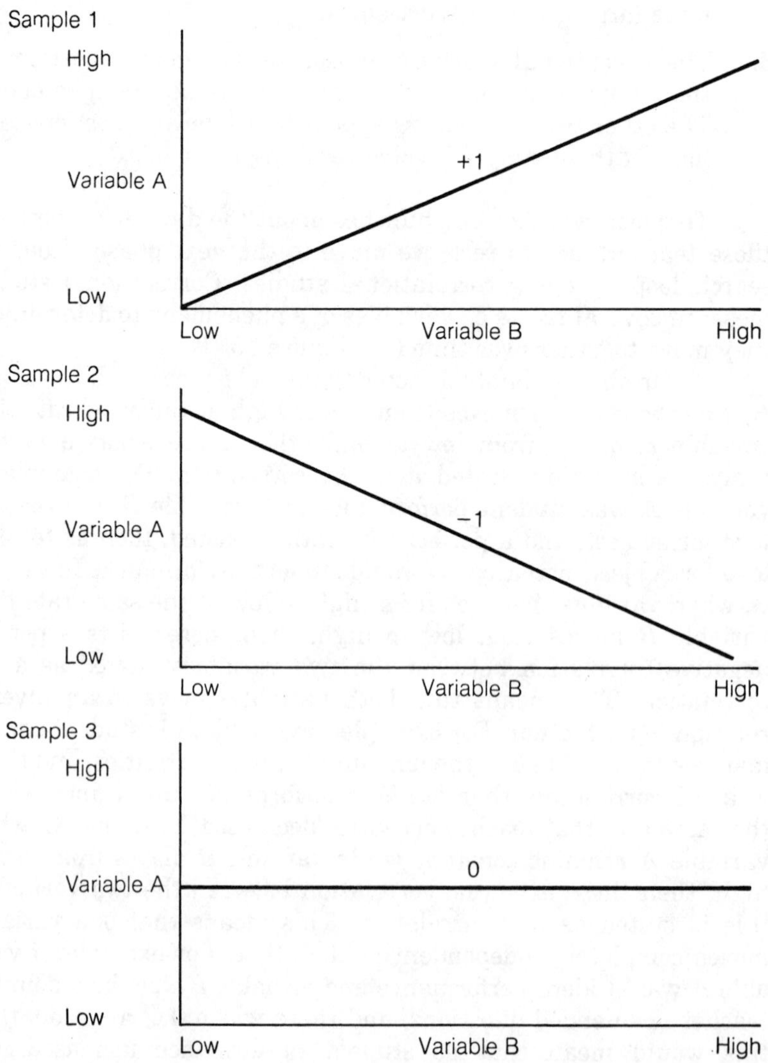

lation. It would be above .70, highly related but not perfectly so. The same correlation computations can be made for three, four, or more variables to determine their overall relationship to each other as well as the relationship between any two. However, diagramming and explaining the scores is best left to textbooks on statistics.

Returning to our example of studying differences in social studies teachers, we would want to find out if our hunches about these differences do indeed correlate between the four exceptional and the twelve other teachers. We might proceed to do a correlational study. From our descriptive study of students' achievement on tests, students' attitudes, and a number of students' projects completed, we know that these four teachers' classrooms score consistently high. We might put together a composite score for classroom student performance by combining achievement, attitude, and projects completed. On the composite performance we rank the teachers' classrooms from 1 (the lowest performance) to 16 (the highest). To test our hunches about why these student outcomes are different, we measure teacher variables of teacher love for subject, teacher assignments, and teacher open-ended questionnaires. We wish to see if there is a correlation between the various teacher variables and the composite student performance.

We might devise ways to measure our hunches about teacher variables:

1. Teacher love for subject: Recording the total amount of outside books read, visits to museums and libraries, and lectures attended.

2. Teacher assignments of individual and small group activities: Counting the percentage of classroom time given to individual and small-group activities that depart from the textbook.

3. Open-ended questions asked during a class period: Observing classrooms at random times and tallying the amount of questions that ask for a nonrecall answer.

We collect our data by having teachers fill out a survey in which they list outside activities related to their teaching topic, and we conduct three random classroom visits to count amount of activity time and questions. We rank each of our three teacher variables from 1 to 16 (lowest to highest). We now have four rankings:

Variable A = composite student performance including achievement, attitudes, and projects completed.

Variable X=teacher love for subject.

Variable Y=teacher allocated time for activities.

Variable Z= teacher open-ended questions.

The next step is to see if the student and teacher variables positively correlate. Our major hypothesis would be that they will. We can figure the total performance of students with the teacher variables rankings (see Figure 13–2).

According to our correlation study, there exists a strong positive correlation with teacher ranking on student outcomes and open-ended questions (+.86) and teacher ranking on student outcomes and love for subject (+.77), but a very weak correlation with activities (+.07). Our correlation studies have now supported two of our hunches and eliminated a third. The correlation study does not tell us cause and effect, however. We haven't been proved wrong about our hunches that teacher love for subject and teacher open-ended questions create higher outcome classrooms, but there

FIGURE 13–2   Correlations of Composite Performance of Students with Teacher Love, Allocated Time, and Open-Ended Questions

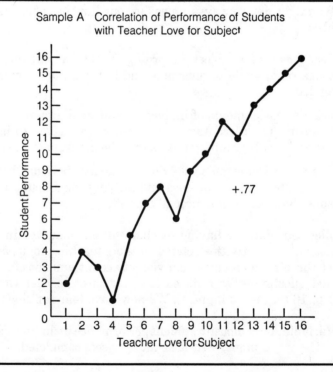

Sample A   Correlation of Performance of Students with Teacher Love for Subject

+.77

Student Performance

Teacher Love for Subject

FIGURE 13-2 (*continued*)

Sample B Correlation of Performance of Students with
Teacher Allocation of Time for Independent Action

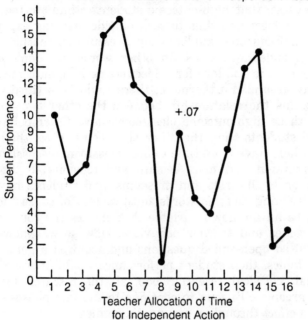

Teacher Allocation of Time
for Independent Action

Sample C Correlation of Performance of Students with
Teacher Open-Ended Questions

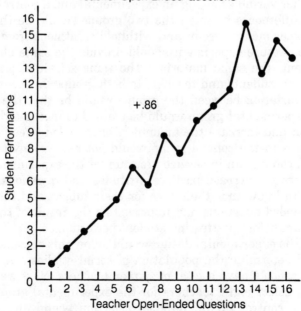

Teacher Open-Ended Questions

is still no proof that we are right. An alternative explanation could be the reverse: that high-outcome students stimulate teachers to love their subject and thus to seek outside learning experiences. Perhaps high-outcome students put pressure on teachers to ask more open-ended questions. In other words, we don't know if teacher questions and love for subject create high outcomes, or the other way around. Furthermore, there could be a third variable that explains the relationship between the other two variables. Perhaps these high-outcome classrooms have fewer behaviorally disturbed students than the other classrooms. If so, then maybe these teachers have more time to hold classroom discussions without interruption and more leisure and tension-free time after school to go to libraries and museums, and students have more time for learning. In other words, until we test for cause and effect, it might be an unknown variable that creates the conditions for high outcomes and teacher behaviors. How do we know that if teachers used open-ended questions and acquired a genuine love for their topics, then student performance would improve? In the traditional, classical research loop, all the research lights are flashing green, telling us to continue to the last phase—seeking cause and effect through experimental studies.

Pure experimental study attempts to remove alternative explanations for correlation of variables. The only way we can know for sure that certain variables cause certain outcomes is to control all other variables, using an experimental and a control group. The only differences between the two groups should be that we treat the experimental group and withhold treatment from the control group. A pure experiment should provide the same physical environment, the same materials, the same schedule, and the same range of students and teachers to both groups. In the example, the only variation between the groups would be that the teachers in the experimental group would be trained to increase their love for subject and increase the amount of open-ended questions, and the teachers in the control group would not receive any training. We would conduct an in-service program for the experimental group of teachers to increase positive attitudes and questions. We would want to know that their love for their subject and the amount of open-ended questions had improved as the result of the in-service program before posttesting student performance.

The experimental design would follow this sequence. First, we would determine the population of social studies classrooms. The three schools have a total of sixteen teachers. Next we would *randomly* select eight teachers for the experimental group and eight for the control group. Random selection would ensure that the same range in terms of asking open-ended questions and love for subject existed in both groups of teachers.

Second, we would pretest all control and experimental students on achievement, attitude, and extra projects completed.

Third, we would treat the experimental group with an in-service program on question asking and positive attitude and would give no special treatment for the control group.

Fourth, after the in-service program and after documenting improvement in asking questions and in the attitudes of the experimental group, we would posttest students in both experimental and control groups on an alternative form of the same pretest instruments that measured student attitude, achievement, and projects completed. The differences between the pre- and posttest scores of the experimental and control groups would be mathematically analyzed to determine statistical significance. Usually, differences in scores between groups are considered significant at the .05 level or lower. That means there is only a 5 percent possibility that the results are due to chance alone; we can be 95 percent confident that the differences found are a result of the experiment.

If the results of the experiment showed that the experimental group made significant gains over the control group, we could say the increase in teacher open-ended questions and love for subject had caused the increase in student achievement, attitudes, and extra projects. An implication of the study would be to give the same in-service program to all social studies teachers.

The Classical Research Loop Applied to Special School Projects: The Case for Quasi-Experiments

When a special project is launched, such as a new curriculum (say, remedial mathematics) or a new technology (say, computer-assisted instruction), it is difficult to apply the classical research loop with its emphasis on experimental design to the variable world of schools. Descriptive studies, used to understand and form hunches about what is transpiring in schools, can be done more readily. In fact, descriptive study, referred to as qualitative, naturalistic, or ethnographic research, has become an increasingly useful methodology for researchers and evaluators (Eisner 1983). Correlation studies continue to be the most popular type of research in education. Collecting available information and then seeing how one measure relates to another can be done with little disruption to the school. On the other hand, pure experimental studies are difficult to conduct. In most cases, it is impossible to split students and teachers randomly into experimental and control groups and withhold a potentially beneficial treatment from one group. Ethical and political considerations often make pure experiments unfeasable. To counter such difficulties, Campbell and Stanley (1963) derived a new form of study known as *quasi-experimental,* which was an adaptation of experimental design to the realities of schools. It has become a widely used and accepted research methodology for evaluators.

Quasi-experimental researchers accept that randomly assigned groups of teachers and students within identically controlled environments are an unrealistic goal. Instead, quasi-experimental research uses volunteers or preselected groups who are already involved in a particular program. For example, one would not randomly assign students to a remedial reading program or randomly assign teachers to a particular workshop. More often the researcher has to work with a preestablished group as the experimental group. Quasi-experimental design treats the preselected or volunteer group as the experimental group. Then the researcher chooses a *comparable* group who would not receive the same treatment. The comparable group functions as the control group. The researcher must establish that the two groups are comparable. Remedial reading students could be matched with other students in the same school who would have qualified for the remedial program, or students participating in a new reading program could be compared to students in another school in the same system with equivalent socioeconomic background and similar reading test scores from previous years. Therefore, the gains in reading of students in the school receiving the new reading program can be analyzed against those of the students in the adjacent school using the traditional reading program. A further example of a quasi-experimental design would be to compare the effects of in-service training on a group of volunteer teachers with the effect on nonvolunteers who are comparable in age, experience, and academic background. Teacher B, who does not volunteer, is matched with teacher A, who does volunteer, because they are of the same age, have the same amount of experience, and have completed the same level of graduate work. Another use of quasi-experimental design involves comparing a group's performance to its own past performance. For example, students in a new junior high school math program perhaps have averaged a gain of 0.7 year in past years. Their gain over the current year in the new program could be compared to past gains.

Every research design has flaws. Pure experimental design with random groups and controlled conditions provides results that are generalizable and conclusive, but it is very difficult to perform.

Quasi-experimental design with comparable groups and less controlled conditions provides results that are less conclusive, but it is easier to do. In designing a study, the researcher always has to balance feasibility against definitiveness.

Statistical versus Educational Significance

The discussion of classical research and quasi-experimental research of special school projects should include the issue of statistical significance versus educational significance. An uninformed consumer of educational research can be impressed by statistical significance and lose sight of educational significance. *Statistical significance* is the mathematical analysis of scores that gives a confidence level about the truth of the results. *Educational significance* includes the overall benefits of using a particular treatment program. For example, if we study the results of an in-service program for social studies teachers and find that student attitude gains from the experimental teachers were significant at the .01 level over student attitude gains from the control group, does this mean that all social studies teachers should undergo the in-service? Maybe, but maybe not. Besides the obvious need to see whether there were other student gains—in achievement, attendance, or work completed—we also need to consider the *magnitude* of the gain against its *cost*. If we had tested attitudes of 100 students in both experimental and control groups and found that on a nine-point scale the experimental students increased from a pretest average score of 5.0 to a posttest score of 6.5 and the control students increased from a pretest average of 5 to a posttest score of 6.1, the 0.4 difference might be statistically significant at the .01 level. The instructional supervisor would have to consider whether a 0.4 difference on a nine-point attitudinal scale is worth the in-service cost, including teacher time, expense for consultants, administrative work, and so on. Decisions about educational significance can be aided greatly by knowledge of statistical significance, but a human judgment must decide on overall benefits.

Some Cautions about Achievement Tests

The misuse of achievement tests can give schools inaccurate results, leading to inaccurate evaluation. For example, many schools evaluate the success of their basic skills programs by comparing the previous year's standardized test scores with the current year's scores. Unfortunately, only a comparison of alternative forms of the same test will yield valid results. Likewise, schools might use the same publisher's test in early fall and late spring and find large but inaccurate gains because the scores in late spring were normed to the fall population of test takers. Another common error in using achievement tests for evaluation is the lack of pre- and posttest scores for *each* student. Often the average pretest scores of a group of students will be compared to the average posttest scores of the same group, even though the group at the end of the year is seldom the same group as at the beginning. Some students will have moved away, been suspended, been reassigned; new students will have replaced them. Only the scores of those students who participated in the project both at the beginning and at the end can be used for program evaluation.

A further problem with achievement tests is using the score on the selection test for a program as the pretest and then using an alternative form of the same test as the posttest. This is a common problem with federally funded and state-funded compensatory programs in schools. If a remedial reading program or a gifted education program uses an alternative form of the original screening test as a posttest, the results will be hopelessly skewed because of what is called *regression toward the mean*. If we test all students on an achievement test and then retest the lowest and highest scorers on the following day, the low scorers will test significantly higher and the high scorers will test significantly lower. This is true because of the test, not the students. Therefore, using a form of the test used to screen high or low students as a posttest for program evaluation will show gains or losses that have nothing to do with the program. The easiest way to prevent this problem is to use a different test, not from the screening test, for pre- and posttest evaluation. (A supervisor who plans to use achievement tests for program evaluation should read the excellecnt and inexpensive federal publication entitled *A Practical Guide to Measuring Project Impact on Student Achievement,* No. 1, U.S. Office of Education, Washington, D.C.)

Many of the aforementioned problems with achievement tests are eliminated by using criterion-referenced tests instead of nationally normed tests. A *nationally normed test* gives grade equivalence scores in comparison to students all across the country. A *criterion-referenced test* gives the percentage of correct responses. Therefore, pre- and posttest scores of criterion-referenced tests more accurately demonstrate what a student has learned.

Combining Approaches: Description and Quasi-Experiment

Now that we understand the classical research loop and adaptations to special school project research, we can borrow procedures, techniques, and methods for school evaluation. We can use descriptive, correlation, and quasi-experimental research as part of evaluation. Instead of the step-by-step progression of the classical loop, we can use a particular research methodology or combine several methodologies. Evaluation that uses descriptive study can be combined with a correlational or quasi-experimental study. For example, if we evaluated an in-service program by using a quasi-experimental study, we also might conduct interviews, case studies, and participant observations to try to determine what other changes were occurring in the classrooms and in the minds of students and teachers involved in the experiment. Such description might account for the *fidelity* (degree of implementation) and *serendipity* (side effects of the in-service program), whereas the experimental study would account for the *outcome*. Combining different approaches can provide a deeper and more comprehensive evaluation.

Overall Instructional Program Evaluation

Evaluating the overall instructional program is different from evaluating special projects. In such an overall evaluation, decision makers can choose to refine existing practices or to launch special projects. This section will mention two such overall program evaluations: the cybernetic model of William Cooley and the self-study model of the National Study of School Evaluation. The supervisor would not necessarily be the data collector or analyzer of such comprehensive evaluation models but would more likely see him- or herself in the role of organizer and coordinator.

William Cooley, past president of the American Educational Research Association and director of program evaluation for the Pittsburgh Pennsylvania public schools discusses his cybernetic model, used for evaluating both individual schools and an entire school system:

> It involves developing and monitoring a variety of performance indicators. Then whenever an indicator moves into an unacceptable range, an attempt is made to determine just where that condition is most severe. Focused corrective action is then taken which I call tailoring practice [Cooley 1983, p.7].

It is interesting that Cooley combines process and product measures into performance indicators of school or school system rather than focusing evaluation on an individual program. He believes that a school or school system should first evaluate what it is currently doing in total via the use of indicators and should attempt through in-service programs and direct assistance to fine tune the existing system before launching and evaluating new programs.

Cooley classifies performance indicators according to three constructs: (1) efficacy of the system, (2) quality of present experience, and (3) equality of educational opportunity. The first construct, *efficacy,* consists of indicators that measure entering students' abilities, interests, progress in school, and achievement. The second construct, *quality* of school life, consists of indicators that focus on the richness of the school experience, such as teacher attitudes, the physical and aesthetic work environment, and the organizational climate of classrooms and schools as perceived by students and faculty. The third construct, *equality* of educational opportunity, consists of indicators that measure the fairness of the educational system, such as the progress, attendance, achievement, attitudes, and opportunities of minority students compared with those of the majority population of students (that is, do racial-minority students succeed academically in the same ratio as racial-majority students from year to year?). Cooley believes that evaluation based on these three constructs should measure multiple levels of performance at the classroom, grade, department, school, and district levels.

Let's examine briefly how a cybernetic evaluation system might work with a hypothetical example. (Cooley and his associates have been using this evaluation model since 1978 with the Pittsburgh schools.) Suppose that in our school system we have determined (via a needs assessment and planning process as outlined in Chapter Eleven) that an acceptable range of the efficacy of the school system would be that 90 percent of students pass to the next grade; an acceptable range of quality of school life would be that 80 percent of students perceive the school environment as enjoyable and supportive; and an acceptable range for equality of educational opportunity would be that students of minority populations are represented proportionally in accelerated classes. We then use multiple measures to determine if the indicators fall in the acceptable range. After collecting our data, we find they are acceptable except for the quality of school life. After analyzing the classroom climate surveys and student interviews, we find that only 70 percent of students perceive the environment as an enjoyable and supportive one. By aggregating the information at the classroom, grade, department, and school level, we find that fewer than 50 percent of freshman students see the school as supportive, as opposed to 85 percent of upperclassmen and women. We then can target our improvement on the freshman class and, with freshman students, teachers, parents, and guidance counselors, plan ways to improve the quality of school life.

It is crucial that the tests, surveys, and observation forms used are actual indicators of the constructs. Obviously, if a school system wants to evaluate but uses inaccurate measures, the results will be worthless. For example, if one indicator for quality of school life was the number of classroom discipline referrals sent to the principal, an unacceptable range could be corrected by simply having the principal refuse to accept teacher referrals. The indicator would show an acceptable range without the quality of school life being improved. Students might still be creating discipline problems, but those problems would not show up in the number of discipline referrals. Therefore, multiple indicators should be used and revised if they do not appear to be measuring the construct.

The Self-Study Model

The self-study model of program evaluation was developed by two complementary organizations, the National Study of School Evaluation for Elementary Schools (NSSEES) (1973) and the National Study of Secondary School Evaluation (NSSSE) (1969). The National Study of School Evaluation originated in 1933 with the aim of developing effective instruments and procedures for schoolwide evaluation. Its workbooks and manuals form the basis of the school accreditation process used by the New England Association of Schools and Colleges, the Middle States Association of Colleges and Secondary Schools, the Southern Association of Colleges and Schools, the North Central Association of Colleges and Secondary Schools, the Northwest Association of Secondary and Higher Schools, and the Western Association of Schools and Colleges. (If, after reviewing the following self-study plan, the reader is interested in further details, the manuals can be ordered from the address given in the reference section.)

The model is based on the premise that "Self-study is to improve the quality of the school's program through the means of self-evaluation, introspection, and comprehensive examination of what is happening to children in the school environment." (National Study of School Evaluation 1973, p.4). Furthermore, the study consists of four parts (National Study of School Evaluation 1973, p. 8):

1.   Self-analysis of the school's program and services.

2.   Objective reaction to the school's analysis by a visiting committee.

3.   Oral and written reports to the school by the chair of the visiting committee.

4.   A resultant program of continuous improvement by the school itself.

A self-study steering committee of between five and seven members is appointed. They in turn appoint subcommittees of faculty to prepare various sections of the self-study. The sections are *school and community demographics, philosophy and objectives, curriculum learning areas, curriculum overview, individual faculty data, school staff and administration, student activities program, learning media services, student personnel services, school plant,* and *plans and priorities.* For each section, the manual provides a format for the subcommittee to check on whether the school philosophy and objectives are relevant and being accomplished. Data is collected by means of teacher-designed tests, criterion-referenced tests, observations, checklists, and surveys. The various National Study of School Evaluation manuals contain validated instruments that a subcommittee can choose to use. Each subcommittee completes its report by showing the degree to which the school is achieving its objective, and makes recommendations for correcting weaknesses. The subcommittee's report goes to the entire faculty for reactions and approval (NSSSE 1983).

In the next stage of the evaluation process, the steering committee selects a visiting team of outside educators with expertise in the various sections of the self-study. A chairperson of the visiting team is also selected. Visiting committees usually consist of between four and fifteen members, depending on the size of the school. The committee visits the schools and has free access to observe, interview, and survey students, teachers, administrators, and parents. The visiting committee's task is to determine the accuracy of the school's self-study and to measure school accomplishment against the school's own objectives. The committee then writes a report of fact finding, strengths, weaknesses, and recommendations for each section of the study, as well as an overall evaluation with prioritized recommendations for the school as a whole. If the visiting team is being used for regional accreditation purposes, they will make a recommendation with respect to accreditation. At the conclusion of the visit, the report is summarized orally to the faculty, and the chairperson of the visiting committee compiles and edits a comprehensive written report that is given to the school's steering committee.

The school's steering committee reads the written report and then develops a plan for acting on the recommendations. The self-study takes approximately six to nine months to complete, the visiting committee spends three to four days visiting, and the completed written report is delivered within three weeks after the visit. The improvement plan developed by the steering committee usually is implemented over several years.

Other Considerations for Evaluation

There are some considerations that arise for a supervisor regardless of the type of evaluation to be employed.

Who Should Evaluate?

Only professors of educational evaluation from the University of Georgia should be hired as program evaluators. (This is a paid advertisement by my colleagues from the Center for Educational Research and Evaluation at the University of Georgia.) If only the answer were so simple! Whether the supervisor, a team of faculty members, central office personnel, or private consultants should evaluate depends on the particular school's resources and the purpose of the evaluation.

Most school systems have scarce financial resources. If they are concerned with formative evaluation, they might proceed by using their own personnel. The teachers and coordinators of school programs could form an evaluation committee and conduct their own data collection and analysis. Since the purpose of the evaluation is to improve the program, there is no reason that participants and supporters (perhaps with the assistance of someone with specialized skills), should not evaluate. On the other hand, if the evaluation is for summative purposes—to determine if a particular project is to continue or not—then it is best to have persons external to the projects conducting the evaluation, so that there is no perception of bias or conflict of interest. Most state- and federally funded school projects require such unattached persons as evaluators.

When looking for evaluators, the supervisor might check with other school systems and acquire a list of prospects. She should check on references. The standards for evaluators presented in the *Standards for Evaluations of Educational Programs, Projects, and Materials* (Stufflebeam 1981) would serve as a guide to hiring ethical and competent persons. As in any profession, those who call themselves evaluators span the entire spectrum. The majority are persons of fine character, but there are a few charlatans. An evaluator should be interviewed to determine his or her view of evaluation, how she or he would proceed, and whether or not he or she will be the type of person in whom others would confide.

One way to remove bias when using school system personnel for evaluation is to use the adversary model (Worthen and Rogers 1980). The adversary model presents two polarized evaluations of the same program. One evaluator or team is commissioned from the beginning to collect data to show that the program is *not* working and should be discontinued. The other evaluator or team is commissioned from the beginning to collect data to show that the program *is* working and should be continued. Since the evaluations have opposing positions to begin with, the sum of the two visions gives a comprehensive review of facts and interpretations for a superintendent or school board to consider before making a final judgment. The pro and con evaluations can be conducted as a trial, with a judge or jury listening to the development of each argument, considering the merits of each position, and then rendering a judgment.

How Should an Evaluation Be Reported?

After collecting the results of tests, observations, surveys, interviews, and testimonials, how should the evaluation be reported? The answer is largely determined by the audience. Most school board members and superintendents will not read a 200 page technical report on the raw data, statistical treatments, and evaluation methodologies. They are interested in the results and conclusions. Evaluators should issue a condensed five- to ten-page report with simple graphs and charts that explain the results and conclusions. The technical report should be available to decision makers as a reference to the summarized paper. Any reader of the condensed paper who is confused or desires more information about certain parts of the paper can check the complete technical report. On the other hand, if the audience for the evaluation report consists of people with sophisticated evaluation skills, then a complete technical report would be in order.

The same caution is advised when giving oral reports of evaluations to parents, newspaper reporters, and school board members. The oral report should be a summary of results, not a long, detailed report with arcane language that will only confuse the listener.

What Is the Supervisor's Role in Evaluation?

A supervisor cannot be personally involved in every evaluation. Instead, he should be responsible for seeing that evaluation of special projects and of the overall instructional programs is ongoing. The supervisor, whether he be school principal, department head, lead or master teacher, district director, or assistant superintendent, should constantly remind himself and the faculty of two questions (Hamilton 1980):

1. Is what we are doing working?

2. How does it work?

Answers to those questions can be gathered through informal means such as surveys, interviews, and group discussions, or through more formal means of observations, questionnaires, and tests. Only as we remind ourselves of these questions and seek answers can actions be taken that improve instruction. Chapter Eighteen will show how such asking and answering can be an integral supervisory task of everyday school life.

Summary

Educational evaluation has been influenced heavily by educational research design. Descriptive, correlational, and quasi-experimental designs are often used to determine the value of an education program. We must be cautious in selecting instruments that measure what we truly wish to find out about a program. Various types of educational evaluations are used for special projects and for the overall instructional program. It is not sufficient to know intuitively that a program is good or bad. Rather, decisions about revising, improving, or discarding need to be made with multiple sources of information. The cybernetic and self-study models permit the gathering of the information needed to make productive instructional decisions.

EXERCISES

ACADEMIC

1. Locate one descriptive study, one correlational study, and one quasi-experimental study in educational research. Write a summary of each study. Include in each summary a description of the study's purpose, participants, methodology, results, and conclusions.

2. Choose a topic of educational study of significance to supervision. Write a paper taking the topic through the classical research loop, outlining ideas for a descriptive study, a correlational study, and an experimental study related to the chosen topic.

3. Compare and contrast experimental with quasi-experimental research. Refer to at least four outside sources in the paper.

4. Compare and contrast quantitative research with qualitative research. Refer to at least four outside sources in the paper.

5. Write a paper entitled "Criteria for Effective Evaluation of a School's Instructional Program." Refer to at least four outside sources in your paper.

FIELD

1. Interview the individual in a school district who is ultimately responsible for instructional program and special project evaluation about procedures for carrying out such evaluations. Write a report summarizing the interview and evaluating the school district's instructional program and special project evaluation methods.

2. Interview a person who has served on a self-study team as part of a school evaluation. Include questions on the interviewee's role and function as a team member, self-study methods used by the team, team conclusions and recommendations, changes ultimately made as a result of the self-study, and the interviewee's reactions to his or her participation. Prepare a report on the interview.

3. Develop a written plan for evaluating a specific area of an instructional program with which you are familiar (for example, a K-6 math program, a senior high school Spanish program, a remedial reading program).

4. Interview a supervisor to determine his or her views on the three universal concerns about evaluation addressed in the chapter: Who should evaluate? How should an evaluation be reported? What is the supervisor's role in evaluation? Prepare a written or verbal report on the interview.

5. Visit a school or system that is currently attempting to follow one of the evaluation models discussed in Chapter Thirteen or cited in the chapter references or suggested readings. Discuss problems the school or system is experiencing in attempting to follow the selected model; note deletions, additions, and modifications the school or system has made in its use of the model. Prepare a report on your investigation.

DEVELOPMENTAL

1. Begin to analyze judgments made by educational leaders and others regarding instructional programs to determine which decisions are based on comprehensive evaluation and which are based on cosmetic, cardiac, colloquial, curricular, or computational methods.

2. Begin an in-depth investigation of alternative models for instructional program evaluation.

3. If the opportunity presents itself, volunteer for membership on a school self-study team or a visiting school evaluation team.

REFERENCES

Campbell, D. T., and Stanley, J. C. 1963. Experimental and quasi-experimental designs for research of teaching. In N. L. Gage, ed., *Handbook of research on teaching*. Chicago: Rand McNally.

Cooley, W. W. 1983. Improving the performance of an educational system. *Educational Researcher* 12(6):4–12.

Eisner, E. W. 1983. Anastasia might still be alive, but the monarchy is dead. *Educational Researcher 12*(5):23–24.

Gage, N. L. 1982. Seminar in educational research, Stanford University, Winter.

Hamilton, S. F. 1980. Evaluating your own program. *Educational Leadership,* 1980, *37*(6):545–551.

National Study of School Evaluation. 1973. *Elementary school evaluative criteria: A guide for school improvement.* Arlington, Va.: National Study of School Evaluation.

National Study of School Evaluation. 1983. *K-12 school evaluative criteria: A guide for school improvement.* Falls Church, Va.: NSSE.

National Study of Secondary School Evaluation. 1969. *Evaluative criteria for the evaluation of secondary schools.* Washington, D.C.:NSSE.

Payne, D. 1983. Personal conversation with Dr. David Payne, director of the Center for Research and Evaluation, University of Georgia, June 6.

Popham, W. J. 1975. *Educational evaluation.* Englewood Cliffs, N.J.: Prentice-Hall.

A practical guide to measuring project impact on student achievement. Number 1 in a series of monographs on evaluation in education. Under contract OEC-0-73-6662, U.S. Office of Education, Washington, D.C.

Scriven, M. 1967. The methodology of evaluation. In R. E. Stake, ed., *Perspectives on curriculum evaluation.* AERA monograph series on curriculum evaluation, No. 1. Chicago: Rand McNally.

Stufflebeam, D. 1981. *Standards for evaluations of educational programs, projects, and materials.* New York: McGraw-Hill.

Wolfe, R. 1969. A model for curriculum evaluation. *Psychology in the schools 6:*107–108.

Worthen, B. R., and Rogers, W. T. 1980. Pitfalls and potentials of adversary evaluation. *Educational leadership 37*(6):536–543.

PART IV

CONCLUSION

Part IV was devoted to the technical skills the supervisor needs in assessing, planning, observing, researching, and evaluating the instructional program. Let's highlight some of these skills. Chapter Eleven on assessing and planning looked at organizing personal plans; managing time; flow charting; conducting needs assessments; management by objectives; Gant charts; program evaluation and review techniques; and planning, programming, and budgeting systems. Chapter Twelve on observing dealt with description and interpretation; quantitative uses of categorical frequencies, performance indicators, and visual diagramming; and qualitative uses of narrative, participant involvement, focused questionnaires, and educational criticism. Chapter Thirteen discussed research and evaluation skills, including types of evaluation; the classical research loop with descriptive, correlational, and experimental study; and applied school research with the use of quasi-experimental design, the cybernetic model, and the self-study model.

The technical skills of Part IV have concluded the prerequisites needed by a supervisor in implementing the supervision function (see Figure IV–1). With knowledge about schools, teachers, and self; with interpersonal skills matched to developmental characteristics of teachers; and with technical skills in assessing, planning, observing, researching, and evaluating, the supervisor can function knowingly and skillfully in the realm of instructional improvement and can carry out the five developmental tasks of supervision.

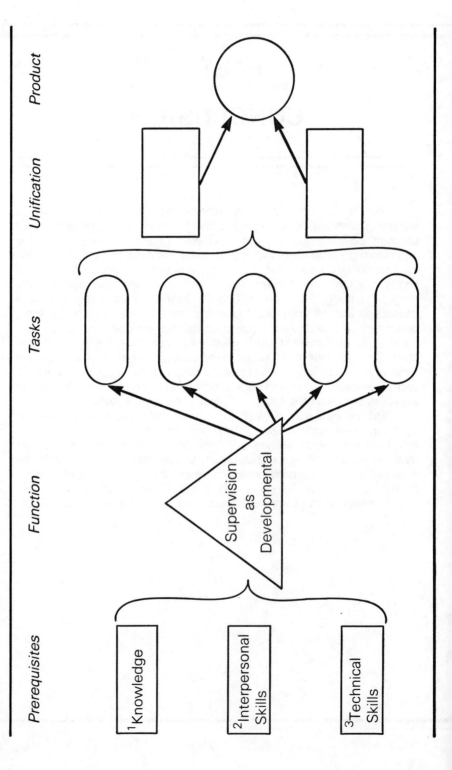

FIGURE IV-1 Supervision for Successful Schools

Prerequisites   Function   Tasks   Unification   Product

Supervision as Developmental

[1]Knowledge
[2]Interpersonal Skills
[3]Technical Skills

PART V

Tasks of Supervision

INTRODUCTION

If one has responsibility for the improvement of instruction, what does one do? We've accounted for what the supervisor needs to possess in terms of knowledge, interpersonal skills, and technical skills. What are the tasks of supervision that can bring about improved instruction? They are direct assistance to teachers, in-service education, curriculum development, group development, and action research. How does instruction improve?

Direct assistance: The supervisor can provide one-to-one feedback to teachers to improve instruction.

In-service education: The supervisor can provide learning opportunities to teachers to improve instruction.

Curriculum development: The supervisor can provide for changes in teaching content and instructional materials to improve instruction.

Group development: The supervisor can provide for instructional problem-solving meetings among teachers to improve instruction.

Action research: The supervisor can provide teachers with ways to evaluate their own teaching to improve instruction.

Each of these tasks is directly related to improved instruction. A supervisor needs to take responsibility for these tasks if a school is to become increasingly effective. Part V will detail how these tasks can be performed so that teachers take individual and collective responsibility for instructional improvement.

CHAPTER FOURTEEN

Direct Assistance to Teachers

Direct human assistance to help teachers improve instruction can come from different sources. This book has contended that someone needs to take responsibility for the supervisory function of direct assistance to ensure that teachers receive feedback, are not left alone, and are involved as part of a collective staff. Research by Dornbush and Scott (1975) and Natriello (1982) has shown that teachers who receive the most classroom feedback are also most satisfied with teaching. Other research studies have shown that teachers in need of assistance tend to seek out first fellow teachers and second supervising or administrative personnel (Lortie 1975, pp. 75–77). Direct assistance to teachers is one of the crucial elements of an effective school (Edmonds 1982). Keeping the frequency and source of direct assistance in mind, we will look at an established structure for assisting teachers and then at some alternative ways of implementing the structure.

Clinical Procedures for Using Observations

Although there are multiple ways of observing, the structure or steps for conducting observations with teachers is relatively standard and accepted, and has a respectable research base (Sullivan 1980; Reavis 1977). In fact, over 90 percent of school administrators in a southern and a midwestern state have cited their knowledge of the use of this structure with teachers (Bruce and Hoehn 1980). The structure, commonly referred to as *clinical supervision,* is derived from the pioneering work of Morris Cogan with supervisors of intern teachers at Harvard University. Cogan's *Clinical Supervision* (1973) and Robert Goldhammer's book, also entitled *Clinical Supervision* (1969), are publications resulting from this pioneer work. Since then numerous refinements and alterations of clinical supervision have been made (Goldhammer,

Anderson, and Krajewski 1980). Those desiring an in-depth study of the research and development of clinical supervision can find references at the end of this chapter. The structure of clinical supervision can be simplified into five sequential steps:

1. Preconference with teacher.
2. Observation of classroom.
3. Analyzing and interpreting observation and determining conference approach.
4. Postconference with teacher.
5. Critique of previous four steps.

Step 1

At the *preconference,* the supervisor sits with the teacher and determines (1) the reason and purpose for the observation, (2) the focus of the observation, (3) the method and form of observation to be used, (4) the time of observation, and (5) the time for postconference. These determinations are made before the actual observation so that both supervisor and teacher are clear about what will transpire. The purpose of the observation, as mentioned in Chapter Twelve, should provide the criteria for making the remaining decisions on focus, method, and time of observation.

Step 2

The next step, *observation,* is the time to follow through with the understandings of the preconference. The observer might use any one observation or combinations of observations. Methods include categorical frequencies, physical indicators, performance indicators, visual diagramming, space utilization, detached open-ended narratives, participant observation, focused questionnaire, and educational criticism. The observer should keep in mind the difference between *descriptions* of events and *interpretations.* Interpretation should follow description.

Step 3

The *analysis* and *interpretations* of the observation and determination of approach are now possible. The supervisor leaves the classroom with her observations and seeks solitude in an office or corner. She lays out the recorded pages of observations and studies

the information. The task might be counting up frequencies, looking for recurring patterns, isolating a major occurrence, or discovering which performance indicators were present and which
were not. Regardless of the instrument, questionnaire, or open-
ended form used, the supervisor must make sense out of a large
mass of information. Then the supervisor can make interpretations
based on the analysis of the description. Figure 14–1 is a form that
can be used to organize this task.

A case study might help to clarify this worksheet. Supervisor
A has completed a verbal interaction instrument for students and
teacher. She reviews the ten sheets, tallies the columns, and writes
in the worksheet under analysis:

1.   The teacher asked 27 questions and received 42 answers.

2.   Out of 276 total verbal moves, 6 were student to student; the
     other 270 were teacher to student or student to teacher.

3.   ...

The supervisor, knowing that the purpose of the lesson was to
encourage student involvement, now makes interpretations on the
worksheet *corresponding* to the analysis:

1.   The teacher encouraged students to answer questions.

2.   There was little interaction among students.

3.   ...

FIGURE 14–1

Worksheet for Analysis and Interpretation of Data
A. Analysis: Write the major findings of your observation. Write down
               only what has been taken directly from your observation.
   1.
   2.
   3.
   4.
   5.
B. Interpretations:Write below what you believe is desirable or not
               desirable about the major findings.
   1.
   2.
   3.
   4
   5.

Note the relationship between analysis 1 and interpretation 1. There is clear documentation of evidence leading to the supervisor's judgment.

Let's provide one more case, this time of supervisor B doing a participant observation. The supervisor reads through his brief classroom notes, picks out the most significant events, and writes under analysis:

1. James, Tyrone, Felix, and Sondra asked me about the assignment they were supposed to be doing.

2. Kirk and Felipe were talking with each other about sports the three times I overheard them.

3.   . .

From this analysis the supervisor makes the following interpretation:

1. The teacher was not clearly communicating the directions to some students.

2. At least a couple of students were not interested in the class work.

3.   ...

Although one could argue with the supervisor's interpretation, it is readily apparent how it was logically derived from the recorded descriptions.

The last determination for the supervisor to make in step 3 of the clinical structure is to choose the interpersonal approach to use with the teacher in the postconference. Remember the nondirective, collaborative, and directive orientations to supervision explained in Chapters Seven, Eight, and Nine? Should the supervisor be *directive* by presenting his observations and interpretations and then demonstrating, standardizing, and reinforcing an assigned plan of teacher improvement? Should the supervisor be *collaborative* by sharing the observation, allowing the teacher to present her own interpretations, and negotiating a mutual contract for future improvement? Should the supervisor be *nondirective* by explaining his observations and encourage the teacher to analyze, interpret, and make her own plan. The supervisor needs to consider the individual teacher's level of abstraction and level of commitment in deciding the approach as explained in Chapter Ten.

Step 4

With the completed observation form, completed analysis, and interpretation form, and with the chosen supervisory interpersonal approach, the supervisor is ready to meet with the teacher in a *postconference*. The postconference is held to discuss the analysis of the observation and, finally, to produce a plan for instructional improvement.

The first order of business is to let the teacher in on the observation—to reflect back to the teacher what was seen. Then the supervisor can follow the chosen approach—directive, collaborative, or nondirective. The responsibility for developing a future plan will either reside with the supervisor, be equally shared, or belong to the teacher. The conference ends with a plan for further improvement. Figure 14–2 can be used to develop such a plan.

FIGURE 14–2   Plan for Instructional Improvement

Postconference Date _____ Observed Teacher _____

Time _____   Peer Supervisor _____

Objective to be worked on:

Activities to be undertaken to achieve objectives:

Resources needed:

Time and date for next preconference:

The *objective* is a statement of what the teacher will attain for the next observation: "I will improve student-to-student interaction by 50 percent in group discussions." *Activities* are a list of preparation points to accomplish the activity: "(1) Practice pausing at least three seconds before answering a student response. (2) Practice using open-ended questions. (3) Set up ongòing mini debates." *Resources* are the materials and/or people needed to do the activities: "(1) Read book on *Leading Discussion Groups*. (2) Attend workshop on "Involving Students." (3) Observe Mr. Filler when he holds a science discussion." *Date* and *time* specify when the teacher will be ready to display his or her improvement. Such a plan—whether teacher-, supervisor-, or jointly designed—should be clearly understood by both parties before they leave the postconference.

Step 5

The *critique* of the previous four steps is a time for reviewing whether the format and procedures from preconference through postconference were satisfactory and whether revisions might be needed before repeating the sequence. The critique might be held at the end of the postconference or in a separate conference after a few days. It need not be a formal session but can be a brief discussion consisting of questions such as: "What was valuable in what we have been doing?" "What was of little value?" "What changes could be suggested?"

The five steps are now complete, and a tangible plan of future action is in the hands of the teacher. The supervisor is prepared to review the plan in the next preconference and reestablish focus and method of observation.

Peer Use of Clinical Supervision

The number of teachers that a supervisor has will influence the frequency of clinical observations conducted by the supervisor. An English department head who teaches five periods a day and has fifteen staff members will have a difficult time conducting full clinical cycles with every teacher during the school year. A principal of a large school, without assistants to delegate administrative and disciplinary responsibilities, will find it an overwhelming task to meet and observe each teacher frequently. From experience, we know the frustration of starting a preconference only to be interrupted by an irate parent, a breakdown of the plumbing system, or two misbehaving students. A supervisor cannot provide direct assistance to teachers unless she establishes priority, energy, and time for doing so. Other nonsupervisory matters will have to be ignored, delegated to others, or simply put off. Most often it is direct assistance to teachers that receives the lowest priority. This sad state of affairs is shown by the evidence that the overwhelming majority of school teachers receive little or no direct assistance (Natriello 1982). Most teachers state that supervisors do not visit them for the purpose of providing help. In most cases, when a supervisor or administrator is in the classroom, he is there to pass on school information or to pick up attendance records.

If a supervisor is convinced of the critical need to provide direct assistance to teachers and cannot do it alone, the question is, "Who else can do it?" This is where the technical skill of planning becomes important. The supervisor has to determine the amount of time he has available for direct assistance, how many teachers can be seen in that time, and which teachers should be given special attention. Then the supervisor needs to determine how else assistance for all teachers can be provided on a regular continuous basis. Authorities on clinical supervision believe the cycle should be conducted a minimum of twice a year with each teacher (see Snyder, Johnson, and MacPhail-Wilcox 1982).

Since teachers naturally turn to each other for help more often than to a supervisor, and since supervision is concerned primarily with improving instruction, not with summative evaluation (renewal of contracts), teachers helping teachers can become a formalized and well-received way of assuring direct assistance to every staff member. If teachers become proficient in observation skills and the format of clinical supervision, then the supervisor can take on the role of trainer, scheduler, and trouble-shooter: *trainer* by preparing the teachers for the task; *scheduler* by forming teams or trios of teachers who take responsibility for preconferencing, observing, and postconferencing with each other; and *trouble-shooter* by consulting with teams of teachers who are experiencing difficulties and with individual teachers who need more specialized attention. The use of teachers helping teachers via clinical supervision has been labeled *peer supervision* or *colleagueship* (Alfonso and Goldsberry 1982). Research by Roper, Deal, and Dornbush (1976); Goldsberry (1980); and Mohlman (1982) has shown positive results with peer supervision. The research has shown mostly gains in attitudes and perceptions of teachers; more studies focusing on changes in teacher behaviors and student outcomes are necessary to determine whether peer supervision works as well as clinical supervision by a supervisor. However, the reality of tight budgets and large teachers/supervisor ratios remains. If direct assistance is a worthy task for instructional improvement and if a supervisor cannot provide it on a regular basis, then the choice is either to have teachers provide help to each other or simply not to offer the help.

Obviously, the way to begin such a program is *not* to call a staff meeting and announce: "Since I can't see each of you as much as I would like, why don't you start to visit each other? Go to it!" Without planning and resources, disaster is inevitable. To be suc-cessful, peer supervision needs components of training, scheduling, and trouble-shooting. Let's take each in turn.

Training

To begin, at least three 45 to 60 minute orientation meetings are necessary. Later there is a need for at least one in-progress meeting and one culminating meeting. The first orientation meet-ing involves explaining the concept of peer supervision; laying out the procedures, the format, and the amount of time required of each teacher; and, most important, determining the willingness of teachers to participate. As concerns emerge, the supervisor must decide with staff on possible modifications to accommodate as many teachers as possible. The second orientation session is with those teachers still interested in participation. The focus is on ways of observing classrooms according to the purpose of the observations (see Chapter Twelve). A videotape or film of a short class period might serve as a trial exercise in different ways of observing. Ex-perimentation with various types of observation would be followed by discussion and clarification of methods and forms. At the end of this session the participants would need to agree on the composition of peer supervision teams. They might be chosen at random or by grade level or common instructional concern. The third orientation session is for the purposes of announcing and then detailing each of the five steps of clinical supervision. Role playing of the entire se-quence of preconference, observation, analyzing and interpreting, postconference, and critique is useful.

A standard form for writing instructional improvement plans should be reviewed. The form should be simple and easy to fill out. Each peer member should understand that a filled-out plan is the object of the first four clinical steps and the basis for beginning the next round of supervision. Once the program is underway, a time should be set for a midpoint session (approximately three to six weeks later, after each participant has completed the clinical cycle as both peer supervisor and object of supervision). This meeting should be spent sharing successes and failures of clinical procedures and formats (*not* discussing individual teacher performances), with participants suggesting improvements for the next cycle. Toward the end of the year, a culminating meeting should be held to summarize the advantages and disadvantages of using peer supervision and making a recommendation on whether to continue the program for the following year.

Let's emphasize that the program should be based on *agreement* and *voluntarism*. If an entire staff is willing to be involved, that's fine; but if only three teachers are willing, it is still a beginning and a previously unavailable source of help for those three teachers. See Appendix E for an example of how one instructional supervisor initiated such a program.

Scheduling

A teacher will have a more difficult time becoming enthusiastic about a project if it means increasing the amount of personal time and energy expended beyond an already full day. Because peer supervision will require additional time, the program should be voluntary, at least in the beginning. Greater participation of teachers is likely if the supervisor can schedule time for peer supervision during the school day. For example, placing teachers together in teams that share the same planning or lunch periods would allow for pre- and postconferences during the school day. Hiring a few substitutes for two days, twice a year, would allow teachers to be relieved of class duties so they can observe their peers. One substitute could relieve six classroom teachers for one period at a time. Relief could also be found by having the titled supervisor (we mean you!) occasionally substitute for a teacher for one class period. This would enable the teacher to observe and also would give the supervisor a glimpse into the operating world of the classroom. Another way of freeing time for peer observations is for teachers to release each other by periodically scheduling a film, lecture, or some other large-group instruction so that two classes could be taught by one teacher. Whatever the actual schedule used to release teachers for peer supervision, preplanning by supervisor and teachers is needed to ensure that teachers can participate without extreme personal sacrifice. Research on lasting classroom change has shown that having scheduling time for teachers during the school day is critical (Humphries 1981).

Another issue is that of arranging teams of teachers. As in most issues in education, there are no hard and fast rules. Generally teachers should be grouped with each other so that they are comfortable together but not necessarily at identical levels of expe-

rience and/or competence. It may be useful to put experienced
teachers with new ones, superior teachers with adequate ones, or
adequate teachers with struggling ones.

Cognitive psychologists have demonstrated that an individual's thinking becomes more abstract and varied when he or she
interacts with persons at higher levels of mental organization
(Kohlberg 1969). Such matching enables a person to consider ideas
he or she would not have thought of; the novelty of the ideas spurs
the person to rethink problems. If the groupings are too disparate—
a concrete thinker with a highly abstract thinker, or a struggling
teacher with a self-assured teacher—then little of such sparking of
ideas will occur. There must be some degree of understanding and
comfort to begin with. Hence it is undesirable to match people who
think alike but also undesirable to match those who think too differently. The goal is to match people who are different but still can
respect and communicate easily with each other.

Cognitive matching will work if there are enthusiastic participants who are willing to be matched. A supervisor working
with staff who are skeptical about using peer supervision in the
first place might be better served by forgetting cognitive matching
and instead allowing self-selection of teams. Each teacher could
present anonymously a list of teachers he or she would like to work
with. The supervisor could then match up preferences. The choices
are between an ideal way to match people based on cognitive
growth, and a practical way to match them based on people's need
for security with a new program. The practical match might be
best when starting the program; after peer supervision becomes a
familiar ongoing activity, the supervisor could rearrange teams
toward greater cognitive matching.

Trouble-Shooting

The third component of establishing a peer supervision program is the close monitoring of peer progress. The supervisor
should be available to peer teams as a resource person. For example, what happens when the preconference concludes with an
agreement to observe a teacher's verbal interaction in the classroom, and the peer supervisor is at a loss about where to find such
an observation instrument? The training program should answer
such questions, but orientation meetings cannot cover all possible
needs. The supervisor, therefore, needs to monitor needs of peer
teams and be able to step in to help.

An elaborate monitoring device is not necessary. The supervisor simply might wander around the halls and check with peer

supervisors every few weeks. At periodic faculty meetings, she might ask peer supervisors to write a note on their team progress. The supervisor should be sure that books, films, tapes, and instruments on clinical supervision and methods/instruments for observations are catalogued and available to teachers in the professional library. A list of such clinical supervision resources can be found at the end of this chapter.

Now that the supervisor can attend to *training, scheduling,* and *trouble-shooting,* a peer supervision program can be implemented. The initial implementation of such a program undoubtedly will create more work for the supervisor. However, the initial work is less than would be necessary for providing clinical supervision to every teacher two or three times a year. If it is important enough to supervisor and staff, the time spent at the start in preparing for the program will pay off with ongoing instructional improvement of teachers.

Other Means of Direct Human Assistance

It is 10:30 A.M. and Ms. Golan, the reading supervisor, is on her way to present the recommended reading budget for next year to the principal. Principal Malone told her last week that the recommendations were to be in today by 11 A.M. if he was to have them for his luncheon meeting with the superintendent. Ms. Golan has worked on the budget day and night for the last three days and finally has it finished. She needs to explain some of the budget items to Principal Malone personally. Suddenly, someone catches her by the arm and gently spins her around. It's Phillip Arostook, the remedial reading teacher, who says: "Boy, am I glad you're here. I have a meeting with Mr. and Mrs. Cougar at noon. They want my head. They claim I've been neglecting their son William, and that he's not learning anything. They want him out of my class. How do I handle this? I need your help!"

This incident is typical of the numerous unplanned occasions on which one is called to provide direct human assistance. Clinical supervision is focused on long-term, carefully planned instructional improvement. There is still the matter of immediate needs, however. It is just as important for teachers to have someone to confer with in handling the short-term issues that arise each day. What would you do (or what have you done) in Ms. Golan's place? Ms. Golan could handle the situation by (1) telling Phillip she'll be back to see him in a half an hour; (2) telling Phillip she is pressed for time and can speak to him only for a few minutes on her way to the principal's office; (3) telling Phillip she's sorry but she has no time and he'll have to handle it on his own; or (4) sending the budget with a note to the principal via a student, forgetting about explaining the budget, and then calmly sitting down with Phillip. Ms. Golan (and Phillip) would have been better off if there were an established procedure for handling frequent needs for human assistance. The procedure should be premised on *accessibility, arranged time,* and *delegation.*

Human help needs to be physically available and *accessible.* On a daily basis, the supervisor should visit in the lounge or in classrooms with teachers before school, during breaks, and after school. Of course, the supervisor cannot hold lengthy conversations with every teacher daily and also have time for much of anything else. Therefore, the supervisor might consider brief check-ins with teachers—taking the time to pause and speak with a certain number of teachers each day to ensure that by the end of the week every teacher has had the opportunity to bring up classroom concerns. Often such a brief exchange will alert the supervisor to a teacher's concern that should be followed up with a scheduled conference.

The supervisor's schedule also needs to have *arranged weekly times* set aside for such conferences. The supervisor might plan a particular afternoon every week to follow up on teacher concerns. Teachers know that the supervisor will be in the lounge or office every Thursday afternoon to listen and help. Finally, the supervisor needs to consider *delegation.* The supervisor can use these Thursday afternoon times to provide personal help, can refer the concern to a specialist such as the school counselor or reading teacher, or can use the time for teachers to share instructional concerns and help each other. For example, some schools set aside every other Thursday for voluntary after-school meetings where teachers share discipline problems and plan concrete ways to help each other (see Glickman and Esposito 1979). More about specific procedures and structures for efficient meetings can be found in Chapter Seventeen on group development.

Let's return to the case of Ms. Golan and Phillip Arostook. If Ms. Golan had planned for accessibility, scheduled time, and delegation, the crisis situation could have been prevented, with both the budget report and Phillip's need for counseling being satisfied. She would have known from checking in with Phillip that he was having difficulties with William. With a scheduled time for conferences, they could have reviewed the matter and scheduled a meeting with the parents.

The hectic life of schools—even when accessibility, arranged time, and delegation are planned—will still create unusual dilemmas for the supervisor (as anyone involved in education well knows). Planning for direct human assistance will reduce the number of such dilemmas if teachers know they will be able to speak to their supervisors weekly to discuss serious problems and find resources to meet their needs. Such supervisory attention to ongoing concerns creates a climate of confidence and purpose rather than one of confusion and frantic reaction to unexpected crises.

Differences between Direct Assistance and Formal Evaluation

Formal evaluation is quite different from the direct assistance being discussed. *Formal evaluation* is performed to determine whether or not a teacher measures up to a standard of acceptable work—that is, to sum up the value of the teacher. *Direct assistance* is concerned with helping a teacher assess and work on his or her own classroom needs—that is, to form a focus for future improvement. Therefore, observation of teachers for purposes of direct assistance should be distinct from observation for decisions about renewal or nonrenewal of contracts. Direct assistance involves helping the teacher in continuous reassessment and change. When the task is one of getting a teacher to meet a prescribed level of performance—whether established by school administrators, central office, school board, or principal—then the procedures used for working with teachers are less supervisory and collegial and more administrative and directive.

Ideally, it is best to keep these tasks separate. Supervision as a function concerns itself with improvement of classroom instruction. Administration as a function concerns itself with the overall maintenance of school operations, including the contractual aspects of teacher performance, which might include dress, attendance, punctuality, record keeping, and extra school assignments. Supervision focuses on direct assistance for improving classroom instruction. Administration focuses on satisfactory performance in all contractual matters. To delineate these differences further, let's look at two examples of conferences, one for purposes of formal evaluation and the other for purposes of direct assistance.

Example A

Mrs. Readell, the supervisor, sits down with Mr. Hopewell, the teacher, and reports her evaluation: "Mr. Hopewell you have performed well in almost all aspects of the teacher evaluation. I have rated you as satisfactory on all categories under instruction, discipline, dress, school relationships, and extra school duties. The one area I have marked unsatisfactory is in the paperwork category. Your quarterly attendance records have been late for the last two quarters. Although I have recommended strongly that you be rehired, I do want you to get those attendance records in on time. Without them, we are delayed in receiving our state attendance allotments."

Example B

Mr. Sonjan, another supervisor, sits down with Mr. Hopewell and begins: "Well, Mr. Hopewell, as we agreed, I observed those three boys in the back of the classroom. These are the frequency charts, and the results are that they spend over 80 percent of their time off task, talking and passing notes to each other. Notice how for the first ten minutes they were fairly attentive, but in the last twenty minutes you had to stop and speak to them seven times. What do you suppose is happening?" Mr. Hopewell responds, "I was aware that they lose attention, but not that dramatically! I think I need to give them shorter but more frequent activities." Mr. Sonjan: "Maybe if you had them sit up closer where you could check their work more often, they would be more attentive."

These examples should highlight the differences between formal evaluation and direct assistance. In teacher evaluation the concern is with adequate performance, as shown in example A. The teacher is either doing well or not, according to a single, prescribed standard for all teachers. If the teacher has met the standards, then no further attention is needed. In direct assistance the concern is exclusively instruction-related and focuses on the teacher's own professional needs, as shown in example B. Instruments and forms used can vary from teacher to teacher. Observation times and methods are agreed on, and improvement is ongoing *regardless of* the competence level of the teacher. Instructional improvement is relative; there are always changes that might make the classroom better. Therefore, instructional improvement is continuous, whereas teacher evaluation is periodic. Other writers have noted these differences, calling direct assistance *formative evaluation* and formal evaluation *summative evaluation* (see McGreal 1982). Many writers of supervision texts (Harris 1975; Oliva 1976) believe a supervisor should have a staff relationship with teachers in order to be responsible totally for direct assistance (that is, helping teachers to help themselves), whereas administrators such as school principals should have line relationships *over* teachers so as to be totally responsible for formal evaluation. The rationale for these distinctions is understandable. A teacher is more prone to allow an observer to see the real classroom, warts and all, if the observer is present solely to help. A teacher is more prone to confide in a staff person. When the observer is in the role of evaluator, the teacher is more likely to hide the real classroom and, instead, give a rehearsed and stilted performance to meet the standards of the evaluation form. The teacher will be reluctant to discuss what is wrong or inadequate in his own teaching if the supervisor might use the information to document unacceptable teaching standards. Simply put, individuals speak more easily about their real selves to a friend than to a boss. Since help with real classroom problems can be provided only if a supervisor can see the real classroom, a staff relationship with teachers is helpful.

Most school organizations reflect this separation through job descriptions. Any combination of distinct roles might do—principals as evaluators and assistant principals, department heads, lead and master teachers, or peer teachers as direct assistors; or central office personnel as evaluators and principals as direct assistors. This book, however, treats supervision as a function, not as a particular position or role. Our concern is that direct assistance be provided. Which persons or positions provide the help can vary from system to system, depending on school resources. However, if a school is to become more successful with instruction, the task of direct assistance *must* be performed.

In many school systems, one or more persons are expected to do both formal evaluation and direct assistance. Can such dual responsibilities be done well? Can a person do a credible job if he or she is responsible for both improving and judging a teacher. The answer might surprise the reader, it is *yes*. It can be done, but with difficulty and only by an individual who can maintain a relationship of trust and credibility with teachers. Ask yourself: Is there someone who you would trust to evaluate you for contract renewal purposes as well as to assist you with your own professional improvement? Could you let your hair down with this person? There probably is someone, but it must be a very special person. Only if you believed that the person is *primarily* concerned with helping you would you be comfortable, receptive, and willing to reveal your areas of greatest need. The point is that to do both jobs well is an extraordinary accomplishment. In a school system that has supervisors whom teachers thoroughly trust and respect, dual responsibilities are possibile. More often, teachers have a natural wariness toward those higher up in the organization. Therefore, separating the roles is often advisable.

Summary

Regardless of how or where the responsibilities reside, no school or school system can hope to improve instruction if direct assistance is not provided to teachers. To leave classroom teachers alone and unobserved in their classrooms, without professional consultation and without school resources tailored to their unique needs, is a statement (intended or not) that teaching is unimportant. The message to teachers is that what is important is keeping your class quiet, your doors shut, and your problems to yourself. Assuredly, this is not the message we want to give.

A different message can be given by arranging for observation, feedback, and discussion of classroom improvement. Clinical supervision is a recognizable structure for assistance that peers can use to help each other. Furthermore, supervisors can be accessible, arrange contact times, and refer specialists to teachers. Direct assistance separated from formal evaluation will help teachers confide, improve, and move with each other toward collective action.

EXERCISES

ACADEMIC

1. Locate three research studies on clinical supervision. Write a summary of each study, including purpose, participants, methodology, results, and conclusions.

2. Write a paper (a) giving advantages and disadvantages of having supervision done by a formally designated supervisor, and (b) giving advantages and disadvantages of having supervision performed by other teachers (peer supervision). Refer to at least three outside sources in your paper.

3. Locate three research studies on peer supervision. Write a summary of each study, including purpose, participants, methodology, results, and conclusions.

4. Assume you are a supervisor who has been asked by the superintendent to begin a program of clinical supervision by peers in one of the district's medium-sized schools. Prepare a written plan for introducing clinical supervision to all the school's teachers, training a volunteer group of teachers in

the clinical process, selecting teams (matching teachers), scheduling an initial round of clinical cycles, and monitoring the peer supervision program.

5. A traditional question debated in supervision is whether a single supervisor should be involved in both direct assistance and summative evaluation of teachers, or whether these two functions should be performed by different supervisors? Find one author (other than the author of this book) on each side of this issue. Write a paper summarizing the arguments of each author.

FIELD

1. Interview a supervisor who follows the clinical model in direct supervision of teachers on the practical advantages and disadvantages of clinical supervision. Prepare a report on your interview.

2. Arrange to supervise a teacher using the clinical model (preconference, observation, analysis and interpretation, postconference, critique). Record the preconference, postconference, and critique on audiotape, and write a summary of the clinical cycle.

3. Conduct a group interview with a team of teachers involved in peer supervision on the specifics of the peer supervision program, problems encountered, and perceived value of peer supervision for instructional improvement. Prepare a report on the interview.

4. Prepare a survey instrument to be completed by teachers that (a) defines direct assistance, (b) asks teachers to list the types of direct human assistance they desire from supervisors, and (c) asks teachers to list the types of direct human assistance they desire from other teachers. Distribute the survey to at least ten teachers, and request that they respond anonymously, in writing, to the two survey questions. Collect the surveys, and process and analyze response data. Prepare a report on which types of direct human assistance the respondents desire from supervisors and from fellow teachers.

5. Interview a school administrator who has primary responsibility for providing direct human assistance to teachers *and* summative evaluation of teachers. Ascertain whether the ad-

ministrator attempts to separate these two functions, and if so, how he or she attempts to maintain such separation. Question the administrator on the advantages and disadvantages of such dual resonsibility. Prepare a report on your interview.

DEVELOPMENTAL

1   Begin an in-depth study of the development of clinical supervision by comparing three major works in clinical supervision, such as Goldhammer (1969); Cogan (1973); and Goldhammer, Anderson, and Krajewski (1980).

2. Begin an in-depth study of peer supervision, beginning with Alfonso and Goldsberry (1982).

3. As you continue your readings on the tasks of supervision, note the interrelationship of direct assistance with the other tasks of supervision and how previously discussed knowledge and skills of supervisors are common prerequisites for each task.

REFERENCES

Alfonso, R. J., and Goldsberry, L. F. 1982. Colleagueship in supervising. In T. J. Sergiovanni, ed., *Supervision*. Alexandria, Va.: Association for Supervision and Curriculum Development.

Bruce, R. E., and Hoehn, L. 1980. Supervisory practice in Georgia and Ohio. Paper presented at the annual meeting of the Council of Professors of Instructional Supervision, Hollywood, Fla., December.

Cogan, M. 1973. *Clinical supervision*. Boston: Houghton-Mifflin.

Dornbush, S. M., and Scott, W. R. 1975. *Evaluation and the exercise of authority*. San Francisco: Jossey-Bass.

Edmonds, R. 1982. On school improvement. *Educational Leadership 40*(3): 13.

Glickman, C. D., and Esposito, J. P. 1979. *Leadership guide for elementary school improvement*. Boston: Allyn and Bacon, pp. 233–250.

Goldhammer, R. 1969. *Clinical supervision: Special methods for the supervision of teachers.* New York: Holt, Rinehart and Winston.

Goldhammer, R.; Anderson, R. H.; and Krajewski, R. J. 1980. *Clinical supervision: Special methods for the supervision of teachers,* 2nd ed. New York: Holt, Rinehart and Winston.

Goldsberry, L. F. 1980. Colleague consultation: Teacher collaboration using a clinical supervision model. Unpublished Ed. D. diss., University of Illinois, Urbana–Champaign.

Harris, B. M. 1975, *Supervisory behavior in education,* 2nd ed. Englewood Cliffs, N.J.: Prentice-Hall.

Humphries, J. D. 1981. Factors affecting the impact of curriculum innovations on classroom practice: Project complexity, characteristics of local leadership and supervisory strategies. Unpublished Ed.D. diss., University of Georgia.

Kohlberg, L. 1969. Stage and sequence: The cognitive-development approach to socialization. In D. Goslin, ed., *Handbook of socialization theory and research.* Chicago: Rand-McNally.

Lortie, D. C. 1975. *School teacher: A sociological study.* Chicago: University of Chicago Press, pp. 75–77.

McGreal, T. L. 1982. Effective teacher evaluation systems. *Educational Leadership, 39*(4):303–305.

Mohlman, G. G. 1982. Assessing the impact of three inservice teacher training models. Paper presented at the annual meeting of the American Educational Research Association, New York, March.

Natriello, G. 1982. The impact of the evaluation of teaching on teacher effect and effectiveness. Paper presented at the annual meeting of the American Educational Research Association, New York, March.

Oliva, P. F. 1976. *Supervision for today's schools.* New York: Harper & Row.

Reavis, C. A. 1977. A test of the clinical supervision model. *Journal of Educational Research 70*:311–315.

Roper, S. S.; Deal, T. E.; and Dornbush, S. 1976. Collegial evaluation of classroom teaching: Does it work? *Educational Research Quarterly,* Spring, pp. 56–66.

Snyder, K. J.; Johnson, W. L.; and MacPhail-Wilcox, B. 1982. The implementation of clinical supervision. Paper presented at the annual meeting of the Southwest Educational Research Association, February.

Sullivan, C. G. 1980. *Clinical supervision: A state of the art review.* Alexandria, Va.: Association for Supervision and Curriculum Development.

SUGGESTIONS FOR ADDITIONAL READING

Acheson, K. A., and Gall, M. D. 1980. *Techniques in the clinical supervision of teachers.* New York: Longman.

Boyan, N. J. and Copeland, W. 1978. *Instructional supervision training program.* Columbus, Ohio: Merrill.

Champagne, D. W., and Hogan, R. C. 1977. *Supervisory and management skills: A competency-based training program for middle managers of educational systems.* Pittsburgh: Program of Curriculum and Supervision, University of Pittsburgh.

Cogan, M. L. 1973. *Clinical supervision.* Boston: Houghton-Mifflin.

Glickman, C. D. 1981. *Developmental supervision: Alternative practices for helping teachers improve instruction.* Alexandria, Va.: Association for Supervision and Curriculum Development.

Goldhammer, R. 1969. *Clinical supervision: Special methods for the supervision of teachers.* New York: Holt, Rinehart and Winston.

Goldhammer, R.; Anderson, R. H.; and Krajewski, R. J. 1980. *Clinical supervision: Special methods for the supervision of teachers,* 2nd ed. New York: Holt, Rinehart and Winston.

Reavis, C. A. 1978. *Teacher improvement through clinical supervision.* Bloomington, Ind.: Phi Delta Kappa Educational Foundation.

Sullivan, C. G. 1980. *Clinical supervision: A state of the art review.* Alexandria, Va.: Association for Supervision and Curriculum Development.

Wingspan: The Pedamorphosis Communique 1(1)(1220 Broadway, Suite 605, Lubbock, Texas 79401). Issue devoted to clinical supervision.

CHAPTER FIFTEEN

In-Service Education

Bob Jeffries, director of staff development, calls six school principals into his office to plan for the upcoming in-service day. He begins by explaining that the in-service program will begin with a morning session attended by the entire school system faculty, to take place in the high school auditorium. The afternoon will consist of individual school activities, with the principal being responsible for whatever transpires. He asks the principals: "What might we do for the morning session?" One principal suggests that at this time of year teachers could use an emotional lift, and that an inspirational speaker would be good. Another principal adds that she had heard a Dr. Zweibach give a great talk entitled "The Thrill of Teaching" at a national principal's conference last summer. She thinks he would be a terrific speaker. Bob Jeffries likes these suggestions and tells the principals he will call Dr. Zweibach and make arrangements for his appearance.

On the in-service day 238 teachers file into the auditorium and fill all but the first eight rows of seats. Mr. Jeffries makes a few introductory remarks about how fortunate "we" are to have Dr. Zweibach with "us" and then turns the session over to Dr. Zweibach. A rumpled, middle-aged university professor walks to the microphone and launches into his talk on the thrill of teaching. Within ten minutes, signs of restlessness, boredom, and bitterness are evident throughout the audience. Twelve of the teachers are sitting through a talk they had heard Dr. Zweibach deliver verbatim two years earlier at a teacher convention. Fifteen others are thinking about the classroom work they could be doing to prepare for next semester and wondering, "Why in the world are we sitting through this talk?" Another twenty-two teachers have become impatient with Dr. Zweibach's continual reference to the academic high school settings where he found teaching thrills. Their own work settings are vocational, special education, and elementary; they can't relate what he is saying about high schools to their world. Eventually some teachers begin to correct papers, read, or knit; a few appear to fall asleep. On the other hand, nearly half the members of the audience remain attentive and give Dr. Zweibach a rousing ovation when he concludes. The other half appear relieved that the talk is finally over and they can return to their own schools. Upon leaving the auditorium one can overhear such remarks as "What a great talk!" and "Why do we have to put up with all this in-service crap?"

This depiction of an in-service day is typical of many school systems. Some teachers find it valuable, but many do not. In-service days have been referred to as "the slum of American education, neglected and of little effect" (Wood and Thompson 1980). In-service is often viewed by supervisors, administrators, and teachers as a number of days contracted for in the school calendar that simply need to be endured. The two crucial questions that will shape this chapter are: (1) Why is in-service needed? (2) How should it be planned and conducted? A supervisor with responsibility for in-service cannot hope to make every activity interesting and valuable to every teacher, but he or she can expect in-service to be, overall, of value and interest to most if not all staff members. The ultimate outcome of in-service should be improved instruction for students.

Research on Effective Staff Development

Considerable research exists on effective in-service programs (ERIC 1980; Dillon-Peterson 1981; Hough and Bishop 1981). Let's focus on some of these findings, with a particular look at the works of Berman and McLaughlin (1978); Lawrence (1974); Mohlman, Kierstead, and Gundlach (1982); and Joyce and Showers (1980, 1982).

The Rand Corporation was contracted by the federal government to conduct a four-year study of three hundred educational projects (Berman and McLaughlin 1978). The researchers surveyed 852 administrators and 689 teachers, and conducted on-site observations of projects. Two years later they resurveyed 100 projects and revisited 18 sites where the innovative projects had continued beyond their funded period. The researchers found that successful projects had common characteristics of in-service (see McLaughlin and Marsh 1978; ERIC 1980). The findings were that:

1. Training was concrete, continual, and tied to the world of the teacher.

2. Local resource personnel provided direct follow-up assistance to teachers after in-service activities.

3. Peer observation and peer discussion provided teachers with reinforcement and encouragement.

4. The school leader participated in the in-service activities.

5. Regular project meetings were held with teachers for problem solving and adapting techniques and skills of the innovation that were not working as expected.

6. Released time was used for teachers instead of monetary payment for after-school work.

7. In-service was planned with teachers prior to and during the project.

Humphries's study on curriculum innovation of thirty-six schools in Georgia from 1980 to 1981 affirmed the findings of Berman and McLaughlin. Humphries found that collaborative planning of in-service was a particularly powerful explanatory variable related to program success (Humphries 1981).

Lawrence (1974) reviewed ninety-seven studies of in-service programs and separated effective programs from less effective ones. The findings of effective programs are similar to those of the Rand study but contain some additional information. The findings were:

1. Individualized in-service activities are more effective than large-group activities.

2. Programs that incorporate demonstrations, trials, and feedback of ideas are more effective than lecturing and reading of ideas.

3. In-service programs are more successful when teachers are active planners and help each other.

Mohlman, Kierstead, and Gundlach (1982) developed an in-service program for basic skill instruction for secondary school teachers. The program incorporates the findings already cited as well as the recent research of Joyce and Showers (1980), Stallings (1980), and Mohlman (1982). Joyce and Showers have shown that in-service programs that use presentation, demonstration, and practice as well as classroom feedback and coaching are more successful than programs that do not use feedback and coaching. In other words, teachers acquire and use in-service skills more readily when there is follow-up into their own classrooms. Stallings has shown that small-group problem solving workshops in which six to seven teachers share and experiment show greater results than workshops with large groups.

Finally, Mohlman has compared three different in-service models: The first contained presentation, demonstration, practice, and feedback; the second contained presentation, demonstration, practice, and feedback followed by peer observation; and the third contained presentation, demonstration, practice, feedback, and trainer coaching. She found participants acquired more classroom skills with the second model of peer observation. The trainer-coaching model ranked second in skill acquisition, and the model that did not have peer observation or coaching ranked last.

The Mohlman, Kierstead, and Gundlach model, now being used in a pilot study with the California Department of Education, incorporates various elements of effective in-service. It includes:

1. Small-group workshops spaced three weeks apart.

2. Peer observations.

3. Postobservation analysis and conferencing focused on skills introduced in workshops.

4. Classroom experimentation and modification of implemented skills.

The major findings of effective in-service programs can be summarized in an in-service planning checklist (see Table 15–1). When reviewing or developing a plan for in-service, the supervisor can check to see if the established components of effectiveness are provided.

TABLE 15–1   Checklist for Planning In-Service

Participants involved in planning	_____
Planning, long-term	_____
Released time for participants	_____
Training, concrete and specific	_____
Small-group workshops	_____
Peer observations and feedback	_____
Demonstration, trial, and feedback in workshops	_____
Feedback and coaching in classrooms after workshops	_____
Regular participant meetings for problem solving, experimentation and alterations	_____
Instructional and school leaders participating in activities	_____

Individual Teacher-Based In-Service

There are many ways to determine topic priorities for in-service programs. Chapter Eleven detailed the techniques of eyes and ears, official records, third-party review, written open-ended surveys, check and ranking lists, and the Delphi technique. Any of these techniques would give a planning committee an idea of in-service topics desired by particpants. For example, the director of staff development might survey the teaching personnel of the school system for individual priorities and might find that *discipline* appears as the top-priority topic for both elementary and secondary teachers. This does not mean, however, that the planning committee can be assured that if they find an expert on discipline to work with staff throughout the school year, they will have a successful in-service program. When teachers check off a topic such as discipline as their top priority, *those individual checks mean different things to different people.* An eleventh-grade teacher who checks discipline thinks, "I want to learn how to handle those big, tough, obnoxious students who keep making me back down." Another eleventh-grade teacher checks the discipline box thinking, "I want to learn how to conduct class discussions so students will listen more attentively to each other." A seventh-grade teacher checks the discipline box thinking, "I want to encourage self-discipline and have students take on more responsibility for their homework, studying for tests, and asking for help." An in-service program on discipline that does not account for what individual teachers mean will be a hit-or-miss affair. The content of a general session on discipline will, by chance, fit the needs of some and miss those of others. A consultant who is an expert on teaching assertive behavior will be of real benefit to the eleventh-grade teacher who is being intimidated by students; the same consultant would be of some benefit to the eleventh-grade teacher who wants to conduct classroom discussions but of little benefit to the seventh-grade teacher who desires students to develop self-discipline. To be relevant, in-service needs to be planned not only according to prioritized topics but also according to the individual meanings ascribed to the topics.

Gene Hall and his associates at the Research and Development Center for Teacher Education have made substantial contributions to the planning of in-service programs based on individual meaning to participants. They found that teachers have different levels of interest, commitment, and needs when it comes to instructional changes. As in our example on discipline, they found that an innovation such as individualized instruction, mastery learning, or team teaching has different meanings to individuals and that teachers are concerned with different aspects of the proposed topic.

How does one find out what a teacher means by his or her priority for in-service? As Hall and associates found, the best way to find out is simply to ask. If discipline emerges as a school system's number one priority for in-service, a follow-up form might be sent to teachers. A simple open-ended form has been developed by Newlove and Hall (1976):

WHEN YOU THINK ABOUT DISCIPLINE, WHAT ARE YOU CONCERNED ABOUT? Do not say what you think others are concerned about, but only what concerns you *now*. Please write in complete sentences, and please be frank.

From reading the responses, the in-service planning committee can group the concerns into different categories. Some may be concerned with assertiveness, some with leading discussion groups, some with giving students more self-responsibility, and some with schoolwide rules. Common concerns could be handled through large-group instruction; more individualized concerns could be handled by various choices of small-group workshops. An additional way of using concerns as a guide to planning in-service is for a school or school system to propose a program innovation. Hall, Wallace, and Dossett (1973) found that teacher concerns about a particular program innovation could be grouped into stages that would provide information about the focus of in-service. These stages of concern are found in Figure 15–1.

If a school system or individual school had decided to implement a new program such as mastery learning in mathematics, they could administer the concern survey and find whether staff were largely in the awareness, informational, personal, management, consequence, collaboration, or refocusing stage. Hall, Loucks, Rutherford, and Newlove (1975) have proposed matching stages of concerns with level of utilization to decide on the focus of in-service. Teachers with concerns at the awareness, information, or personal stage, and whose current level of utilization of an innovation is low, should have in-service that focuses on orienting, providing information, discussing the rationale for the innovation, and demonstrating the personal benefits of the change. Teachers with management and consequence concerns, who also have begun to use the innovations in their classrooms, should have in-service that focuses on the mechanics, routine, and refinement of the skills through workshop practice and classroom application. Those who have collaboration or refocusing concerns as well as proficiency in utilizing the innovation should have in-service based on integration of individual skills with those of other colleagues and should be encouraged to reevaluate and modify the innovation.

The work of Hall and his associates has added individual concern and utilization of innovations as factors to be considered when planning in-service. The knowledge that teachers want help in discipline (or any other topic or program) is simply not enough information for planning effective programs. Soon we will see that other information about teachers also can be used for planning in-service.

FIGURE   15–1   Stages of Concern about the Innovation

---

0   AWARENESS: Little concern about or involvement with the innovation is indicated.

1   INFORMATIONAL: A general awareness of the innovation and interest in learning more detail about it is indicated. The person seems to be unworried about himself/herself in relation to the innovation. She/he is interested in substantive aspects of the innovation in a selfless manner such as general characteristics, effects, and requirements for use.

2   PERSONAL: Individual is uncertain about the demands of the innovation, his/her inadequacy to meet those demands, and his/her role with the innovation. This includes analysis of his/her role in relation to the reward structure of the organization, decision making and consideration of potential conflicts with existing structures or personal commitment. Financial or status implications of the program for self and colleagues may also be reflected.

3   MANAGEMENT: Attention is focused on the processes and tasks of using innovation and the best use of information and resources. Issues related to efficiency, organizing, managing, scheduling, and time demands are utmost.

4   CONSEQUENCE: Attention focuses on impact of the innovation on students in his/her immediate sphere of influence. The focus is on relevance of the innovation for students; evaluation of student outcomes, including performance and competencies; and changes needed to increase student outcomes.

5   COLLABORATION: The focus is on coordination and cooperation with others regarding use of the innovation.

6   REFOCUSING: The focus is on exploration of more universal benefits from the innovation, including the possibility of major changes or replacement with a more powerful alternative. Individual has definite ideas about alternatives to the proposed or existing form of the innovation.

Source: Reprinted from Richard M. Bents and Kenneth R. Howey, "Staff Development—A Change in the Individual." In *Staff Development/Organization Development: ASCD 1981 Yearbook,* © 1981. Reprinted by permission of the Association for Supervision and Curriculum Development, Alexandria, Va. Original concept from G. E. Hall, R. C. Wallace, Jr., and W. A. Dossett, *A Developmental Conceptualization of the Adoption Process within Educational Institutions,* © 1973. Adapted by permission of the Research and Development Center for Teacher Education, University of Texas, Austin.

Conceptual and Psychological States

McKibbin and Joyce refer to David Hunt's principle of "optimal mismatch." Training environments should be oriented just above the level at which someone functions most comfortably. If the optimal mismatch is achieved, the teacher can function adequately but is pulled toward greater development (McKibbin and Joyce 1980, p. 254). Increasingly, in-service programs are planned to incorporate optimal mismatch of activities with conceptual and psychological levels of teachers (Thies-Sprinthall 1981; Oja 1981; McCarthy 1982; Wilsey and Killion 1982).

Chapter Four discussed how conceptual thinking of individuals moves from concrete and restrictive to abstract and multiperspective. Individuals with particular thought structures are able to process and respond to certain modes of training. For example, a concrete thinker is better able to respond to demonstrations of specific, isolated skills; an abstract thinker is better able to respond to discussion and making independent decisions on how to apply new skills. Let's reiterate the levels of abstract thinking discussed in Chapter Four (see Table 15–2).

Putting teacher abstraction aside momentarily, let's think of Hall's work on major stages of concern. The major stages of teacher concerns are *orientation* concerns ("What is this skill, project, or topic? What will it do for me?"); *integrating* concerns ("How can I make this skill better in my classroom? How can I rearrange my instruction to make this skill, project or topic more effective?"); and *refinement* concerns ("How can I share and work with others to make this practice part of our team?")

The amount of emphasis to place on particular activities in an in-service program can be shown by displaying a graph with teacher concerns on the vertical line and teacher abstraction on the horizontal line (see Figure 15–2).

Teachers who have a low level of abstraction and whose concerns are with orientation would benefit from in-service training that demonstrates the benefits of the new practice, skill, or program. Since they are hesitant, unaware, and inexperienced in applying the necessary skills, in-service with such individuals or groups must focus on giving information and providing specific demonstration and practice. Finally, the workshops should focus on teachers' understanding of the personal advantages of the proposed changes. It would be foolish to move in-service into the integration phase until teachers have the willingness, confidence, and ability to implement the new skills.

Teachers at moderate levels of abstraction and concerns with integration would benefit from in-service that focuses on classroom practice with several cycles of observation, feedback, and coaching given by peers and supervisors. Obviously, the beginning activities of explanation and demonstrations are necessary in any in-service program, but the major focus for this group should be the application of skills into their classroom settings.

The third group of teachers displayed on the graph are those with high levels of abstraction and refinement concerns. In-service for such persons should be focused on experimentation, modification, brainstorming, and group problem solving to improve on skills and practices already implemented. Since these teachers are already well informed and able to apply the new skills, the first two in-service phases, demonstration and application, can be dismissed quickly.

TABLE 15–2   Levels of Abstract Thinking

Low	Moderate	High
Confusion about situation	Can define situation by focusing on one dimension	Can define situation by drawing on relationships between several sources of information
Doesn't know what can be done	Can think of several responses	Can relate the information to changes in classroom practice
Asks to be shown	Has difficulty in thinking of consequences of changing the situation	Can generate many alternative responses
Have habitual responses to varying situations		Can evaluate the consequences of each response and choose the one most likely to succeed

FIGURE 15–2   Level of Abstraction and Concern as Focus for In-Service

| | Abstraction | | |
	Low	Moderate	High
Orientation	*Demonstration of skill* ⁘ INFORMATION EXPLANATION, *DEMONSTRATION* AND WORKSHOP PRACTICE— SHOW PERSONAL BENEFITS	*Demonstration of skills* Information explanation, *Demonstration* and workshop practice— show personal benefits	*Demonstration of skills* Information explanation, *Demonstration* and workshop practice— show personal benefits
Integration	Classroom practice and observation, Direct assistance and peer supervision Application of skills	CLASSROOM PRACTICE ⁘ AND OBSERVATION, DIRECT ASSISTANCE AND PEER SUPERVISION APPLICATION OF SKILLS	Classroom practice and observation Direct assistance and peer supervision Application of skills
Refinement	*Improving skills* modification of classroom practice through teams. Brainstorm and group problem solving	*Improving skills* modification of classroom practice through teams. Brainstorm and group problem solving	*IMPROVING SKILLS* ⁘ MODIFICATION OF CLASSROOM PRACTICE THROUGH TEAMS, BRAINSTORM AND GROUP PROBLEM SOLVING
Concern			

⁘ = emphasis for inservice

The Experience Impact of In-Service Activities

As we acquire information on faculty members' varying thinking, needs, and utilization of new practices, and as we match those individual characteristics with a particular focus for in-service programs, we also need to think about the order of activities most suitable for a particular focus. Ben Harris (1980) has listed the array of in-service activities with a description of each activity according to sensory involvement, group size, experience, and type of objective. The supervisor and in-service committee can consider the chart shown in Table 15–3 in choosing the order of various activities. Harris defines sensory involvement, group size, and objective as follows:

> Sensory involvement refers to the physiological senses utilized by the participant. Only those clearly used in the activity are included. Each of the senses is listed in order of importance for learning. For instance, "(19) Panel Presenting—Audio, visual" indicates listening is most important, while visual involvement with the several panelists is less important for participant learning.
>
> Group size indicates the group that probably represents optimum use of the activity. For many activities, both larger and small groups are feasible, but effectiveness may be sacrificed or special arrangements may be required.
>
> Type of objective refers to the outcomes that are most probably and clearly possible under normal conditions of use of the activity. Other objectives are always potentially possible, of course. For instance, a lecture could be so dramatically presented as to have affective outcomes. Testing could be employed under special circumstances to produce affective outcomes. The interview could relate to problem solving in ways that model and hence produce problem-solving skills. [Harris 1980, pp. 77, 81].

Experience impact is the degree to which the individual participant will be totally involved on each dimension of senses, interactions, experience control, focus, activeness, originality, and reality. The experience impact score was derived by totaling the scores on each dimension (1 = low, 3 = high) for each dimension of the activity. The total score is an estimate of the impact on the individual. Although Harris's experience impact scale is theoretically derived and not empirically tested, it has much commonsense appeal when deciding on activities.

Table 15-3   Basic Activities for In-Service Education Session Design

Activity	Sensory Involvement	Group Size	Experience Impact	Type of Objective
1. Analyzing and calculating	Visual, kinesthetic	Ind.	16	Cognitive
2. Brainstorming	Audio, visual, oral	Med.	13	Cognitive
3. Buzz session	Audio, oral	Sml.	14	Cognitive, affective
4. Demonstrating	Visual, audio	Med.	12	Cognitive
5. Discussing, leaderless	Audio, oral, visual	Sml.	10	Cognitive
6. Discussing, leader-facilitated	Audio, oral, visual	Ind.	11	Cognitive, affective
7. Film, television, filmstrip viewing	Visual, audio	Med.	10	Cognitive affective
8. Firsthand experience	Audio, oral, visual, kinesthetic	Ind.	21	Skill, cognitive, affective
9. Group therapy	Audio, oral, visual	Sml.	16	Affective
10. Guided practice	Kinesthetic, visual, audio	Ind.	19	Skill, cognitive
11. Interviewing, informative	Audio, oral	Ind.	9	Cognitive
12. Interviewing, problem-solving	Audio, visual, oral, kinesthetic	Ind.	15	Cognitive
13. Interviewing, therapeutic	Audio, oral, visual	Ind.	17	Affective
14. Lecturing	Audio	Lrg.	7	Cognitive
15. Material, equipment viewing	Visual, kinesthetic	Med.	12	Cognitive
16. Meditating	Kinesthetic	Ind.	12	Affective, cognitive
17. Microteaching	Audio, visual, oral	Sml.	18	Skill, affective
18. Observing systematically in classroom	Visual, audio	Sml.	13	Cognitive, affective
19. Panel presenting	Audio, visual	Lrg.	8	Cognitive
20. Reading	Visual	Ind.	14	Cognitive, affective
21. Role playing, spontaneous	Audio, visual, oral	Sml.	16	Affective
22. Role playing, structured	Audio, visual, oral	Sml.	18	Cognitive, skill
23. Social interaction	Audio, visual, oral	Sml.-Med.	13	Affective, cognitive
24. Tape, radio, record listening	Audio	Lrg.	7	Cognitive, affective
25. Testing	Audio, kinesthetic	Med.	16	Cognitive
26. Videotaping or photographing	Visual, kinesthetic	Ind.	16	Cognitive
27. Visualizing	Visual	Lrg.	9	Cognitive
28. Writing or drawing	Visual, kinesthetic	Ind.	12	Cognitive

Source: B. M. Harris, *Improving Staff Performance through In-Service Education.* Reprinted by permission of Allyn and Bacon. Adapted from Ben M. Harris, *Supervisory Behavior in Education,* 2nd Ed., © 1975, p. 73. Adapted by permission of Prentice-Hall, Inc., Englewood Cliffs, N.J.

Let's look at how we can use this experience impact of activity for planning in-service with three hypothetical situations involving various groups of teachers concerned with discipline.

Situation 1

Group 1 consists mostly of teachers who readily use corporal punishment for most student infractions. They are unaware of and reluctant to use other approaches to discipline. Their concern is with how to get students to "shape up." Behavior problems are viewed as student problems, not problems for which the teacher might share responsibility.

Assessment of Situation 1.   We can identify this group as in the *orientation stage* of concern with a *low or concrete level of abstraction.* They appear to need in-service that will focus both on demonstration of new approaches and on discussion of the personal benefits of using new approaches.

Selection of Activities.   The criteria for choosing activities are that they should provide specific, demonstrated skills but be non-threatening and of low experience impact.

Planners of in-service consider the list of experience impact activities (Table 15–3). They might choose to begin with these five activities:

1. *Panel presenting:* A group of representative teachers will discuss their current difficulties with discipline, what they have tried, and what they would like to do in the future. This is a low-impact, cognitive, large-group activity that involves the visual and audio senses.

2. *Discussing, leader-facilitated:* The next activity will have small groups of teachers discuss their own attitudes, problems, and thinking about new approaches to discipline. This small-group activity is of modest experience impact; involves audio, visual, and oral senses; and will provide a chance for teachers to assess their own beliefs.

3. *Lecturing:* An expert on discipline will present discipline approaches that have been found to be efficient in reducing teacher time for handling troublesome students. This low-experience, audio, cognitive, and large-group activity provides a concrete understanding for the teachers of the benefits and use of specific skills.

4. *Demonstration:* An activity in which an expert shows the teachers how to use the skills explained in the previous lecture. The expert might actually work with a group of students in front of the teachers, or show a videotape of such work, or use teachers to

play the roles of students. This activity is of low experience impact, involves the visual and auditory senses, is a cognitive activity, and can be done with a medium-sized group.

5. *Role-playing, structured:* Teachers will now be asked to try out the demonstrated skills in a nonthreatening, gamelike situation. Teachers are assigned roles and asked to use the new skills. This activity uses all the senses, helps a teacher gain confidence in being able to use the practiced skills later in a real classroom setting, is best done in small groups, and provides for cognitive learning.

Situation 2

Group 2 comprises mostly teachers who have been dissatisfied with their current classroom discipline practices and have been attempting in a random fashion to do things differently. They read articles on discipline in popular teacher magazines and are aware of some of the new practices. They are experiencing difficulties in selecting and integrating new practices (a time-out area, new classroom rules, a reinforcement system) into their instruction. Many of the new practices have been started haltingly but stopped when unforeseen problems arose. This is indicative of the integration stage. The teachers want to improve discipline, are willing to continue to work on improvement, but desire help in organizing and streamlining their actions.

Assessment of Situation 2. We can identify this group as being concerned with management and consequence, with a willing attitude toward new practices. Yet their level of abstraction about such practices is moderate. They can define their discipline problems, have a sense of changes that might be made, but are uncertain about making these changes on their own.

Selection of Activities. Activities should provide classroom practice, direct observation, coaching by an expert, peer observation, and peer supervision. The focus of in-service would be on applying skills in the ongoing classroom. The experience impact should be relatively high, using all senses, and should involve each teacher with practice in his or her own classroom. The sequence of activities might be as follows:

1. *Demonstrating:* This relatively low experience impact activity, conducted by an expert or by teachers themselves, serves as a review of the various discipline practices that might be used. Discipline practices that have been used by teachers in the group could be demonstrated to the entire group. Thus the in-service begins on a cognitive, informational basis.

2. *Role playing:* This higher-impact activity will consist of individual teachers selecting one or two of the previously demonstrated skills and practicing those skills in a workshop setting. An example might be a role-playing triad. One teacher might be a disruptive student in class, a second teacher would practice a skill of dealing with the disruptive student, and a third teacher would be an observer giving feedback to the teacher after the scenario was concluded. The actors would then switch roles until each teacher had a chance to practice and receive feedback.

3. *First-hand experience:* The teachers will then try out the new skill over a period of time in their classroom and keep a report of their progress. This real experience then serves as the basis for future guided practice and observation.

4. *Guided practice:* This activity will incorporate the use of another person, perhaps a supervisor, in reviewing the teachers' first-hand progress with the skill and reviewing what the teacher will attempt to practice during a short classroom observation. The teacher will demonstrate the skill prior to the session, and the supervisor will suggest corrections. The teacher will then demonstrate the same skills during the classroom observation. This activity is of high impact, involves all the senses, and is real.

5. *Discussion, leader-facilitated:* The teachers will step away from the classroom with an activity that provides a chance to discuss in small groups the future work needed to consolidate their new practices into the ongoing classroom routine. They might explain their needs, receive suggestions from other teachers, and arrange to observe each other. The activity leader helps each individual teacher to organize classroom practice and arranges for peer classroom visits.

6. *Systematic observation in classroom:* This technical, moderate-impact activity will prepare teachers to observe each other. They will learn how to focus on the specific classroom practices they have learned as a result of in-service. They will be given observation forms and use these forms on trial tapes. This activity is of moderate experience impact, is both cognitive and affective in nature, and is best done in small groups.

7. *Guided practice:* This highly involving activity will repeat itself. This time teachers will guide and observe each other's practice rather than having the formal supervisor do so. Teachers will have the opportunity to learn how others are using the in-service skills and be able to provide feedback to each other. This activity is of high experience impact, involving all the senses.

At this point, implementation of new practice should be well established, and a new focus for in-service will emerge.

Situation 3

Group 3 consists of teachers who are highly proficient with respect to discipline. They are confident in their ability to handle classroom disruption but believe that discipline could be even more productive if teachers used complementary discipline approaches from classroom to classroom. They realize that from time to time even the best teacher will confront a situation with an individual student or small group of students that will strain his or her tolerance. They are concerned with ways to help each other when stressful discipline situations occur, and they are concerned with adopting mutual practices to improve discipline throughout the school.

Assessment of Situation 3.   Here we see a group of teachers with refinement concerns: collaboration and refocusing. They view discipline in highly abstract ways by considering multiple options for dealing with disruptive students. They have a history of being decisive and thorough in implementing new procedures.

Selection of Activities.   The activities chosen should be ones that help teachers reflect on current individual practice and think about ways to complement each other. The first activities might be cognitive, collaborative, and of low experience impact. The next phase might be implementation activities, which are of high experience impact. Implementation might be followed by collaborative activities to revise and refine team practices. Let's follow a sample sequence of activities on discipline that should build individual discipline skills into consistent team skills.

1. *Analyzing and calculating:* Teachers will individually express how teaming efforts could help their own classrooms. Teachers will fill out a form and then read what they have written to the entire group. This activity, of moderate experience impact, allows for each person's thoughts to be considered by the entire group before they discuss the merits and demerits of ideas.

2. *Discussion, leaderless:* Teachers will work in small groups to discuss common ways to support each other in the area of discipline. They might be grouped according to grade level, department, or adjoining classrooms. Some solutions a small group could decide on might include a system of signals to call on other teachers to leave their classrooms to help when a particular teacher finds him- or herself facing an emergency, or a reinforcement system for certain students that would be consistent from classroom to classroom. This cognitive, low-impact activity serves as preparation for the implementation phase.

3. *Role-playing, structured:* The team will practice among themselves the new practices to be used. For example, a consistent reinforcement system might be practiced by having teachers role play responding to different disruptive behaviors and then determining whether teachers have applied consistent rewards and sanctions. This activity is very close to reality. It is of higher experience impact than the previous two activities and is basically cognitive.

4. *First-hand experience:* This activity will usher in the experimentation phase, and teachers will keep notes on the progress of the plan. They are now individually responsible for their own parts in the team plan. The activity is of the highest experience impact, involving all senses, with both cognitive and affective involvement.

5. *Buzz session:* The individuals will return to an activity that enables them to reflect on the first-hand experience and discuss their progress reports. They reveal happenings, actions, and feelings about the plan. This low-impact activity allows teachers to be empathetic and reflective about each other's progress and involvement. This session is a time for generating feelings and thoughts without judging individual progress.

6. *Discussion, leaderless:* This activity kicks off the cycle of refining and changing team practices. Team members have learned from the first-hand experience and have shared in the buzz session what they perceive to be happening. In this activity, they agree as a team on changes to be made before going on to the next phase of role playing and first-hand experience.

Sequence of Activities and Variations in Plans

The sequencing of in-service activities appropriate to groups of teachers has been described as one way of selecting activities. Other activities could have been chosen according to teachers' needs. In-service will have a greater chance of positive reception and will be more likely to promote enduring teacher change if teachers' individual and group characteristics are considered. As a rule of thumb, experience impact of activities should proceed from low to high. For teachers with concerns of orientation and personal benefits, activities should be of relatively low experience impact. We cannot expect teachers to implement new skills without having a chance to understand and accept the benefits of such skills. Teachers will not be committed to change until they themselves see the need for change. For teachers concerned with management and consequences of new skills in the classroom (integration concerns), activities should move from moderate to high experience impact. These teachers want practical applications, lectures and discussions. Finally, teachers who have refinement concerns— working as teams with others beyond their own classroom walls— desire in-service programs on collaborative planning; implementation activities should be of high experience impact.

These explanations have depicted groups of teachers as largely homogeneous. In the three situations the teachers were of similar levels of concern and abstraction. Teacher concern and degree of abstraction are not always closely related, however. For example, a teacher could have a low-level, orientation concern about an in-service topic but might be a highly abstract thinker. He or she might be able to process new information quickly and be ready for immediate application of new practices. Therefore, in-service that is planned only according to teacher concerns and not in relation to degree of abstraction could run into trouble, causing participants impatience and boredom. Pacing of activities is therefore an important consideration. For teachers of moderate and high levels of abstract thinking, quick pacing of activities is needed. For teachers of low abstract ability, slower, more repetitive activities are more appropriate.

Most school faculties, departments, and grade levels are not composed of teachers with identical stages of concern and/or abstraction. Therefore, the ideal plan would be to have different in-service programs for subgroups of teachers—one program that emphasizes demonstration, another that emphasizes application, and still another that emphasizes improving skills through teamwork. A less ideal but more realistic solution would be to develop an in-service plan that meets the needs of the majority of teachers and provides individual options for those with different needs. In-service aimed at promoting discussion about instructional matters among knowledgeable professionals can help achieve a school-wide commitment to "a cause beyond oneself," which is a key characteristic of successful schools.

The Nuts and Bolts

We have covered a great deal of information for planning in-service, but the best planning is useless if the supervisor forgets the nuts and bolts of in-service. What value is an excellent speaker who lectures in a room where the acoustics garble every word? What good is a fast-paced microteaching demonstration if it conflicts with other teacher meetings so that few can attend? What good is an exciting role-playing activity whose participants have had no chance to eat, unwind, or use the restroom during the previous two hours? If one is going to the trouble to plan in-service, then one should go the extra step to ensure an environment that enables participants to be responsive and comfortable.

Let's list six important considerations:

1. *Prepare speakers by telling them exactly what they are expected to do.* If a speaker is invited to conduct an activity, make sure he or she understands the assignment. Speakers will do whatever they normally do unless someone tells them elsewise. Most speakers have their own topics, their own rehearsed presentations, and their own formats. If a speaker is expected to demonstrate a particular skill (for example, asking higher-order questions) or to include role playing (scripts of classroom discussions), *tell him or her so.* Speaker and participants are both in an embarrassing situation when the speaker, through no fault of either party, is not doing what the participants have been led to expect.

2. *Check the facility beforehand for seating arrangements, media, and acoustics.* Make sure the facility is appropriate to the activity. For example, small-group discussions in an auditorium give teachers stiff necks and a stiffer attitude toward the next in-service. See that all equipment is operating correctly. Check microphones, cassettes, and overheads. Move around the room to see if displays on screen or walls can be viewed clearly by everyone. Have at hand spare bulbs and replacement equipment in case of an equipment failure.

3. *Provide refreshments and transition time at the beginning.* Tell participants where the restrooms are. Provide drinks and snacks. Informally greet the participants at the door and tell them when the session will begin. When formally beginning, inform participants when other breaks are scheduled.

4. *Check the comfort of the room.* Beforehand, check whether the room will maintain a comfortable temperature. Find out if the heating or cooling system is turned off at the time of the meeting and, if so, arrange to have the system operating. Estimate the temperature of the room when it is full. A room that feels comfortable when only a few people are present can become oppressively hot when full to capactiy.

5. *Have materials run off and a plan for easy dissemination to participants.* Prior to the session, check with the leader of the activity to make sure all desired materials will be prepared. Also before the session, figure out a distribution system for materials. Often a table next to the entrance with collected materials and a person responsible for telling entrants to pick up the materials is sufficient.

The Nuts and Bolts

FIGURE 15–3   In-Service Evaluation

We would like your feedback to plan future in-service sessions. Please circle the number closest to your feelings and provide comments in the space provided on the form. If you need more space, feel free to use the back of the sheet. As you leave, please drop this form in the box on the back table.

In-Service Topic _____

Date _____

	Poor	*Satisfactory*	*Good*	*Excellent*
1. The session today was	1	2	3	4

Comments _____

_____

_____

2. The organization of the session was	1	2	3	4

Comments _____

_____

_____

3. The meeting room was	1	2	3	4

Comments _____

_____

_____

4. The materials were	1	2	3	4

Comments _____

_____

_____

Suggestions for future meetings: _____

_____

_____

6. *Have evaluation forms for participants to fill out after the session.* Asking participants to evaluate the session allows existing problems to be corrected before the next session. A simple form to be filled out anonymously by participants can be seen in Figure 15–3.

Summary

For in-service education to be meaningful to teachers and to transfer into instructional improvement, it must be geared to the stages of teachers' concerns and thoughts. Research on successful in-service programs has shown an emphasis on involvement, long-term planning, problem-solving meetings, released time, concrete training, small-group workshops, peer feedback, demonstration and trials, coaching, and leader participation in activities. Consideration for individual and group characteristics can help make in-service more relevant to the participants. Research on stages of concern has shown that teachers differ according to awareness, informational, personal, management, consequence, collaboration, and refocusing needs. Teachers also vary from concrete to abstract in their thinking about particular in-service topics. The experience impact of in-service activities also can be used to choose activities with particular groups. Nuts-and-bolts considerations—informing speakers; checking facilities; and providing refreshments, materials, and evaluation—can increase the comfort and attentiveness of teachers. It's time to change the perception that in-service education is a waste of teachers' time to the perception of in-service as time well spent.

EXERCISES

ACADEMIC

1. Write a paper defining and discussing the concept of *the coaching of teaching*. Include descriptions of successful in-service coaching techniques found in the professional literature.

2. A small group of senior high teachers have requested an in-service program on making better use of open-ended ques-

tions during class discussions. The teachers are at a moderate level of abstraction, and their concern is at the integration stage. Outline a plan for an in-service program for these teachers on the requested topic.

3. A small group of elementary teachers from the same school have requested an in-service program on strategies for more effective team teaching. All these teachers have had considerable experience in team teaching, but they wish to improve their skills in this area. The teachers are at a high level of abstraction, and their concern is at the refinement stage. Outline a plan for an in-service program on team teaching for these teachers.

4. A general needs assessment, administered districtwide, has revealed that the number one perceived need of teachers in the district is for increased communication skills. Prepare a plan for assessing *specific* needs of various groups of teachers within this general topic, and include teachers in planning an in-service program that will meet their group and individual needs.

5. Write a paper summarizing three recent research studies on in-service education not discussed in this chapter. Include the purpose, participants, methodology, results, and conclusions of each study. Analyze the findings in terms of whether they are congruent with research findings cited in this chapter.

FIELD

1. Evaluate the needs assessment process a school district employs in planning in-service programs. As part of your evaluation, interview teachers to determine whether decisions on in-service activities reflect actual teacher needs. Include recommendations for improvement of the needs assessment process in your report.

2. Attend an in-service session for teachers. Evaluate the in-service session in terms of (a) the extent to which the session reflects the major research findings on effective in-service programs, (b) whether varying levels of abstraction and stages of concern are taken into consideration, (c) organization, (d) facilities, and (e) materials. Note informal reactions of teachers attending the session. Include suggestions for improving future in-service sessions.

3. Interview five teachers concerning a program innovation that is being proposed or introduced in their school. On the basis of the interviews, attempt to classify each teacher according to his or her stage of concern about the innovation.

4. Interview an individual who has considerable experience at planning in-service sessions on the practical aspects of preparing for such sessions. Ask him or her to relate past experiences that illustrate potential problems to avoid, eventualities to consider, and areas in which special preparation is necessary. Prepare a report on your interview.

5. Interview the individual in charge of staff development on a school system's long-range staff development program. (Be sure the school system *has* a long-range staff development program before arranging the interview!) Prepare a report describing and evaluating the program.

DEVELOPMENTAL

1. As you attend in-service activities over a period of time, observe the experience impact of different activities on various groups of teachers (the effects of high- and low-impact activities on teachers of various levels of abstraction and concern).

2. Develop a file of ideas for in-service activities. Research on successful in-service programs can serve as a planning source. Activities can be developed for individuals and groups at various stages of concern and abstraction. Experience impact can be considered when designing activities for teachers of different concern and thinking levels.

3. Volunteer to help plan and implement in-service activities in your school or school system. Try to incorporate the research on effective in-service into the plans.

REFERENCES

Berman, P., and McLaughlin, M. W., 1978. *Federal programs supporting educational change*, Vol. 8. *Implementing and sustaining innovations*. ED 159 289. Santa Monica, Calif.: Rand Corporation.

References

Dillin-Peterson, B., ed. 1981 *Staff development/organization development.* Alexandria, Va.: Association for Supervision and Curriculum Development.

ERIC. 1980. ERIC Research Action Brief—Clearinghouse on Educational Management, No. 10. EA 012 256. Eugene: University of Oregon.

Hall, G. E.; Loucks, S. F.; Rutherford, W. S.; and Newlove, B. W. 1975. Levels of use of the innovation: A framework for analyzing innovation adoption. *Journal of Teacher Education* 26(1):52–56.

Hall, G. E.; Wallace, R. C., Jr., and Dossett, W. A. 1973. *A developmental conceptualization of the adoption process within educational institutions.* Austin: Research and Development Center for Teacher Education, University of Texas.

Harris, B. M. 1975. *Supervisory behavior in education,* 2nd ed. Englewood Cliffs, N.J.: Prentice-Hall.

———. 1980. *Improving staff performance through in-service education.* Boston: Allyn and Bacon.

Hough, M. J., and Bishop, L. J. 1981. *An annotated resource guide to current literature on staff development in education.* Athens, Georgia: Department of Curriculum and Supervision, p. 73.

Humphries, J. D. 1981. Factors affecting the impact of curriculum innovations on classroom practice: Project complexity, characteristics of local leadership, and supervisory strategies. Unpublished Ed.D. diss., University of Georgia.

Joyce, B., and McKibbin, M. 1982. Teacher growth states and school environments. *Educational Leadership* 40(2):36–41.

Joyce B., and Showers, B. 1980. Improving in-service training: The message of research. *Educational Leadership* 37:379–385.

———. 1982. The coaching of teaching. *Educational Leadership* 40(1):4–10.

Lawrence, G. 1974. *Patterns of effective in-service education: A state of the art summary of research on materials and procedures for changing teacher behaviors in in-service education.* ED 176 424. Tallahassee: Florida State Department of Education.

McCarthy, B. 1982. Improving staff development through CBAM and 4 MatTM. *Educational Leadership* 40(1):20–25.

302

IN-SERVICE EDUCATION

McKibbin, M., and Joyce, B., 1980. Psychological states and staff development. *Theory into practice (TIP)* 19(4):248–255.

McLaughlin, M.W., and Marsh, D.D. 1978. Staff development and school change. *Teachers College Record* 80(1):69–94.

Mohlman, G. G. 1982. Assessing the impact of three in-service teacher training models. Paper presented at the annual meeting of the American Educational Research Association, New York.

Mohlman, G. G.; Kierstead, J.; and Gundlach, M. 1982. A research-based in-service model for secondary teachers. *Educational Leadership* 40(1):16–19

Newlove, B. W., and Hall, G. E. 1976. *A manual for assessing open-ended statements of concern about an innovation.* Austin: Research and Development Center for Teacher Education, University of Texas.

Oja, S. N. 1981. Adapting research findings in psychological education: A case study. Presentation at the annual meeting of the American Association of Colleges for Teacher Education. Detroit, February.

Stallings, J. 1980. Allocated academic learning time revisted or Beyond time on task. *Educational Researcher,* December.

Thies-Sprinthall, L. 1981. Promoting the conceptual and principled thinking level of the supervising teacher. Unpublished research funded by St. Cloud State University, 1978 and 1979. Reported in Educating for teacher growth: A cognitive developmental perspective. Paper presented at the annual meeting of the American Educational Research Association, Los Angeles, April.

Wilsey, C., and Killion, J. 1982. Making staff development programs work. *Educational Leadership* 40(1):36–38, 43.

Wood, F. W., and Thompson, S. R. 1980. Guidelines for better staff development. *37*(5):374–378

SUGGESTIONS FOR ADDITIONAL READING

Bishop, L. J. 1976. *Staff development and instructional improvement. Plans and procedures.* Boston: Allyn and Bacon.

Dillon-Peterson, B., ed. 1981. *Staff development/organization development*. Alexandria, Va.: Association for Supervision and Curriculum Development.

Educational Leadership 40 (1), October 1982. Entire issue on the coaching of teaching.

Harris, B. M. 1980. *Improving staff performance through in-service education*. Boston: Allyn and Bacon.

Joyce, B. R., and Showers, B. 1983. *Power in staff development through research on training*. Alexandria, Va.: Association for Supervision and Curriculum Development.

Rubin, L., ed. 1978. *The in-service education of teachers*. Boston: Allyn and Bacon.

CHAPTER SIXTEEN

Curriculum Development

Imagine we have just heard about a phenomenal new chemistry curriculum that has been field-tested in twenty-seven school systems throughout the United States and has resulted in a 100 percent student success rate. The curriculum has been created by some of the most distinguished chemists and educators in the country. All students in grades ten, eleven, and twelve who have been taught by the new curriculum have scored in the upper 10 percent of a nationally normed chemistry achievement test. Furthermore, their attitudes toward chemistry are far superior to those of comparable high school students who have been taught by other chemistry curricula.

To verify this success story, we travel to some of the school sites, review the curriculum materials, and look over test results. We find it's true, and we decide the curriculum should be used immediately in our schools. We will need to purchase the materials and hire a consultant to show teachers how to use the curriculum. We believe we will have immediate success.

The truth is that, if we proceed as planned, we probably will not achieve much success with this curriculum. Teachers will use it half-heartedly and keep returning to their old lecture notes and traditional instructional activities. Within a few years most of the new materials will be lost or abandoned. Ten years from now, stacks of the new curriculum materials might be gathering dust in the school attic.

From the late 1950s to the early 1970s, the National Science Foundation allocated millions of dollars for the development of such new curricula. University scholars were hired to develop materials to improve instruction in elementary and secondary science and mathematics. The U.S. Office of Education similarly spent large sums of monies to hire subject specialists to develop curricula in English and social studies. The curricula were carefully constructed, field-tested, revised, and tested again—only to be resisted, misused, and abandoned when implemented in public schools.

Some of the best curricula developed, such as "Man: A Course of Study" (MACOS) and the Physical Science Study Committee's physics course (PSSC) showed overwhelming student success during the pilot phase, yet they are hardly used now. A series of reports on the results of twenty years of federally supported curriculum development concluded that nearly all such curricula have been bypassed by schools (See Ponder 1979; Yager and Stodghill 1979; Gibney and Karns 1979). Why is this so? Doll (1982, p. 313) explained: "It seems likely that an important reason many of the massive curriculum projects ... proved so disappointing is that they did not take into account the differing situations in which the projects were expected to take root."

One lesson to be learned by supervisors is that it makes no difference how good a curriculum is if teachers will not use it. To think of any curriculum as being teacher-proof—the label used for those federally supported curricula—was a mistake. *Teacher-proof* implies that the curriculum is so complete and detailed that it is immune to teacher practice and belief. Since then we've learned a multimillion-dollar lesson: Curricula cannot be teacher-proof as long as schools are loosely coupled organizations.

Loosely coupled is a term that refers to an organization in which there is an absence of continual monitoring of the work force. A tightly coupled organization, on the other hand, is characterized by managers closely monitoring the work force. Schools are loosely coupled because teachers are surrounded by four walls; only infrequently does anyone with managerial control see what they do. Educators know among themselves (but keep the fact from the public) that *basically teachers do whatever they want to do*. Therefore, in a loosely coupled organization, unless a teacher really desires to implement a curriculum, he or she won't. No one is going to stand over a teacher six hours a day, 180 days a year to see that the curriculum is being implemented. On those rare occasions when a person in authority does stand over a teacher, the teacher can usually give the person what he or she is expecting and then return to the usual method once the authority is gone. Therefore, any notion of a curriculum being teacher-proof simply flies in the face of reality. For a curriculum to be implemented by teachers, they have to be involved in choosing, adapting, and developing it. It must serve the needs of teachers, and they must want to use it.

Sir Alex Clegg wrote disparagingly of such so-called teacher-proof materials:

> I have no time whatever for any system which re-
> cruits high-powered thinkers to contour and foist a cur-
> riculum on the schools. This cannot work unless we be-
> lieve that the teacher of the future is to be a low-grade
> technician working under someone else's instructions
> rather than a professional making his own diagnoses
> and prescribing his own treatments [cited in Tanner and
> Tanner 1980, p. 629]

Denver Superintendent Jesse H. Newlon knew about curriculum
and loosely coupled organizations as far back as 1922, when he
originated the Denver plan, which gave curriculum development
and implementation to committees of teachers. Tanner and Tanner
wrote of Newlon as a person of

> ... deep and abiding faith in the teacher as a profes-
> sional. Because of this confidence and because he be-
> lieved that the study of curriculum problems was the
> best possible kind of inservice training, Newlon put
> teachers at the heart of the curriculum-making pro-
> cess. . . . [Tanner and Tanner 1980, p. 341]

The eight-year study completed in 1942 confirmed Newlon's
idea of the teacher at the heart of curriculum. In this historic
study, thirty private and public secondary schools were selected on
the basis of having a nontraditional, non-college-preparatory curriculum. Instead, the curriculum was unique to each high school
and was developed by the high school faculty. The students who
graduated from these thirty schools were matched with students
who graduated from high schools having a traditional, college pre-
paratory curriculum with little faculty involvement in curriculum
development.

Both groups of students were followed through college. It was
concluded from the study that graduates of the innovative, teacher-
involved schools had higher grade point averages; received more
academic honors; and were found to be more precise, systematic,
objective, and intellectually curious than were those who graduated from the traditional, non-teacher-involved schools (Aiken
1942). It was clear that schools operating with teacher involvement
in curriculum development provided a better education than did
schools operating without such involvement.

Thirty-three years later, the Rand Corporation found that
lasting and successful curriculum implementation projects were
characterized by "mutual adaptation." The Rand researchers found
that when teachers were involved in selecting, revising, and

changing an externally prescribed curriculum, the curriculum took hold and lasted (Berman and McLaughlin 1978).

It is clear that in order for schools to be successful, teachers need to be involved in curriculum development. The issues that remain for the supervisor are: (1) In what *ways* can curriculum be developed? (2) To what *degree* should teachers be involved?

In What Ways Can Curriculum Be Developed?

Curriculum, for purposes of this book, is: the content of instruction; what is intentionally taught to students in a district, school, or classroom; the guides, books, and materials that teachers use in teaching students. The elements of curriculum are sequence and continuity, scope, and balance (Doll 1982, pp. 141–146). *Sequence* is the ordering of learning experiences, and continuity is the length or duration of such experiences. *Scope* is the range of learning experiences to be offered. *Balance* is the degree and amount of topics, subjects, and learning experiences that adequately prepare students. A curriculum is developed by deciding: (1) What should students learn? (2) What is the order of content for the student to follow? (3) How is the learning to be evaluated? (see Firth and Newfield, 1984).

Decisions about curriculum are influenced by priorities of state and federal governments, values of professional educators and local community, knowledge of student development, current economics, and future societal conditions. Ultimately, what goes into a curriculum is derived from a philosophical decision about the purpose of schools (Glickman and Esposito 1979, pp. 29–38). For example, an essentialist philosophy is reflected by a curriculum that emphasizes rote learning, memorization of facts, and academic achievement. An experimentalist philosophy is reflected by a curriculum that emphasizes social activism, trial-and-error learning, and cooperation. An existentialist philosophy is reflected by a curriculum that emphasizes individual awareness, creativity, and self-exploration.

Philosophical emphasis can be detected further by the format used in writing curriculum. We will describe behavioral-objective, webbing, conceptual-mapping, and results-only formats. Curricula that follows a behavioral-objective format are reflections of essentialism. Curricula that follow a webbing or conceptual-mapping format are reflections of experimentalism. Curricula that follow a results-only format are reflections of existentialism. We will take each in turn.

Behavioral-Objective Format

Predetermined knowledge, facts, and skills are written in curriculum guides in a linear cause-and-effect format. The curriculum developers determine what is to be learned, state the learning as a behavioral objective, specify the teaching/learning activities, and conclude with a post-test to see if the objective has been achieved. The progression is

Objective   Activity   Evaluation

Figure 16–1 is an example of a behavioral objective guide written for a fifth-grade social studies class. Curriculum developers break their unit into the most important facts or skills that cover the subject. They write behavioral objectives for each fact or skill. Each behavioral objective involves a sequence of activities and evaluation. The teacher who uses such a curriculum guide is expected to follow the sequence of activities and administer the evaluation. Recycling activities might be included in the guide for those students who do not pass the evaluation. Each behavioral-objective plan is tightly sequenced so that one objective is mastered before a student moves to the next (for example, after identifying and spelling the original thirteen American colonies, the next objective might be identifying and spelling those states that came into the Union from 1776 to 1810). Another example of a behavioral objective curriculum format is given in Appendix F.

FIGURE 16–1   Behavioral-Objective Format

Behavioral objective: At the end of the week, students will recall and spell the original thirteen colonies at a 100 percent level of mastery.

Activities:
1. Lecture on thirteen colonies.
2. Students fill in map of thirteen colonies.
3. Students read pp. 113–118 of text and do assignments on p. 119 as homework.
4. Call on students at random to spell the various colonies.

Evaluation: Ask students to recall the names and spell correctly each of the thirteen original colonies on a sheet of paper.

Most school curricula that have been written in the last decade follow a behavioral-objective format. It is particularly easy to use in subjects such as mathematics and physical sciences, where skills are obvious and facts are clear (2 plus 2 is always 4, for example, but is war always justifiable?). So prevalent has been the behavioral-objective format in curriculum writing in the last ten years that many educators know of no other way to write curricula. Before this current period, behavioral objectives were virtually unknown and curriculum formatting was largely of the webbing variety.

Webbing and Conceptual Mapping

Curriculum can be written in a format that shows relationships of activities around a central theme. William Kilpatrick popularized this type of curriculum in writing about the work unit (Kilpatrick 1925). Instead of predetermining the knowledge or skills, the curriculum developer determines the major theme, related themes, and then possible student activities.

The webbing format can be conceived of in this way:

2. Related theme   2. Related theme
3. Activities   3. Activities
4. Possible outcomes   4. Possible outcomes

1. SUBJECT THEME

2. Related theme   2. Related theme
3. Activities   3. Activities
4. Possible outcomes   4. Possible outcomes

An actual web on environmental issues might look like Figure 16–2.

After the activities have been written, the curriculum developers write possible learning outcomes: "Students will be able to identify four major environmental issues," "Students will be able to argue and give evidence for both the pro and con sides of both issues," "Students will take a personal stance on each issue." In planning activities, developers consider multimodes of learning via reading, writing, listening, and constructing, and then integrate many fields of knowledge around a central theme. Notice how the theme of environmental issues integrates activities in sociology, mathematics, economics, history, journalism, physics, and biology. Included in the guide are the resources needed to conduct the activities. In our example, resources might include tape recorders, newspapers, books, and community volunteers.

A webbing curriculum guide would contain a blueprint of the web followed by sections for each related theme with activities, possible outcomes, and resources needed. Notice that the web curriculum includes possible outcomes and allows for the possibility of others. In a behavioral-objective curriculum, activities are controlled toward predetermined ends. In a webbed curriculum, activities lead to possible and unanticipated learning. Another example of a webbed curriculum guide is given in Appendix G.

A webbed curriculum is useful in subjects that emphasize affect, attitude, and social learning, and where answers to problems are not clear-cut. Courses such as art, music, social science, and language are prime subjects for such an approach.

FIGURE 16–2   Webbing Format

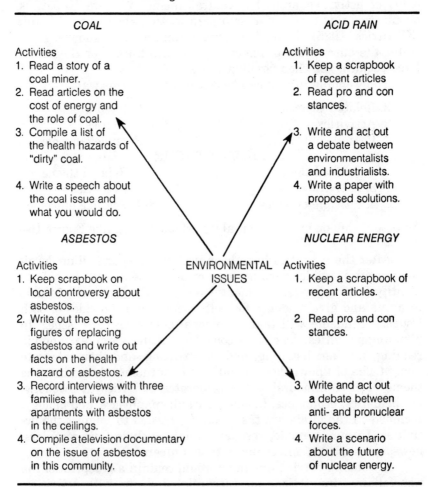

COAL	ACID RAIN
Activities	Activities
1. Read a story of a coal miner.	1. Keep a scrapbook of recent articles
2. Read articles on the cost of energy and the role of coal.	2. Read pro and con stances.
3. Compile a list of the health hazards of "dirty" coal.	3. Write and act out a debate between environmentalists and industrialists.
4. Write a speech about the coal issue and what you would do.	4. Write a paper with proposed solutions.

ASBESTOS — ENVIRONMENTAL ISSUES — **NUCLEAR ENERGY**

ASBESTOS	NUCLEAR ENERGY
Activities	Activities
1. Keep scrapbook on local controversy about asbestos.	1. Keep a scrapbook of recent articles.
2. Write out the cost figures of replacing asbestos and write out facts on the health hazard of asbestos.	2. Read pro and con stances.
3. Record interviews with three families that live in the apartments with asbestos in the ceilings.	3. Write and act out a debate between anti- and pronuclear forces.
4. Compile a television documentary on the issue of asbestos in this community.	4. Write a scenario about the future of nuclear energy.

Conceptual Mapping Format

Posner and Rudnitsky (1982) have developed a curriculum format called conceptual mapping that is an interesting integration of webbing and behavioral objectives. It includes the following:

1. Rationale for the course including the overall educational goals.
2. List of intended learning outcomes for the course, categorized according to type of learning.
3. Conceptual maps depicting the relationship among the important ideas to be learned in the course.
4. Instructional plan describing a) what each unit is about, b) what learning outcomes each unit is intended to accomplish and c) what general teaching strategies could be used in each unit to accomplish the intended learning outcomes.
5. Evaluation plan describing behavioral indicators for each high-priority intended learning outcome (main effects), together with a list of some unintended, undesirable learning outcomes (side effects) to be on the lookout for (Posner and Rudnitsky 1982, p. 8.)

Conceptual mapping uses both webbing and behavioral-objective curricula. It provides the teacher with specific directions for accomplishing predetermined skills, as well as general strategies for teaching concepts.

Results-Only Format

A results-only format for curriculum provides teachers with the widest latitude for using materials, activities, and methods. Such a curriculum specifies the goals and general learning about a subject, theme unit, or course. The guide might include ways to evaluate the learning. For example, a results-only guide in elementary reading might specify the following skills to be learned:

Comprehension

1. Develops powers of observation.
2. Classifies by name, color, shape, size, position use.
3. Anticipates endings to stories.
4. Discriminates between fact and fantasy.

5. Understands who, what, when, where, how, and why phrases.

6. Recalls a story sequence.

7. Reads to find the main ideas of a story.

8. Reads to draw a conclusion.

9. Compares and contrasts stories.

It is then left to the teacher to determine when and how to teach these skills. The teacher is held accountable only for the results, not for the procedures used.

Bloom's Taxonomy as a Guide For Choosing Formats

Benjamin Bloom's taxonomy of learning might serve as a guide for determining the specificity and structure of curriculum formats (see Table 16–1). His lower-level learnings—(1) memory and (2) translation—are based on students recalling and demon-

TABLE 16–1   Bloom's Taxonomy

Category Name	Description
1. Memory	Student recalls or recognizes information.
2. Translation	Student changes information into a different symbolic form or language.
3. Interpretation	Student discovers relationships among facts, generalizations, definitions, values, and skills.
4 Application	Student solves a life problem that requires the identification of the issue and the selection and use of appropriate generalizations and skills.
5. Analysis	Student solves a problem in the light of conscious knowledge of the parts and forms of thinking.
6. Synthesis	Student solves a problem that requires original creative thinking.
7. Evaluation	Student makes a judgment of good or bad, right or wrong, according to standards designated by students.

Source: G. Manson and A. A. Clegg, Jr., "Classroom Questions: Keys to Children's Thinking?" *Peabody Journal of Education 47,* No. 5 (March 1970): 304–305. Reprinted by permission of Peabody Journal of Education.

strating known answers. His intermediate levels of learning—(3) interpretation, (4) application, and (5) analysis—are based on students using logic to find sequential, verifiable knowledge. His higher levels of learning—(6) synthesis and (7) evaluation—are based on combining various knowledge, facts, skills, and logic to make unique personal judgments. Therefore, *behavioral objective* formatting might be more appropriate for lower-level learning, *webbing* and *conceptual mapping* might be more appropriate for intermediate levels of learning, and a *results-only* format might be more appropriate for higher levels of learning. A use of all formats in the same curriculum would provide balance to all levels of learning.

Curriculum Format as Reflective of Choice Given to Teachers

Previously we noted the rough approximation of curriculum formats with educational philosophy: behavioral objectives and essentialism, webbing and experimentalism, results only and existentialism. The less specificity and detail a curriculum has, the greater the choice given to teachers to vary instruction according to the situation. Figure 16–3 illustrates the enlargement of teacher choice by curriculum.

Picture being in a curriculum cone where, at the behavioral-

FIGURE 16–3 Curriculum Format as a Reflection of Teacher Choice: The Curriculum Cone

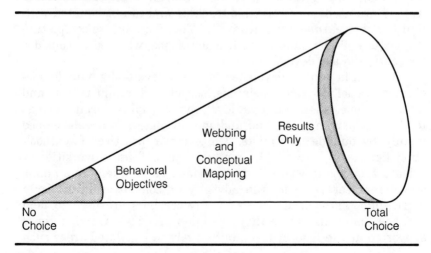

objective bottom, a teacher can barely budge. As the teacher moves toward the webbing and conceptual-mapping area he or she finds room to move hands, feet, elbows, and knees. At the results-only end of the cone, the teacher can extend fully. If the teacher is allowed to step out of the curriculum cone, then there are no limits on where and how he or she can move. Behavioral-objective formats predetermine the *what* and *how* of teaching as much as possible in a loosely coupled organization. Webbing and conceptual-mapping formats focus on themes and relationships of possible activities for teachers but give them a choice of actual activities, duration of activities, and evaluation methods. A results-only format focuses on generalized learning and gives teachers the latitude to proceed as they wish.

It would appear relatively easy to match teacher's stages of development to curriculum formats. It is not so easy, however. We need to look further at type and degree of involvement in curriculum development.

How Curriculum Is Developed and Used

If a school has decided to use a behavioral-objective format, that does not necessarily mean that classroom teachers have little choice about how to teach. Perhaps the teachers have chosen to use that format; perhaps they wrote the curriculum themselves. Also, an elaborately detailed behavioral objective curriculum could be presented to teachers as a reference guide to use as they wish. Simply knowing the format of the curriculum would not tell us how much choice was given to teachers. Although behavioral curricula usually are used as prescriptive teaching and can be equated with limiting choice, this is not always so. Therefore, before completing the picture of curriculum and teacher choice, we need to consider how curricula are developed.

Curricula can be developed at many levels—by outside specialists, school district specialists, school curriculum teams, and teachers alone. At the national level, commercial materials such as textbooks, learning kits, and audiovisual materials are developed mainly by outside specialists. The common practice of textbook publishers is to hire subject matter experts from universities or private agencies to write their materials. There might be a public school representative on the advisory or consulting board for a curriculum textbook, and occasionally teachers are used to field test the materials before they are mass produced. Curriculum is supported at the federal level, but largely in legislated areas such as education for the handicapped, bilingual education, and vocational education. At the state level, departments of education have become increasingly active in curriculum development. Many states have legislated statewide competency tests for student promotion and graduation and have developed curriculum guides for local schools to ensure the teaching of those competencies. (For example, in the state of Georgia, there now exist mandated and state-developed minimum curricula in every subject area for grades K–12.) At the local level, some school systems have written their own curriculum guides for coordinating instruction across grade levels. This is done either by having curriculum specialists at the district level write the guides themselves or by having such specialists work with representative teams of teachers (perhaps with community and student representation). Rarely do local schools turn curriculum development over entirely to teachers and provide them with support services such as a curriculum specialist.

We can think about levels of curriculum development according to Figure 16–4 (Oliva 1982, p. 54). Most curricula are devel-

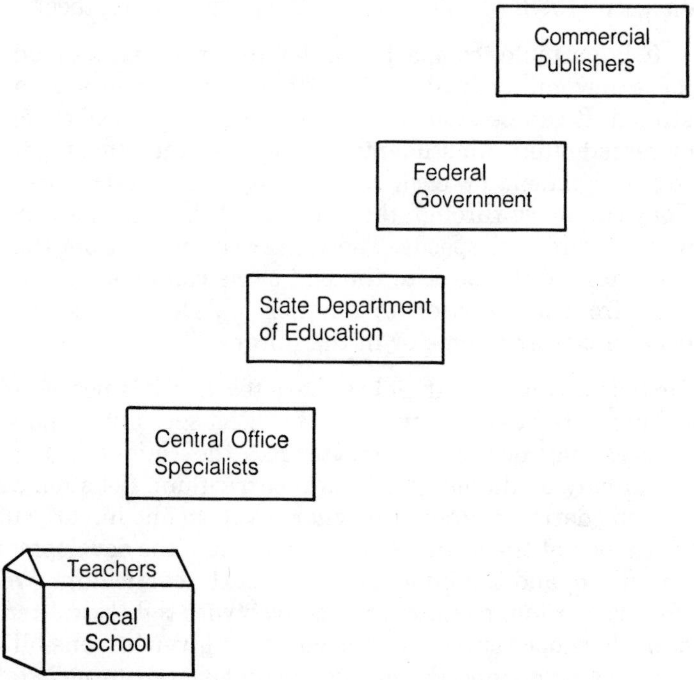

FIGURE   16–4   Illustrations of Levels of Curriculum Development

oped at the state, federal, and commercial levels. Commercial companies are by far the greatest producers of curricula. In other words, most curricula are produced far away from the local teacher and the local schools.

Jessie H. Newlon noted in the early 1920s: "No program of study will operate that has not evolved to some extent out of the thinking of teachers who are to apply it" (Saylor et al. 1981, p. 16). The fact that curriculum development is largely done far away from local schools might help explain why so many schools are floundering and ineffective. On the other hand, local involvement in curriculum development might explain the success of those schools that are effective (Goodlad 1984, pp. 235–238).

We cannot say all externally developed curricula are bad and all internally developed curricula are good. We must consider not only the formatting and development but also the implementation of curricula before making a judgment of worth. Commercial textbooks will not disappear from the educational horizons. Greater school effectiveness will not be found by simply removing external curricula and having teachers create their own. After all, the fact that external curricula, particularly textbook curricula, have survived so long means they must be serving a useful purpose.

Jackson (1969, p. 130) wrote of the purpose of textbooks:

> It is portable, compact, and enduring. It can be read for a few minutes at a time or for many hours at a stretch. It can be studied or skimmed quickly, read once, or reread often. All students can be given the same reading assignment or each can be given a different one. They can move through the material at the same pace or at very different speeds. The reader can move from the beginning of the book to the end or he can jump erratically from one section to another. . . . He can use his book in class, at home or in the library.

Textbooks can be a valuable aid to a teacher. It is not necessary for teachers to recreate the wisdom of subject specialists and scholars in developing new curricula. Instead, they might fit together what is already available into a total curriculum. Let's remember that, in considering degree of teacher involvement in curriculum, we need to look at the format of the curriculum, the development of the curriculum, and the implementation of the curriculum. We can allow for teacher judgment and choice even with tightly written and externally developed curricula if teachers are given responsibility to alter, expand, or change them. The current and historical state of affairs with respect to curriculum development is the familiar "tail wags dog" story. Curriculum developers, mainly textbook publishers, shape school curricula rather than local schools shaping and adapting external materials to their curriculum.

As Kirst and Walker (1971) wrote:

> The bold fact is that most teaching in our schools is and must be from a textbook or other commercial package. We do not trust teachers to write their own materials, we do not give them the time or money, and we insist on standardization. So long as this is true, the suppliers of teaching materials will have a potentially powerful effect on the curriculum.

Teachers can be trusted, given time and money, and given the freedom to develop curricula. If they still choose to use textbooks, it will be their curriculum and no one else's.

Levels of Teacher Involvement in Curriculum Development

Tanner and Tanner (1980) wrote of teachers and local schools functioning in curriculum development at one of three levels: (1) imitative-maintenance (2) mediative, and (3) generative. Teachers at level 1 are concerned with maintaining and following the existing curriculum. Teachers at level 2 look at development as refining the existing curriculum. Teachers at level 3 are concerned with improving and changing the curriculum according to the most current knowledge about learning and societal conditions. Tanner and Tanner explain these three levels according to Table 16–2.

Level I: Imitative-Maintenance

> Teachers operating at Level I rely on textbooks, workbooks, and routine activities, subject by subject. Skills are treated as dead ends rather than as means of generating further learning. Ready-made materials are used without critical evaluation, resulting in a multiplicity of isolated skill-development activities. (The already segmental curriculum is further fragmented.) The imagination of the teacher does not go beyond maintaining the status quo. This teacher would like to think that he or she has less freedom than he or she may actually have for curriculum improvement. In the secondary school, concern for curriculum development is largely confined to each departmental domain.

TABLE 16–2   Levels of Teacher Involvement in Curriculum Development

Level	Locus	Tasks and Activities	Principal Resources
Level I: Imitative-maintenance	Microcurriculum Established conditions Segmental treatment	Rudimentary Routine Adoptive Maintenance of established practice	Textbook, workbook, syllabi (subject by subject), segmental adoption of curriculum packages, popular educational literature School principal
Level II: Mediative	Microcurriculum Established conditions Segmental treatment Awareness of emergent conditions aggregate treatment macrocurriculum	Interpretive Adaptive Refinement of established practice	Textbook, courses of study (subject by subject with occasional correlation of subjects), multimedia, adaptation of segmental curriculum packages, professional literature on approved practice Pupils, teacher colleagues, helping teacher, supervisor, curriculum coordinator, parents, community resources, school principal, in-service courses
Level III: Generative-creative	Macrocurriculum Emergent conditions Aggregate treatment	Interpretive Adaptive Evaluative problem-diagnosis problem-solving Improvement of established practice Search for improved practice	Textbook, courses of study (across subjects and grade levels), alternative modes of curriculum design, professional literature on research and approved practice, multimedia, projects Pupils, teacher colleagues, helping teacher, supervisor, curriculum coordinator, parents, community resources, school principal, in-service courses, outside consultants, experimental programs, professional conferences and workshops

Source: Daniel Tanner and Laurel N. Tanner, *Curriculum Development: Theory into Practice*, 2nd ed., p. 637. Copyright © 1980 by Macmillan Publishing Co., Inc., New York. Reprinted by permission.

When change is made, it is made on the adoption level, without adaptation to local needs. As shown in Table 16–2, curriculum development at this level is plugging in the package to the existing situation without attention to the resulting interactions. Teachers at this level tend to be left alone to struggle with innovations that are handed to them from above. Schools are turned inward, with the principal as the sole resource for classroom assistance.

Level II: Mediative

Teachers at Level II are aware of the need to integrate curriculum content and deal with emergent conditions. (Societal problems such as the energy crisis and children's questions about things that interest and concern them are examples of emergent conditions.) Although teachers at this level may have an aggregate conception of curriculum, implementation does not go beyond the occasional correlation of certain subjects. The focus of curriculum remains segmental; theory remains divorced from practice; curriculum improvement remains at the level of refining existing practice.

Yet teachers at the second level of curriculum development do not blindly plug in an innovation or curriculum package to the existing situation. The necessary adaptations, accommodations, and adjustments are made (see Table 16–2). Teachers are aware of and capitalize on a range of resources for curriculum improvement, including pupils, parents, and peers; and they utilize resources beyond the local school. Teachers are consumers of professional literature on approved practices and tap the resources of the university through in-service courses. The mediative level is a level of awareness and accommodation. Teachers are attracted to, and can articulate, new ideas but their efforts to improve the curriculum fall short of the necessary reconstruction for substantive problem solving.

Level III: Creative-Generative

As shown in Table 16–2, teachers at Level III take an aggregate approach to curriculum development. Ideally, the curriculum is examined in its entirety by the teacher and the whole school staff, and questions of priority and relationship are asked. While individual teachers can and should be at the generative-creative level, a macro-curricular approach requires cooperative planning for vertical and horizontal articulation.

Granted that teachers as individuals usually cannot create new schoolwide curricula, an individual teacher can establish continuities and relationships in his or her own teaching and with other teachers. Teachers at Level III use generalizations and problems as centers of curriculum organization. They stress the broad concepts that specialized subjects share in common, and they use and develop courses of study that cross subject fields. These are aggregate treatments.

Teachers at the third level of curriculum development think about what they are doing and try to find more effective ways of working. They are able to diagnose their problems and formulate hypotheses for solutions. They experiment in their classrooms and communicate their insights to other teachers.

Teachers at this level are consumers of research and seek greater responsibility for curriculum decisions at the school and classroom levels. They exercise independent judgment in selecting curriculum materials and adapt them to local needs. They regard themselves as professionals and, as such, are continually involved in the problems of making decisions regarding learning experiences. To this end, their antennae are turned outward to a wide range of resources [Daniel Tanner and Laurel N. Tanner, *Curriculum Development: Theory into Practice*, 2nd ed., pp. 636, 638–639]. Copyright © 1980 by Macmillan Publishing Co., Inc., New York. Reprinted by permission.

Integrating Curriculum Format with Developers and Levels of Development

To integrate what we know about curriculum format, developers, and development, we can refer to Figure 16–5. When the developers are either outside the school system or from the district level and the curriculum is in a tightly prescribed behavioral-objective format, development will be primarily *imitative*, characterized by teachers following the course of study. When the developers are intermediate teams of teachers led by district specialists and the curriculum is written in a conceptual map or web with objectives and suggested activities, development will be primarily *mediative,* characterized by teachers revising and adapting the course of study to their immediate situation. When curriculum developers are teams of teachers using specialists as resource persons or individual teachers with a results-only curriculum format that identifies what students should learn and leaves activities to the teacher, then development is *generative,* characterized by ongoing creativity.

Of course, there are other variations of these combinations. For example, the developers could be an inside team of teachers using a behavioral-objective format that would be generative development. Once that curriculum was written and became a prescriptive curriculum mandated for all teachers, however, it would become imitative. Figure 16–5 shows the integration between format, developers, and development.

Matching Curriculum Development with Teacher Development

A progression of curriculum development matched with teacher development might look like Figure 16–6. The supervisor might think of his or her staff in terms of the commitment, abstraction,

FIGURE 16–5 Integrating Curriculum Format with Developers and Levels of Development

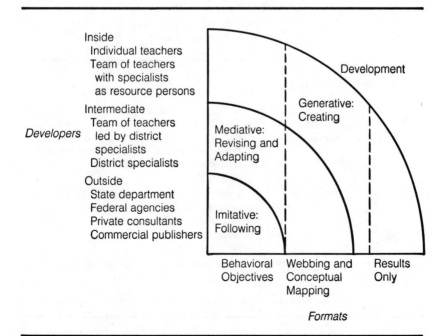

and expertise they currently bring to curriculum and then determine if the current curriculum is appropriately matched with teachers' level of curriculum functioning. If the present curriculum is inappropriate to teachers' development, then readjustments to the curriculum would be in order.

A staff that has a low level of curriculum functioning—as displayed by little commitment to change, little ability to suggest possible changes, and little curriculum expertise—would be appropriately matched with an outside-developed, behavioral-objective, and imitative curriculum. They should be allowed to make minor revisions in adapting the curriculum to their classrooms. On the other hand, a staff that has a moderate level of curriculum functioning, as displayed by a desire to change; can think of possible changes; but lack expertise in writing curriculum would be appro-

FIGURE 16–6 Progression of Curriculum Matched with Characteristics of Staff

Staff Characteristics	Low	Moderate	High
Commitment to curriculum change	Low commitment to change	Would like to make change	Eager to make change
Abstraction in thinking about curriculum	Low ability to think about possible changes	Can think of some possible changes	Has many suggestions
Expertise in curriculum procedures	Low expertise in how to proceed	Does not know how to write curriculum	Knows how to proceed

Curriculum Characteristics

Developers	Outside developers	Outside developed but substantially revised by team of teachers led by specialists	Internally developed by team of teachers with specialists as resource
Format	Behavioral-objective, highly structured	Eclectic format using behavior objectives, webbing, and/or conceptual map	Results-only, with suggested activities
Development	Imitative, with allowance for minor revisions	To be mutually adapted	To be discussed and changed continually

priately matched with a curriculum originally developed by outside experts but substantially revised by an internal team of teachers led by a curriculum specialist. The format of the curriculum might be eclectic in its use of behavioral objectives, webbing, and conceptual maps. Throughout the development and implementation, teachers should have problem-solving meetings for purposes of curriculum adaptation. Finally, a staff that is at a high level of curriculum functioning as displayed by initiating and suggesting ways to change and that knows how to proceed in creating curriculum would be appropriately matched with an internally developed curriculum. The format should emphasize results only and suggested activities, and should be continuously open to revision.

The supervisor should keep in mind the question: "How does one increase teacher control over curriculum making?" If a staff has been appropriately matched—for example, low-functioning staff with an imitative curriculum—and successful implementation is occurring, then the supervisor should plan for the next cycle of curriculum development to give teachers additional responsibilities by serving on decision-making teams under the leadership of a curriculum specialist. This would lead to more mutually adaptive curriculum and at the same time continue to stimulate and increase teacher commitment, abstraction, and expertise.

The supervisor also might think about using curriculum matching when working with individual teachers for improving classroom instruction. Some teachers with low levels of abstraction, expertise, and/or commitment would benefit, at least initially, from a highly prescriptive curriculum. Other teachers with moderate or mixed levels of abstraction, expertise, and commitment would benefit from the use of an eclectic curriculum that offered choices of two or more texts or guides. The highly abstract, committed, and expert teacher would benefit from having the freedom to pick, choose, and create his or her own plans.

Summary

Teachers will implement curriculum successfully if they have been involved in its development and can adapt it to their specific classroom and school situation. The failure of the teacher-proof curriculum movement should remind us that imposing curriculum from outside is useless. Instead, the questions for supervisors to consider have to do with type and degree of curriculum development. The supervisor can pick from three arenas. One arena consists of format, which includes behavioral objectives, webbing, conceptual mapping, and results only. The second arena consists of sources of development, ranging from teachers to district-level personnel, state and federal experts, and commercial writers. The third arena consists of types of involvement, which include imitative, mediative, and generative. Based on teachers prior experiences and knowledge of curriculum, the supervisor should choose format, sources, and types of curriculum development that will increase teachers' choice and commitment to curriculum implementation.

EXERCISES

ACADEMIC

1. Review one of the reports on the results of federally supported curriculum development referred to in Chapter Sixteen. Prepare a written summary and discussion of the highlights of the chosen report.

2. Prepare a written summary and discussion of one of the following:

    a. The Denver plan.

    b. The eight-year study.

    c. The Rand Corporation study.

3. Summarize the recommendations of two curriculum textbook authors providing each of the following in a school curriculum.

    a. Sequence and continuity.

    b. Scope.

    c. Balance.

4. Create one or two sample pages of curriculum guides that reflect each of the following formats for curriculum development:

    a. Behavioral-objective format.

    b. Webbing format.

    c. Results-only format.

5.   Summarize, analyze, and evaluate conceptual mapping curriculum as described by Posner and Rudnitsky (1982).

FIELD

1.   Examine a curriculum guide of a school with which you are *not* familiar. What philosophy of education is reflected by the curriculum guide? What national, regional, and local priorities are reflected? What examples of knowledge of student development, current economics, and predicted future societal conditions can be derived from the guide? What format was used in developing the curriculum? What categories from Bloom's taxonomy are evident in the curriculum objectives? What parental, central office, teacher, and student influences are recognizable? What commercial publishing influences can be discerned? Does the guide reflect an imitative-maintenance, mediative, or generative level of curriculum development? Was the guide most likely developed by outside developers with minimal revision, by outside developers with substantial revision, by a team of teachers led by a specialist, or internally by a team of teachers with specialists as resource people?

   Write a paper answering each question and provide examples from the guide to support your answers.

2.   Examine the living curriculum of a school (what is actually taught) to determine how the development of that curriculum has been significantly affected by one of the following:

   a.   The federal government.

   b.   The state department of education.

   c.   The local community.

   d.   Parents of students attending the school.

   e.   Central office personnel.

   f.   Teachers.

   g.   Students.

   Write a paper discussing the effects of the chosen entity on the development of the school's living curriculum.

3.   Examine a so-called canned curriculum, including the teacher's guide, teacher-proof texts and/or materials, programmed methods of measuring student progress, and all other major

components of the program. Prepare a report describing and evaluating the selected curriculum. If your report is a verbal one, display and discuss physical components of the curriculum as part of your presentation.

4. Interview a teacher to determine to what extent the schools' curriculum guide determines what he or she teaches. Probe for other influences on what is taught (for example, what the teacher was taught when he or she was a student, the text being used, other teachers, administrators, nationally normed achievement tests, and so on). Prepare a report summarizing and analyzing the interview.

5. Observe a working meeting of a curriculum development or curriculum review committee. What is the prevailing educational philosophy of the group? What influences (government, community, parental, administrative, commercial publishers) are influencing the group's decision making? What are some characteristics of individual members of the group (levels of commitment, abstraction, expertise)? Is the curriculum development taking place at an imitative, mediative, or generative level? What curriculum development format (behavioral objective, webbing and conceptual mapping, or results only) is in evidence? Prepare a report on your observation, including answers to each of these questions. Support your answers with descriptions of behaviors or artifacts observed at the meeting.

DEVELOPMENTAL

1. Volunteer for membership on a curriculum development or review committee.

2. Examine the writings of authors on educational supervision to compare their positions on the role and function of the supervisor in curriculum development.

3. Over a period of time, compare a school's written curriculum with its living curriculum (what is actually taught from day to day). How much congruence is there between the formal curriculum and what is actually taught?

REFERENCES

Aiken, W. M. 1942. *The story of the eight year study.* New York: Harper.

Berman, P., and McLaughlin, M.W. 1978. *Federal programs supporting educational change,* Vol. 8. *Implementing and sustaining innovations.* Ed 159 289. Santa Monica, Calif.: Rand Corporation.

Barths, R. S. 1980. *Run school run.* Cambridge, Mass.: Harvard University Press.

Brubaker, D. L. 1982. *Curriculum planning: The dynamics of theory and practice.* Glenview, Ill.: Scott, Foresman.

Cremin, L. A. 1976. *Public education.* New York: Basic Books.

Doll, R. C. 1982. *Curriculum improvement: Decision making and process,* 5th ed. Boston: Allyn and Bacon.

Firth, G. R., and Newfield, J. W. 1984. Curriculum development and selection. In J. M. Cooper, ed., *Developing skills for instructional supervision.* New York: Longman.

Gibney, T., and Karns, E. 1979. Mathematics education, 1955–1975: A summary of the NSF findings. *Educational Leadership 36*(5): 356–359.

Glickman, C. D., and Esposito, J. P. 1979. *Leadership guide for elementary school improvement.* Boston: Allyn and Bacon.

Goodlad, J. I. 1984. *A place called schools.* New York: McGraw-Hill.

Jackson, P. W. 1969. Technology and the teacher. In Committee for Economic Development, *The school and the challenge of innovation.* New York: McGraw-Hill.

Kilpatrick, W. H. 1925. *Foundations of method.* New York: Macmillan.

Kirst, M., and Walker, D. 1971. An analysis of curriculum policymaking. *Review of Educational Research 41*(5): 479–509.

Oliva, P. F. 1982. *Developing the curriculum.* Boston: Little, Brown.

Ponder, G. 1979. The more things change ... the status of social studies. *Educational Leadership 36*(7): 515–518.

Posner, G. J., and Rudnitsky, A. N. 1982. *Course design: A guide to curriculum development for teachers,* 2nd ed. New York: Longman.

Saylor, J. G., Alexander, W. M.; and Lewis, A. 1981. *Curriculum planning for better teaching and learning,* 4th ed. New York: Holt, Rinehart and Winston.

Stenhouse, L. 1975. *An introduction to curriculum research and development.* London: Heinemann Educational Books.

Tanner, D., and Tanner, L. W. 1980. *Curriculum development theory into practice,* 2nd ed. New York: Macmillan.

Venezky, R. L., and Winfield, L. R. 1979. *Schools that succeed beyond expectations in teaching.* Studies in Education Technical Report No. 1. Newark: University of Delaware.

Yager, R. E., and Stodghill, R. 1979. School sciences in an age of science. *Educational Leadership 36*(6): 439–445.

SUGGESTIONS FOR ADDITIONAL READING

Brubaker, D. L. 1982. *Curriculum planning: The dynamics of theory and practice.* Glenview, Ill.: Scott, Foresman.

Doll, R. C. 1982. *Curriculum improvement: Decision making and process, fifth edition.* Boston: Allyn and Bacon.

English, F. W., ed. 1983. *Fundamental curriculum decisions.* Alexandria, Va.: Association for Supervision and Curriculum Development.

Foshay, A. W. 1980. *Considered action for curriculum improvement.* Alexandria, Va.: Association for Supervision and Curriculum Development.

McNeil, J. D. 1981. *Curriculum: A comprehensive introduction,* 2nd ed. Boston: Little, Brown.

Oliva, P. F. 1982. *Developing the curriculum.* Boston: Little, Brown.

Posner, G. J., and Rudnitsky, A. N. 1982. *Course design: A guide to curriculum development for teachers,* 2nd ed. New York: Longman.

Suggestions for Additional Reading

Saylor, J. G.; Alexander, W. N.; and Lewis, A. 1981. *Curriculum planning for better teaching and learning,* 4th ed. New York: Holt, Rinehart and Winston.

Stenhouse, L. 1975. *An introduction to curriculum research and development.* London: Heinemann Educational Books.

Tanner, D., and Tanner, L. N. 1980. *Curriculum development theory into practice,* 2nd ed. New York: Macmillan.

Tyler, R. W. 1950. *Basic principles of curriculum and instruction: Syllabus for education 305.* Chicago: University of Chicago Press.

CHAPTER SEVENTEEN

Group Development

Learning the skills of working with groups to solve instructional problems is a critical task of supervision. This chapter deals with using group observations, changing group leadership styles, dealing with dysfunctional members, resolving conflict, preparing for meetings, and facilitating large-group involvement.

Professional people who are brought together to deal with pressing mutual problems have the right to expect results. Meetings that drag on with seemingly endless and unfocused discussion are morale breakers. Participants become reluctant, apathetic, and sometimes hostile toward future meetings. They might even suspect that the group leader is deliberately leading them astray, so that the group's inability to decide can be used as an excuse for the leader to do whatever he or she wishes. Whether the leader's intent is to create confusion or he or she truly desires a group decision, the lack of clear results erodes unity and common purpose. We already know how important unity, common purpose, and involvement are in developing a cause beyond oneself related to school success.

Groups that work productively, efficiently, and harmoniously generally have a skillful leader. Unfortunately, since being part of a group is such an everyday occurrence in professional, personal, and social life, we seldom stop to think about what makes some groups work well and others fail. It is unrealistic for the leader of a new group to expect the group to proceed naturally in a professional, concise manner. A leader needs to be conscious of the elements of a successful group, select clear procedures for group decision making, be able to deal with dysfunctional behavior, use conflict to generate helpful information, and determine appropriate leadership style. We now turn to these considerations.

Dimensions of an Effective Group

There are two dimensions of an effective professional group (Bales 1953): the task dimension and the person dimension. The *task* dimension represents the content and purpose of the group meeting. The task is what is to be accomplished by the end of the meetings. Typical tasks of professional groups might be deciding on a new textbook, writing a new instructional schedule, coordinating a particular curriculum, or preparing an in-service plan. An effective group, obviously, accomplishes what it sets out to do. The *person* dimension of an effective group is the interpersonal process and satisfaction participants derive from working with each other. Concern and sensitivity to participants' feelings create a climate of desiring to meet with each other from week to week to accomplish and implement the group task.

Let's explain these two dimensions in a different way. Specific task behaviors seen in a group are clarifying the group's purpose, keeping discussions focused, setting time limits, and appraising group progress toward the goal. A leader who says, "We're getting off the track; let's get back to discussing textbooks," is exhibiting a task behavior. Specific person behaviors seen in a group include recognizing people for their contributions, smiling, injecting humor, and listening attentively. A leader who says, "Fred, I'm following what you've been saying; it's a point worth considering," would be demonstrating a person behavior. Imagine a group that exhibits only task behaviors. The meeting would be formal, cold, and tense. People would not receive feedback, would not be encouraged, and probably would swallow hard before addressing the unsmiling, staring faces. Such a group would accomplish its task quickly, with little mutual support. The decision would be quick because participants would wish to remove themselves from the tense environment as soon as possible. The formality of the sessions would prevent in-depth discussions of feelings, attitudes, and differences of opinion. Decisions would be made on the basis of incomplete information and commitment from group members. The implementation of the decision would be problematic at best.

Next imagine a group that exhibits only person behaviors. There would be much personal chatter, humorous story telling, and frequent back slapping and touching. People would be smiling and laughing. The image of a raucous cocktail party might characterize a group with all person behaviors and no task behaviors, and the morning-after hangover is also analogous to the extent of accomplishment of a meeting devoid of task behaviors. People would enjoy each other's company for its own sake. Everyone would have a wonderful time, but little would be done.

Little's study of six urban, desegregated schools (three elementary and three secondary schools) provides evidence that the two schools identified as "high success" on teacher involvement in schoolwide projects held meetings that encompassed both personal and task behaviors (Little 1982). Little (1982, p. 331) described the successful schools in this way:

> Teachers engage in frequent, continuous, and increasingly concrete and precise talk about teaching practice.... By such talk, teachers build up a shared language adequate to the complexity of teaching, capable of distinguishing one practice and its virtues from another, and capable of integrating large bodies of practice into distinct and sensible perspectives on the business of teaching.

As Little has shown, successful schools have collegial, industrious meetings. Teachers involve themselves with each other in professional dialogue to accomplish better schoolwide instruction. In summary, productive groups have meetings that emphasize both task and person dimensions. It falls to the group leader to ensure that both dimensions are present.

Group Member Roles

First the leader needs to determine what behaviors are indicative of roles already in existence. Are some members displaying task roles and/or person roles? What roles are ongoing? Are certain roles lacking? Remember that both task and person roles are functional to group performance. Another set of roles and behaviors, called *dysfunctional,* distract a group from task and person relations. Dysfunctional roles, unlike functional roles, are a concern when present. We begin by listing and briefly describing the most common functional member roles. Then we will explain dysfunctional roles.

Task Roles

The following descriptions are adaptations from those listed by Benne and Sheats (1948).

Initiator-contributor: Proposes original ideas or changed ways of regarding group problem of goal or procedure. Launches discussion, moves group into new areas of discussion.

Information seeker: Asks for clarification in terms of factual adequacy. Seeks expert information and relevant facts.

Opinion seeker: Asks for clarification of values pertinent to the group undertaking or to propose suggestions. Checks on other's attitudes and feelings toward particular issues.

Information giver: Provides factual, authoritative information or gives own experience relevant to the issue.

Opinion giver: Verbalizes his or her own values and opinions on the group problem; emphasizes what the group should do.

Elaborator: Picks up on other's suggestions and amplifies with examples, pertinent facts, and probable consequences.

Coordinator: Shows the link between ideas and suggestions, attempts to pull diverse proposals together.

Orienter: Clarifies the group's position, gives a state-of-the-scene review. Summarizes what has been discussed, points out where discussion has departed from the goal, and reminds the group of their ultimate goal.

Evaluator-critic: Evaluates the proposals of the group against a criteria of effectiveness. Assesses whether proposals are "reasonable," "manageable," "based on facts," and derived through fair procedures.

Energizer: Focuses the group to move toward decisions. Challenges and prods group into further action.

Procedural technician: Facilitates group discussion by taking care of logistics. Sees that the group has the necessary materials for the task (paper, pencils, chalk, and so on).

Recorder: Writes down the group's suggestions and decisions. Keeps an ongoing record of what transpires in the group.

A group needs these member roles to keep moving toward accomplishing its task. A leader can use these descriptions to figure out what roles are missing. Additional roles might need to be assigned to group members or incorporated by the leader. For example, if a group has many opinion givers but no information givers, then decisions would be made on the basis of feelings without regard to actual experience or knowledge. A leader would need to consider ways to add more information giving. Perhaps he or she could assign people to gather more knowledge or ask outside experts for assistance. Likewise, if a group has many opinion givers and information givers but lacks orienters and coordinators, then the members may be talking past each other. There would be a lack of direction and a lack of synthesis of the relationships between member's ideas. The leader would need to plan ways to coordinate discussions. As a final example, a group might contain most of the task roles except for a procedural technician or recorder. Such a group probably would converse easily but would bog down on recalling what has been said. The leader who knows what roles are needed can ask for a volunteer to be a recorder and summarizer. Knowledge of task roles and behaviors enables a leader to assess what roles are evident and what further roles need to be assigned. The leader might take on some of the missing roles, assign them to others, or add particular persons to a group.

Person Roles

Similarly, the knowledge of person roles and behaviors provides a guide to the group leader.

Encourager: Affirms, supports, and accepts the contribution of other members. Shows warmth and a positive attitude toward others.

Harmonizer: Conciliates differences between individuals. Looks for ways to reduce tension between members through nonthreatening explanations and humor.

Compromiser: Offers to change his or her proposals for the good of the group. Willing to yield position or to acknowledge own errors by meeting other opposing ideas halfway.

Gatekeeper or expediter: Regulates flow of communication by seeing that all members have a chance to talk. Encourages quiet persons to speak and puts limits on those who dominate the conversation. Proposes new regulations for discussions when participation becomes unbalanced.

Standard setter, ego ideal: Appeals to group's pride by not letting group members give up when trouble occurs. Exudes confidence that the group is a good one and can make sound decisions.

Observer and commentator: Monitors the working of the group. Records who speaks to whom, where and when most roadblocks occur, and the frequency and length of individual members' participation. Provides feedback when the group wishes to evaluate its procedures and processes.

Follower: Is willing to accept the decisions of the group and follow them even though he or she has not been active or influential in those decisions. Serves as a listener to group discussion.

The seven person roles provide human satisfaction and group cohesiveness. People feel positive about meeting and talking with each other and comfortable enough to express their ideas. As a result, meetings are seen as pleasant times to continue the group's work. When person roles are missing, a group may face severe difficulties in making acceptable and committed decisions. Without person behaviors and roles, only the strongest, most assured, and vocal members will speak. Decisions might be made that more timid persons strongly reject but the group may not know that such strong disapproval exists. Again, it is the group leader's responsibility to see if people roles are evident. If roles are missing, then he or she can confront the group with their absence, pick up the role(s) him- or herself, quietly suggest particular roles to existing members, or add to the group other individuals who more naturally play such roles. *Both task and person roles, when not already in existence, need to be added.*

Dysfunctional Roles

Dysfunctional roles and behaviors are those that are conspicuous in their presence. Such roles and behaviors disrupt the progress towards a group goal and weaken group cohesiveness.

Aggressor: Personally attacks the worth of other members. Belittles and deflates the status, wisdom, and motivation of others. Examples of such verbal attacks are, "That's the most ridiculous thing I've ever heard," "You must be crazy to suggest. . . ."

Blocker: Sees all opinions and suggestions by group members as negative. Opposes any decision being made and stubbornly refuses to propose alternatives. Examples of such blocking statements are: "That's a terrible idea," "I don't want to do that," "It's futile to do anything."

Recognition-seeker: Uses the group setting to receive personal attention. Examples of such behaviors are dropping books, scattering papers, coughing incessantly, pretending to be asleep, raising hand and then forgetting what one would have said.

Self-confessor: Uses the group to ventilate personal feelings not related to the group's task. Talks about personal problems or feelings of inadequacy whenever he or she can see ways to slip such confessions into the group discussion. Examples of self-confessing statements are, "This discussion reminds me of when I was a little child and the weight problem I had," or when the group is talking about differences of opinion, "You should hear my son and me fight; I don't know what to do about him."

Playboy or playgirl: Displays lack of interest and involvement by using the group setting to have a merry time. Distracts other members from the group's purpose. Tells private jokes, passes notes, makes faces at others, plays cards, and so on.

Dominator: Asserts superiority in controlling group discussion and dictates what certain members should do. Claims to know more about the issue under discussion and have better solutions than anyone else. Has elaborate answers to almost every question and monopolizes the discussion.

Help-seeker: Tries to gain group's sympathy by expressing feelings of inadequacy or personal confusion. Uses such self-derogation as reason for not contributing: "This is all too confusing for me," "I can't make a decision on my own," "Why ask me? I can't help."

Special-interest pleader: Has no opinion or suggestions of his or her own but instead speaks for what others would say or do. Cloaks own bias by using an outside group: "We couldn't do that. Do you know what the school board would think?" "If those parents down in the local restaurant ever heard that we were going to change . . ."

Dysfunctional roles are fairly self-evident in a group. The leader's responsibility is to reduce or eliminate such dysfunctional roles before they severely harm the morale and efficiency of the group. He or she might try to understand the dysfunctional member's reason for acting as an aggressor, playboy, special interest pleader, etc., and then might either confront the person privately or provide changes within the group to satisfy the unmet needs that are leading to the dysfunctional behavior. Methods for dealing with dysfunctional behaviors will be discussed shortly, but first let's focus on leadership styles matched with maturity levels of groups.

Changing Group Leadership Style

If a group lacks either task or person behaviors, the leader can choose a style that will fill the void. A group that exhibits much initiative, information, and competitiveness (high task) as well as hostility, aggression, and bitterness (low person) could benefit from a leadership style that is encouraging, praising, harmonizing, and humorous (high person). A group that exhibits much positive camaraderie (high person) but is being uninterested, apathetic, or uninformed (low task) could benefit from a leadership style that presses for information, sets goals, and enforces procedures (high task).

The work of Hersey and Blanchard (1969, 1977) on what they call the "life-cycle theory of leadership," also known as *situational leadership* is a comprehensive theory of leadership style in response to group characteristics. Hersey and Blanchard identified four styles of leadership based on the relative emphasis on task and relationship (person) behavior:

Style 1 (S1): High task, low relationship. This is an autocratic style, whereby the leader tells the group members what is to be done, when, and by whom. The leader makes decisions for the group. This style is similar to directive supervision as detailed in Chapter Nine. One word that describes this style is *telling*. The leader determines both the process and the content of decision making.

Style 2 (S2): High task, high relationship. This is a democratic style, whereby the leader actively participates with the group both as a facilitator of the decision-making process and an equal member contributing his or her own ideas, opinions, and information. This style is similar to collaborative supervision as explained in Chapter Eight. One word that describes this influencing style is *selling*. The leader attempts to influence both the processes and the content of decision making by being a persuasive equal.

Style 3 (S3): High relationship, low task. This is an encouraging and socializing style whereby the leader promotes cohesion, open expression, and positive feelings among the members but does not influence or interfere with the actual decision. (The leader's role is one of clarification, encouragement, and reflection.) The style is similar to nondirective supervision as described in Chapter Seven. Note that the leader participates by helping members express their ideas, opinions, and needs but does not participate in the sense of offering his or her own ideas, opinions, and needs. The leader participates in the process but not in the content of decision making.

Style 4 (S4): Low relationship, low task. This is a hands-off or laissez faire style whereby the leader turns the task over to the group and does not participate in any manner. The leader tells the group what the task is and then physically or mentally removes him- or herself from any further involvement. One word that describes this style is *delegating*. The leader is involved in neither the process nor the content of decision making.

Hersey and Blanchard believe effective leadership is based on matching leadership style to the maturity level of the group. The maturity of a group depends on the particular task. The same group could be of high maturity with one task and low maturity with another. Maturity can be assessed according to the characteristics of motivation, responsibility, and education:

Motivation is the group's degree of interest and enthusiasm with respect to the task.

Responsibility is the degree of commitment the group has shown in completing previous tasks.

Education or *experience* is the degree of information and expertise the group possesses about the task.

The leader can assess the maturity of the group according to these levels.

A *low mature group* (M1) would have little motivation for the task, no previous record of success as a group, and little knowledge or insight into the task.

A *low to moderately mature group* (M2) would have some motivation, responsibility, and knowledge or would be high on one of the three characteristics and low on the other two. For example, a science curriculum committee might be highly motivated but might not have worked together previously as a group (low responsibility) and might be unaware of the newly developed science curriculum (low expertise).

A *moderate to high mature group* (M3) would be motivated, responsible, and knowledgeable or would be high on two of the three characteristics. For example, they might be of high motivation and knowledge but of unproved or low responsibility.

A *high mature group* (M4) would be a group that was highly motivated, responsible, and knowledgeable. The group would have shown on many occasions its ability to work productively.

Situational leadership matches leadership style to the maturity level of the group (see Figure 17–1 on matching and directionality of a developing group). An M1 group is best matched with a *telling* autocratic style (S1). An M2 group is best matched with a *selling,* democratic style (S2). An M3 group is best matched with a *participating,* encouraging style (S3). An M4 group is best matched with a *delegating,* laissez-faire style (S4).

Hersey and Blanchard's theory was originally called life-cycle leadership but is now more commonly referred to as situational leadership. This is an unfortunate change in terminology, because *life cycle* connotes development or growth in both leader and group behaviors, an implication that is missing from the term *situational.* Groups are complex human entities that respond to the gradual shifting of a group leader's external control in the same manner that an individual teacher will respond to gradual shifting of supervisory control. In other words, an M1 (low-maturity) group with an S1 (telling and autocratic) leadership style will not develop greater maturity until the leader gradually allows them to gain greater internal control. An unmotivated group might work most efficiently with S1 leadership at first. As the group gains experience, as members become acquainted with each other, and as the group acquires expertise, the leader should be alert to those signals of increasing maturity and provide for greater group involvement by shifting to an S2 leadership style. It is conceivable that a group working on a long project might complete the entire life cycle by beginning with S1 (telling) leadership and concluding with S4 (delegating) leadership. A group leader might work toward eliminating his or her control over the group. The ultimate goal should be for a group to provide its own task and person behaviors and not be dependent on formal leadership.

Dealing with Dysfunctional Members

The fact that a group is made up of individuals with varying temperaments and motivations is important when thinking about ways to work with groups. Dealing with individuals, particularly

FIGURE 17-1 Matching and Directionality of a Developing Group

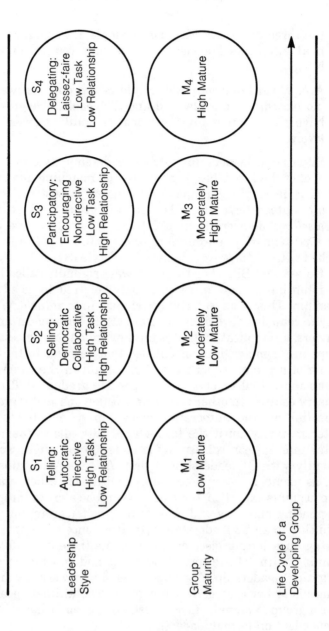

those who display dysfunctional behaviors, is an additional responsibility of a group leader.

If the leader has observed the group at work and has determined that his or her own leader behaviors are appropriate for most members of the group, yet there continue to be a few dysfunctional members, then individual treatment might be in order. The procedure for treating a dysfunctional member is (1) observe the member, (2) try to understand why the member is acting unproductively, (3) communicate with the member about the behavior, (4) establish some rules for future behavior, and (5) redirect the unfavorable behavior (Corey and Corey 1977; Kemp 1964). Each step of this procedure will be amplified.

1. *Observe the member:* When and with whom does the dysfunctional behavior occur? What does the group member do, and how do others respond? For example, a dominator might start monopolizing the conversation as soon as he or she walks into the meeting. Other people might be interested in the dominator's talks for the first few minutes of the meeting but become increasingly annoyed as the dominator continues. They might roll their eyes, yawn, fidget, or make comments to each other.

2. *Try to understand the member:* Why does the member persist with dysfunctional behavior? Does he or she know the behavior is unproductive? Is the behavior being used to mask some underlying emotion? For example, a playboy might be insecure about his own worth and pretend not to care rather than exposing his thoughts to the scrutiny of the group.

3. *Communicate with the member:* What can you communicate about the group member's behavior and the situation? Describe the situation and the behavior to the member without denigration. Instead of saying, "You're being an aggressive son of a gun" say: "I've noticed that you speak loudly and angrily to Sara. At the last meeting you told her to keep her mouth shut." Tell the dysfunctional member the effect of the behavior on you as group leader: "When you tell Sara to shut up and tell Bob that he's stupid, it starts an argument that takes time away from the meeting. I can't complete the agenda on time when those arguments take place" (see Gordon 1980).

4. *Establish some rules for future behaviors:* Either ask the member to suggest some rules that he or she can abide by in the future, or tell the member your future rules, or establish them jointly. Regardless of which tactic is chosen, the leader should think of rules that would minimize further disruptions to the group. For example, with a self-confessor the leader might say,

"The next time you have a personal problem, come speak to me privately about it," or with a dominator, "I'm going to enforce a two-minute limit on every member's participation," or with a blocker, "If you don't think we're on the right course, tell us your objection once and only once."

5. *Redirect the unfavorable behavior:* Pick up on the group member's dysfunctional behavior, and try to make it functional. A dominator can be assigned the role of recorder, summarizer, or time keeper. A playboy can be given an opening time for sharing a funny story to relax the group before starting official business. An aggressor can be asked to play devil's advocate and argue the position of an adversary.

The five steps outlined here will help us understand and deal with individual dysfunctional behavior. The steps are predicated on the leader confronting the dysfunctional member in private. Dysfunctional behaviors that occur infrequently and in isolated situations might simply be ignored. The leader can respond to infrequent misbehaviors or make light of them: "Sara, I guess you really got wound up today; perhaps we might hear from someone else now." Only incessant behaviors that distract the entire group need to be dealt with via direct confrontation. Confrontation is not easy but is necessary at times for the sake of the group.

Resolving Conflict

The key to a productive group is the way ongoing conflict is resolved. Conflicts are particular disagreements that occur between two or more members at a particular time. *Conflict is not necessarily dysfunctional.* In fact, research has shown that successful groups exhibit much conflict (Johnson and Johnson 1982, pp. 228–230). A group can make wise decisions only when there is a wealth of information and ideas to consider. Information and ideas are generated through conflict. To suppress conflict is to limit the group's decision-making capacity. Therefore, the leader should encourage conflict, not stifle it. Of course, conflict, if not handled correctly, can degenerate into adversarial and harmful relations. It is not conflict that is bad; it is the way the leader deals with it that determines its value.

Conflict occurs when there is a disagreement over ideas. The leader should keep the disagreement focused on the ideas and not on the personalities of the members. The following procedure for handling conflict serves as a ready reference for the group leader:

1. Ask each member to state their conflicting position.

2. Ask each member to restate each other's position.

3. Ask each member if conflict still exists.

4. Ask for underlying value position; why do they still stick to the position?

5. Ask other members of the group if there is a third position that synthesizes, compromises, or transcends the conflict. If not, reclarify the various positions. Acknowledge that there exists no apparent reconcilation, and move the discussion to other matters.

The following is an application of conflict resolution procedures to a high school meeting:

> The supervisor from the central office has called a meeting of the English high school department heads to discuss possible changes in the tenth-grade English curriculum. The topic of composition writing comes up, and two department heads begin to argue. Mrs. Strick of Toofarback High School says: "We need to require three formal compositions each semester from each tenth grader. Each composition should be graded according to spelling, punctuation, and format. I'm sick and tired of seeing kids coming into the eleventh grade without being able to put a sentence together!" Mr. Ease of Space High School objects: "Are you serious? Six technical compositions a year should just about kill any remaining interest that tenth graders have in writing. That is a ridiculous idea!"

The language supervisor, Mr. Cool, is now aware of a conflict and wants to capitalize on these varying points of view in providing information to the group. At the same time, he is aware of emotional intensity in this conflict (words such as "sick and tired" and "ridiculous") and wishes to soften the emotion and promote the ideas. So he uses step 1 and asks each member to state their conflicting position.

> "Mrs. Strick and Mr. Ease, you both have definite ideas about the requirements of technical compositions. We are interested in fully understanding what you think. Would you each take a few minutes and further explain your positions?"

After Mrs. Strick and Mr. Ease have stated their positions, the supervisor moves to step 2 by asking each member to restate each other's position.

> "Now that you have stated your position, I want to make sure that you fully understand each other. Mrs. Strick, would you please paraphrase Mr. Ease's position, and Mr. Ease, would you repeat Mrs. Strick's position." Mrs. Strick says: "Mr. Ease thinks that technical writing assignments are a waste of time and students lose interest." Mr. Ease replies: "No, I didn't say they are a waste of time; but if such assignments are frequent, students learn to hate English class." Mr. Ease then restates Mrs. Strick's position: "You're saying that tenth graders need skills in the basics of writing. Technical required compositions would ensure proper spelling, grammar, and format." Mrs. Strick replies, "Yes, that's what I'm saying."

Now that both positions have been made and paraphrased, Supervisor Cool goes to step 3 and asks if conflict still exists.

> He asks Mrs. Strick and Mr. Ease: "Are you both still far apart about composition requirements for tenth-grade English?" Mrs. Strick nods, but Mr. Ease says: "Well, not as far apart as at the beginning. I'm not against some technical writing requirements. It's the number, three for each semester, that hangs me up. I could accept one per semester." Mrs. Strick replies: "Well, I can't. If they are going to write correctly, they must do it frequently. Three compositions a semester is just the minimum!"

Mr. Cool, knowing that Mrs. Strick is adamant about her position, goes to step 4, asking for the underlying value:

> Mr. Cool asks Mrs. Strick: "Could you explain why technical composition writing is important to you?" Mrs. Strick says: "Kids today don't get any basics in writing. Everything is creativity, expression, write it like you speak it in the streets! I was taught standards of good manners and proper English. If these kids are to succeed in later life, they have to know how to write according to accepted business and professional standards. I'm not being hard-nosed for my own sake. It's them I'm concerned about!" Mr. Cool turns to Mr. Ease and says: "What about you? Why do you disagree?" Mr. Ease replies: "I

don't completely disagree, but I'm against making tenth-grade English class a technical writing drill. Writing should be a vehicle for expression and students should love, not dread, it. They should be able to write personal thoughts, juggle words and formats, and not worry about every comma and dotted *i*. Let them play with words before pushing standards at them. I don't write letters with one-and-a-half-inch margins to my friends or in my diary—why should kids have to? Sure, there is a need for them to learn to write formally, but not at the expense of hating to write!"

Mr. Cool restates the conflict to the group: "We have an obvious disagreement between Mrs. Strick and Mr. Ease. Mrs. Strick believes there should be at least three technical compositions per semester in the tenth grade. Mr. Ease believes there should be less emphasis on technical writing and more on expressive writing."

Supervisor Cool goes to step 5, *Asking other members of the group if there is a third position that can be taken*. Some members might side with one over the other; suggest a compromise (one technical composition in the first semester, two in the second semester); or offer a new alternative (let's require a three-week minicourse of technical writing and let each school decide the type of work and assignments). If the conflict between Mrs. Strick and Mr. Ease does not resolve itself, the supervisor acknowledges that the conflict remains: "We understand the difference of opinion that you both have, and we can't find a ready solution." Then she moves to other matters: "Eventually the committee will have to decide or vote on what to do about required assignments. For now, we'll leave this particular issue and discuss the tenth-grade testing program."

Conflict cannot and should not be avoided. Conflict, if encouraged and supported, will enable a group to make better decisions. It is the group leader's handling of conflict that makes the difference. The group should have the feeling that it is all right to disagree and that when someone does disagree, he or she will be able to make his or her full position known.

Preparing for Group Meetings

A group can proceed more easily with its task if the leader has made certain preparations. Preparation includes setting an agenda, writing guided discussion questions, and determining procedures for large group involvement.

GROUP DEVELOPMENT

Agendas

A group has to be clear on its task and purpose. Why are they meeting? What are they to accomplish? Is there to be a product? An agenda distributed several days before the actual meeting will inform members of the reasons for the meeting and what will be accomplished. The agenda need not be elaborate. See Figure 17–2 as a sample agenda. Notice how the agenda includes a brief explanation and a breakdown of items. Time limits for each item provide members with a sense of priorities as well as the assurance that the leader plans to end on time. Keeping to starting and ending times displays respect for group members' personal schedules.

Guided Discussion

When meeting with a small group to discuss an issue, it is helpful to have in mind the type of questions to ask. Typically, questions to be asked will shift during a meeting. At the beginning of the meeting the leader usually spends time clarifying the topic for discussion. During the meeting, the leader uses open-ended questions that allow for seeking, elaborating, and coordinating of ideas, opinions, and information. At the conclusion of the meeting,

FIGURE 17–2   Sample Agenda

To: All physical education teachers
From: Morris Bailey, athletic director
Subject: Agenda for the meeting of February 23 in Room 253, 3:30–5:00

Next Thursday will be the last meeting before voting on the revisions of our student progress forms. Remember, bring any progress forms you have collected from other school systems. Sally and Bruce are to report on the forms provided by the state Department. At the conclusion of the meeting, we are to make specific recommendations of changes.

Agenda

I.	Review purpose of meeting	3:30–3:40
II.	Report from Sally and Bruce on state Department forms	3:40–4:00
III.	Report on other school system forms	4:00–4:20
IV.	Discussion of possible revision	4:20–4:40
V.	Recommendations	4:40–5:00

See you Thursday. Please be on time!

---

the leader asks questions that summarize what has been accomplished and what remains to be done.

A list of discussion questions that might help as a reference are presented in Figure 17–3. Prior to a meeting, the leader might review the questions in Figure 17–3 and write down specific questions concerning the topic to have before him or her. When the discussion stalls, the leader can look at his or her notes and ask one of the preselected questions. A discussion guide helps the leader ensure that the topic will be thoroughly examined.

Procedures for Large-Group Involvement

With small groups of up to ten members, all members have a chance to actively participate throughout the decision making pro-

FIGURE 17–3   Questions for Use in Leadership Discussion

Questions Designed to Open Up Discussion

1. What do you think about the problem as stated?

2. What has been your experience in dealing with this problem?

3. Would anyone care to offer suggestions on facts we need to better our understanding of the problem?

Questions Designed to Broaden Participation

1. Now that we have heard from a number of our members, would others who have not spoken like to add their ideas?

2. How do the ideas presented so far sound to those of you who have been thinking about them?

3. What other phases of the problem should be explored?

Questions Designed to Limit Participation

1. To the overactive participant: We appreciate your contributions. However, it might be well to hear from some of the others. Would some of you who have not spoken care to add your ideas to those already expressed?

2. You have made several good statements, and I am wondering if someone else might like to make some remarks?

3. Since all our group members have not yet had an opportunity to speak, I wonder if you would hold your comments until a little later?

Questions Designed to Focus Discussion

1. Where are we now in relation to our goal for this discussion?

continued

FIGURE 17-3   continued

---

2. Would you like to have me review my understanding of the things we have said and the progress we have made in this direction?

3. Your comment is interesting, but I wonder if it is germane to the chief problem that is before us.

Questions Designed to Help the Group Move Along

1. I wonder if we have spent enough time on this phase of the problem. Should we not move to another aspect of it?

2. Have we gone into this part of the problem far enough so that we might now shift our attention and consider this additional area?

3. In view of the time we have set for ourselves, would it not be well to look at the next question before us?

Questions Designed to Help the Group Evaluate Itself

1. I wonder if any of you have a feeling that we are blocked on this particular question? Why are we tending to slow down?

2. Should we take a look at our original objective for this discussion and see where we are in relation to it?

3. Now that we are nearing the conclusion of our meeting, would anyone like to offer suggestions on how we might improve our next meeting?

Questions Designed to Help the Group Reach a Decision

1. Am I right in sensing agreement at these points? (Leader then gives brief summary.)

2. Since we seem to be tending to move in the direction of a decision, should we not consider what it will mean for our group if we decide the matter this way?

3. What have we accomplished in our discussion up to this point?

Questions Designed to Lend Continuity to the Discussion

1. Since we had time for partial consideration of the problem at the last meeting, would someone care to review what we covered then?

2. Since we cannot reach a decision at this meeting, what are some of the points we should take up at the next one?

3. Would someone care to suggest points on which we need further preparation before we convene again?

Source: Produced in group development course at the University of Georgia.

cess (Hare 1976, pp. 230–231). When the number of group members is large, however, it becomes difficult for everyone to participate actively. For example, what does a curriculum director do
when there is an important curriculum decision to make involving
over a hundred teachers? What does a school principal do when
there is an important rescheduling decision to make that involves
a faculty of seventy persons? Seventy-five to a hundred teachers
sitting in a cafeteria to discuss an issue would be an exercise in
folly. At best, only a few brave souls would speak up, and the
leader would have no sense of what others thought. If the leader
truly wants the involvement of all members in making a decision,
then tightly planned procedures are necessary. With all the procedures about to be described, faculty should clearly understand the
decision-making method to be used for the final decision (majority
vote, consensus, frequencies, and so on).

Three different procedures will be explained. An example involving a staff of seventy-five teachers brought together for the
purpose of deciding on how to allocate the use of six new microcomputers in the high school resource center will be used. All three
methods are based on breaking the entire group into subgroups of
seven to twelve and having a representative committee of one
member from each subgroup. Please refer to Figure 17–4 as the
three procedures are explained.

Procedure A, postrepresentational, begins with Step 1. The
leader convenes the entire group and explains the task and procedures to be used, and the method of decision making. Step 2 is
assigning the seventy-five faculty members to seven subgroups of
ten to eleven members each. The leader should have decided on
assignments of subgroups according to logical criteria (grade level,
content field, or years of teaching experience). Grouping can be
made horizontally (teachers of the same grade, content field, or
teaching experience) or vertically (teachers from different grade
levels, content fields, or years of teaching experience). The subgroups are given the assignment to discuss the topic, make recommendations, and select a representative both to report the group's
position and to be a member of the representative committee. After
the subgroup meeting, the representatives report orally on their
subgroup's position to the entire faculty. After each subgroup has
reported, the entire faculty recesses. In step 3 the representative
committee, consisting of the seven representative members, meet
on their own to recommend or decide the use of the microcomputers. In step 4 the entire faculty reconvenes to hear the representative committee's recommendation or decision. Again, the leader
should have made clear at the beginning whether the representa-

GROUP DEVELOPMENT

FIGURE 17–4   Three Procedures for Large-Group Decision Making

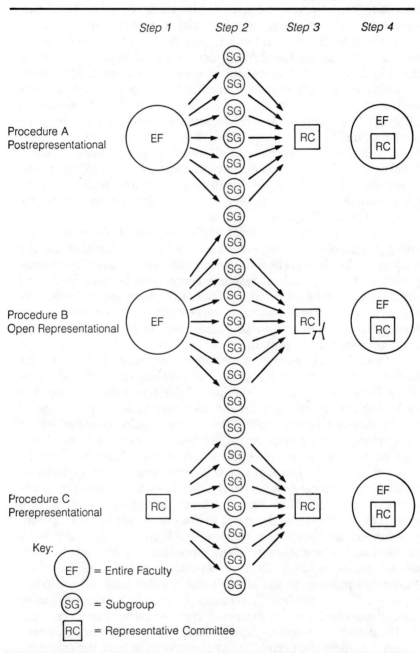

Step 1   Step 2   Step 3   Step 4

Procedure A
Postrepresentational

Procedure B
Open Representational

Procedure C
Prerepresentational

Key:

EF = Entire Faculty

SG = Subgroup

RC = Representative Committee

tive group would come to the faculty with a recommendation or a decision. If it was to be a recommendation, then the entire faculty would vote on the proposal; if it was to be a decision, then the entire faculty would listen to the decision.

The advantages of the postrepresentative procedure is that a decision can be made after only a few meetings. The disadvantage is that subgroup members might feel that hidden influences are affecting the representative committee. Since most faculty members (in the example, sixty-eight out of seventy-five) are omitted from the representative committee meeting, speculation might abound about what transpires in the representative group. However, since each faculty member helped to choose the representatives, trust in their work should prevail.

Procedure B, open representation, is similar to procedure A except that an open chair or open forum is added to the representative committee. This procedure provides an opportunity for every faculty member to have input throughout the decision-making process. Step 1 is an explanation to the entire faculty of the task. Step 2 involves subgroup meetings with the election of a representative and a report of the subgroup's position to all faculty. Step 3 is a meeting of the representative committee with an invitation for any other faculty member to attend and participate. The representative committee deliberates in an open meeting. Times are built into the meeting for the use of an open chair or open forum where outside faculty might make comments. The open chair is at the table of the representative committee. An outside member can take the seat and speak for a certain length of time (usually two minutes), and then must relinquish the seat. Outside members are limited to a certain number of appearances. An open forum is similar except that an outside member does not physically have to move to a chair. He or she can raise his or her hand and speak when called on. Certain times at the beginning, middle, and closing of the meeting are established for outside-member participation. The representative committee can then consider outside-member contributions throughout their deliberations. In step 4 the representative committee makes its recommendation or decision to the entire group.

The advantage of open representation is the elimination of suspicion. All members, whether representatives or not, can be involved. A faculty member cannot rationally complain that he or she was excluded from the process. The open chair or forum invites participation but does not require it. Those faculty members who are indifferent about the decision or trust the representative group or have other priorities are under no pressure to attend. On the other hand, those faculty members who care intensely or are distrustful have an opportunity to participate. For these various reasons, it is important to schedule the representative group meetings at a time that is convenient for all faculty members. (Releasing seven representatives from teaching duties for a 11:00 A.M. meeting and calling it an open meeting is not good enough. The disadvantage of open representation is duration. Allowing input from other members throughout the process will slow down the proceedings of the representative groups. The leader might consider the trade-off. Is it more important to have some involvement for a quicker decision or greater involvement for a slower decision?

Procedure C, prerepresentational, is the quickest of all but is predicated on the greatest amount of trust between faculty and leader. It begins with a selected representative group *before* the entire faculty convenes. In step 1 the leader selects a seven-member committee that he or she believes best represents the entire faculty. The representative committee meet on their own to develop tentative recommendations to the entire faculty. In step 2 the representative committee report their tentative recommendations to the entire faculty for the purpose of gathering reactions. Reactions are gathered by each member of the representative committee sitting with a subgroup of faculty. The subgroups, having just heard the representative committee's report, can now tell the representative member what they think. The representative member takes careful notes and at the conclusion of the subgroup meeting summarizes the reactions and tells the subgroup that he or she will personally give those reactions to the representative committee at their next meeting. In step 3 the representative committee reconvenes by themselves; listens to the report of each subgroup's reactions; and then decides whether to revise, change, or keep the original recommendation. In step 4 the representative committee gives their recommendation (to be voted on) or decision (to be implemented) to the entire faculty.

The critical element in procedure C is the leader's selection of the representative committee. The leader might be open to the criticism that the representative committee was selected on the basis of allegiance to the leader's own views and, therefore, the process was manipulated. However, if faculty trust the leader's motives and understand the criteria for selection of the committee, then the procedure should be effective.

The three procedures are alternative ways to have large-group involvement on important decisions. The task has to be important, of concern, and effect each person in order to justify such involvement. If the task is not important, if persons are indifferent and the effect will be minimal, then the leader should not subject the faculty to such procedures. Decisions of lesser importance should be made in less involving ways. As a rule of thumb, decisions no one cares about should be made by the leader, decisions that already have been made by superordinates should simply be reported, and decisions that concern and affect some and not others should be made by those concerned and affected. The use of any of these large-group procedures should be reserved for only the most crucial and widely impacting decisions.

Summary

This chapter examined the knowledge and skills needed to help professional groups develop. Particular emphasis was put on the supervisor's role in terms of behaving, confronting dysfunctional members, resolving conflict, and preparing for meetings.

The theme of looking at professional groups in a developmental manner should be familiar by now. As a group works together, the leader needs to practice skills that enable the group to become more cohesive, responsible, and autonomous. Eventually the leader would hope to lessen his or her own control and influence so that the group becomes a wise and autonomous body.

EXERCISES

ACADEMIC

1. Assume you are the leader of a group that is very person-oriented but is routinely failing to attend to tasks for which it is responsible. Assume further that you have determined that the roles of initiator-contributor, coordinator, orienter, and energizer are missing and that their absence is largely responsible for the group's failure to attend to assigned tasks. Write a paper explaining what steps you can take to make sure these task roles become present.

2. Assume you are the leader of a group that is generally functioning well but contains a blocker and recognition-seeker, each of whom is reducing the effectiveness of the group. Write

a paper discussing plans for dealing individually with each of these group members to eliminate or reduce their dysfunctional behaviors.

3. Summarize three small-group research studies. Include a discussion of the purpose, participants, methodology, results, and conclusions of each study. Analyze the findings in terms of whether they are congruent with information presented in this past chapter.

4. Assume you have been charged with leadership of a meeting at which a department/team of nine teachers will decide on a new textbook series to be used by those teachers. (You may decide the subject area and grade or age levels for which the text is to be used.) Prepare a written plan for leading the group meeting. Include a general format, an agenda, your plan for opening the meeting, and a discussion guide with preselected questions.

5. Assume you have been assigned to organize a meeting of 130 teachers who are to decide on a proposal to adopt a building-wide system of discipline. Write a paper discussing the procedure and specific strategies you will use in facilitating a group decision on the proposal.

FIELD

1. Record and analyze an audiotape of yourself leading a group decision-making process. Determine any leadership deficiencies you exhibited during the discussion. Was there a lack of preplanning for the meeting? Was your leadership lacking in facilitation of task or person behaviors? Did you fail to deal effectively with a dysfunctional member? Did you fail to handle conflict properly? Based on your analysis, prepare a self-improvement plan to be followed in a second group session. If possible, analyze an audiotape of a second meeting to see if you improved your leadership in the selected areas.

2. Assign task, people, and dysfunctional roles to various members of a simulated group decision-making meeting. After the simulation, allow each member of the group to express personal reactions to the behaviors of the various role players. Hold a group discussion on how each member affected the group's effectiveness.

3. Hold a one-to-one meeting with a dysfunctional group member of a real group that you lead. The conference should aim to improve that individual's in-group behavior. Write a summary of the conference and its results.

4. Prepare for and lead a real-life small-group meeting. Prepare a written evaluation of your small-group leadership.

5. Prepare for and lead a large-group decision-making process, using one of the procedures for large-group involvement discussed in this chapter. Write a report on the success of the process.

DEVELOPMENTAL

1. Using knowledge and skills you have acquired in group development, continue to facilitate long-range development of a group of which you are a leader or member.

2. Begin an in-depth study of one of the following areas:

   a. Small-group research.

   b. Group counseling skills.

   c. Leadership style.

   d. Organizational management.

   e. Group discussion/interaction.

3. Begin a file of group development activities. Each group activity can be summarized on an index card and classified according to categories that are useful for you.

REFERENCES

Bales, R. F. 1953. The equilibrium problem in small groups. In T. Parsons, R. F. Bales, and E. A. Shils, eds., *Working papers in the theory of action.* Glencoe, Ill: Free Press, pp. 111–161.

Benne, D. D., and Sheats, P. 1948. Functional roles of group members. *Journal of Social Issues* 4(2):41–49.

Corey, G., and Corey, M. 1977. *Groups: Process and practice.* Monterey, Calif.: Brooks/Cole, pp. 39–47.

Gordon, T. 1980. *Leadership effectiveness training—L.E.T.* New York: Bantam Books, Chap. 9.

Hare, A. P. 1976. *Handbook of small group research,* 2nd ed. New York: Free Press, pp. 230–231.

———. 1982. *Creativity in small groups.* Beverly Hills, Calif.: Sage Publications, pp. 17–53.

Hersey, P., and Blanchard, K. H. 1969. Life-cycle theory of leadership. *Training and Development Journal 23*(5):26–34.

———. 1977. *Management of organizational behavior: Utilizing human resources.* Englewood Cliffs, N.J.: Prentice-Hall.

Johnson, D. W., and Johnson, F. P. 1982. *Joining together: Group theory and group skills.* Englewood Cliffs, N.J.: Prentice-Hall, pp. 11, 228–230.

Kemp, C. G. 1964. *Group process: A foundation for counseling with groups.* Boston: Houghton Mifflin, pp. 352–360.

Little, J. W. 1982. Norms of collegiality and experimentation: Work-place conditions of school success. *American Educational Research Journal 19*(3):325–340.

SUGGESTIONS FOR ADDITIONAL READING

Corey, G., and Corey, M. S. 1977. *Groups: Process and practice.* Monterey, Calif.: Brooks/Cole.

Hare, A. P. 1982. *Creativity in small groups.* Beverly Hills, Calif.: Sage Publications.

Hyman, R. T. 1980. *Improving discussion leadership.* New York: Teachers College Press.

Johnson, D. W. 1981. *Reaching out,* 2nd ed. Englewood Cliffs, N.J.: Prentice-Hall.

Johnson, D. W., and Johnson, F. P. 1982. *Joining together: Group skills,* 2nd ed. Englewood Cliffs, N.J.: Prentice-Hall.

Napier, R. W., and Gershenfeld, M. K. 1981. *Groups: Theory and experience,* 2nd ed. Boston: Houghton Mifflin.

Phillips, G. M.; Pedersen, D. J.; and Wood, J. T. 1979. *Groups discussion: A practical guide to participation and leadership.* Boston: Houghton Mifflin.

Sanford, G., and Roark, A. E. 1974. *Human interaction in education.* Boston: Allyn and Bacon.

Simpson, D. T. 1977. Handling group and organization conflict. In *Annual handbook for group facilitators.* LaJolla, Calif.: University Associates.

CHAPTER EIGHTEEN

Action Research: The Integrating Task for Schoolwide Improvement

The famous social scientist Kurt Lewin devoted his career to studying democracy and the relationship of individuals within groups. His contributions ushered in the school of Gestalt psychology, group dynamics, and the concept of action research. He argued that social research needs to be based on actions groups take to improve their conditions. Social research should not be based on controlled experiments removed from real conditions. As people plan changes and engage in real activities, there needs to be fact finding to determine if success is being achieved and if further planning and action are necessary (Lewin 1948, p. 206).

Stephen Corey applied Lewin's concept of action research to education. He argued that traditional research is done mainly by researchers outside the public school and has little influence on school practice. Corey (1953, p. 9) wrote:

> Learning that changes behavior substantially is most likely to result when a person himself tries to improve a situation that makes a difference to him ... when he defines the problem, hypothesizes actions that may help him cope with it, engages in these actions, studies the consequences, and generalizes from them, he will more frequently internalize the experience than when all this is done for him by somebody else, and he reads about it. . . . The value of action research . . . is determined primarily by the extent to which findings lead to improvement in the practices of the people engaged in the research.

Action research in education is, therefore, a study conducted by colleagues in a school setting of the results of their activities to improve instruction. Although an individual teacher can conduct action research, in most cases it is best done as a cooperative endeavor by faculty attempting to improve on a common instructional concern. Action research implies that practitioners are the researchers. Although the objectivity and rigor of research methodology can be questioned by classical researchers (see Chapter Thirteen on the classical research loop), the benefits of the process for students and teachers seem to outweigh the loss of experimental purity.

How Is Action Research Conducted?

There is little mystery about action research. Refer to the previous sections on interpersonal skills and technical skills to see how a supervisor works with teachers and what techniques are chosen for implementing a plan.

First, the supervisor chooses an interpersonal approach to use with the action research team. The action research team is composed of teachers who represent the entire faculty. The choice of interpersonal approach is shown in Table 18–1.

Based on characteristics of teachers, including their ability to think abstractly about instructional problems, their commitment to making changes, their experience with instructional change, and their expertise with instruction, the supervisor determines a general interpersonal approach. She might choose to be nondirective by using behaviors of listening, reflecting, clarifying, and encouraging and allow teachers to make their own decisions. She might choose to be collaborative by stressing behaviors of presenting, problem solving, and negotiating and, therefore, aim for a mutual, democratic decision. She might choose to be directive by presenting, problem solving, directing, and standardizing and using the teachers as an advisory group.

Second, the team conducts a needs assessment of faculty and collects base-line data to determine common objectives for improvement of instruction.

Techniques for conducting a needs assessment can be chosen from the following list:

■ Eyes and ears.

■ Official records.

- Third-party review.
- Written open-ended survey.
- Check and ranking lists.
- Delphi.

(Explanations of each assessment technique can be found in Chapter Eleven).

Third, the team brainstorms activities that will cut across supervision tasks. The team can respond to these four questions corresponding to supervisory tasks:

1. What type and frequency of *direct assistance* needs to be provided to teachers to improve our instructional concern?

2. What *curriculum development* needs to be made in course content, curriculum guides, lesson plans, and instructional materials in order to improve our instructional concern?

3. What learning opportunities such as lectures, workshops, demonstrations, courses, and visitations need to be provided

TABLE 18–1   Choosing an Interpersonal Approach

Interpersonal Behaviors	Decision

Nondirective:
  listening
  reflecting
  clarifying
  encouraging
	high teacher/low supervisor

Collaborative:
  presenting
  problem solving
  negotiating
	equal teacher/equal supervisor

Directive:
  presenting
  problem solving
  directing
  standardizing
	low teacher/high supervisor

Characteristics of teachers Abstraction Commitment Experience Expertise	

via *inservice education* for faculty to improve our instructional concern?

4. What meetings and discussions need to be arranged as part of *group development* for faculty to share and improve on our instructional concern?

Each task of supervision is explained in Chapters Fourteen, Fifteen, Sixteen, and Seventeen.

Fourth, the team makes a plan relating activities to objectives. Techniques for writing plans are as follows:

- Simple flow chart.

- Management by objectives (MBO).

- Gant chart.

- Program evaluation and review technique (PERT).

- Planning, programming, budgeting system (PPBS).

A description of each planning device can be found in Chapter Eleven.

Fifth, the team determines ways to observe the progress of the action plan as it is implemented in classrooms. Observations can be made with the use of the following instruments:

- Categorical frequency.

- Physical indicator.

- Performance indicator.

- Visual diagramming.

- Space utilization.

- Detached open-ended narrative.

- Participant open-ended observation.

- Focused questionnaire.

- Educational criticism.

Use of these instruments is explained in Chapter Twelve.

Sixth, the team chooses a research and evaluation design that will enable them to analyze data, determine whether objectives have been met, and what further changes need to be made. Choices can be made from these designs:

■ Descriptive.

■ Correlational.

■ Experimental.

■ Quasi-experimental.

■ Cybernetic.

■ Self-study.

■ Adverserial.

To understand the uses of each design, refer to Chapter Thirteen.

Action Research: Vehicle for a Cause Beyond Oneself

Action research is used in many schools under various names ranging from "organizational development committees," to "leadership councils," to "quality circle groups." Regardless of the name, action research is a beautiful vehicle for bringing together individual teacher needs with organizational goals to achieve a cause beyond oneself.

We previously detailed each task of supervision (direct assistance, curriculum development, in-service, and group development) separately. In reality, any effort to improve instruction must relate each task to the others. It is time to soften the boundaries between the tasks and show how action research can be the vehicle for their integration.

Action research is focused on the needs to improve instruction as perceived by the faculty. As instructional improvements are identified, faculty and supervisor plan related activities to be implemented in each of the tasks of supervision (see Figure 18–1).

Think of action research as a huge meteor falling into the middle of the supervision ocean. As it hits, it causes a rippling of water that activates the four seas of direct asistance, in-service, curriculum development, and group development. The rippling of water continues to increase force until a giant wave gathers and crashes onto all instructional shores, sweeping away the old sand of past instructional failures and replacing it with the new sand of instructional improvement. Stepping away from the beach, we might look at some examples of action research related to supervisory activities.

FIGURE 18–1   Action Research as the Core of Related Supervisory Activities

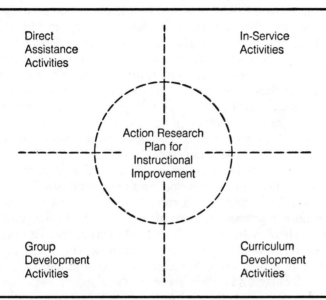

Direct Assistance Activities

In-Service Activities

Action Research Plan for Instructional Improvement

Group Development Activities

Curriculum Development Activities

Examples of Action Research

The attention given to effective and successful schools has been a stimulant to action research in schools. Brookover's studies of improving schools (Brookover et al. 1979), Edmond's studies of effective schools (1979), Rutter et al.'s study of effective high schools (1979), Little's study of successful schools (1982), Berman and McLaughlin's study of successful program implementation (1978), and the Phi Delta Kappa Commission on Schools with Good Discipline (Wayson et al. 1982) have all reported the collective participation of faculty in planning action research as a characteristic of successful schools.

Many schools have formed groups that are engaged in action research. For example, in Portsmouth (N.H.) Junior High School, an action research team of teachers recently planned a study to see if teacher satisfaction and morale would improve by changing the way classrooms were scheduled (Barret and Blomquist 1983). The school principal reduced teacher duties and grouped students by ability, thinking that such changes would increase teacher satisfaction. Teachers were pre- and posttested on a teacher burnout inventory. Surprisingly, there was no significant change. The action research group then studied why such administrative changes had little effect on teacher perceptions. The committee conducted personal interviews and written surveys of the faculty. They discovered that teachers with the highest scores on burnout perceived themselves as being least involved in schoolwide decisions. On the other hand, the teachers with the lowest scores on burnout perceived themselves as being the most involved in schoolwide decisions. The action research team therefore concluded that the issue of scheduling was less significant to teacher satisfaction than the issue of involvement in schoolwide decisions. As a result of the action research investigation, the following year the principal involved every faculty member in making schoolwide decisions. The action research project was instrumental in identifying and focusing on successful interventions (Oja 1984).

Another example of action research comes from an elementary school in Georgia. The school had been committed to mastery learning and had experienced considerable student success. However, teachers expressed concern about the lack of consistent classroom and school rules and enforcement procedures. The principal agreed to form a representative committee composed of seven teachers. The action research committee met and, with input from the entire faculty and administration, developed a set of common expectations for students and enforcement procedures for classroom teachers, specialists, lunchroom monitors, bus drivers, and principals. At the same time, in-service activities aimed at improving teacher management methods were held. Teachers altered the curriculum by teaching students the new rules and procedures. They met as a group on an ongoing basis to brainstorm and problem-solve further improvements. Supervisors and peers observed each other and provided feedback on progress. The committee collected information on teachers' perceptions of improved student behavior, decreases in referrals to the principal's office, amount of time for classroom instruction, and improved student achievement. The committee conducted a simple pre- and posttest evaluation four weeks and then three months after the new procedures had been implemented. The results showed major improvement. The committee decided to keep the new policies in effect and to continue monitoring progress.

An excellent example of long-term action research conducted over several years was done by the faculty of the Annehurst (Ohio) school. A leadership committee of teachers worked with their school principal and several university consultants to improve their schoolwide instruction over a three-and-a-half-year period. The objective of their action project was to individualize instruction, to provide multilevel and varied materials suitable for each student, and to implement team teaching (Mills 1981). The product of the project has been the creation by the faculty of a widely acclaimed curriculum, entitled the Annehurst Curriculum Classification System (Frymier 1977). The evaluation of student progress since implementation of the action plan has shown a major increase in student achievement for over six years (Cornbleth 1981).

In these three examples of action research, some researchers would frown on the lack of control groups and question the validity of the measures taken. However, all the schools reported much greater staff interaction, professional talk, and common purpose as a result of these action research projects. It might well be that the studies and results of action research are less important than the process of teachers being asked to be reflective and collective in their thinking. The prevailing view of research as being done by those at universities and the results handed down to teachers has been described by Sykes (1983, pp. 90–91): "[Traditional research] accords precious little room to the sort of reflection-in-action in which the best practitioners engage. ... We have largely failed either to establish reflection-in-action as an aim of professional education or to encourage inquiry as a professional norm for individual teachers and as an institutional norm for schools."

In two out of the three examples of action research, the teachers probably did not know they were conducting something called action research. If asked what they were doing, they probably would have answered: "We were trying to improve our instructional program as a staff by assessing, planning, observing, researching, and evaluating." Obviously, some people were taking responsibilities for the supervisory function of seeing that school-wide instructional improvement could occur. When a supervisor provides the conditions, organizes the people, and sees that the group has available to them technical skills and expertise, instruction will improve. The norms of despair, isolation and loneliness, conformity, and concrete and restricted thought fall by the wayside as teachers become researchers; they are replaced by norms of abstraction, commitment, and a cause beyond oneself.

Summary

Action research is a vehicle for combining all the tasks of supervision into an integrated whole. Once a faculty determines a direction for improvement, they can plan activities in direct assistance, in-service education, curriculum development, and group development to reach their goals. The supervisor begins by determining an interpersonal approach for working with the faculty based on teacher characteristics of abstraction, commitment, experience, and expertise. Once the representative faculty committee is formed, the supervisor helps the group conduct a needs assessment, write a plan, select data collection instruments, and decide on an evaluation design. Action research is a task that brings together individual faculty needs with schoolwide instructional goals to create a successful organization.

EXERCISES

ACADEMIC

1. Assume you have been assigned the task of speaking in favor of a proposal to provide funding for action research at the next school board meeting. Write your speech, telling how you and your staff will carry out such research and what the benefits will be. To attempt to convince the school board, include in your speech references to sources other than this book.

2. Describe two action research projects that have been reported in the literature and not discussed in this book.

3. Select an objective for instructional improvement that can be adapted to action research. Based on that objective, prepare a written plan for an action research project. Make sure that procedures for conducting action research listed in this chapter are addressed in your plan.

4. Briefly describe an action research project that might be carried out by a small group of teachers facilitated by a supervisor. Next, describe the knowledge and skills the supervisor would need in order to lead the group successfully in the action research. Rely on previous chapters of this book for your answer.

5. Create a model for evaluating action research projects. Components of the model should provide for evaluation of needs assessment, objectives, planning and sequencing of activities, implementation of activities, measurement techniques, and data analysis. Each component should be accompanied by

critical questions to be asked concerning the appropriate phase of the action research project.

FIELD

1. Plan and carry out a short-term, individual action research project. Report on the action research, its results, your conclusions, and your recommendations.

2. Observe, evaluate, and report on an action research project currently being carried out in a school setting. Include a discussion of whether all four tasks of supervision have been integrated in the action research.

3. Describe an instructional improvement recently introduced in a school with which you are familiar. Suggest how the innovation could have been tried out as action research before being fully implemented. Your suggested plan should meet all the requirements (necessary procedures, integrated supervision tasks) for authentic action research.

4. Determine an instructional improvement that would benefit a school with which you are familiar. Suggest how each of the four tasks of supervision would be met in relation to your instructional improvement objective:

    a. What direct assistance would have to be provided to facilitate the instructional improvement?

    b. What curriculum development would have to be made?

    c. What in-service education activities would be necessary?

    d. What types of group development would faculty need?

5. Interview faculty and supervisors of a clearly successful school to determine whether action research is carried out in that school. If so, do faculty members participate collectively in planning for action research? What is the mechanism for such participation (curriculum council, research committees, circle groups)? What are some examples of action research that have been carried out?

    If the selected school does not conduct action research, are teachers allowed opportunities for professional interaction, discussion of ideas for instructional improvement, and reflective and collective thinking? If so, how are such opportunities provided?

    Prepare a report on your interviews.

DEVELOPMENTAL

1. Volunteer to supervise or participate in a long-range group action research project within an educational setting.

2. Take advantage of future opportunities to hold discussions with those involved in school action research. Such discussions can help you generate your own ideas for action research projects and effective supervision of action research.

3. Continue to explore the literature and research on action research. Begin a file of articles appropriate for sharing with educators interested in action research.

REFERENCES

Barret, W., and Blomquist, R. 1983. An evaluation study of junior high school scheduling. A presentation as part of the collaborative Action Research–Teachers as Researchers Symposium of the annual meeting of the American Educational Research Association, Montreal, April 13.

Berman, P., and McLaughlin, M. W. 1978. *Federal programs supporting educational change,* Vol. 8: *Implementing and sustaining innovations.* ED 159–289. Santa Monica, Calif.: Rand Corporation.

Brookover, W.; Beady, C.; Flood, P.; Schweiter, J.; and Wisenbaker, J. 1979. *School social systems and students' achievement: Schools can make a difference.* New York: Praeger.

Corey, S. M. 1953. *Action research to improve school practices.* New York: Teachers College Columbia University.

Cornbleth, C. 1981. Curriculum materials can make a difference. *Educational Leadership 38*(7):567–568.

Edmond, R. 1979. Effective schools for the urban poor. *Educational Leadership 37*(1):15–24.

Frymier, J. R. 1977. *Annehurst curriculum classification systems: A practical way to improve instruction.* West Lafayette, Ind.: Kappa Delta Pi.

Lewin, K. 1948. *Resolving social conflicts.* New York: Harper and Brothers.

Little, J. W. 1982. Norms of collegiality and experimentation: Workplace conditions of school success. *American Educational Research Journal 19*(3):325–340.

Mills, T. 1981. The development of Annehurst school. *Educational Leadership 38*(7):569.

Oja, S. N. 1984. Studies of relationship of teachers' conceptual levels with collaborative action research. Paper presented at the annual meeting of the American Educational Research Association, New Orleans, April.

Rutter, M.; Maughan, B.; Mortimore, P.; Ouston, J.; and Smith, A. 1979. *Fifteen thousand hours: Secondary schools and their effects on children.* Cambridge, Mass.: Harvard University Press.

Social Circle (Ga.) Elementary School. 1983. Schoolwide discipline project. Social Circle, Georgia, Fall.

Sykes, G. 1983. Contradictions, ironies, and promises unfulfilled: A contemporary account of the status of teaching. *Phi Delta Kappan 65*(2):87–93.

Wayson, W. W.; DeVoss, G. G.; Kaeser, S. C.; Lasley, T.; and Pinnel, G. S. 1982. *Handbook for developing schools with good discipline.* Bloomington, Ind.: Phi Delta Kappa.

SUGGESTIONS FOR ADDITIONAL READING

Action for curriculum improvement, 1951 yearbook. 1951. Washington, D.C.: Association for Supervision and Curriculum Development.

Corey, S. M. 1953. *Action research to improve school practices.* New York: Teachers College, Columbia University.

Elliott, J. 1978. What is action research in school? *Journal of Curriculum Studies 10:*355–357.

Elliot, J., and Adelman, C. 1973. Supporting teacher research in the classroom. *The New Era 54:*210–213, 215.

Frymier, J. R. 1977. *Annehurst curriculum classification system: A practical way to improve instruction.* West Lafayette, Ind.: Kappa Delta Pi.

Kelley, E. C. 1951. *The workshop way of learning*. New York: Harper & Brothers, 1951, Chaps. III–V, pp. 12–62.

Lasky, L. R. 1978. Personalizing teaching: Action research in action. *Young Children 33*(3):58–64.

Oliver, B. 1980. Action research for in-service training. *Educational Leadership 37*:394–395.

Rainey, B. G. 1973. Action research: A valuable professional activity for the teacher. *The Clearing House 47*:371–375.

Schaefer, R. V. 1967. *The school as a center of inquiry*. New York: Harper and Row.

Taba, H., and Noel, E. 1957. *Action research, A case study*. Washington, D.C.: Association for Supervision and Curriculum Development.

PART V

CONCLUSION

The purpose of this section was to make instructional improvement and school success a realistic goal. We have looked at the five tasks of supervision that have direct impact on instructional improvement: direct assistance, in-service education, curriculum development, group development, and action research. Emphasis was given on how the use of each task can unite teacher needs with organizational goals (see Figure V–1).

We were able to use prerequisites of knowledge, interpersonal skills, and technical skills to function in the realm of supervision and apply it to the five tasks. Chapter Fourteen on direct assistance examined clinical procedures for observations, peer supervision, accessibility, arranged time, delegation, and separating direct assistance from formal evaluation. Chapter Fifteen looked at in-service education in terms of research findings of successful in-service, teacher concerns, conceptual and psychological states of teachers, and experience impact of activities. Chapter Sixteen on curriculum development examined varying formats for writing curriculum, the range of developers of curriculum, and degree of teacher involvement. Chapter Seventeen on group development studied the supervisor's role in the group with attention to task and person behaviors, confronting dysfunctional members, resolving conflict, preparing for meetings, and lessening leadership control as the group becomes cohesive. Finally, Chapter Eighteen on action research showed how teachers can become researchers on their own instructional problems. Such research integrates the four previous supervisory tasks and unifies teacher needs with organizational goals to promote collective action.

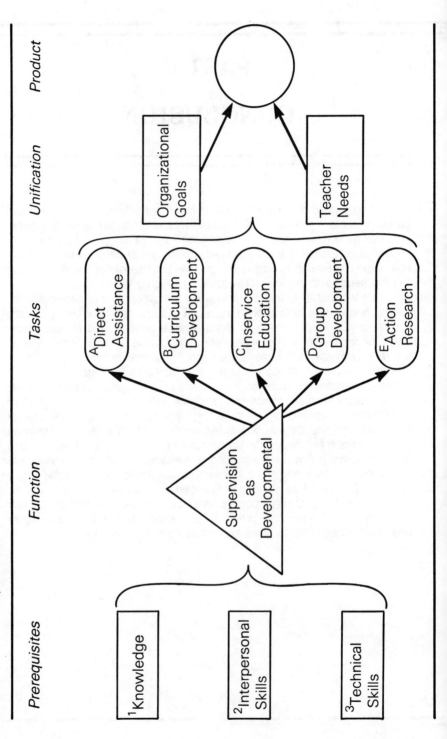

FIGURE V–1   Supervision for Successful Schools

Prerequisites

¹Knowledge

²Interpersonal Skills

³Technical Skills

Function

Supervision as Developmental

Tasks

ᴬDirect Assistance

ᴮCurriculum Development

ᶜInservice Education

ᴰGroup Development

ᴱAction Research

Unification

Organizational Goals

Teacher Needs

Product

PART VI

Function of Supervision

Introduction

Chapter Two introduced five research-based propositions about supervision.

- Proposition 1: *Supervision can enhance teacher belief in a cause beyond oneself.*

- Proposition 2: *Supervision can promote teacher sense of efficacy.*

- Proposition 3: *Supervision can make teachers aware of how they complement each other in striving for common goals.*

- Proposition 4: *Supervision can stimulate teachers to plan common purpose and actions.*

- Proposition 5: *Supervision can challenge teachers to think abstractly about their work.*

Chapter Three looked at the obstacles to supervision. We listed those obstacles as three propositions.

- Proposition 1: *Supervision cannot rely on the teaching career to provide motivation for continual instructional improvement.*

- Proposition 2: *Supervision cannot rely on the existing work environment of schools to stimulate instructional improvement.*

- Proposition 3: *Supervisors cannot assume that all teachers are reflective, autonomous, and responsible for their own development.*

Chapter Four detailed the need for looking at teachers in a developmental manner and proposed the following:

- Proposition 1: *Supervision, to be effective, must be a function that responds to the developmental stages of teachers.*

- Proposition 2: *Supervision, to be effective, must be a function that responds to adult life transitions of teachers.*

Finally, Chapter Five concluded Part II of prerequisite knowledge with propositions about supervisory beliefs and actions.

- Proposition 1: *Supervisors should use a variety of practices that emanate out of various philosophical and belief structures with developmental directionality in mind.*

- Proposition 2: *As supervisors gradually increase teacher choice and control over instructional improvement, teachers will become more abstract and committed to improvement and a sense of ethos or a cause beyond oneself will emerge.*

The subsequent sections of the book explained the technical and interpersonal skills a supervisor needs to carry out the five tasks of supervision. Each task of supervision was carefully outlined with respect to how its delivery to teachers could help them move toward higher stages of professional development and collective action. We will conclude with the meaning of the function of development as it applies to supervision for school success.

CHAPTER NINETEEN

Development, School Success, and Cathedrals

The major thesis of this book has been that supervision must be viewed and applied as a developmental function for school success. In conclusion, we wish to summarize what is meant by development and school success. There are two possible meanings when one speaks of development that are complementary and of equal importance.

> The first meaning of development as a supervisory function is the use of instructional-change strategies that move from persuasive to facilitative.

> The second meaning of development as a supervisory function is the determination of supervisory intervention according to individual and group characteristics of teachers.

We will take a closer look at both of these meanings.

Developmental View of Change Strategies for Instructional Improvement

Zaltman and Duncan (1977) identify four strategies that a change agent can use on or with a target group. The strategies are labeled *power, persuasive, reeducative,* and *facilitative.*

> *Power strategy* is the use of formal authority and control over the target group to force them to change according to the agent's plan. The change agent can use rewards, negative reinforcements, or punishment to achieve compliance.

> *Persuasive strategy* is the use of logic and wisdom to convince

the target group that change needs to be made according to the change agent's plan. The agent appeals to the target group's common sense and emotions to achieve their following.

Reeducative strategy is the use of new information provided by the change agent to the target group for the group to determine their own plan. The agent asks the group to rethink what they currently do based on ideas, opinions, and facts not previously considered.

Facilitative strategy is the delivery of resources by the change agent to the target group after the group has determined its plan. The agent serves as a helper in terms of supplying goods, giving technical services, and removing obstacles from the path of the target group's plan.

With these change strategies, we can see how moving from power to facilitative strategies moves the locus of control for the plan of action from the change agent to the target group. A power strategy is a plan the agent forces on the group. A persuasive strategy is a plan by the agent that depends on the group's willingness to follow. A reeducative strategy gives the target group control over the plan based on the agent supplying new information. A facilitative strategy gives complete control to the group to plan, with the agent assisting in the implementation.

Technical skills for supervision can be used in any of the four change strategies, but should they be used? One can use skills of planning and assessing, observing, researching, and evaluating to coerce, persuade, reeducate, or facilitate teachers. Power strategies have little place in public education that undergrids a democratic society. The use of power in public education is simply wrong. Furthermore, even if power were not wrong, in such a loosely coupled institution as school, implementation cannot be constantly monitored and will not work. What is defensible in schools is the use of persuasive, reeducative, and facilitative change strategies used with the aim of increasing teachers' control over instructional improvement.

Therefore, we can think of three change strategies as developmental or growth-oriented. Over time, persuasive strategies should be replaced by reeducative strategies, which should in turn be replaced by facilitative strategies. The inner strategies for each task of supervision can be viewed in a similar developmental manner (see Table 19–1).

A change strategy for a group of teachers with little experience working with each other and characterized by low abstraction and committment would be *persuasive.* Direct assistance would be furnished by directive, informational interpersonal behavior by the supervisor. In-service would focus on demonstration of skills with emphasis on explanation, workshop practice, and described personal benefits. Curriculum development would be primarily *imitative,* characterized by externally developed and prescribed curriculum. Group development would have a supervisor assuming the *selling* posture by providing a high task and high person orientation. Action research would be *led* by the *supervisor,* with teachers' input into a plan for instructional improvement.

A change strategy for a group of teachers who have worked together and possess moderate or mixed degrees of abstraction and commitment would be a *reeducative* strategy. Direct assistance would be provided via collaborative supervisory interpersonal skills. In-service would emphasize *application of skills* with classroom practice, observation, and peer supervision. Curriculum development would be *mediative,* characterized by a team of teachers led by district specialists revising and adapting existing curriculum. Group development would have supervisor leadership, characterized by *participating* with teachers in the structure and content of meetings. Action research would be *shared* between supervisor and teacher in determining future instructional improvements.

A change strategy for an experienced, highly abstract and committed faculty would be *facilitative.* Direct assistance would be given through *nondirective* interpersonal behaviors of the supervi-

TABLE 19–1 Developmental Directionality: Change Strategies with the Tasks of Supervision

	Change Strategy		
	Persuasive	*Reeducative*	*Facilitative*
Direct assistance	Directive informational	Collaborative	Nondirective
In-service	Demonstration of skills	Application of skills	Improving skills
Curriculum development	Imitative	Mediative	Generative
Group development	Selling	Participating	Delegating
Action research	Supervisor leadership	Shared leadership	Teacher leadership
Task of supervision			

sor. In-service would be centered on *improving skills* through modification of existent classroom practice by teams of teachers engaged in brainstorming and problem solving. Curriculum development would be *generative,* characterized by teachers creating their own curricula with the resource assistance of specialists. Group development would be approached by a supervisor as *delegating* the structure and content of the meetings to teachers. In the same manner, action research would come from the *leadership of the teachers,* where they would plan, act, research, and use the supervisor as a consultant.

A supervisor uses his or her own knowledge about self, characteristics of faculty, and skills for planning supervisory tasks to determine the change strategy to use. There exists no scientific precision or algorithm for determining a faculty's level of experience, abstraction, and commitment. Supervision for successful schools is a developmental function that increases teachers' choices, stimulates teachers' thinking, and encourages collective action—a cause beyond oneself. Therefore, one meaning of supervision as developmental is the strategic movement from persuasive to reeducative to facilitative change. The other meaning of supervision as developmental is responding to teachers as growing, dynamic professionals.

Developmental View of Teachers

We have reiterated in previous chapters how teachers' thinking, concerns, and commitments change over their careers. A beginning teacher simply does not have the same concerns or responses to instructional problems as more experienced and successful teachers do. Optimal career development of teachers shows movement from egocentric to altruistic concerns and from concrete to abstract thinking. The most successful schools are characterized by teachers who can think in complex and differentiated ways and who view instruction as a team or schoolwide effect. Common cause, common action, challenging ideas, professional talk, and visibility of effort are what is meant by the concept of a cause beyond oneself as the key to successful schools. One simple point of this book is that most teachers do not enter a school with the optimal, collective capacity to think and act. A cause beyond oneself is not inherent in schools. In fact, most often the norms of the work environment of schools and the established career patterns of teaching work against such development. For teachers to achieve higher stages of professional development, the supervisor needs to respond to the individual and group's present stage and to alter the work environment in ways that stimulate, challenge, and provide options for them. Therefore, the second meaning of development is to view teachers as growing adults who will become more professional and successful as they are provided with a work environment that demands choice, autonomy, dialogue, and reflection.

Current Concerns with Teaching: Within and Without

Currently there is a healthy national concern with upgrading the teaching profession. The National Commission on Excellence in Education has proposed (1) providing college scholarships to attract more intelligent and achievement-minded students into teacher education, (2) raising teacher salaries to compare more favorably with salaries in private industries, and (3) creating financial career ladders to pay teachers substantially higher salaries when they achieve certain plateaus (U.S. Department of Education 1983, pp. 30–31). The aim of these three proposals is to attract and keep more capable people in the profession by providing financial incentives. There is little opposition to such proposals, and many states already have legislated substantial pay increases. Teaching should be a more extrinsically rewarded profession. Yet I am convinced that changing the outer conditions for teachers without making subsequent changes in the internal conditions in their work life will not substantially improve instruction. Improving the external conditions without improving the internal conditions is similar to baking a loaf of bread and having a beautiful, smoothly textured crust, only to bite into a moldy and unmixed core. We obviously need a profession that is satisfying from both within and without.

The Carnegie Foundation study of high schools, directed by Ernest Boyer, spoke to these internal conditions of school in this way (Boyer 1983, p. 159):

> In 1981, more than one-third (36 percent) of the high school teachers said they would not or "probably" would not go into teaching if they had to do it over again. This is almost twice as many (19 percent) as felt that way in 1976, and almost three times as many (13 percent) as felt that way in 1971.

> In sum, the teachers' world is often frustrating, frequently demeaning, and sometimes dangerous. The re-

sult for many teachers is a sense of alienation, apathy, and what is now called "teacher burnout."

John Goodlad, upon completing the most comprehensive study of schools ever undertaken in the United States, concluded (Goodlad 1984, pp. 193–194):

> In general the practicing teacher—to the degree we can generalize from our findings—functions in a context where the beliefs and expectations are those of a profession but where the realities tend to constrain, likening actual practice to a trade ... a question arises as to whether the circumstances can be made conducive to developing in all teachers the behavior a profession entails. By its very nature a profession involves both considerable autonomy in decision making and knowledge and skills developed before entry and then honed in practice. The teachers in our sample, on the whole, went into teaching because of those inherent professional values. However, they encountered in schools many realities not conducive to professional growth.

Boyer and Goodlad, two of our most distinguished educators, have concluded from their extensive research that the work environment of schools is not conducive to the professional development of teachers and to the success of schools. Only when supervisors attend to individual differences in teachers and improve what Boyer (p. 159) refers to as "the intellectual climate of the school" will teachers become more abstract in their thinking and committed to improving instruction for students.

The Door Is Open

At a luncheon, I once discussed public education with an executive of a large corporation who was serving as chairperson of a Governor's Task Force to finance excellence in public education. The executive spoke words to this effect: "I've followed funding for public education ever since I was a local school board member, and I see the history of education as times of opening or closing doors. We've had the door closed for quite a while, but it's open again, and while it's open we're going to do our darnedest to improve the salaries of teachers."

The executive's words reinforced the current excitement in

public education. If we can go beyond the rhetoric, and I think we will, and upgrade the external conditions of schools, then at last we will be close to having it all. The door always has been open to improve schools from within; now the public is showing a willingness to improve schools from without. Only we, as supervisors, can improve the internal conditions of schools. Many supervisors have made their schools centers of teacher inquiry, autonomy, and dialogue. We certainly have enough information available to us about supervision, interpersonal skills, technical skills, tasks, the nature of change, and the psychology of individual and group development to make all our schools better places. The door for improving internal conditions will never close; it's simply a matter of whether or not we care to step in and make a difference.

The Role of Supervision and Supervisor

We began this book by defining the key to successful schools as instructional supervision that fosters teacher development by promoting greater abstraction, commitment, and collective action. The aim of supervision is to bring faculty together as knowledgeable professionals working for the benefit of all students. The role of supervision is to change the attitude of many schools that a classroom is an island unto itself to an attitude that faculty is engaged in a common schoolwide instructional task that transcends any one classroom—a cause beyond oneself.

Supervisors—whether they be building-level persons such as school principals, department heads, or instructional lead teachers or master teachers; districtwide persons such as assistant superintendents, curriculum directors, subject area specialists, or consultants; or school-level generalists (early childhood, elementary, middle school, or secondary)—can play an important part in improving schools. The critical tasks for such improvement are direct assistance, curriculum development, in-service education, group development, and action research. Each of these tasks can be planned to enhance teacher development and collective action. Districtwide and building-level supervisors can work together to implement such plans. Rarely can one person do it all; but on the other hand, rare is the situation where supervisors concerned with instructional improvement cannot begin. We know that school success can be achieved when supervisors attend to those tasks that enable teachers to develop individually and collectively (Pratzner 1984).

What Is School Success?

Ironically, we have left the definition of school success to the end of this book. This has been done with a purpose, however. The rationale for a school faculty making its own collective definition of school success should be apparent. In referring to studies of successful schools to support many of the propositions of this book, I was referring to schools that were achieving what they had set out to do, regardless of what those goals were. Some schools prioritize academic learning and achievement as their criteria for success. Some prioritize creativity and self-directed learning. Other schools prioritize problem solving, community involvement, and social cooperation as their criteria for success. Many schools want it all: They want to be successful in academics, creativity, self-directed learning, problem solving, community involvement, and social cooperation (Goodlad 1984, pp. 33–60). Although I personally prefer schools that strive to have it all, that decision should be a local school matter. It is in the clarity of common purpose that purposeful action to improve instruction takes place.

With an understanding of what is meant by improved instruction and school success, we can fill in the remaining circle on the diagram of supervision for successful schools that has served as the organization of this book (see Figure 19–1).

A Final Note

This book has been written to help those who function in the realm of supervision to bring about school success. Supervision, thought of as a developmental function, enables the supervisor to screen techniques, skills, procedures, and tasks according to their potential for enabling teachers to move to greater levels of reflection, choice, and collective action.

As we close, I ask the reader to think about this story:

> A man was walking by a building site one day, and he saw some workers working near a great pile of stones. Going up to one of the workers, he asked, "What are you doing?"
>
> The worker said, "I'm a stonecutter, and I'm cutting stones."
>
> The man went up to a second worker and asked, "What are you doing?"
>
> The second worker said, "I'm a stonecutter, and I'm trying to make enough money to support my family."

FIGURE 19-1 Supervision for Successful Schools

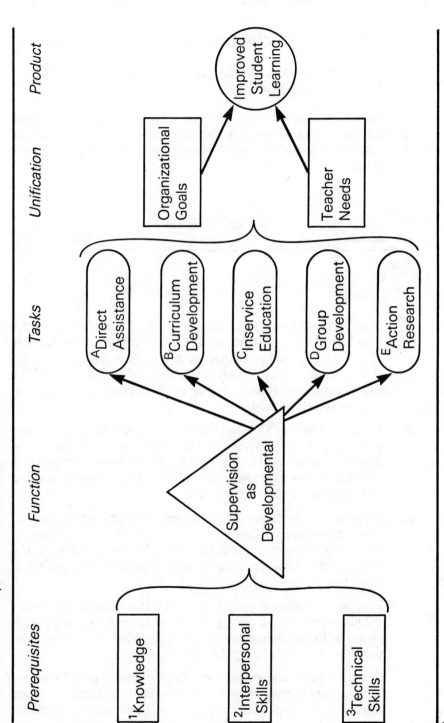

Prerequisites

¹Knowledge

²Interpersonal Skills

³Technical Skills

Function

Supervision as Developmental

Tasks

^ADirect Assistance

^BCurriculum Development

^CInservice Education

^DGroup Development

^EAction Research

Unification

Organizational Goals

Teacher Needs

Product

Improved Student Learning

The man went up to a third worker and asked, "What are you doing?"

The third worker said, "I'm a stonecutter, and I am building a cathedral."

This book is not for those supervisors who work to cut stones or those supervisors who work only for financial security. Instead, this book is for those who work to make schools public cathedrals of learning.

EXERCISES

ACADEMIC

1. Find in the literature a description of an educational leader who has turned an unsuccessful school into a successful one. Which of the change strategies discussed in this chapter did the supervisor use? Report on actions related to each of the five tasks of supervision that he or she carried out while turning the school around.

2. If Boyer (1983) or Goodlad (1984) were asked to write a three-page paper on "What Makes Effective and Successful Schools," what would each of them say in his essay? Assume the role of one of these authors and, on the basis of reading their studies, write such a paper.

3. Prepare a report comparing and contrasting conclusions and recommendations found in the national study *A Nation at Risk: The Imperative for Educational Reform* (1983) with the views of this book on steps needed to improve the quality of education in our schools.

4. Prepare a report on recent efforts by individuals and groups outside of education and government to provide concrete assistance to education and educators. What have they proposed, and what is being done?

5. Diagram your own model for effective supervision. Provide a written explanation of each component of your model. Explain the scope, arrangement, sequence, and relationship of model components.

FIELD

1. Attempt to carry out one (or more) of the tasks of supervision, and use change strategy (persuasive, reeducative, or facilitative) appropriate for the teacher(s) you are working with. Report on your efforts and results.

2. Interview a supervisor on practical problems that must be considered to bring about change within a typical public school system. Prepare a report on your interview. Include your own ideas on how appropriate knowledge, skills, roles, functions, processes, tasks, and strategies discussed in this book can be applied to overcome or reduce problems described by the interviewee.

3. Prepare a photo or written essay about schools, students, teachers, and supervisors that has as its theme "A Cause beyond Oneself," and that reflects the meaning this book attaches to this phrase. Share the essay with others.

4. Paint or sculpt a work of art that symbolizes the developmental function of educational supervision. Share the work of art with those interested in supervision as a developmental function.

5. Create a collage in which the key ideas of the text are represented. Share the collage with others who have read this text.

DEVELOPMENTAL

1. Begin a file of newspaper, magazine, and journal articles describing ideas and efforts of individuals and organizations both in and outside of education for achieving success in education.

2. Use selected readings from other texts on educational supervision to compare authors' ideas on specific issues you consider crucial to your own education and development in supervision.

3. Use opportunities as they arise to test out this book's ideas on supervision within your own particular work setting. Through such exploration, determine which of the proposals and suggestions are of most value to your own development and that of others.

REFERENCES

Boyer, E. L. 1983. *High school: A report on secondary education in America*. New York: Harper & Row.

Goodlad, J. I. 1984. *A place called school: Prospects for the future*. New York: McGraw-Hill.

Pratzner, F. C. 1984. Quality of school life: Foundations for improvement. *Educational Researcher 13*(3):20–25.

U.S. Department of Education. 1983. *A nation at risk: The imperative for educational reform*. Washington, D.C.: U.S. Department of Education, April.

Zaltman, G., and Duncan, R. 1977. *Strategies for planned change*. New York: Wiley.

APPENDIX A

What Is Your Educational Philosophy?

Instructions

Please check the answer under each item that best reflects your thinking. You may also want to check more than one answer for any one of the questions.

1. What is the essence of education?

   A. The essence of education is *reason* and *intuition*.

   B. The essence of education is *growth*.

   C. The essence of education is *knowledge* and *skills*.

   D. The essence of education is *choice*.

2. What is the nature of the learner?

   A. The learner is an experiencing organism.

   B. The learner is a unique, free choosing, and responsible creature made up of intellect and emotion.

   C. The learner is a rational and intuitive being.

   D. The learner is a storehouse for knowledge and skills, which, once acquired, can later be applied and used.

Source: "What is Your EP: A Test Which Identifies Your Educational Philosophy," by Patricia D. Jersin, appears in *Clearing House* Vol. 46, January 1972, pp. 274–278. Reprinted by permission of Fairleigh Dickinson University. (The reader may note that Jersin has identified four philosophies. Since we are of the mind that educational *practice* is reflected in three, we would subsume her philosophies in this way—Perennialism (belief in changeless knowledge) grouped with Essentialism, Progressivism as Experimentalism, and Existentialism as itself.)

3. How should education provide for the needs of man?

A. The students need a passionate encounter with the perennial problems of life; the agony and joy of love, reality of choice, anguish of freedom, consequences of actions and the inevitability of death.

B. Education allows for the needs of man when it inculcates the child with certain essential skills and knowledge which all men should possess.

C. The one distinguishing characteristic of man is intelligence. Education should concentrate on developing the intellectual needs of students.

D. Since the needs of man are variable, education should concentrate on developing the individual differences in students.

4. What should be the environment of education?

A. Education should possess an environment where the student adjusts to the material and social world as it really exists.

B. The environment of education should be life itself, where students can experience living—not prepare for it.

C. The environment of education should be one that encourages the growth of free, creative individuality, not adjustment to group thinking nor the public norms.

D. Education is not a true replica of life, rather, it is an artificial environment where the child should be developing his intellectual potentialities and preparing for the future.

5. What should be the goal of education?

A. Growth, through the reconstruction of experience, is the nature, and should be the open-ended goal, of education.

B. The only type of goal to which education should lead is to the goal of truth, which is absolute, universal, and unchanging.

C. The primary concern of education should be with the development of the uniqueness of individual students.

D. The goal of education should be to provide a framework of knowledge for the student against which new truths can be gathered and assimilated.

6. What should be the concern of the school?

   A. The school should concern itself with man's distinguishing characteristic, his mind, and concentrate on developing rationality.

   B. The school should provide an education for the "whole child," centering its attention on all the needs and interests of the child.

   C. The school should educate the child to attain the basic knowledge necessary to understand the real world outside.

   D. The school should provide each student with assistance in his journey toward self-realization.

7. What should be the atmosphere of the school?

   A. The school should provide for group thinking in a democratic atmosphere that fosters cooperation rather than competition.

   B. The atmosphere of the school should be one of authentic freedom where a student is allowed to find his own truth and ultimate fulfillment through non-conforming choice making.

   C. The school should surround its students with "Great Books" and foster individuality in an atmosphere of intellectualism and creative thinking.

   D. The school should retain an atmosphere of mental discipline, yet incorporate innovative techniques which would introduce the student to a perceptual examination of the realities about him.

8. How should appropriate learning occur?

   A. Appropriate learning occurs as the student freely engages in choosing among alternatives while weighing personal responsibilities and the possible consequences of his actions.

   B. Appropriate learning takes place through the experience of problem-solving projects by which the child is led from practical issues to theoretical principles (concrete-to-abstract).

   C. Appropriate learning takes place as certain basic readings acquaint students with the world's permanencies, inculcating them in theoretical principles that they will later apply in life (abstract-to-concrete).

D. Appropriate learning occurs when hard effort has been extended to absorb and master the prescribed subject matter.

9. What should be the role of the teacher?

A. The teacher should discipline pupils intellectually through a study of the great works in literature where the universal concerns of man have best been expressed.

B. The teacher should present principles and values and the reasons for them, encouraging students to examine them in order to choose for themselves whether or not to accept them.

C. The teacher should guide and advise students, since the children's own interests should determine what they learn, not authority nor the subject matter of the textbooks.

D. The teacher, the responsible authority, should mediate between the adult world and the world of the child since immature students cannot comprehend the nature and demands of adulthood by themselves.

10. What should the curriculum include?

A. The curriculum should include only that which has survived the test of time and combines the symbols and ideas of literature, history, and mathematics with the sciences of the physical world.

B. The curriculum should concentrate on teaching students how to manage change through problem solving activities in the social studies . . . empirical sciences and vocational technology.

C. The curriculum should concentrate on intellectual subject matter and include English, languages, history, mathematics, natural sciences, the fine arts, and also philosophy.

D. The curriculum should concentrate on the humanities; history, literature, philosophy, and art—where greater depth into the nature of man and his conflict with the world are revealed.

11. What should be the preferred teaching method?

    A. *Projects* should be the preferred method whereby the students can be guided through problem-solving experiences.

    B. *Lectures, readings,* and *discussions* should be the preferred methods for training the intellect.

    C. *Demonstrations* should be the preferred method for teaching knowledge and skills.

    D. *Socratic dialogue* (drawing responses from a questioning conversation) should be the preferred method for finding the self.

Scoring the Test

This test is self-scoring. Circle the answer you selected for each of the questions checked on the test (Table A–1). Total the number of circles below each column.

Implications

The four answers selected for each of the questions in this multiple-choice test represent positions on educational issues being taken by hypothetical spokesmen from the major educational philosophies heading each column—Progressivism, Perennialism, Es-

TABLE A–1   What Is Your EP?

	Progressivism	Perennialism	Essentialism	Existentialism
1	B	A	C	D
2	A	C	D	B
3	D	C	B	A
4	B	D	A	C
5	A	B	D	C
6	B	A	C	D
7	A	C	D	B
8	B	C	D	A
9	C	A	D	B
10	B	C	A	D
11	A	B	C	D

sentialism, and Existentialism. If, in scoring your test, you find that a majority of your choices, no matter how much doubling up of answers, falls in a single column, you are selecting a dominant educational philosophy from among the four. For example, if you find your totals: Progressivism (9), Perennialism (1), Essentialism (3), and Existentialism (2); your dominant educational philosophy as determined by this test would be *Progressivism* (9 out of 15 choices being a majority). If you discover yourself spread rather evenly among several, or even all four, this scattering of answers demonstrates an eclectic set of educational values. Indecisiveness in selecting from the four positions could indicate other values and beliefs not contained within one of these major educational systems.

In all formal systems of philosophy, an important measure of the system's validity is its consistency. Your consistency in taking this test can be measured by comparing the answer you selected for item #1 that identifies *essences* with your other answers. The more of the remaining 10 responses you find in the same column where you circled item #1, the more consistent you should be in your educational philosophy. The fewer of the other 10 responses in the same column as item #1, the more you should find your responses contradicting one another—a problem inherent in eclecticism. Again, keep in mind, lack of consistency may also be due to valuing another set of educational beliefs, consistent in themselves, but not included as one of the possible systems selected for representation here.

APPENDIX B

Skill Practice in Nondirective Behaviors

This exercise is best done in triads, with one person being the supervisor, the second being the supervisee, and the third being the observer.

The supervisor is responsible for adhering to the directions, keeping the conference on track, and finally having the supervisee come up with his or her own plan. The supervisee is to select a real problem, preferably a professional one, about which he or she needs to make a decision within the next few days or weeks. It should be a problem to which he or she already has given some thought but has not decided what to do. It might have to do with a problem of personnel, scheduling, budgets, or community relations. The observer should read through this entire exercise and note the instructions given to the supervisor. The observer should have a watch or clock to tell the supervisor when to stop each activity. The observer is the enforcer of time limits. During the conference, the observer should take notes on the supervisor's behavior. Look at body posture, tone of voice, facial expressions, and phrasing of sentences. Try to determine if the supervisor is making his or her opinion know in subtle ways. Keep your notes for the end of the exercise, when you will be asked to give your observations to the supervisor.

This exercise is set up as a series of timed mini-activities. These mini-activities are only approximations of an actual supervisor-supervisee conversation, as one obviously does not repeatedly stop and start or necessarily adhere to strict time frames. The times are being used to highlight the flow of the conference and to emphasize critical supervisory behaviors when using a nondirective approach.

The supervisee has given some thought to the problem before beginning the conference. The supervisor and supervisee are seated face to face. The observer sits a few feet away, able to see both participants. Now we are ready to begin.

Activity 1: *Initiating the meeting: Listen to the supervisee's problem—3 minutes.*

Reflecting the problem: 1 minute.

The supervisor can begin with words such as "Could you tell me about the problem that you shortly need to make a decision about?" The supervisor then sits back and listens for a full 3 minutes. *Do not talk;* show you are listening by maintaining eye contact, nodding head, looking quizzical, and so on. After the 3 minutes are over (the observer should say "stop"), the supervisor is to paraphrase accurately and succinctly the essence of the problem. The supervisor is not to provide elaborations or interpretations. After 1 minute the observer should say "stop."

Activity 2: *Verifying and adding to the identified problem: Clarifying, encouraging, and reflecting—5 minutes.*

This activity is for the purpose of extending the supervisee's thinking about the problem. The supervisor should first ask the supervisee to verify the accuracy of the 1 minute summary of the problem. The supervisee should be encouraged to add, correct, or elaborate on the supervisor's summary. Afterwards the supervisor should ask questions to add information. Questions are to ask, not suggest! Questions that might be used are: "Could you tell me some more about . . . ?" "What do you think about . . . ?" "When does this happen?" "How does it come about?" "Why does that occur?" or "Who else is affected?" Avoid statements such as, "Don't you think that you (we) should . . . ?" "I think that . . . don't you?" which are really disguised suggestions, personal statements, and opinions. When the supervisee responds, if the supervisor is unsure of what is being said, he or she should reflect back the statement. This activity concludes the problem identification phase of the conference. After 5 minutes, the observer should say "stop."

Activity 3: *Problem solving: Generating possible actions—5 minutes.*

The supervisor asks the supervisee to give possible actions that might be taken to solve this problem: "What could you think of doing?" The supervisee should feel free to respond imaginatively. Targeting a certain number of alternative actions, such as three to five, often helps a supervisee propose a range of possibilities. The supervisor should again listen attentively, reflect back to the teacher what has been said, and encourage the teacher to continue. The supervisor must be conscious of not interfering or judging the supervisee's proposals. The supervisor might write down each proposed action and, toward the end of the 5 minutes, read the list back.

Activity 4: *Problem-solving: Narrowing down the choice and presenting a decision—10 minutes.*

The supervisor now asks the supervisee to decide on the merits of the many possible actions by asking a question such as, "Which actions do you think would work best? Why?" If the supervisee is not sure, the supervisor can return to each listed possible action and ask for advantages and disadvantages. Once one or two clear actions have been decided on, the supervisor asks the supervisee to restate what is going to be done. After 10 minutes the observer should say stop.

Activity 5: *Standardizing and restating the plan—5 minutes.*

At this point the chosen action is to be formalized by the supervisor by asking the *when* and *how* questions: "When will the plan be implemented?" "In what stages?" "How will you go about it?" "How will you know it is successful?" The supervisor concludes the meeting by reflecting back to the teacher the final plan: "So I now understand that you will . . ." and pauses to see if the paraphrase has been accurate. The observer says "stop" after 5 minutes.

The five activities totaling 28 minutes conclude the exercise. Immediately afterward, each participant is asked to discuss the following with each other:

First, the observer should give feedback to the supervisor based on his or her observations.

Second, the supervisee should give feedback to the supervisor by responding to these questions:

1. What made you believe that the supervisor understood you? did not understand you?

2. In what ways could you pick up on what the supervisor believed about the problem?

3. How did the supervisor help you analyze and solve the problem? How did he or she interfere?

Third, the supervisor should ask him- or herself these questions and respond:

1. Did you interject any of your own ideas or interpretations of what the speaker was saying?

2. What was your mind doing while you were listening?

3. Were some encouraging statements inconsistent with what you were actually feeling? If so, how did you act?

Fourth, each participant should now write one to three words describing their experience of using nondirective behaviors, being the recipient of nondirective behaviors, or observing nondirective behaviors. After writing the descriptions, they should be shared and the discussion might end with a consideration of the merits and demerits of nondirective supervision.

APPENDIX C

Skill Practice in Collaborative Behaviors

The upcoming exercise should be done with three individuals, one playing the role of the supervisor, one being the supervisee, and the other being the observer. The observer is asked to sit apart and watch the supervisor. The following questions might serve as a guide to the observer.

What evidence shows that the supervisor is accepting the supervisee as an equal?

How does the supervisor steer the conference toward a shared decision?

What nonverbal behaviors are characteristic of the supervisor?

What verbal behaviors are characteristic of the supervisor?

How does the supervisor resolve conflicts about ideas? Both the supervisor and the supervisee are to respond with real ideas and solutions. Remember this is a conference of equals, with the supervisor having the added responsibility of guiding the conference.

Figure C–1 can be used for this exercise or, if there are other problems more relevant and demanding of a joint solution between supervisor and supervisee, they can be used instead. The result of this practice conference is for the supervisor and supervisee to commit themselves to two specific actions. Figure C–2 can be filled out at the end of the conference.

To save time on identifying the various concerns with teacher evaluation, the explanation and questions in Figure C–2 are provided. Both supervisor and supervisee individually should read and respond *before* beginning the meeting. In the practice activities, we will refer to the supervisor as female and the supervisee as male.

APPENDIX C

FIGURE C–1   Issue of Teacher Evaluation

   Formal evaluation of teachers for contract renewal is a sticky issue. Many teachers claim that there are no generic qualities of good teachers and that, even if there were, there are no *realistic* instruments available for collecting information on such qualities. Therefore, many believe that evaluation is often an arbitrary, subjective, personality contest: If the evaluator likes the teacher, he or she receives a good evaluation; if not, then the teacher receives a poor one. There is some interest in taking evaluation responsibilities away from the school principal. Some alternatives to principal evaluation are to give the responsibility to central office personnel, to an outside team of state Department of Education personnel, or to groups of peer teachers; or to allow teachers to do their own self-evaluation.

   As an educator, where do you stand on this and other issues of teacher evaluation? Please check your response to the following questions:

1. The principal should have major responsibility for formal teacher evaluation for contract renewal.   Yes ☐   No ☐   Maybe ☐

2   To ensure objectivity, an evaluator should not be involved in an ongoing program for helping the evaluated teacher improve instruction.   Yes ☐   No ☐

3. Beginning teachers. should be evaluated more closely than tenured teachers.   Yes ☐   No ☐

4. Please check those persons who should be responsible for formal evaluation of teachers:
   A.   The school principal   ☐
   B.   Central office personnel   ☐
   C.   State Department of Education representative   ☐
   D.   Peer teachers   ☐
   E.   The individual teacher (self-evaluation)   ☐

5. When a principal does evaluate, he or she should be able to call in the following person(s) to receive a second opinion on a teacher whose performance is questionable.
   A.   Another teacher in the same school   ☐
   B.   Central office consultant   ☐
   C.   Another teacher from the local teacher association   ☐
   D.   An assistant principal   ☐
   E.   A department head   ☐

6. Should a teacher have the right to select another person to evaluate him- or herself if there is substantial disagreement with the evaluator?   Yes ☐   No ☐

Activity 1: *Identifying the problem as seen by teacher and supervisor—10 minutes.*

Using the questionnaire as a beginning point, the supervisor asks the supervisee to present his general beliefs about evaluation. Then the supervisor presents her own position. The supervisor might suggest that they each read through their responses to the questions on teacher evaluation and give a brief rationale for each response. Each person's position should be checked for understanding. The supervisor should ask the supervisee to identify his position (*clarifying*), understand the supervisee's position (*listening*), and verify the supervisee's position (*reflecting*). After understanding the supervisee, the supervisor can provide her own point of view (*presenting*) and seek teacher's understanding (*clarifying*).

When the supervisor speaks, she should present her thoughts clearly and forcefully. She should tell what she thinks about the issue and not qualify, excuse, or hedge her statements. Avoid statements that begin with "Others think . . . ," "I'm not sure but . . . ," "I guess . . ." Instead, use words such as "It is my belief . . . ," "In my own experience . . ." "According to what I know . . ."

Each person should speak for up to 5 minutes. The time is for understanding each other's initial positions, not discussing them. The observer should stop this activity after 10 minutes.

Activity 2: *Problem solving: The supervisor asks for suggestions of actions—5 minutes.*

The supervisor asks for possible ideas about what should take place in a good program of teacher evaluation: "If you were respon-

FIGURE C-2   Collaborative Conference Contract

Issue: Teacher Evaluation

General Position
  We agree that teacher evaluation should be:

Specific Actions
  We agree that we would commit ourselves to the following activities in a teacher evaluation program.

1.

2.

---

sible for teacher evaluation, what would you want to see happen?" The supervisor might suggest that they both privately write down a list of actions before exchanging and discussing the lists. They then can read their lists of activities to each other. This time is for generating many ideas. Criticizing and evaluating ideas are to be avoided. The aim of the activity is to gather a list from both supervisor and supervisee. The observer should stop this activity after 5 minutes.

Activity 3: *Encouraging and negotiating—5 minutes.*

The supervisor now inaugurates a discussion of each other's ideas. She accepts conflict over ideas as a way of gathering additional information for better decisions; she looks for commonalities as well as differences. The supervisor encourages the supervisee to judge the advantages and disadvantages of her ideas, and she likewise critiques the supervisee's ideas. The supervisor then might say: "Let's see where we agree and disagree" or "In what ways are we saying the same things?" The observer should allow 5 minutes for this activity.

Activity 4: *Finding and agreeing with an acceptable plan—15 minutes.*

The supervisor asks that they find a general position about evaluation with which they both can agree: "Where do we stand on teacher evaluation?" They should write that statement down under "General Position" in Figure 8–3. Next they must find at least two activities they agree would happen if they were responsible for teacher evaluation: "What would we specifically do?" Those actions are written into the contract. This activity should be concluded by the observer after 15 minutes.

After the practice conference of 30 minutes, the observer is asked to provide feedback to the supervisor pertaining to the guide questions. The supervisee can also respond to the same guide questions. He or she might respond in particular to any times when he or she was feeling pressure by the supervisor to agree. If the conference did not result in a completed contract, all three participants might discuss how such an approach could be more successful in a real conference. Each participant should write a one- to three-word description of personal feelings about being part of a collaborative conference. The feedback session concludes with the participants discussing the advantages and disadvantages of the collaborative approach.

APPENDIX D

Skill Practice in
Directive Behaviors

This exercise again involves three persons—a supervisor, a supervisee, and an observer. While the supervisor practices directive behaviors, the supervisee will play the role of a strong-willed teacher. The observer is to watch for the following: How does the supervisor give a directive? Is it clear, does it have a rationale, and how does the supervisor try to gain teacher compliance? Is there evidence of anger, resentment, or coercion? How does the supervisor assert him- or herself? In what ways does the supervisor show understanding of the teacher's position?

All persons should read the scenario, and the supervisor should take a few minutes preparing for the conference. The following scenario might appear to be far-fetched, but it is based on an actual high school incident. (You might substitute a similar incident that has recently occurred in your own locality.) The critical point of the exercise is that the teacher thinks far differently from the supervisor about this issue and the supervisor believes that, for the good of the instructional program, the teacher must understand and comply with the directive. To make the exercise a bit more interesting, we will define the science supervisor as having no organizational authority over teachers. Instead, the supervisor has a staff relationship with the teacher and must convince the teacher of his expertise. Please read the following scenario:

> You, the science supervisor, have visited Ms. Truxhall's classroom several times in the last week and have been amazed at the number and types of skeletons that students have brought to the class. Ms. Truxhall, as a part of her anatomy unit, has been showing students

how to preserve skeletons from dead birds and animals. Yesterday Ms. Truxhall had asked your advice about student, Johnny Fridgemore, bringing in a human skeleton. Johnny is an average student a bit on the tough side but from a caring home. According to Johnny, the skeleton belonged to his grandfather who was a medical doctor. You thought it would be all right. Ms. Truxhall then told Johnny to bring it in.

Today, you read in the morning paper a story about a local cemetery being vandalized. One of the graves had been dug up and the remains were missing. The story had been circulating around the school and some students had been overheard joking about Ms. Truxhall's grave diggers. You do not believe that Johnny Fridgemore robbed a grave to get the skeleton and that his explanation is true but still you are bothered about the skeleton in the classroom. The talk around school could easily filter to parents and the community. In your opinion, nothing wrong has been done but trouble could be brewing. To avoid trouble, you decide to meet with Ms. Truxhall and tell her, for the time being, to tell Johnny to take the skeleton home. Little do you know how adamant Ms. Truxhall is going to be about your decision. Ms. Truxhall is going to insist that since Johnny has done nothing wrong that it is absurd to ask him to take home the skeleton. In fact, she believes to do otherwise would show a lack of confidence in Johnny. You will be just as insistent that the skeleton be taken home.

Activity 1: *Disclosing the supervisor's position and listening to the teacher—8 minutes.*

The supervisor begins the meeting by presenting to the teacher his perception of the problem: "As I see it, the problem is . . ." He explains why the problem exists and why changes must be made: "If no changes are made, then . . ." He makes clear that this is a serious concern and that he, in the interests of all, will take responsibility for the consequences of the decision: "I think you must know how strongly I feel because . . ." He discloses what should be done: "As of now, I believe that you must . . ." Next, the supervisor *clarifies* the teacher's understanding by asking for the teacher's view of the problem. He *listens* carefully to what the teacher has to say. This activity has a time limit of 8 minutes (approximately 5 minutes for the supervisor's position and approximately 3 minutes for the teacher's position).

Activity 2: *Determining and detailing teacher change—10 minutes.*

The supervisor should be mentally checking his own perception of the problem against the teacher's perception and determine if there exists any new information to alter the original solution. After mentally *problem solving,* the supervisor directs the teacher in what he believes must be done. This is done by such statements as "It is clear to me that . . . ," "I feel strongly that . . . ," and "I urge you to . . ." Such declarative statements are followed by a rationale for why the solution is correct. The teacher is asked for her reactions to the directive: "Please react to what I've just said." Based on the teacher's reaction, the supervisor may or may not decide to make changes in the details of the plan (standardizing): "Based on your reactions, I can see some revisions; tomorrow morning I want you to . . . ," or "I understand your reservations about my directive, but still I believe it is necessary to . . ." At this time the supervisor fills in details of time, place, and persons responsible for carrying out the plan. The observer should stop activity 2 after 10 minutes.

Activity 3: *Repeating and following up on expectations—5 minutes.*

If the teacher is satisfied and offers no further opposition, then the meeting is over. However, if the teacher continues to argue the detailed plan—"I don't agree . . . ," "It won't work . . . ," "It isn't fair . . . ," then the supervisor should use the broken-record method and keep repeating the plan. The supervisor wants the teacher to understand the firmness of his conviction; therefore, as the teacher argues, the supervisor counters with acknowledgment of the argument and persistence with the plan: "I understand that you don't think it's fair (it's wrong, it won't work), but I still want you to . . ." If the teacher continues to reject the supervisor's directives after several repetitions, then the supervisor can conclude with a final repetition of the directive, the rationale, and the choice for the teacher. If the supervisor is in a staff position (as is the case in this exercise) he can say: "This is what I believe and why. I am convinced that it is the right course of action, but if you don't agree, I can't make you do it. However, let's be clear: What you are planning to do, I think is wrong." If the supervisor is in a line position, then he can hold power over the teacher: "There's no purpose in arguing this matter further. I want you to do the following. If you refuse, I will consider it a case of insubordination and will document the matter at contract-renewal time." The observer should stop activity 3 after 5 minutes.

These three activities, totaling a maximum of 23 minutes,

conclude the exercise. A follow-up discussion between supervisor, supervisee, and observer should now take place. This discussion might take place as follows:

1.   The observer shares his or her notes in responding to the focused questions that preceded this exercise.

2.   The supervisee as a recipient of the directive approach might respond to the same questions. When did she feel particularly frustrated or angry? Did the supervisor convince her of the rightness of the action, or did the supervisor resort to coercion? Was the supervisor up front and clear about where he stood? How did the supervisor act when the teacher disagreed?

3.   The supervisor might share his feelings about being directive. Was it easy, was it difficult, in what ways, and at what times?

4.   Each participant might write a one- to three-word description of what it was like to take part in a directive conference. Read and discuss the responses. Finally, the participants should examine the advantages and disadvantages of using directive behaviors.

APPENDIX E

Example of Letter Initiating Peer Supervision

Dear teachers,

Whenever I drop into a classroom to deliver a note, or books, or to ask you about something, etc., I am constantly impressed with the quality and depth of instruction I see daily at Columbia Elementary. I've been trying to figure out how teacher A can share his or her expertise in an area with teachers B, C, D, and E, who would benefit from the sharing of that expertise. Also, teachers go to workshops or in-services and pick up all kinds of instructional tips. Why not share it with other teachers? I guess what I'm trying to illustrate is that we have a wealth of knowledge among us right here at Columbia Elementary. Let's help each other out!

Okay, now to the mechanics. One person needs to be the coordinator, and since I'm not responsible for students all day, I'm volunteering. I will make a visit to every teacher's classroom (at a time each teacher suggests) and make general notes on things such as how you keep up with kids' work (individual file folders? a box for each subject? answer sheets for kids to check own work and record the grade?); your forms of classroom management (tokens? marbles? points to best groups for free time?); the style of your room (rows? circles? groups?); etc. After school or during your break I'll show you my observation sheet, and you can fill me in on areas I wasn't sure of. I'll keep all this information in my room in a folder. I'll also give you a questionnaire about les-

Source: Reprinted by permission of Mrs. Mary Anne S. Mount, instructional supervisor, DeKalb County Schools, Decatur, Georgia.

sons you've developed that worked out the way you wanted them to, so there will also be records relating to subject matter.

After I have all that information, teachers can come and say things like, "I'd like to see how different teachers keep up with kids' daily work." I would look through the file and find teacher X who uses individual file folders and teacher Y who has children check their own work. I would go to teachers X and Y and ask them if teacher Z could observe them and at what times. I'd take over teacher Z's class during those times. I hope even veteran teachers will want to see how other teachers do things.

Now I want your feedback. Please fill out the next two pages and return to me by Tuesday, 11-18-80.

You are doing an exceptional job, teachers. Let's share it.

Mary Anne Mount

Name _____

Circle (Yes) if you want the statement on the observation form. Circle (No) if you don't want the statement on the observation form.

1. Keeping up with student work   Yes   No
   (file folders, subject boxes, etc.)

2. Arrangement of classroom   Yes   No
   (rows, circles, groups)

3. Form(s) of classroom management   Yes   No
   (tokens, checks, work for free time, etc.)

4. Handling routine interruptions   Yes   No
   (hall passes signed; Just get up and
   get them passes, etc.)

What else do you want on the form? Feel free to use the back. _____

_____

_____

_____

Example of Letter Initiating Peer Supervision

Any comments? suggestions? Feel free to use the back. _____

_____

_____

_____

Name _____

Year You Teach _____

Room Number _____

Reading levels you feel most comfortable teaching:

_____

Math levels you feel most comfortable teaching:

_____

Your favorite subjects to teach:

_____

_____

A short synopsis of some of your favorite lessons to teach (see next page for example):

_____

_____

_____

_____

_____

_____

Examples

Seventh-Year Newspaper Unit

Takes two weeks, forty minutes per day. Students first are introduced to different sections of the newspaper (and the types of articles in each section) as a whole group, with much discussion and use of the overhead projector. Then the class elects an editor and votes for a title for their newspaper. Students sign up for three different types of articles they must submit to the editor for corrections. They make the corrections and resubmit the articles. When the articles are acceptable, they are compiled by the class editor into an attractive newspaper. The newspaper is displayed in the media center. I have two centers and several worksheets to go along with this unit.

Introducing Primary Students to Telling Time

Takes three days, twenty minutes per day. I introduce the concepts of hours, half hours, and clockwise movement. I've made a clock for each child to use at his or her desk, which makes checking easy. I have worksheets, letters to parents explaining how they can help teach time at home, and a bulletin board for this lesson.

APPENDIX F

Example of Behavioral-Objective Curriculum

Family Living

Objectives (minimum three hours)

The learner will:

1. Describe the range of family characteristics.

2. Explain roles and responsibilities of family members.

3. Describe physical and emotional changes related to maturity.

Performance Indicators

The learner will:

1.11 Describe at least five ways in which families today may differ from one another.

2.11 Explain at least five roles and responsibilities of family members.

3.11 Describe at least five physical and emotional changes related to maturity.

Source: *Health Education for Georgia Middle Grades, A Competency Based Approach*, p. 22. Reprinted by permission of the Georgia Department of Education, Atlanta, Georgia, 1982.

Content Outline

I. Family life

    A. Importance of the family

        1. Influences psychosocial development.

        2. Influences physical development.

        3. Serves as major cultural institution.

    B. Range in characteristics

        1. Extended family.

        2. Nuclear family.

        3. Single-parent family.

        4. Childless through multiple children family.

    C. Roles and responsibilities

        1. Types of roles and responsibilities.

        2. Influences on assumption and delegation of roles and responsibilities:

            a. Age.

            b. Capabilities.

            c. Relationship to other family members.

            d. Family tradition.

            e. Sociocultural-religious.

II. Maturation

    A   Physical changes

    B. Emotional changes
        Note: For guidelines, films, pamphlets, guest speakers, etc., see your principal, curriculum director, or designated person for sex education guidelines and approved teaching materials.

Instructional Activities

1.11 Have students conduct a survey to determine the variety of family units prevalent. Chart results.

2.11 Have students query a variety of families to determine what roles and responsibilities are carried out by whom, and reasons why those particular members were chosen for the role responsibility.

2.12 Have students try to complete charts labeled "Toys and Games for Boys," "Toys and Games for Girls," and "Toys and Games for Both." Discuss students' feelings as they try to fill out the charts.

3.11 First have students compare how they are alike and different in physical and emotional characteristics at present. Then have students describe how they individually have changed physically and emotionally since first grade and how they believe they will change by twelfth grade.

APPENDIX G

Webbing Curriculum

FIGURE G–1   Literature Web

Oral Activities

Interview the elephants about their heroic rescue.

Discuss other ways Amos might have rescued Boris.

Share a time when you helped someone and it made you feel good.

Compare the shape of the boat and the shape of Boris. Stress similarities.

Construction Activities

Show paintings and sketches about whaling from *The Story of Yankee Whaling.*

Glue beans and peas on boards in whale shapes.

Make papier-maché whales.

Carve soap in the shapes of elephants, mice, or whales.

Writing

Write a list of items *you* would take on a long trip.

Write a paragraph about a good friend and what you like about him or her.

Write a journal that Amos might have kept.

Write another title for the story.

Arrange a choral reading of the attached list of poems.

Read some of the related stories and compare and contrast.

Additional Activities:

List unfamiliar words in vocabulary notebooks.

Using the *Third Junior Book of Authors*, find out what William Steig has done besides children's books.

Show filmstrip "Creating a Fable" from *English Composition for Children* (Pied Piper Productions, 1975). Create an original fable.

Science and Mathematics

Make a chart on the characteristics of mammals and discuss why all the characters in the story belong to this group.

Make a transparency showing a size comparison between an average sperm whale and familiar items such as cars, school buses, desks, and classrooms.

Find out why whales must sound and live in water.

Find out how the sperm whale population has fluctuated over the years.

Make a ship model.

AMOS AND BORIS
by William Steig

Dramatization

Make the four characters into sock or stick puppets and act out the story.

Act out three scenes:
1. The first time Boris sounds
2. Amos finding Boris on the beach
3. Amos and Boris saying good-bye

Pantomime the whole story.

Geography

Locate the Ivory Coast of Africa on a map or globe.

Pinpoint the Seven Seas on a map or globe.

Show the typical migration routes of sperm whales on a map or globe.

Related Books to Read

The Fables of Aesop: 143 Moral Tales

Andy and the Lion

The Lion and the Rat

"Stand Back", Said the Elephant, "I'm Going to Sneeze"

My Friend John

Listening Activities

Listen to the tape of William Steig reading his own story (*Famous Author/Illustrator Filmstrip Library*, Miller-Brody Productions, 1975).

Listen to a tape of the voices of humpback whales.

Listen to a recording of *La Mer* by Claude Debussy.

Source: Developed by Sibley Veal for *Amos and Boris*. From C. J. Fisher and L. A. Terry. *Children's Language and the Language Arts*, 2nd edition. Copyright © 1982 by McGraw-Hill Company, New York. Reprinted by permission of McGraw-Hill Company.

Indexes

Author Index

417

AUTHOR INDEX

Subject Index

420

SUBJECT INDEX

premise of, 80, 143, 169–170
supervisor's role in, 80, 148
when to use, 151–152, 156, 169,
170–172, 376–377
with groups, 145–149
with individuals, 143–145
Dissatisfiers. *See* Motivational factors
Dysfunctional behaviors, 335–336,
341–342
Dysfunctional group members, 330,
339–342, 353, 371

Educational criticism, 223–226,
227, 228, 361
Educational philosophy, 75, 76–80,
84, 85, 86
Educational Resources Management System (ERMS), 199
Effective schools. *See* School effectiveness
Ego development:
adult, 46–47
of teachers, 51, 52, 60
Eight-year study, 306
Equal Opportunity Act, 34
ERMS. *See* Educational Resources
Management System
Essentialism, 75, 76–77, 79, 80, 84,
307, 313
Evaluation, 7, 95, 183, 232, 233, 234,
241–250, 251, 271, 366, 376
(*see also* Action research)
and achievement tests:
cautions about, 243–244
criterion-referenced, 244
nationally normed, 244
compared with research, 234, 251
components of, 233
formative, 233, 271
of instructional program, 245–
249, 251
report, 250
of special projects, 241–245, 251
standards for, 249–250
summative, 233, 264, 271
supervisor's role in, 245, 251
who should conduct, 249–250
Existentialism, 75, 76, 79–80, 84,
85, 86, 307, 313
Experimentalism, 75, 76, 77–78,
79, 80, 84, 85, 86, 307, 313

Eyes and ears assessment, 192,
282, 359

Flow chart, 189–190
Focused questionnaire observation,
222–223, 226, 227, 228, 361

Gant chart, 195, 197–198, 202, 361
Graduate Record Exam, 35
Group decisions, 330, 331, 335,
337, 338, 342, 345, 347–353
Group development, 5, 6, 7, 19,
257, 330–353, 361, 365, 371,
376–378, 381
Group dimensions, 331–332
Group leader, 330, 332, 333, 334,
335, 336, 337, 338, 339, 341,
342, 345, 346, 347, 349, 352,
353
Group maturity, 172–174, 338–
339, 340
Group meetings, 330, 345–353,
361, 371
agenda for, 346
guided discussion in, 346–347
large-group involvement in,
349–353
through open representation,
351–352
through postrepresentation,
349–351
through prerepresentation,
352–353
Group roles:
dysfunctional, 332, 335–336
person, 332, 334–335
task, 332–334, 335

Hygiene factors, 163–165
and hierarchy of needs, 164–165

Idealism, 76–77
Improvement of instruction. *See* Instructional improvement
Informational environments, 168–
170, 174, 175
Innovation, utilization of, 280,
282–284, 319
Inquiry, 365, 381
In-service education, 5, 9, 67, 257,
278–298, 360–361, 365,
371, 376–378, 381